Hijacking History

Hijacking History

*How the Christian Right Teaches History
and Why It Matters*

KATHLEEN WELLMAN

OXFORD
UNIVERSITY PRESS

OXFORD
UNIVERSITY PRESS

Oxford University Press is a department of the University of Oxford. It furthers
the University's objective of excellence in research, scholarship, and education
by publishing worldwide. Oxford is a registered trade mark of Oxford University
Press in the UK and certain other countries.

Published in the United States of America by Oxford University Press
198 Madison Avenue, New York, NY 10016, United States of America.

© Oxford University Press 2021

Library of Congress Control Number: 2021029409
ISBN 978–0–19–757923–7

DOI: 10.1093/oso/9780197579237.001.0001

1 3 5 7 9 8 6 4 2

Printed by Sheridan Books, Inc., United States of America

For friends and colleagues at Southern Methodist University

Contents

Preface   ix

Acknowledgments   xiii

Abbreviations   xv

Introduction: Why This Book?   1

1. The Publishers and Their Books   17

2. What Christianity?   31

3. What Is History?   45

4. The Beginning of History   59

5. Misguided Ancients   79

6. Medieval Darkness, a Dim Renaissance   95

7. The Triumph of Protestant Truth   113

8. The Fruits of the Reformation   127

9. What Reason Wrought   145

10. "As a City on a Hill"   157

11. The Christian Nation   169

12. Christian Colonialism and Capitalism   189

13. Bad Ideas and Deplorable Politics   209

14. The Wages of Sin   227

15. Evil Abroad and at Home   247

16. The Righteous Right   269

Conclusion: Toward End Times or Christian Hegemony   293

Notes   307

Index   353

Preface

I became concerned about the issues that define this book when I learned about the 2010 history standards mandated by the State Board of Education (SBOE) of Texas for 2014 textbooks. Those standards, known as Texas Essential Knowledge and Skills (TEKS), imposed ahistorical stipulations on teaching history in Texas. Several introduced rather bizarre requirements for treating world history within my own areas of expertise, among them the obligation to acknowledge Thomas Aquinas and John Calvin's influence on the founding of the United States. In other words, students had to recognize that two theologians—a medieval Catholic and a Protestant Reformer—exerted decisive influences on eighteenth-century Americans. One of the most ideological members of the SBOE, Cynthia Dunbar, argued for excluding Thomas Jefferson from the Founding Fathers because of his ties to the Enlightenment. Other standards, including those which systematically deemphasized slavery or insisted on the Christian roots of American government, provoked historians' outcries. Nonetheless, the controversial TEKS of 2010 were mandated for inclusion in textbooks to be reviewed by external experts commissioned by the SBOE before adoption in 2014.

How could such ahistorical standards for teaching history have been accepted by the SBOE? Where had these strikingly ahistorical ideas come from? The first question had some obvious answers. School board members in many states are elected in districts explicitly gerrymandered to provide safe seats for one party or another. Like candidates for other elective positions, school board candidates represent their parties' extreme wings. Education has long been a hot-button issue in Texas and such elections often attract candidates with extreme views. In 2010, most Texas SBOE members were extremely conservative. The history standards they implemented reflected their beliefs and those of the experts whose opinions they solicited. An expert was anyone endorsed as such by two board members. Conservative, handpicked "experts" weighed in on whether or how standards should be modified. The battle over standards exposed a hollow notion of "expertise" as self-promoting, ideologically sanctioned, and impervious to evidence or scholarship.

When the textbooks conforming to the new TEKS were available for review by outside reviewers in the spring of 2014, I volunteered to evaluate world history textbooks but was not chosen. Mark Keogh, then a candidate for the Texas House of Representatives as a member of the Tea Party, was selected. His prior professional experience was as a car salesman, although he had retired to run a ministry and, in 2018, was elected county judge of Montgomery County, Texas. The Texas Freedom Network (TFN), an organization dedicated to protecting religious freedom and civil rights, highlighted my example to show what the SBOE sought in outside evaluators. It compared my credentials as a historian, then chair of Southern Methodist University's history department, with extensive publications and a long teaching career, to Keogh's, whom the board deemed more appropriate. I was just one of the many academics rejected in favor of reviewers who would more reliably ensure that the textbooks presented the "right" historical narrative.

Nonetheless, I read some textbooks to see how publishers had implemented the standards I found most peculiar. To my relief, they had clearly been flummoxed by the stipulation to include Thomas Aquinas and John Calvin; they merely inserted their names into lists of religious thinkers. I was, however, disconcerted by the frequent mentions of Moses. Textbooks eagerly espoused him as fundamental to morals, laws, and documents crucial to the American founding. I was not then aware just how crucial Moses and "Mosaic Law" are to the claim that America was founded as a Christian nation. That was just one of my discoveries as I tried to understand these highly unorthodox views.

As these TEKS were directed toward an explicit rewriting of history, I wondered about sources for their views and, more generally, what the history they promoted was intended to convey. In exploring the sources of these ideas, I became especially intrigued by the three most prominent Christian curricula, published by Abeka Books, Bob Jones University Press, and Accelerated Christian Education, which are the central focus of this book. These are all long-standing, conservative Christian publishers whose wares served the private schools that proliferated after desegregation but are now used by homeschoolers and in charter schools and private schools with publicly funded vouchers.

Initially, I wanted to see if these curricula gave clues to the TEKS. They proved to be an especially useful source for understanding them. I focused on world histories for high school students, typically grade ten or eleven, because the textbooks offered the most expansive historical overview, both chronologically and geographically, with extensive global implications. I found that these curricula articulated an idiosyncratic but generally consistent narrative fundamentally at odds with that of the historical profession. As I explored them, I found their account ever more disquieting but also recognized how loudly it resonates in the public sphere, spread by an extensive array of conservative Christian media.

My efforts to understand and contextualize these Christian textbooks directed me beyond world history to American religious and political history. These curricula not only read human history as a gloss on the Bible but also impose their understanding of American history first on European history and then on the globe. They use world history to take positions in crucial debates about America—its founding, national character, and presumed purpose. These textbooks thus offer an entrée into America's sense of itself, its past, and its place in the world. They allow readers to revisit intense debates about education and raise questions about religion and its role in American political culture. My exploration of the origins of ideas shaping these curricula led me into the history of the political and Christian right in America.

I have engaged seriously with these curricula to make my fellow historians and educators, the parents of children using these materials, and Americans concerned about the education of future citizens more aware of the powerful but historically questionable narrative they advance and the dangers it poses to a democratic society.

Acknowledgments

This book is dedicated to my friends and colleagues at Southern Methodist University (SMU), where I have benefited from the friendship and intellectual stimulation of a community of engaged scholars and teachers across disciplines, who share a commitment not simply to scholarship and teaching but also to one another and our students. Many of them have been sounding boards; this book has directly benefited from their support and intellectual generosity. At an early stage in this project, the honors program invited me to deliver a Gartner Lecture to students and faculty. That opportunity made me aware that many SMU students had used the curricula I was examining. Their feeling of having been miseducated gave me a sense of urgency about completing this work. A semester-long Writing Fellowship from the Center for Presidential History gave me the time to complete a draft of the manuscript.

I have been especially fortunate to spend my academic life in the Clements Department of History. My colleagues' commitment to excellence is inspiring. Their engagement with our community has also made it a notably happy and sustaining academic department. I have enjoyed being part of it even when contending with the many, inevitable challenges of being department chair. The history department sponsored a workshop that brought together colleagues from a variety of disciplines to read a draft of the manuscript. I benefited from the thoughtful comments of SMU colleagues Mark Chancey, John Chávez, Richard Cogley, Crista DeLuzio, David Doyle, Brian Franklin, Erin Hochman, Thomas Knock, Bruce Levy, and Laurence Winnie, and of David Brockman of the Baker Institute for Public Policy at Rice University. Their enthusiasm for the project was a great source of encouragement. This project took me out of my usual areas of expertise. I am especially grateful to David Brockman and Mark Chancey for their extensive commentary on religious history and issues; to Thomas Knock for his thoughtful comments on American politics; to Erin Hochman for her insights on modern European politics; and to Jill Kelly for her comments on these textbooks' treatments of Africa and colonialism. I appreciate as well generous comments of my departmental colleagues, who read a draft of the last chapter and the conclusion for a departmental colloquium. Mark

Chancey, Richard Cogley, Thomas Knock, and April Shelford of American University provided invaluable comments during the final stage of completing this book.

I have enjoyed working with Oxford University Press. I appreciate Theodore Calderara's support for the book and his shepherding of it from the manuscript through the review process to publication. It has been a pleasure to work with assistant editor Zara Cannon-Mohammed and production manager Solani Vohra. I appreciate the careful attention of copy editor Leslie Stafford to my manuscript.

As always, my family has been the most important source of support. My children, Matthew and Elizabeth Sepper, both once undergraduate history majors, are now accomplished adults with well-honed historical sensibilities. They, like my son-in-law, Navid Vazire, deploy insight and wit in any discussion—lawyers all! My daughter-in-law, Najma Sepper, is a new and most welcome addition to the family. I hope that the next generation, my young grandsons Joe and James Vazire, will develop a keen interest in history and appreciate that history matters. I am most grateful that I have the love and company of my husband, Dennis Sepper, through all of life's adventures as well as the joys and occasional frustrations of academic lives lived in tandem.

Abbreviations

Abeka* *World History and Cultures in Christian Perspective.* 3rd ed. Pensacola, FL: Abeka Books, 2010.

Abeka+ *History of the World in Christian Perspective.* 5th ed. Pensacola, FL: Abeka Books, 2014.

AbekaUS Michael R. Lowman. *United States History in Christian Perspective: Heritage of Freedom.* 3rd ed. Pensacola, FL: Abeka Books, 2009.

BJU* *World History.* 3rd ed. Greenville, SC: BJU Press, 2007.

BJU+ Dennis Bollinger. *World History.* 4th edn. Greenville, SC: BJU Press, 2013.

BJUUS Timothy Keesee and Mark Sidwell. *United States History.* 4th edn. Greenville, SC: BJU Press, 2012.

ACE *Self-Pac of Basic Education, Social Studies.* Lewisville, TX: Accelerated Christian Education, 1974.

ACEUS ACE *Social Studies: American History.* 4th ed. Accelerated Christian Education, 2007, 2011 revision.

Introduction

Why This Book?

This book is motivated by a profound sense that history matters. As Arthur Schlesinger Jr. put it, "history is to the nation as memory is to the individual. As a person deprived of memory becomes disoriented and lost, not knowing where he has been or where he is going, so a nation denied a conception of its past will be disabled in dealing with its present and its future."[1] But not all historical accounts enhance historical memory. This book raises an alarm about a deliberately constructed and promoted Christian, right-wing historical narrative, one that is not only inaccurate, but dangerous as well. That narrative does not simply misrepresent the past; it shapes the present in ways that have come home to roost in contemporary political and religious debates and seeks to influence the future. A recent op-ed posed a central question this book addresses: "What if the inability of Americans to agree on our shared history—and on the right way to teach it—is a cause of our current polarization and political dysfunction, rather than a symptom?"[2]

The impact of our view of the past on our understanding of the present can be seen in the debate over Confederate symbols, to take a prominent recent example. In a 2015 *Washington Post* op-ed, James Loewen argued that one reason for Americans' support for Confederate symbols is that we have been misinformed by history textbooks, which downplay slavery as the cause of the Civil War.[3] When *The Diane Rehm Show* featured that topic several days later, guests singled out the Texas Essential Knowledge and Skills standards (TEKS) as a prime source of this misinformation.[4] The 2010 TEKS downplayed the role of slavery as a cause of the Civil War, giving it far less significance than sectionalism and states' rights, even though every Southern state cited slavery as its reason for secession. Only in 2018 did the State Board of Education finally concede that the expansion of slavery played "a central role in states' rights, sectionalism and the civil war."[5]

Minimizing slavery as a cause of the Civil War has had an impact. In 2011, 48% of Americans polled believed that states' rights were *the* cause of the

Hijacking History. Kathleen Wellman, Oxford University Press. © Oxford University Press 2021.
DOI: 10.1093/oso/9780197579237.003.0001

Civil War.[6] In 2015, a McClatchy-Marist poll asked the somewhat different question of whether slavery was *the* cause of the Civil War; 41% of those polled said it was not.[7] A high school geography textbook, published in 2014 by McGraw-Hill and written to conform to the TEKS, went further, noting that "the Atlantic Slave Trade between the 1500s and 1800s brought millions of *workers* from Africa to the southern United States to work on agricultural plantations," without acknowledging that they were enslaved. In response to media furor, the caption was corrected.[8] This example illustrates how textbook histories can distort our understanding of the past and influence our present.

As media coverage of such stories shows, issues involving American history textbooks resonate with the American public and prompt historians' responses.[9] But flagrant distortions in world history curricula may be more difficult to detect. The subject is less familiar to parents of school-age children and general readers and, perhaps on the face of it, less contentious. More worrisome, the public and even professional historians are largely unaware of curricula that teach an explicitly right-wing religious and political world history.

This book examines a topic with broad and increasingly crucial ramifications for Americans' understanding of the world and history, for education, and for political, religious, and economic debates in contemporary America: the way world history is taught to conservative Christian children. It focuses on world history curricula produced by the three most significant Christian publishers of educational materials—Abeka Books, published by Pensacola Christian College; Accelerated Christian Education produced by an educational materials company; and the publisher Bob Jones University Press's textbooks. These publishers became influential in the 1970s as evangelicals developed materials explicitly for the mushrooming Christian school movement, and their textbooks have become popular among homeschoolers as well.

Why are these curricula important? Published by fundamentalist publishers, they have an influence that has extended far beyond the confines of fundamentalism. Fundamentalist views have penetrated the evangelical community and nondenominational Christian schools. Their views, as indeed the textbooks insist, increasingly define American Christianity. These curricula's narrative of Christian history has been grafted onto right-wing political and economic positions. And right-wing political interests have promoted these views.

These books claim to present the "Christian" perspective on history. But they recount a polemical, Protestant, right-wing understanding of government, economics, and religion that claims to be both "true" and sanctioned by God. World history gives these publishers wide chronological and geographical scope, but their reading of history is often glaringly inaccurate and frequently idiosyncratic. Historians might dismiss them as ahistorical or, on some points, as laughably erroneous, as indeed some columnists and satirists have done.

My study takes a different tack. It treats their content seriously because, even though these textbooks are not well known or studied, the history they advance has sunk deep roots in American conservative religious education and is increasingly spread by right-wing institutions and popular media.

The positions these textbooks articulate resound in public debate. They influence discussions about education by providing an alternative to the history usually taught in the public schools. They not only tap into a rich context of European and American political and religious debates since the nineteenth century but also introduce distinctive and often unconventional perspectives on contemporary cultural issues. They proclaim their positions as "Christian" and, as such, unquestionably true and diametrically opposed to other histories they disdain as secular. Their current prevalence exposes the successful alliance among evangelicals, conservative legislators and school boards, and corporations interested in reshaping educational agendas to advance such views.

The increasing use of these curricula at a time when college education in central humanities disciplines has been hollowed out raises further concern about their content. For countless high school students, these curricula or others like them will be their last formal exposure to the study of history. With diluted college requirements, fewer college students take postsecondary history courses. Even universities that require college history courses allow students to submit Advanced Placement courses to attest to a post-secondary understanding of history, even though college professors do not typically consider such courses comparable to college-level courses. (In 2015, over 600,000 students took AP history exams.[10]) Without college history courses, students have fewer opportunities to critically reappraise or enhance their secondary school understanding of history.

These Christian world histories should also provoke questions about how far into our education system or indeed our society their historical narrative has penetrated. While historians have cause to bemoan historical illiteracy, these curricula pose bigger but different problems by deliberately promulgating a narrative that is not, at root, historical at all and may prove particularly difficult to challenge or refute. These materials are explicitly intended to inoculate students against more critical historical thinking or evidence. These curricula should raise concern for universities and the historical profession. The University of California rejected high school courses using these curricula as so violating historical and scientific consensus that they failed to meet their entrance requirements.[11] Will other colleges and universities accept courses based on these curricula from applicants?

The success of intelligent design in penetrating the science curricula of public schools offers a cautionary tale about the efficacy of political and religious conservatives in introducing educational content that runs counter to the current state of knowledge. Although these history curricula construct and aggressively promote a distinctive history, the arguments they use are akin to the circular and thus largely irrefutable reasoning that promoted intelligent design as a legitimate alternative to evolutionary biology. The methods used, the constituencies appealed to, and many of the institutions involved are those that mobilized to promote creationism in public schools.[12]

Scientists have been less effective than one would hope in discrediting challenges to evolution. Perhaps they were so committed to accuracy or so careful not to overstate their case that they failed to make it. Perhaps they considered intelligent design too patently unscientific to merit serious refutation. As Stephen J. Gould put it, creationists "had a vernacular misunderstanding of the word 'theory,'" even though evolution is a theory in the same way that gravity is a theory.[13] Perhaps scientists were insufficiently aware of strategies the religious right developed after the Supreme Court ruled in 1987 that teaching creationism in public schools was unconstitutional. Relabeled as "intelligent design," creationism gained a place in science curricula as an alternative "theory."[14]

Successes in undermining the teaching of biology should heighten concern about deliberate distortions of history. Historians might dismiss conservative Christian textbooks, assuming an idiosyncratic narrative could not possibly challenge a well-developed historical consensus. But the teaching of history has long generated controversy; the right attacked it as insufficiently "pro-American" during the Cold War or uncritical of the civil rights movement and the culture of the 1960s. Donald Trump's 1776 Commission produced an ahistorical but entirely positive history of the nation to contest recent works that incorporate the crucial role slavery played in the nation's history. Attacks on the teaching of Critical Race Theory (CRT) have little to do with the theory but rather object to teaching about slavery and race.

History, like science, is thus targeted for an ideological counternarrative.[15] The story of Texas's social science standards offers a revealing example of such an attempt. In 2010, the State Board of Education of Texas successfully rewrote the required standards (TEKS) for social science, inserting positions dear to the Christian right. Most notably, the TEKS stipulated that history and government textbooks claim that Moses was a critical influence on the American founding.[16] In November 2018, the State Board of Education again reaffirmed this stipulation. Some board members expressed eagerness to integrate a Christian worldview even more extensively into the TEKS.[17]

The TEKS tell an important story about how school boards advance a conservative Christian narrative.[18] In this book, the TEKS function primarily as a noteworthy and chilling example of an effective campaign to insert that narrative into public school history instruction in one of the nation's largest textbook markets, but one that has an even more outsized influence because many other states adopt Texas's textbooks. The other influential market is California, differentiating red and blue state history textbooks.[19] But Texas is far from the only state promoting an alternative history, incorporating contentions of the religious and political right. Local school boards in Colorado enacted similarly ahistorical requirements, including the ludicrous claim that America had never experienced political protest. High school students knew enough history to protest this absurdity. Alternative history is frequently found in state legislators' proposals, intended to ensure that students' understanding conforms to theirs.[20]

Historical expertise can be challenged, discounted, or ignored much in the way that scientific authority has been in discussions of evolution. Discrediting historians undermines historical knowledge, the legitimacy of the historical profession, and the very idea of expertise. Reactionary state school boards cavalierly dismiss professional historians as left-leaning elitists, intent on undermining America's obvious exceptionalism, and their scholarship as irrelevant to state standards for history.

Texas again offers an illuminating example. When the State Board of Education chose experts to recommend changes to the standards for social studies for Texas, Cynthia Dunbar, who later taught law at Jerry Falwell's Liberty University, insisted on John Calvin's importance to the American founding. David Barton of WallBuilders, which is explicitly dedicated to reversing the separation of church and state, was another consulted "expert."

Mary Helen Berlanga, a Democratic member of the board, objected: "They are not experts, they are not historians . . . they are re-writing history, not only of Texas but of the United States and the world."[21] A leader of this effort was Don McLeroy, a Texas dentist and member of the board's conservative majority. McLeroy was staunchly committed to making the Bible the basis of history instruction. He praised the board's efforts in resisting historians' criticisms as balancing left-wing academics and "standing up for true American history."[22] Board members promoted their understanding of American history as "true" and dismissed historical arguments or evidence to the contrary as wrong or partisan.

Recent battles over history standards suggest that the war is fought at the state level and in local schools and churches. For decades, the Christian right has advanced slates of candidates for school board elections and successfully mobilized voter turnout in some states to elect majorities.[23] Somewhat underground, that campaign has sunk deep roots and evaded the scrutiny of the public and historians. This book attempts to raise awareness about the views a Christian-focused world history promulgates and to what ends. It urges historians, parents, and other engaged citizens to read history textbooks with a thoughtful and critical eye.[24]

Initially, these curricula were tightly identified with fundamentalism, a narrower movement than evangelicalism, with which it overlaps, but they are now promoted as "Christian." Evangelicals have increasingly subscribed to some fundamentalist positions—anti-evolution, for example. As evangelicalism has become more culturally mainstream, its influence on American Christianity and national politics has grown significantly, and has become central to the national conversation since the election of Donald Trump incontrovertibly demonstrated its political clout.[25] This book brings these Christian curricula, with which several generations of students have been educated, into our understanding of this movement's polemical use of history and, more broadly, of the evolution of the Christian right.

These curricula have played a distinct role in the history of education in America, primarily because every challenge to public schooling since the 1920s expanded their reach, increasing their diffusion in the educational marketplace and their influence. They are thus marketed to and used by an increasing array of Christian private schools, in voucher programs, and in homeschooling.[26]

In the nineteenth century, Catholic immigrants established parochial schools to protect their children from America's predominantly Protestant culture, epitomized by use of the Protestant Bible in public schools. When Catholics challenged compulsory school attendance laws, the Supreme Court sided with them. Its ruling sustained parents' rights to make decisions about their children's education as well as the state's right to regulate education. With their rights affirmed, evangelical parents too began to remove their children from the public schools to avoid influences they considered dangerous. They were initially most concerned about the teaching of evolution, but by the 1950s public schools became heated battlegrounds over integration and church-state relations. Much discontent with public schools was found on the political right. Groups like the John Birch Society battled allegedly liberal textbooks in the 1950s, and religious conservatives similarly charged that textbooks introduced "moral relativism" or subjects they considered inappropriate, like sex education. Supreme Court rulings (*Engel v. Vitale*, 1962 and *Abington v. Schempp*, 1963) against prayer and Bible reading in the public schools pushed many conservative Christians to take their children out of public schools they saw as atheistic. In the 1970s, some groups condemned textbooks that introduced students to multiculturalism, feminism, or evolution as unpatriotic and unchristian.[27] Conservative activists have consistently mobilized to challenge public school education: from the religious conservatives in Kanawha County, West Virginia, who asserted that a new curriculum exposed their children to dangerous ideas, to Mel and Norma Gabler, who waged a prodigious battle to maintain Judeo-Christian values in public schools, to Phyllis Schlafly, who saw public schooling as attacking religion.[28] These causes were widely discussed in the burgeoning Christian conservative media during the 1970s and 1980s.

The Christian curricula examined in this book were both inspired by these battles and the beneficiaries of them. They are most immediately connected to the Christian day schools of the 1970s. In addition to wanting control of educational content, many of these schools, sometimes called "segregation academies," wanted to avoid federally mandated desegregation. These schools largely evaded data collection, so their exact numbers cannot be determined. By some accounts, they expanded by 200% from 1965 to 1975 with enrollments of half a million.[29] At one point, three new schools were opening each week.[30] By 1982, there were approximately 11,000 Christian evangelical and fundamentalist day schools enrolling about 1 million students. Enrollments in these schools seems to have remained at that level.[31] These curricula were explicitly produced to serve these schools, and Bob Jones

University Press, Abeka Books, and Accelerated Christian Education were the three most important publishers of materials for them.[32]

When the IRS announced, on the basis of the Supreme Court decision in *Green v. Connally* (1971), that religious schools that refused to desegregate could not claim a tax exemption, the religious right argued—ineffectively, as it turned out—that, because public schools taught the alternative religion of secular humanism, schools teaching Christianity should be equally entitled to federal funds.[33] When that effort failed, the Christian right redoubled its efforts to replace public schools with schools promoting Christian values. In 1990, James Dobson and Gary Bauer published *Children at Risk: The Battle for the Hearts and Minds of Our Kids,* which argued that Christian children should be warriors in "the second Great Civil War."[34]

Publicly funded voucher programs too were created in response to disaffection with the public schools. Their use in religious private schools expanded after *Zelman v. Simmons-Harris* (1994). The Supreme Court determined that, even though 96% of the students in the Cleveland school district involved in the case used vouchers in religious schools, the program did not violate the establishment clause, because vouchers were available for use in both religious and nonsectarian schools.[35] By 2011, some 200,000 students in private and religious schools received vouchers.

Conservative Christian schools have benefited disproportionately from the development and expansion of such programs. While hard data can be difficult to come by, studies suggest that the curricula examined in this book also have a large and increasing share of the market for publicly funded voucher programs.[36] In Louisiana and Florida, when Republican governors Bobby Jindal and Jeb Bush expanded voucher programs, they were used primarily in Christian schools.[37] In those states, the Abeka and BJU curricula featured in this book were widely adopted, although it is strange to imagine histories that identify Catholics as heretics in widespread use in largely Catholic Louisiana. Investigative reporting by the *Orlando Sentinel* in 2018 found that 65% of the private schools in Florida using vouchers adopted one of these three curricula, although the Florida Department of Education is not allowed to track which curricula the 140,000 students receiving these funds use.[38] In 2017, the League of Women Voters of North Carolina also reported on private schools receiving vouchers. They found that 76.7% of voucher funding in North Carolina went to schools with a "literal biblical worldview that affects all areas of the curriculum." Most of them used the Abeka curriculum.[39]

Rebecca Klein of the *Huffington Post* conducted a thorough investigation and assembled a database of some 7,200 schools using vouchers across twenty-seven states and the District of Columbia. Yet it remains extremely difficult, perhaps deliberately, to find comprehensive information. Most states do not require reporting about curricula. Many private schools receiving vouchers are not required to exercise oversight of educational quality. As Klein put it, such schools "can conduct their schools in the manner they believe to be appropriate."[40]

But the dramatic expansion of homeschooling has been the most influential development in enlarging the market for the educational materials this book treats. Homeschooling as we know it today developed in the postwar period in response to both progressive and conservative discontent with the public schools. Progressives saw public schooling as rigid and insufficiently responsive to the needs of the individual child. Conservatives objected to changes in curricula as liberal, irreligious, or too responsive to disturbing changes in American culture.[41]

Various studies estimate that over 2 million students, or 3–4% of American school children, are currently homeschooled. This is approximately the same number of students who attend charter schools, and more than the number currently enrolled in parochial schools.[42] It is impossible to have completely accurate numbers of homeschooled children, especially since states with the largest numbers—California, Pennsylvania, and Texas—do not require parents to register homeschooled children. Twenty-six states do not even require testing of homeschooled students.

The predominant rationale for homeschooling, like that of other alternatives to public schooling, has been conservative, both religious and political. (The progressive impetus has become much less significant over time.) A key figure uniting these interests was the Christian Reconstructionist, Rousas John Rushdoony, who advocated for homeschooling as a Christian obligation and legal right. His views began to influence the religious right in the 1960s. He contended that that modern secular education inappropriately empowered children at the expense of the authority of God, parents, and teachers, allowing the state to encroach on the divinely established authority of parents. He called for the abolition of public schools and denounced them as serving secular interests, which cultivated "autonomy" or what conservative Christian curricula identify as "humanism" and which many evangelicals denounce as "secular humanism"—all of which Rushdoony considered antithetical to biblical law.[43] Rushdoony advocated Mosaic Law as the foundation of government—positions these textbooks as well as the TEKS take.[44] Rushdoony's educational views were significant in fostering the homeschool movement through court cases, in which he was both expert witness and litigant, that paved the way for ever more states to allow home-schooling.[45] His arguments prevailed in the crucial case *Texas Education Agency v. Leeper and Rushdoony* (1994). The Texas Supreme Court found that to exempt private schools from state oversight but not private home schools violated the equal protection clause of the Fourteenth Amendment. Texas then became extremely accommodating to homeschooling, which is virtu-ally unregulated there. Other states followed suit.

The greatest proportion of parents who choose homeschooling do so for religious reasons.[46] Current estimates suggest that between 75% to 90% of those who homeschool their children do so for religious reasons and the vast proportion of them, up to 90%, are conservative Christians.[47] The United States now has several generations who have been homeschooled. Many students being homeschooled are the children and grandchildren of those who had been educated in Christian schools.[48] It is not possible to determine accurately how many students currently use these Christian educational materials or were previously educated with them, although all three of the publishers of these curricula have, at one time or another, claimed that they have the largest share of the homeschool market.[49] The success of these edu-cational materials is increased by the vigorous promotion of them by home-schooling networks and seminars.

The Christian right has challenged public schools not simply from a re-ligious perspective but also from more extreme antigovernment and patri-archal positions. Some contend that government indoctrinates "children for a new social system" in which government will train them to serve the "big state." Some current members of the Kansas State Legislature insist that public schools be called "government schools," for example.[50] In the 2020 State of the Union Address, President Trump repeatedly cited "failing gov-ernment schools."[51]

Some involved in homeschooling promote the more extreme view that the godly family is patriarchal and hierarchical with women subject to the complete authority of their husbands and children to their parents.[52] John Holzman published the *Christian Education Manifesto,* laying out biblical quotations enjoining parental education.[53] Kevin Swanson, a Colorado pastor, argues for patriarchal homeschooling and has developed a strategy to implement that vision in Colorado with hopes of replicating it across the country.[54] Many homeschooling Christian parents believe they are carrying out the fundamental injunction of Deuteronomy 6:7 to "teach them diligently." Homeschooling fairs promoting Christian educational materials typically feature lectures on patriarchy, appropriate gender roles, and Christian courtship.[55]

The Homeschool Legal Defense Association supports homeschooling families. It asserts the absolute authority of parents over children and argues that that parents' right to determine their children's lives is guaranteed by the Fourteenth Amendment right to privacy. That right trumps school attendance laws, they insist.[56] It urges resistance to Child Welfare Laws and Child Protective Services as violations of parental authority.[57] As Chris Klicka, Senior Counsel of the Home School Legal Defense Fund (HSLDA), put it, "God has given the authority and the responsibility of educating children to the parents only."[58] A powerful and effective lobby, the HSLDA has prevailed in court cases attacking regulations or even registration of homeschooling, and many state legislatures have supported its efforts.[59] The political influence of HSLDA and its success in resisting oversight of homeschooling has raised concerns about children's rights and protections from inadequate education and child abuse in the home.[60]

From the establishment of Christian schools, efforts to privatize K–12 education, whether motivated by desire for educational reform, ideology, or crass pillaging of the public treasury, have allowed greater diffusion of educational materials such as these Christian world histories to greater numbers of students. Many who advocate for these alternative forms of schooling are sympathetic to these curricula's religious or political views and intend to make such materials the coin of the educational realm.[61] Homeschooling, motivated primarily by religious concerns and supported by right-wing groups, is crucial to the fusion of the political right with Christianity.

The political right intervenes in education not simply to foster alternatives to public schools but also to shape educational content to promote ideas they favor, many of which they share with the curricula examined in this book. The political right's efforts have become more sophisticated, better funded, and consistently directed to consolidating political and economic control over education.[62] Some state legislatures and school boards actively advance the Christian right's educational mission in the public schools. With many evangelicals and right-wing Republicans serving on school boards in states where the Republican Party controls statehouses, school textbook review committees, appointed by these elected school boards, frequently reflect ideological orthodoxy and a desire to see a "Christian" history of the United States and its hegemony. School board members or even textbook reviewers may well have learned this history in their schools or churches. They might have degrees from fundamentalist universities or seminaries. Believing that "Christian" history is the correct history, they are committed to promoting it.

The alliance between religious and right-wing political interests has attracted investors committed to promulgating a politically conservative history. The wealthy Koch brothers have spread largesse to many universities to establish curricula supporting conservatism as they define it—capitalism extolled, government attacked, and the social safety net or, indeed, any use of public monies in the public interest repudiated. Right-wing political interests, allied with and reinforced by Christian groups, are clearly "on message" in asserting American exceptionalism and its quasi-divine destiny as a unique model of government and society. The Kochs may have little interest in these curricula's religious arguments but support their political views. CRPE (Center on Reinventing Public Education), funded by the Walton Foundation, promotes "free-market education," including charter schools, voucher programs, and other efforts to privatize public schools.[63] ALEC (the American Legislative Exchange Council), largely funded by foundations such as the Charles G. Koch Foundation, the Claude Lambe Foundation, and the Scaife and Coors families, drafts educational legislation to advance corporate interests.[64] ALEC's members buy memberships and then ALEC lobbies state legislatures withbills promoting members' concerns and financial interests. ALEC writes bills on educational policy for virtually every Republican-held statehouse. When ALEC writes the laws, Republican legislatures pass them. Education bills recently or currently before state legislatures attest to a concerted effort of these foundations and think tanks to alter the historical narrative in ways consonant with these Christian curricula. ALEC bills support vouchers for schools using Christian curricula probably because they also promote unfettered capitalism. All these measures tighten bonds between religious conservatives and the political right.

A 148-page *Report and Analysis on Religious Freedom Measures Impacting Prayer and Freedom 2018–2019* outlines the goals of Project Blitz, a coalition of right-wing, Christian nationalist groups, including the Congressional Prayer Caucus and David Barton's Wallbuilders. Its legislative agenda includes promoting public school Bible courses, undermining LGBTQ rights, and asserting that religious freedom justifies public discrimination. They want to persuade legislatures to pass bills, including the Biblical Literacy Act, and issue proclamations, including A Proclamation Recognizing the Importance of the Bible in History and others endorsing Christian Heritage Week and Religious Freedom Day. Project Blitz disingenuously proclaims that its mission is not proselytization, because legislators make up their own minds even though the project furnishes templates to advance these measures.[65]

The relationship between the history propounded in these textbooks and conservative politics has tightened since the Supreme Court's *Citizens United* ruling unleashed floods of corporate money into American political life. Well-funded advocacy is expanding the diffusion of educational materials supporting a right-wing, Christian history as well as making public education an investment opportunity. Significant external money pours into local elections, even for relatively minor positions such as school board members. To cite just one example, the Koch brothers and Jeb Bush were significant donors to three right-wing school board members in Colorado, who then pushed through the previously discussed controversial standards for American history textbooks that only student protest derailed.[66]

That religious and political interests have coalesced to support the diversion of public educational funds into corporate hands and to advance their interests became increasingly obvious in the Trump administration. The Secretary of Education, Betsy DeVos, was a fervent proponent of Christian education and the use of public funds to support it, including through her family foundation, the American Federation for Children. She objected to oversight of schools and their curricula, as she did in Michigan. She supported The Education Savings Account Act, an ALEC bill, to divert funds equivalent to the public school per-student allocation for use as private elementary and high school tuition. She also advocated for the Educational Development Zone Act, which would allow families of any income level to use public school funds to attend private schools in any area deemed economically disadvantaged.[67] Such initiatives' success would further erode public education and expand the diffusion of highly unorthodox and ahistorical materials like the three curricula featured in this book.

A concerted effort to diffuse this distorted and polemical Christian narrative in public schools is well underway. Political and religious propaganda under the guise of a historical narrative, as exemplified by these curricula, have been advanced by reactionary state legislatures and school boards, less interested in history than in using history instruction to promote their beliefs and interests. When ALEC and CRPE, conservative legislators, Project Blitz, and some state boards attempt to stipulate the teaching of a right-wing

Christian American history, they contest the historical consensus about American history most overtly with disturbing ramifications for historians in all fields.

The view of history some on the right promote is disconcerting, but even more jarring is the explicit condemnation of critical thinking in public schools and universities. A plank in the Republican Party of Texas platform of 2016 perhaps makes this clearest: "We oppose the teaching of Higher Order Thinking Skills, critical thinking skills, which focus on behavior modification and have the purpose of challenging the student's fixed beliefs and undermining parental authority."[68]

National ridicule led to the removal of this plank, but the statement remains troubling for what it reveals about the understanding of education by some who make educational policy: education should have no impact on a student's "fixed beliefs." Whatever ideas a student brings to school should remain unchallenged and inviolate. The idea that education should simply corroborate received opinion (what the Enlightenment condemned as "prejudice") is an extreme ramification of a long-standing American suspicion of learning.[69] Fear of exposure to university education is at the heart of the legendary Bob Jones claim that children sent to college return as atheists.[70] A representative of Accelerated Christian Education (ACE) responded to criticism of its curriculum: "We do not believe that education should be nondirective or speculative or that the final interpretation of facts and events should be left up to immature inexperienced minds as mainline secular curricula do."[71]

If education should not expose students to new ideas, what is its purpose? How can a good education or a good history course fail to produce critical thinking as it expands students' exposure to unfamiliar events and ideas? What will education be, if knowledge of the humanities, including history, is stunted, particularly if it deliberately promotes an explicitly religious interpretation, inextricably tied to a political agenda?

The curricula I examine in this book have been the beneficiary of the expansion of alternatives to public schooling. They fueled the Christian school movement. They are adopted by schools with publicly funded voucher programs. They are in wide use by homeschooling parents. Their narratives are promoted by conservative politicians, legislators, and think tanks. As will be obvious, the ideas these curricula assert reach far beyond those who use them directly. They can be found in Christian media of all kinds from many radio and TV programs to megachurch sermons. What makes these curricula significant are the ideas they promote and the ways they have done so. They staked out the terrain for disseminating these materials throughout Christian education since the early 1970s, giving them a long and deep influence.

Why explore the content of these world history textbooks in depth rather than simply sound the alarm? These Christian curricula warrant serious consideration because (1) they penetrate the culture more thoroughly than one might expect; (2) what they select, what they omit, and their rationale for doing so expose their ahistorical but rhetorically effective worldview; (3) the premises of these histories shape an increasingly significant historical narrative but also frame contemporary debates on social and political issues because they are widely promulgated in other venues from blogs to ministries; (4) although they have already had considerable success in penetrating American secondary education, their challenge to the discipline of history has been neither sufficiently analyzed nor contextualized.

These are world histories, but they tell us a great deal about the United States, especially the history of religion and education. They inscribe the history of evangelical Protestantism on world history and present it as a Christian morality play in which American Protestant fundamentalist capitalists are God's chosen instruments. Christian America is preeminent in the world and other cultures disparaged in comparison. Under the guise of "truth" and "Christianity," these curricula articulate positions that have civic implications for the separation of church and state, civil rights, and religious toleration—all essential foundations of pluralistic democracy. These educational materials use history to make explicit arguments about how the past and present should be understood to shape the future. Their claim this is the "true" history that must be restored and imposed deserves to be exposed and contested.

1

The Publishers and Their Books

As the religious right began to flex its political muscle in firm alliance with the Republican Party and demand for educational materials for the mushrooming Christian day schools exploded, Bob Jones University (BJU), Accelerated Christian Education (ACE), and Abeka Books all began publishing to meet this need. These three publishers are committed to an alternative, Christian perspective on all disciplines:[1] BJU offers "Christ-centered resources for education, edification and evangelism"; Abeka Books' motto is "excellence in education from a Christian perspective"; ACE's stated mission is "the world for Christ . . . one child at a time."[2] These publishers stake out their opposition to secularism, liberalism, and humanism—red flags for much of their intended audience. They reject biblical modernism and insist on biblical inerrancy.[3] They oppose much of modern culture.

The dean of the BJU School of Education, Walter G. Fremont, urged his fellow fundamentalists to "face the stark reality that many Christian schools lack direction" to develop materials with a rigorous and consistent religious message. Despite shared concerns, their efforts to formulate a unified position only confirmed divergent views within the fundamentalist camp.[4] Abeka Books offered a "traditional Christian curriculum"; BJU was "conventional"; and ACE claimed that it had the proper fundamentalist perspective.[5] Despite these differences, which seem subtle but appeal to specific constituencies, the promulgators of ACE and the Abeka curricula were all educated at Bob Jones University and thus share deep, common roots in American fundamentalist education.

While these publishing ventures began only in the 1970s, American fundamentalism developed much earlier and largely in response to innovations in American university education adopted from Germany in the 1890s, including the seminar system and a scientific approach to disciplines. Many evangelicals rejected these changes as undermining higher education's Christian foundation. They responded in various ways, but by the 1920s, fundamentalists had defined distinctive, more rigid theological positions and founded Bible institutes and universities to maintain their beliefs and

Hijacking History. Kathleen Wellman, Oxford University Press. © Oxford University Press 2021.
DOI: 10.1093/oso/9780197579237.003.0002

enforce college students' moral behavior. Even fundamentalists could not agree exactly on their central religious beliefs, their standards for behavior, or their response to pressing intellectual issues, particularly evolution. They divided into pre- and postmillennialists, taking different stances on when Christ would return and on what terms, or whether there were successive dispensations or distinct periods of God's relationship with man.[6] They even disagreed on how firmly their differences divided them. Bob Jones College, now Bob Jones University, was founded at this time. It shared these general concerns but has always taken positions characteristic of Southern fundamentalism that continue to influence its curriculum.[7] While the publishing ventures featured in this book were among the first to respond to the demand for alternative educational materials for the new Christian schools, they expanded well beyond the fundamentalist market into the current, broader Christian market and all the venues described in the Introduction.

Accelerated Christian Education (ACE) is independent of any academic institution and is produced by American Educational Products Company, founded in 1970 by Esther and Donald Howard. Based in Hendersonville, Tennessee, with a distribution center in Lewisville, Texas, just north of Dallas, ACE emphasizes its theological purity, allowing only those schools that accept central evangelical beliefs to use their materials.[8] Curricular materials explicitly ally religion with patriotism: the ACE logo is a bald eagle atop the Bible. The first Learning Center to use this curriculum opened in 1970 in Garland, Texas, northeast of Dallas, and it quickly became the curriculum most Christian schools. Its adoption by Christian Liberty Academy Schools (CLASS) initially propelled its growth.[9] By 1980, 8,000 schools as well as significant numbers of homeschoolers in the United States used ACE materials. As other ACE schools were launched across the world, distribution centers opened in the Philippines, Russia, the United Kingdom, and Africa. As the founder of ACE noted, the curriculum "literally reproduced itself around the world."[10] The early 1980s were the high point of the dissemination of ACE's curriculum in the United States. By 2013, its scope had diminished; it claimed to serve 6,000 schools in 145 countries. Nonetheless, its promotional materials proudly proclaim to have educated millions over the past fifty years. ACE hosts national and international competitions for students educated with its materials as well as an annual all-Africa conference. The emphasis on Africa is part of ACE's proselytizing outreach.[11]

ACE cofounder Don Howard proved to be a tireless promoter of its materials as the best and most innovative, child-centered education.[12] Its materials are also called "Schools of Tomorrow." This curriculum quickly became popular; its methods were aggressively promoted as effective and low-cost, described in one analysis as a "school-in-a-kit." ACE provides a complete educational system, including consultants.[13] The company is a $15 million a year operation in fifty countries. Initially, Howard and his partner, Dr. Ronald E. Johnson, a member of the Arizona Governor's Commission on Textbooks, held all shares.[14]

This curriculum may warrant kudos from the assessment industry, as every lesson has "objectives," but its methods have more usually been condemned. The student works through a workbook called a Self-Pac of Accelerated Christian Education, with twelve such packets per subject per grade level. For high school world history, the student reads a short section, a paragraph or two; answers questions about it; and regurgitates the material just read in a short fill-in-the-blank quiz. Every section is followed by a quiz. The correct answers replicate exactly the material previously read; interpretation or analysis is unnecessary. At the end of a Self-Pac, the student takes a fill-in-the-blank test with questions identical to the earlier quizzes. (The ACE curriculum for United States history provides a more extensive narrative than for world history.[15]) Its unappealing, if functional, format perhaps diminishes this curriculum's impact in disseminating its central ideas; the course materials are unrelentingly dull. They have been revised only slightly and infrequently since the 1970s. A new edition added some 400 words to the world history curriculum, for example.[16] The course packs are full of inconsistencies, even in the typefaces within a single Self-Pac, pointing to the sloppy editing and inexpensive production values of these widely distributed curricula.

All ACE schools are strikingly uniform, as stipulated in the Procedures Manual and Administration Manual.[17] As the ACE website attests, only kindergarten and the earliest grade levels require an instructor or parent (because that instruction is based on phonetics). Subsequent levels of instruction require "minimal staffing"; anyone can supervise students working on their own. An ACE training manual even contends that a degree is detrimental to teaching. Online support is available from Lighthouse Christian Academy, which issues "accredited diplomas."[18]

Not surprisingly, the ACE curriculum has been criticized as promoting nothing but rote learning. In its first twenty years of operation alone, ACE was involved in more than 150 lawsuits, primarily over accreditation. When Jonathan Scaramanga, educated in an ACE school, explored ACE educational methods in his University College London doctoral dissertation, he denounced their methods as indoctrination. His dissertation profiled "survivor stories" by former students who critiqued their education as completely inadequate or even abusive.[19] When *The Guardian* and *The Independent* investigated conditions in ACE schools in the United Kingdom, they condemned them as inhumane. Reporters pointed out that students were required to work silently in cubicles and prevented from moving without a supervisor's permission. Corporal punishment was encouraged to keep students on task. They critiqued the quality of education as well. Graduates with ACE diplomas reported that employers did not accept their credentials and that they were inadequately prepared to pursue higher education. Studies revealed that the ACT scores of students educated with these materials were significantly lower than those of students using more orthodox materials.[20]

ACE emphasizes parental authority over all aspects of their children's lives, encapsulated in what they call the GREAT COMMANDMENT, substantiated by Deuteronomy 6:7: "And thou shalt teach them diligently unto thy children, and shalt talk to them when thou sittest in thine house, and when thou walkest by the way, and when thou liest down, and when thou risest up." As ACE insists, students "grow to see God's point of view."[21] Each workbook integrates "biblical truths and character-building principles."[22] These materials are littered with random questions like "is your office neat?" presumably to urge the student to good behavior.

Its workbook format makes glaringly obvious when this curriculum takes extreme or controversial positions or makes fallacious claims, many intended to refute evolution. It baldly states that evolution is a lie and that the Loch Ness monster proves it, presumably showing that dinosaurs roamed the earth with humans.[23] In the same vein, it claims that Japanese fisherman recently found a dinosaur.

ACE has an international presence, with a focus on proselytizing in Africa. One might assume that its curricular material would provoke opposition or intense hostility there, since it consistently portrays Africa as backward. But international objections have been most vehement from Norway, which banned ACE for violating its gender equality act. The Norwegian Equality Board of Appeals presented its case against ACE as a violation of CEDAW (Commission on the Elimination of Discrimination against Women). Labor Party leader Trond Giske read aloud from an ACE workbook, "Since God's word tells us that wives are to subjugate themselves to their own husbands, then this means that wives should obey their husbands. Wives who love their husbands in the way that God intended are happy to submit to their husbands."[24] An ACE spokesman responded that men and women are equal but God stipulated their distinct roles: men are leaders and women are nurturers.

Abeka Books textbooks have also generated controversies. It is the publishing arm of Pensacola Christian College and is named for Rebekah "Beka" Horton, the wife of the college president, Arlin Horton. Founded in 1974, Pensacola Christian College claims to be "an idea that came from God," although it was founded when the Hortons became convinced that their alma mater, Bob Jones University, had adopted secular and progressive religious ideas.[25] In contrast, Abeka Books insists that it offers a "distinctively Christian-traditional, liberal education," training students "competent in their chosen fields of study, knowledgeable of the Bible, capable of rightly divining the Word and the truth of God." Its educational objective is that students be able to "explain biblical teaching regarding the God-ordained institutions of the home, church, and government."[26] Pensacola Christian College also owns the Rejoice Broadcast Network, which broadcasts to two million on the upper Gulf Coast, with another thirty-nine "satellator stations." It broadcasts a weekly television program *Campus Church* nationwide.

The college requires its students to accept a strict code of conduct, based in biblical injunctions and extrapolation where the Bible is silent. Student must abstain from alcohol, tobacco, e-cigarettes, illicit drugs, pornography, sexual immorality, dancing, profanity, obscenity, harassment, abuse, discrimination, gambling, stealing, and satanic practices. It prohibits "sexual communications, including verbal, written, or electronic." Contact between the sexes is so strictly controlled that campus buildings have sex-segregated elevators. A strict dress code is imposed on men and women; women may not wear pants.[27]

These stringent stipulations were not a response to the sexual revolution of the 1960s. Fundamentalist universities widely implemented them in the 1920s to resist new social practices of courtship and marriage, which moved courtship from the familial setting to more public venues.[28] By exercising strict control over the behavior of students, these new universities resisted such changes. Pensacola Community College still exercises great vigilance *in loco parentis,* as other fundamentalist universities have done since the 1920s. While these strictures may seem anachronistic, many were in effect until the

1970s at most American universities.[29] At its founding, Pensacola Christian College maintained them.

Abeka Books developed its publishing venture in the 1970s as fundamentalists became more vocal in the culture wars. The Hortons defined their educational agenda: they intended to preserve theological purity and traditional methods and substance in education. They purchased copyrights for older materials and republished them.[30] Virtually all sources their textbooks cite were written before 1960. Copyright issues may play a role, but the publisher doubtless appreciates sources untainted by more recent scholarship or ideas. Thus the Abeka history textbooks rely on sources that are outmoded or written by religious writers. The Abeka curriculum advocates a return to the appropriate education of earlier days, which, it contends, was "basically the same as that followed by Martin Luther, John Calvin, John Wesley, the English and American Puritans, and the majority of Christians through the ages. It is called traditional education."[31]

With over a million students using its textbooks, Abeka Books is the largest US publisher of Christian textbooks and the largest provider for the homeschool market.[32] The company, valued at $280 million, generates approximately $70 million in revenue, and supports the college.[33] Its K–12 curriculum is now used in more than 10,000 Christian schools. A large, but again unknowable, share of homeschooled students use their textbooks. By 1998, over 225,000 families purchased their textbooks independently of schools.[34] The Abeka Academy Video Streaming enrolls more than 50,000 homeschooled students.[35] The college produces teachers and administrators for K–12 schools. It hosts regular sales events to promote and sell their materials. Several occur each month in a variety of locations in the Dallas area, for example. It also has a massive marketing presence online. The many modes of distribution suggest a wide diffusion of these materials but the lack of reporting requirements for private schools and homeschoolers makes an accurate account of their actual use impossible.

Objections to the content of the Abeka Books focus primarily on its science and history curricula. It was party to a lawsuit brought by Calvary Christian Schools against the state of California after the University of California system refused to accept courses using its materials as fulfilling admission requirements. The State of California maintained that the Abeka Books' science and American history curricula failed to conform to the academic consensus on either subject. When the circuit court found the testimony of professional historians and scientists persuasive, the State of California and the National Center for Science Education prevailed. The Supreme Court declined to hear the case on appeal. Abeka Books was also sued by the federal government for back taxes. It had claimed tax-exempt status as a nonprofit because it channeled its profits back to Pensacola Christian College. In 1995, the IRS ruled that the publishing arm was a for-profit entity and subject to taxation.

The best known of these publishers is undoubtedly Bob Jones University Press. It is the publishing arm of Bob Jones University, an obligatory site for visits by Republican presidential candidates hoping for an evangelical endorsement or a South Carolina primary win. The university has long insisted that it maintains true Christianity or the most orthodox fundamentalism. Founded in 1927 as Bob Jones College in Panama City, Florida, it moved to Cleveland, Tennessee in 1933 before becoming Bob Jones University in 1947 in Greenville, South Carolina. Bob Jones Sr., who smarted under the characterization of fundamentalists as ignorant and backward in the aftermath of the Scopes trial, founded the college to train fundamentalists. Like other early fundamentalists, he advocated withdrawal from worldly corruption and deplored the new, scientific model of university education. His university was established to maintain religious fundamentals and insist on moral behavior. He identified evolutionary theory as a sign of the decline of both and asserted that the new college (as it was then) would resist "all atheistic, agnostic, pagan and so-called scientific adulteration of the Gospel, unqualifiedly affirming and teaching the inspiration of the Bible (both Old and New Testaments); the creation of man by the direct act of God."[36] Bob Jones University has always insisted on an education integrated by the Bible, which, as its faculty wrote in their *Christian Philosophy of Education*, "gives basic truths in God's word as inerrant, divinely inspired and preserved in sixty-six books of the Old and New Testaments."[37]

In the 1940s, Jones stipulated that BJU students were to read Darwin and other proponents of evolution, but they were to be taught that such theories were just guesses. The BJU faculty confidently expected that such teaching would foster an appreciation of creation, as indeed it did. But they also entertained theories suggesting gaps or prolonged periods of geological time between creation and modern history. Such theories then gained the support of many fundamentalist universities even though they challenged strict biblical literalism. It is striking how much more rigidly opposed to evolution BJU's position has become since then.

Throughout its history, the university has been governed by the Jones family; its first four chancellors were family members, although its fifth chancellor, Steve Pettit, is not. With only 95,000 graduates to date, the university's prominence in promoting staunchly conservative, Christian views has given it a greater influence than the number of its graduates would suggest. Furthermore, Bob Jones University has been crucial in training teachers and administrators for the burgeoning number of religious schools. In 1973, it inaugurated graduate study with an MS in school administration "to prepare administrators for a dynamic ministry in the Christian Schools."[38]

Its faculty and the policies the university requires of them preserve its consistent character and ideology. Faculty are not granted tenure and must espouse and support fundamentalist views. For example, science faculty members must now subscribe to Young Earth creationism, the belief that the earth is less than 10,000 years old. The university neither promotes research nor allows academic freedom. Its students must "live obediently under authority."[39] Not surprisingly, there have been several purges of faculty for disloyalty. Unaccredited for much of its history, Bob Jones University is now accredited by the Transnational Association of Christian Colleges and Schools.

Bob Jones University and its chancellors have had a long history of insisting on theological purity and have regularly fallen out with other evangelicals and even other fundamentalists, condemning them as lax or insufficiently committed to the truth. The university claimed a "purest of the pure" status, defined itself in staunch opposition to modern culture, and rigorously separated itself from it. These quarrels provide a useful window into the evolution of both religious movements over the twentieth century.

Baptist fundamentalists, who broke with the main denomination in 1925 as the Southern Baptist Convention, founded Bob Jones University. Throughout the 1930s and 1940s, it retained a consistent commitment to separatism. Its position was somewhat inconsistent. Even as it withdrew from society and looked to the premillennialist expectation of the destruction of society, it also saw the university as an institution building "a city on a hill" to battle society.[40] This stance combines the inherent contradiction of its quest to remake a Christian society with the initial fundamentalist retreat from secular culture. Ironically, this central inconsistency allowed BJU to emerge as a political force on the Christian right.

The university played a prominent and clearly defined role in the Christian right in early twentieth-century politics. It supported Prohibition and nativism, and was virulently anti-Catholic. In 1928, Bob Jones Sr. delivered an impassioned sermon, "The Perils of America," warning that immigrants and cities were great dangers and that the United States must submit to biblical authority. He ardently supported William Jennings Bryan and joined the anti-Catholic campaign against the Catholic Al Smith's presidential campaign in the election of 1928. Jones withdrew from direct political participation once Prohibition, one of his principal causes, had ended in 1933.

But Bob Jones Jr. carried on his father's crusades. In 1960, the university staunchly opposed the presidential campaign of the Catholic John F. Kennedy. Jones criticized the Roman Catholic Church as "not another Christian denomination. It is a satanic counterfeit, an ecclesiastic tyranny over the souls of man. . . . It is the old harlot of the Book of Revelation. . . . all popes 'are demon possessed.' "[41] He invoked "Americanism" as a right-wing code word directed against both desegregation and immigration. He affirmed the mantra "America is a Christian country." Committed to racial separation as biblical, Jones denounced the civil rights movement as the work of Satan.[42] During his tenure, BJU became well known as a venue for speakers advocating segregation and the exodus of the United States from the United Nations. Vestiges of these positions remain evident in its educational materials.

Because of these extreme positions, Jones became embroiled in controversies with other fundamentalists. He previously supported Billy Graham and the National Association of Evangelicals but became disillusioned over compromises they made on social and religious issues. Jones's dispute with Graham reflected a split between separatist-fundamentalists and more ecumenical neo-evangelicals who sought greater cultural influence and more followers. His father, Bob Jones Sr., had earlier denounced even Graham's sharing speaking platforms with Catholics, condemning him for violating 2 John 9–11, which prohibits fellowship with those who do "not abide in the teaching of Christ." Bob Jones Jr. confirmed his father's views.[43]

Bob Jones University's policies on sex, specifically those with racial overtones, also generated controversy. In 2014, an independent report revealed that Bob Jones University told student victims of sexual assault not to report it and instead blamed the victims. In response to the report, the president apologized.[44] But the university's policies against Black students were especially egregious. It did not admit Black students until 1971, and, from 1971 to 1975, Black students had to be married. As recently as 1998, Bob Jones University refused, on biblical grounds, to admit married, mixed-race couples. These policies raised questions about the university's tax-exempt status. Bob Jones III defended restrictions on Black students by using biblical quotations. He insisted, as had his father and grandfather, that God intended racial segregation.[45] These policies made BJU central to conservatism, particularly in the South. Strom Thurmond and Ronald Reagan played influential roles in the political life of the university—Thurmond because of his own segregationist beliefs and Reagan as part of the Republican strategy to recruit Southern Democrats by appealing to Southern racism. Since 1980, many Republican candidates for local and statewide offices and for the presidency have sought the endorsement of BJU to enhance their standing with evangelicals. The university endorsed Reagan, but Bob Jones III later denounced him for choosing George H. W. Bush, whom he called a "devil," as his vice-president.[46]

In the case of Bob Jones University v. United States, the Supreme Court ruled against the university's admission policies as discriminatory. It asserted that the First Amendment did not prevent the IRS from revoking the tax-exempt status of a religious university whose policies contravened central concerns of the federal government. In this case, BJU violated the federal non-discrimination policy. The case was part of the Justice Department's broader effort to enforce the Civil Rights Act. The decision mobilized evangelicals' political engagement, as they saw their tax-exempt status threatened. (Bob Jones University's tax-exempt status was restored in March 2017, when the university merged with its nonprofit elementary school as BJU, Inc.)[47]

Bob Jones University rescinded its policy against interracial dating but only after George W. Bush's visit as a presidential candidate in 2000 generated negative media attention. While the university's endorsement remains one conservative Republicans still seek, BJU has played a less overt political role in recent years. Liberty University with its 100,000 students no likely give conservative politicians a bigger forum. BJU's fourth chancellor, Stephen Jones, son of Bob Jones III, endorsed no one in the 2008 presidential election. The university, nonetheless, continues to influence the Christian right primarily through its publications and its commitment to training school administrators.

While conservatives objected that public schools were teaching "secular humanism" as an alternative religion, BJU Press, in contrast, made the Bible central to every part of the curriculum. So firmly committed to an alternative world view, it even produced The Christian Student Dictionary to eliminate anti-Christian bias in definitions.[48] (Ironically, BJU thus recognizes, much as the Enlightenment thinkers they deplore, that definitions have the power to change first meaning and then thinking.) Despite its earlier separatism from corrupt culture, the university later took more public roles to influence culture and politics.[49]

Bob Jones University, like fundamentalists Pat Robertson and Jim Baker, cultivated a media empire. It published a biblically based periodical, *Faith*, from 1973 to 1986 and, in 1976, introduced a weekly radio program, *Show My People*. The BJU Press, founded in 1973, is the most significant aspect of its expanded outreach efforts. The university's educational philosophy is somewhat more open than that of Pensacola Christian College and insists the faculty be well-trained. However, BJU Dean Walter G. Fremont criticized Abeka Books and other fundamentalist publishers for using early twentieth-century materials. The use of such materials, he charged, introduced progressive content, undermining religious authority and fundamentalism. Thus, BJU Press produced its own materials.[50] Pensacola Christian College countercharged that the university and its curricula were unacceptably liberal.

At present, the press has over a million pre-college students using its textbooks. It offers distance-learning courses and serves the homeschool market. It has an ancillary Academy of Home Education, which maintains school records, administers achievement tests, and issues diplomas. It developed a weeklong Home Education Leadership Program (HELP) and hosted homeschool fairs. Like the other two publishers, BJU Press offers a complete education with online support platforms. BJU LINC (Live Interactive Network Classroom) serves schools without teachers appropriate to the discipline and HomeSat (Home School Access Terminal) for those homeschooling.[51]

The BJU world history textbooks are written by its faculty and staff. The fourth edition identifies its author as Dennis Bollinger, a PhD in history from BJU, who is assisted by the same authors listed on earlier editions. Of the listed contributors, only Bollinger and Carl Abrams are trained historians. Abrams, a BJU graduate, has a PhD in history from the University of Maryland with significant publications to his credit. His area of expertise is American religious history. This publishing house relies on collaborative writing as well as ghostwriting, likely to guarantee orthodox treatment of all issues. Contributors to BJU textbooks typically have academic credentials in church history, church music, or theology. The BJU Press also has a Biblical Integration Team to ensure that all of its publications promote its message. The coordinator of that team is Bryan Smith, who has a PhD in Old Testament

Interpretation from Bob Jones University.[52] This collaborative feature may well explain some of the jarring dissonance in the textbook's narrative.

The in-house character of the publishing arm of the university carries through with the university's extensive hiring of their own graduates as faculty. In 1992–1993, there were 310 faculty; 252 of them were alumni. Forty-nine faculty had doctoral degrees, ten of them from BJU, showing how firmly this university remains an in-house operation.[53] The current catalog reveals that nearly 90% of the faculty have an undergraduate or graduate degree from Bob Jones University.[54]

The BJU world history looks much like a conventional textbook but draws conclusions foreign to standard narratives. It interjects non sequiturs to make a religious point or to give explicit instructions to students on how they are to understand what they have learned. It proudly proclaims that its curriculum is "free of distortions of truth such as evolution and humanism." To make sure students cannot miss these points, the 2007 edition tested two separate kinds of material. A first section includes orthodox exam questions and identification of historical figures and events, and essays requiring discussion of historical information. In other words, it makes the usual demands of a history exam. Another test for each section, called "Thinking with Jesus," requires students to subscribe to the authors' religious interpretation of the period to pass the test. This strategy may well have allowed students to maneuver within both conventional test-taking settings, such as the SAT, yet subscribe to the correct Christian point of view. These dual tests are not included in the most recent edition, but workbooks reinforce a biblical interpretation of historical material.[55]

Although these curricula share a religious tradition and political perspective, there are obvious differences between them, even in format. The BJU world history editions have nearly or over 600 pages of tight print in the textbook's two recent editions. Richly illustrated, it most closely resembles an orthodox history textbook in format. It is much more challenging than the other two. The Abeka textbook editions are just 430–450 pages, with larger typeface and less content. While the BJU curriculum incorporates some more recent scholarship, the Abeka textbook uses old church histories and obviously dated sources. It rejects all historical material written after the 1950s because it reflects the culture of the 1960s. The ACE curriculum does not provide a textbook but rather twelve workbooks, called Self-Pacs, per subject and indicates neither sources nor authors. The author of the Abeka world history, Jerry Combee, with a PhD in government, wrote a number of conservative US histories, including *Designed for Destiny* and *Democracy at Risk: The Rising Tide of Illiteracy and Ignorance of the Constitution.*

This study began by examining the editions of the BJU and Abeka textbooks available in 2014. Both publishers produced new editions in 2016. As is common in textbook publishing, the new editions made few changes but reduced the amount of text. The BJU edition of 2016 includes almost identical content to that of the earlier edition but, with different formatting, it has cut some sixty pages to produce one volume rather than two. The explicitly religious reflections at the end of each chapter have been omitted, but now some are featured in chapter assignments and the accompanying study guide. The final chapter, "To the Present," was reduced from the thirty pages of the earlier edition to fourteen. The Abeka edition of 2016 is some twenty pages shorter and reorganized to make its argument that history tells the story of God's favor to Christians even more explicit. It also reduced its treatment of the history of other parts of the world to focus on its central narrative.

These publishers have been important to the rise of Christian (non-Catholic) education since the 1970s. They appealed to Christians who wanted to protect their children from aspects of modern American culture they saw as threatening. They sought an education that was untainted by "secular humanism" and that would allow them to avoid desegregation. Later Christian parents who chose these curricula likely shared with them an antipathy to the civil rights movement, feminism, and other cultural issues of the 1960s. These curricula, replete with dire warnings about the dangers of mainline American culture, attracted those who wanted to separate themselves from it. Ironically, since they were first published in the early 1970s, the ideas they promote have become more central to American culture.

With many alternatives to public schooling, why would parents still choose the Christian curricula treated in this book for their children? The curricula's appeal is likely both their content and their convenience. Many of those who homeschool their children may well appreciate the complete program of education these curricula provide with textbooks, tests, and study guides. The ACE curriculum even makes an instructor unnecessary, as students work alone; anyone can compare workbook answers to the key provided. The BJU educational materials have demanding content with high production values and extensive illustration. The Abeka textbooks also resemble orthodox materials in format, and the ACE workbooks are accessible. For parents taking on the challenges of homeschooling, the touted intellectual pedigree of the textbooks' authors might be attractive. These materials seem to have the same stamp of authority as other curricula. They also receive strong endorsements from Christian reviewes of homeschool curricula.[56]

For a teacher or a parent looking for educational materials from a "Christian perspective," these curricula would likely seem attractive. Parents and schools that select these textbooks appreciate their insistence on the Bible as the source of knowledge, biblical law as a foundation of society, and parents as authorities over children. Some choosing these curricula may be unaware of their specific history or religious positions but pleased to have a Christian education for their children. Many who homeschool children share religious traditions tied to evangelicalism, especially since many of them were products of the Christian schools of a generation ago. They may also be attached to new megachurches that do not have explicit theological positions but would certainly be sympathetic to the "Christian" designation these curricula use, the adversarial stance toward the modern world they promote, and the political conservatism they reinforce. Parents have chosen to use these Christian curricula. The next chapter considers what Christianity their choice entails.

2

What Christianity?

These history curricula emphatically reject an allegedly erroneous, secular history in favor of a purportedly correct, Christian perspective—the only legitimate way to understand world history. When they use the term "Christian," what do they mean? Although these textbooks do not define it, they clearly believe that they have the correct understanding. Nonetheless, it is difficult to determine exactly what that entails: they admit no real distinctions of creed and stipulate few theological tenets; they are simply "Christian."

This chapter discusses the myriad religious traditions implicit in that term as these textbooks apply it. To do so, it is necessary to briefly follow the history of Protestantism into evangelicalism and crucial to discuss the fracturing of evangelicalism in the nineteenth century over social and political issues, most critically over slavery. This chapter addresses some distinctions between evangelicals and fundamentalists, even though neither group was ever entirely uniform in its beliefs. It is also important to remember that there were no self-styled fundamentalists before the early twentieth century. When fundamentalists broke from evangelicals, it was easier to differentiate the two. Distinguishing between their present manifestations has become harder even for scholars of religion, because fundamentalists differentiate themselves from evangelicals in various and not entirely consistent ways but share many religious and political views. Many fundamentalists now reject the term "fundamentalist" in favor of "evangelical" because of the current pejorative connotations of the former. By separating evangelicalism from Christian nationalism, some evangelicals have recently tried to disassociate themselves from the political positions many evangelicals have taken.[1]

This chapter briefly explores two more extreme views that have permeated both religious communities, although they are often not clearly alluded to or recognized: Christian Reconstructionism and dominionism. This chapter thus teases out many strands within American Protestantism and its history that shape these curricula. They themselves, it must be emphasized, studiously avoid such terms. They instead present every position they take as

Hijacking History. Kathleen Wellman, Oxford University Press. © Oxford University Press 2021.
DOI: 10.1093/oso/9780197579237.003.0003

Christian. Nonetheless, in applying the term "Christian" to historical events, they reveal multiple influences, as this book points out where they occur.

To be Christian unquestionably means to be Protestant for these curricula; Protestants understood "biblical truth." Even the earliest Christians in the centuries immediately after Christ's death did not meet this standard. They were quickly overwhelmed by the heresy of Roman Catholicism. "Christians" arrived with the Reformation and Martin Luther's "true" understanding of Scripture with *sola scriptura* and *sola fides*. "True" is emphatically not Roman Catholic. Anti-Catholicism remained a unifying issue for American evangelicals from the eighteenth century until their sometimes uneasy alliance with Catholics over opposition to abortion in the 1970s. That hostility remains latent in some quarters but is overt in these textbooks.

Luther repudiated Catholicism by expunging its errors, as he saw them, and establishing central, theological tenets of Protestantism, but he did not define a systematic theology. And modern evangelicalism, while embracing Lutheran fundamentals, defines or requires adherence to a coherent, developed theology even less than Lutheranism does. It is theologically tethered to few tenets beyond the authority of Scripture and the belief that salvation was gained by Jesus Christ's death.

Christianity, as these curricula construe it, is indebted to Luther for its fundamental social stance as well. Over their history, American evangelicals periodically retreated from direct involvement in society and politics. At such times, they shared the position Luther advocated when he advised peasants to look to the next life for redress for their dire social ills. After the bloody denouement of the Peasants' War against feudal overlords, Luther urged his followers to retreat from social and political engagement. So too these curricula frequently emphasize that the Christian message has nothing to do with alleviating social problems. For modern evangelicals that stance owes as much to early twentieth-century disputes within evangelicalism over the Social Gospel as to the early Protestant reformer.

These curricula's Christianity is also indebted to the other central figure of the sixteenth-century Protestant Reformation, John Calvin, primarily because the Calvinists who left England, whether Separatists or Puritans, rejected Anglicanism as an insufficiently reformed form of Protestantism. They were the initial English settlers of New England. These textbooks reflect American evangelicalism's roots in the eighteenth-century Calvinist Congregationalist churches. They appreciate Calvin's emphasis on sin, the powerlessness of man, the power of God, and His Covenant with humanity. These textbooks are staunchly Calvinist in their proselytizing zeal and commitment to God's covenant with His chosen as the source of their moral and political empowerment. God works through human history to achieve His ends. That fact alone makes human history important—a fundamental Calvinist tenet.[2] These textbooks, as their evangelical forebears did, excise the stringency from Calvin's theology, including his emphasis on divine predestination to heaven or hell. As early as the 1920s, Calvinists reflected the conflict between theological purity and "institutional pragmatism," as Adam Laats describes it.[3] These curricula do not specify those excisions but rather, again like early evangelicals, emphasize the good news of grace. They most clearly reveal their Calvinist roots in their emphasis on sinfulness, or "total depravity," as Calvin described it. This emphasis may reflect or simply accord with the similar position of the New Calvinism of the 2000s along with its commitment to authority and hierarchy.[4]

Christianity also entails evangelical Protestantism for these textbooks, although that inclusion too is left unspecified.[5] They confirm key characteristics of evangelicalism the noted historian of the movement George Marsden identified: "(1) belief in the final authority of the Bible, (2) the real historical character of God's saving work recorded in Scripture, (3) salvation to eternal life based on the redemptive work of Christ, (4) the importance of evangelism and missions."[6] But evangelicalism, as historians of religion emphasize, has been neither homogeneous nor static.[7] While scholars explore the history of evangelicalism, many evangelicals as well as these textbooks seem largely unaware or unwilling to acknowledge its deeply contested history. Most positions these curricula signal as defining true Christianity emerged from battles within Protestant denominations and within the evangelical community itself from the Reformation to the present.

True Christianity, as these curricula present it, is detached from history and admits no change over time. Christianity is thus either ahistorical or afflicted with historical amnesia, much like modern American evangelicalism. It is ironic that history textbooks treat post-Reformation Christianity as having no history; truth was either accepted or resisted. The irony increases, as these curricula never acknowledge how deeply the history of their religious beliefs is embedded in them. Instead, they record those who believed the truth and spread it. To admit historical change into Christianity would interject contingency into what these textbooks present as unquestionable and unchanging.

Since evangelicals first separated from the Calvinists of New England Congregationalist churches during the eighteenth-century First Great Awakening, they emphasized individual religious experience and emotion over adherence to theological positions. If these curricula focused on theology, they might both undervalue and intellectualize that experience. Since certainty about both salvation and truth is grounded in a personal experience, doctrinal disputes do not hold much interest for most contemporary evangelicals, who instead enjoy an assurance that they are saved.[8] Perhaps evangelicals do not emphasize their history because doing so would highlight the many theological disputes and even schisms among them and, indeed, confirm that they have a contested intellectual tradition rather than a consistent "truth." Such issues may engage scholars but are not part of the evangelicals' general notion of what it means to be a Christian. Their acceptance of the authority of the Bible has by no means produced consensus on how to interpret it. Without a systematic theology to ground it, modern evangelicalism can, however, be more ecumenical, bringing many more into the fold, building larger communities, and serving conversions. Lack of theological specificity has characterized evangelicalism from the outset. It has been, as Timothy Smith describes it, "a kaleidoscope," attracting adherents otherwise defined by their attachment to movements and creeds from Pentecostal to Southern Baptist.[9]

These textbooks and evangelicals more generally do not acknowledge the social and religious dissent that galvanized it initially. Evangelicals opposed the social elites of New England, objecting to Congregationalists' control of both civic and religious hierarchies. Unlike Congregationalist churches, evangelical congregations were more socially inclusive and theologically amorphous. By adopting religious revivalism, evangelicalism attracted converts and spread from New England throughout the South and Midwest. The rejection of social and political elites that fueled early evangelicalism can still be wielded against the educated or elites, even though social status and wealth are increasingly deemed manifestations of divine favor.

These textbooks are inherently providentialist, identifying God's favor throughout history. This view is a ramification of their underlying Calvinism and its understanding of God's successive covenants.[10] Since the nineteenth century, providentialism focused explicitly on the nation, as God both judged the virtue of its rulers and favored it. A report generated by the BJU faculty underscored providentialism as central to teaching American history: one must "emphasize the providential circumstances of its founding and associate its prosperity with obedience to God."[11] This sense of prosperity as a sign of divine favor has been further emphasized and amplified by the "prosperity gospel."[12]

Dispensationalism is a rather arcane position implicit in these curricula's narratives. It is a more defined providentialism, undergirded by a more rigid Calvinism than usually characterizes evangelicalism. For Calvin, God chose to work through unworthy human creatures to fulfill His plan and did so in successive covenants, as His repudiation of the Jews and subsequent adoption of early Christians and then Protestant reformers confirmed. That fact, Calvin believed, made human history important and should inspire his followers to great effort to advance God's plan. Much of the coercive character of Puritan Calvinism was motivated by a desire to impel human beings to advance God's work on earth. Dispensationalism added specificity to this understanding of God's role in history. It divided human history into seven dispensations of God's revelation to man. God dealt with human beings differently in each dispensation, posing diverse challenges and punishments in each period.[13] Thus the Calvinist and providentialist understanding of successive covenants was refined into a distinctive method of historical interpretation.

Integrally related to a providentialist and/or dispensationalist understanding of history is millennialism. By focusing on biblical prophecy, especially on the final thousand years before the Last Judgment, as the key to understanding the present and predicting the future, millennialism offers an overarching way to understand history. During the Second Great Awakening of the early nineteenth century, evangelicals focused on biblical prophecy in eager expectation of the Second Coming of Christ as they worked to prepare for it. Millennialist expectations took diametrically opposed positions on the state of the world and its future. The Civil War dampened progressive social engagement and evangelicals' impetus to reform. Growing social and economic dislocations, including urbanization, industrialization, and floods of Catholic immigrants, called into question earlier optimism that America was enjoying the millennial age. Thus dispensationalism was an explicit response to this sense of crisis within the evangelical movement, but evangelicals divided in response to these social changes. Some approached them with optimism. For them, the Second Great Awakening continued unabated, fueling a postmillennial strain of millennialism. Postmillennialists believed that Jesus would return to earth after a millennium of peace. They expected to work to bring about the righteous kingdom and thus were inspired to reform society, including by crusading for temperance and public education.[14] Some postmillennialists even believed they were already living in the period before the return of Jesus Christ, a belief that made them even more optimistic about their times and propelled their social activism.

Other evangelicals, discomfited by social changes, became less optimistic. For them, the deplorable state of the late nineteenth century meant that they were in a premillennial period *before* Jesus Christ would return to inaugurate the millennium. These premillennialists took a jaundiced view of society and prospects for human improvement. They tended to separate themselves from nonbelievers to prepare for Jesus's imminent return.[15] Dispensationalist premillennialists also believed that the elect would experience the rapture. They would join Jesus Christ. Those, who were not saved, would experience the seven-year period of tribulation before Jesus Christ returned to defeat the antichrist and to inaugurate a millennium of period of peace the saved would enjoy. They saw no need to improve society before the rapture.

Premillennialists' beliefs alienated some evangelicals from the dominant culture at crucial moments in their history. That alienation was clear in the aftermath of the famous Scopes trial of 1925, when Clarence Darrow and William Jennings Bryan faced off over teaching evolution in public schools. The defeat of the anti-evolutionists further isolated a more extreme evangelical subculture.[16] Belief in the rapture was promoted in the Scofield annotated version of the Bible's understanding of end times prophecies, widely disseminated in the 1920s. The rapture is currently taught in Bible conferences at the Dallas Theological Seminary as an article of faith and is the premise of the *Left Behind* series of books by Tim La Haye and the spin-off film.[17]

These Christian curricula unquestionably subscribe to millennialism and more or less overtly look forward to the end times. While they do not stipulate whether they are pre- or postmillennialists, it is safe to assume that they are more sympathetic to premillennialism. Both Bob Jones University and Pensacola Christian College, the sponsoring institutions of two of these curricula, espouse it.

The Christianity of these curricula is rooted in evangelicalism and its history, but they also clearly reflect later disagreements of fundamentalists with evangelicals. Fundamentalism emerged within American evangelicalism in the early twentieth century as a reaction against theological liberalism or biblical modernism. Fundamentalists set themselves apart from other Protestants and even other evangelicals by espousing a central set of beliefs, or fundamentals, including biblical inerrancy, the virgin birth of Christ, substitutionary atonement, the literal resurrection of the dead, and the Second Coming. They contended that Christians who were modernists or liberals were consigned to hell—even their more modernist evangelical brethren.[18] As Marsden put it, "an American fundamentalist is an evangelical who is militant in opposition to liberal theology in the churches or to changes in cultural values or mores, such as those associated with 'secular humanism.'"[19] Since their early twentieth-century disagreements with evangelicals, fundamentalists have opposed accommodation with mainline Protestants or other evangelicals whenever they detect a whiff of theological modernism or ecumenism.

These curricula do not explicitly announce their fundamentalism, although the institutions that produce them are clearly fundamentalist. Their founders announced their personal fundamentalism. Don Howard, cofounder of ACE, proudly proclaimed, "I am a fundamentalist. If I can be any more fundamental than fundamental, that is what I want to be." He announced, perhaps reflecting fundamentalist defensiveness, that "fundamentalism is intellectually sound. It has always prevailed in periods of great intellectual enlightenment."[20] Howard received his PhD from Bob Jones University, which was founded just as fundamentalists broke with evangelicals in the early twentieth century. Pensacola Christian College, integrally connected to Abeka Books, is also a fundamentalist institution. Despite their fundamentalist roots, these textbooks are consistently promoted as "Christian" rather than fundamentalist. Whether they would be as readily adopted as educational materials if they identified themselves as "fundamentalist" rather than simply "Christian" is questionable.

The fact that early American evangelicals formed religious communities as offshoots of mainline Protestant denominations to which they formerly belonged doubtless fostered the theological amalgam that defined its past and shapes its current doctrinal fluidity. Paradoxically, evangelicalism is both fluid and rigid. It is fluid in incorporating new theological elements and political positions, and rigid in distinguishing its adherents from the faithless. Theological dissent has always marked its history. Initially a religious movement opposing the beliefs of established churches, evangelicalism was grounded in dissent, both theological and social, about what it meant to be a Christian. The contentious history of evangelical Protestantism is written into the ways these Christian textbooks understand the past. Without referring to those issues or perhaps even recognizing them, these educational materials write world history as the story of the evolution of their religious views and battles.

By asserting their identity as simply Christian, these curricula blur the theological disputes that separated evangelical and fundamentalist strains from mainline Protestantism from the First Great Awakening of the 1740s to the present. Disputes divided Congregationalists from evangelicals, and Presbyterians, Methodists, and Baptists into more or less evangelical churches, and Baptists from Southern Baptists. Since its early twentieth-century origin, fundamentalism too has redefined itself and re-separated itself from other forms of evangelical Protestantism. In these curricula, these theological schisms disappear into an amorphous Christianity.

Since the 1970s, with the political mobilization of the religious right, some fundamentalist views have been espoused by evangelicals and become more significant both within evangelicalism and in public life. One might say that fundamentalists have moved many evangelicals toward fundamentalism, especially in their views of science and history. As a result, today more evangelicals hold extreme views than they did in earlier periods, and thus some formerly fundamentalist views, notably on evolution, the age of the earth, and Christian nationalism, have become for them more central landmarks of what it means to be a Christian.

American fundamentalists and evangelicals themselves often now resist those labels, considering them too inexact, indiscriminately applied, and difficult to define. Some avoid the terms because of the negative connotations they have acquired. Even Bob Jones University now questions the use of the term "fundamentalist."[21] "Christian," the preferred term, connotes inclusion of any who identify as Christian, even though the views of those associated with these religious communities have narrowed in ways these Christian world histories reveal.

Despite the inclusiveness of the "Christian" designation, narrower, minority religious views became increasingly influential within twentieth-century evangelicalism. An important one is Christian Reconstructionism. It is worth discussing in some detail because it is little known but both significant and implicit in these Christian curricula. Developed initially in the nineteenth century as a minority position within Calvinism, Christian Reconstructionism became a program to challenge the modern world. Its key figures objected to revolutionary politics and the expanding role of the state. Within this minority understanding, differences of emphasis emerged. In 1866, the Presbyterian minister James Orr's (1844–1913) influential series of lectures, published as *The Christian View of God and the World*, challenged biblical modernism and proclaimed his understanding of the Bible as unquestionable truth.[22] His theology, grounded in the New Testament, was moderate, but that of Dutch Calvinist Abraham Kuyper (1837–1920), who initiated neo-Calvinism, had a much more fervent and expansive view of Calvinism. He rejected modernism and emphasized the power of God and the limits of human institutions, especially the state. All institutions must be understood as under God. Calvinism would thus be a powerful force of social transformation.[23]

Kuyper exerted a strong influence on certain sectors of the American religious community through the work of his follower Cornelius van Til (1895–1987). Van Til argued as a fundamental presupposition that the Christian faith is the only basis for rational thought and that the Bible is divine revelation. Without these presuppositions, he contended, there is no way to make sense of the human experience. These presuppositions must simply be accepted and cannot, once accepted, be challenged or refuted. (Van Til's theological position is called presuppositionalism). Even fellow evangelicals pointed out the illogic of this system.[24] Nonetheless, it became significant when it was popularized, particularly by Francis Schaeffer, who gave it great urgency as a social and political message. Schaeffer insisted that all civil government must be under God's law. He adapted his theology to argue for America as a Christian nation. Christian Reconstructionism gave American evangelicalism a theological coherence shaped by a consistent Calvinism with a social imperative. Some of its central positions inform these curricula, grafted onto other positions as Christian truth, as we will see.

It is especially noteworthy that Francis Schaeffer's understanding of history directly maps onto the historical narrative these Christian curricula present. Early Christianity was biblical; medieval Christianity corrupted it; the Renaissance introduced humanism; the Reformation recaptured Christianity and connected Christianity to America. This association suggests either that Christian Reconstructionism has a direct impact on these curricula or that this historical narrative is broadly diffused and accepted within evangelicalism.[25]

What does this variant of Calvinism assert? Christian Reconstructionists are postmillennialists. They believe we are in the last thousand years; they are urgently building the Kingdom of God, which will be established at the Second Coming. Like early Calvinists, they are galvanized by a quest to remake society by applying Old Testament civil codes to establish God's sovereignty over all society. They claim the purest Calvinism with the greatest impetus to political engagement in the interest of God's plan. Several features of Christian Reconstructionism made it particularly adaptable to America. Its emphasis on the covenant between God and modern Americans gave it a clear connection to orthodox Presbyterianism. Its optimistic sense of the millennium as a period in which the godly would be rewarded made it attractive to populists and allowed for an easy grafting onto the later prosperity gospel. Elements of Christian Reconstructionism may well appeal to anti-government sentiment in the current political moment.

When Rousas John Rushdoony developed the theology of presuppositionalism into a movement to challenge "humanism and statism," he espoused intellectual positions enshrined in these textbooks. He attacked the Enlightenment and human reason and asserted that all non-Christian knowledge was sinful. He contended that the American Revolution was fought to establish a Calvinist nation and that the South's loss in the Civil War destroyed Christian orthodoxy in America in favor of a secular state. He favored the application of Old Testament law, including the imposition of the death penalty for a wide variety of offenses. In addition to these positions on history and society, he espoused libertarian economics and supported home-schooling to undermine the influence of the government.[26] Even though Calvinist emphases were crucial to Rushdoony's work, it became especially influential, less because of its theology than its fusion to right-wing politics. In economics, Christian Reconstructionists popularized free-market capitalism as moral and biblical.[27] When Rushdoony's stringent ideas were moderated or camouflaged by some of his followers, they influenced many more mainstream movements within the Christian right, including the Moral Majority of the 1970s. That fusion of Christian Reconstructionism and right-wing politics is now fundamental to what it means to be "Christian" for many Americans. It is characterized by commitment to the transformation of America into their version of a Christian nation—patriarchal, capitalist, with a government of Christians applying biblical law—even if many would likely not subscribe to its most extreme ramifications. Indeed, its theological stringency would likely be quite off-putting to many twenty-first-century evangelicals, as they, unlike Christian Reconstructionists, have repudiated the Calvinist emphasis on predestination and human powerlessness. But contemporary arguments for biblical law or a Christian nation are not widely understood as incorporating rigid Calvinism or the strictures of Leviticus. They might, for example, support "one man, one woman" definitions of marriage without advocating stoning transgressors. They do, however, hearken back to an imagined early America, which, they believe, upheld their views.

Although Christian Reconstructionism does not officially have many supporters, its influence is much greater than its few notable adherents suggest. It exercises a strong, often unrecognized influence within American evangelicalism. Many evangelicals would even reject Calvinism's influence on contemporary evangelicalism. Indeed, when evangelicals broke from Congregationalists in the First Great Awakening, they moderated many of the stringent conclusions of Calvin's theology, most notably his emphasis on double predestination—that is to say, the belief that, in His unquestionable wisdom, God predestines some for heaven and others to hell. But Calvinism has been reintegrated into evangelicalism through these more recent theological traditions, which exert an unacknowledged but profound influence on the understanding of both history and contemporary politics. Prominent figures influenced by Christian Reconstructionist views, including Gary North, Pat Robertson, Herb Titus, Charles Colson, Tim La Haye, Gary Bauer, and Paul Crouch held or hold sway in the corridors of power in Washington. Its political influence is augmented primarily because the Christian right adopted its arguments about the impetus for the Christian to remake his society.

When these world histories promote a revisionist Christian history, they advance antigovernment arguments and insist that biblical law is the source of all law. Underlying their general disparagement of government is the specific claim that government has usurped God's sovereign authority. The most extreme version of this argument has led to dominionism, the notion that Christians are best suited to carry out God's commands in the political sphere. Dominionists, like Christian Reconstructionists, intend to replace American civil law with Old Testament biblical law. While their more extreme views would not likely attract many evangelicals if explicitly spelled out, those views have considerable traction when summarized as a political gloss on Genesis 1:26–27, when God gave Adam dominion over the earth. True Christians must reclaim Adam's authority.[28]

Having become more politically engaged, many evangelicals share radical ideas about the relationship between religion and the state. Whether fundamentalist, neo-Calvinist, Christian Reconstructionist, or of some other evangelical or fundamentalist strain, they insist that society should conform to the Bible. The textbooks too reflect views held by these minority Calvinist strains, even though they never mention them. These ideas have become central to American political discussion, even if those who espouse them may well not be aware of their sources. As Gary North, Rushdoony's son-in-law, notes, "the ideas of the Reconstructionists have penetrated into Protestant circles that for the most part are unaware of the original source of the theological ideas that are beginning to transform them."[29]

Some ideas of Christian Reconstructionism and dominionism have been easily grafted onto conventional ideas of God's special favor toward the United States. Their impact is evident in the current "Christian nation" rhetoric. Readers will recognize these ideas as central to current political debates. In the past, Christian Reconstructionist views would have been relegated to the fringe, but they are now propounded on the floors of many state legislatures, found in school standards set by school boards, and widely disseminated in educational materials.

Many points that these curricula develop cannot be identified as belonging to one of the non-mainline Christian denominations, largely because they assert a generic "Christian" character, as if there had never been disagreements between Christian sects or denominations. They leave unresolved questions that, if discussed, might cause readers to reject their claims or their curricula. For example, whether these texts are pre- or postmillennialist is left unstated. For those attracted to an amorphous popular Christianity, such theological distinctions are unimportant. What matters is personal self-identification as a Christian, saved by a personal relationship with Jesus Christ. When textbooks define fundamental distinctions—biblical law versus humanism, God versus the devil, Christian truth versus non-Christian heresy—they place those using these curricula, students, their teachers, and families, on the right side of such divides. History provides a crucial means to identify those on the wrong side.

Why would parents and schools respond favorably to this notion of Christianity and its social and political ramifications and thus adopt one of these three Christian curricula to teach world history? The fact that these textbooks do not articulate a distinct theological position might attract a broad audience identifying as Christian—fundamentalists, evangelicals, even mainline Protestants. Their theological underpinnings are generally Protestant and more integrally tied to Calvinism. The fact that they are also idiosyncratic, reflecting views held by only a small minority of Protestants, is blurred by presenting its history as "Christian," which may attract the big tent of evangelicals. Evangelicals' emphasis on individual faith experiences rather than on a coherent theology might make them pleased to find in these curricula a firm commitment to a Christian perspective and accept that perspective without being aware that "Christian" includes views derived from recent, minority views. Fundamentalists will find many of their views faithfully reflected in these curricula. Arguments embedded in these textbooks may well resonate within long-standing church or family traditions and be accepted by schools, parents, and students as a result.

While Christian Reconstructionism and dominionism are more extreme positions, they have clearly influenced American popular culture to a degree that has only recently begun to raise alarm in American political circles and to elicit academic analysis.[30] The conventional narrative that Christian fundamentalism left the public sphere, humiliated after the Scopes trial, only to be revived by the efforts of various Washington think tanks and lobbyists has been reappraised by scholars, who document a more consistently politically active Christian right, one that has by now influenced several generations of Americans.[31]

These curricula promote their more extreme religious ideas, such as the restoration of a Christian America, by cloaking them in claims about early American history, appealing to both Divine Providence and American exceptionalism, and presenting them as "biblical truth" and "Christianity." Such ideas are increasingly found in a variety of popular media—television programs, music, popular histories, and films labeled as "Christian." They indicate even less than these textbooks their explicit sectarian or ideological underpinnings. In that sense, they, like these educational materials, conform to American evangelicalism; they are theologically unstructured but adamant that they present the truth. Unencumbered by more specific tenets, "Christian" can appeal to a more expansive public and to the schools and parents choosing to use these curricula to teach history.

3

What Is History?

> All truth . . . comes forth from a single Source. . . . Consequently,
> God's written self-revelation is the starting point of all rational in-
> quiry and the guide to all interpretation of reality. No concept can
> be true that conflicts with the statements of the Scriptures. . . . . The
> Bible is the center of the Christian-school curriculum.[1]

Like most histories, these textbooks ask significant questions of the past. They
are noteworthy for the unorthodox answers they give to questions central
to historical analysis such as: Why have events occurred as they have? Who
were significant agents of history? What have human beings accomplished
and under what circumstances? What can we know about how people lived
in the past? How does history reveal the past and make sense of the present?

The answers these textbooks give to such queries about the past and its
significance are disconcerting. They distort the content and practice of history. Their narrative may astound historians unfamiliar with the religious
right's uses of history. It is curiously retrograde, profoundly shaped by the
Whig notion that any successful group or country was so because of its moral
superiority—a kind of "survival of the historically fittest" or, in this case,
the divinely sanctioned.[2] These curricula are more confident about their
conclusions than historians would be: they claim to know the mind of God
or, at least, how He acted in history. They share the sense that history is *His*
story, "the story of God and His plan for mankind."[3] This chapter addresses
two questions: How do these curricula understand and use history? How does
that understanding differ from how history is usually understood and taught?

The publishers of these educational materials proudly and explicitly differentiate their approach from others. The BJU textbook congratulates its readers
on having found the "best educational materials available." Its histories include "nothing to conflict with Truth and everything to support it. Truth is

Hijacking History. Kathleen Wellman, Oxford University Press. © Oxford University Press 2021.
DOI: 10.1093/oso/9780197579237.003.0004

the pathway as well as the destination." It promotes its sense of history as "standing for the 'old time religion' and the absolute authority of the Bible." The study of history starts with "in the beginning God created the heavens and the earth."[4]

The Abeka Books website takes a firm stance against what it sees as illegitimate conventional history: "The theme of world history texts has been man's supposed progress from savagery toward socialism, from tribal religions toward one-world government." Abeka histories unequivocally "reject the Marxist/Hegelian conflict theory of history in favor of a truthful portrayal of peoples."[5]

When ACE founder Don Howard articulated his views on education, he identified the problem his histories intended to redress: education should be a private, Christian undertaking, but it has become public, fundamentally corrupted by government, and, as a result, immoral.[6] ACE's vice president Ronald Johnson further contended that "children matriculate into Christian school in dire need of spiritual programming . . . restricting secular access to his mind and conditioning with Scriptural principles breaks down the child's carnal resistance against God."[7] These educational materials intend to produce "spiritual programming." As they are rooted in the Bible, their authors can discern God's intentions in the past as a guide to the present and future and provide a true foundation for historical knowledge.

These fundamental premises sharply differentiate these curricula's epistemology from that of historians. These textbooks understand what one can know and how one can know it completely differently. Grounded in faith, they contend that history confirms the Bible as authoritative; it is "God's history" and thus the only reliable way to understand history. The Christian studies history to see the working of God or even to know Him. As the BJU faculty wrote about the study of history, "The spiritual mind can trace the character of the Divine Maker of the ages and discern his ways." Historical study recognizes that "the earthly course of events was begun by an act of God; it is progressively unfolding, revealing God's good purpose in His enjoyable time, and it will be brought to an end by God."[8]

These Christian publishers grant the discipline of history a privileged status, because, as the BJU textbook notes, nearly 60% of the Bible is a historical narrative. Through his familiarity with the Bible and study of history, the Christian can know the past, understand the present, and be prepared "for the future by showing him how people have behaved in the past." As the study of history also predicts the coming apocalypse with the establishment of the kingdom of heaven, the Christian should be optimistic.[9]

For these curricula, the Bible is the crucial text and source. It does not simply recount the history of biblical times. It also provides a method of exegesis to explain subsequent events. The study of history leads the Christian to ask, as the BJU textbook does, "What was God doing in this part of history?" With the Bible as a key, these curricula provide the answer.[10] The Abeka textbook is equally unambiguous in laying out the theological assumptions underlying its historical analysis. "History is the written record of what men have done with the time God has given them." It is "the record of God's dealing with men since the beginning." With this perspective, the student will see "through the lens of Scripture" and learn that "world history often reveals the hand of God in the affairs of nations and the success or failure of civilization in proportion to their submission to or defiance against His will."[11] Since creation, "the study of world history reveals many of the consequences of decisions made by men, leading to triumph or tragedy." The student will appreciate history's sobering lessons and thus judge other civilizations, nations, and individuals accordingly: the godly succeed; the ungodly fail. God gave many injunctions to His people to remember, establishing, the BJU history notes, the significance of history.[12] The Abeka textbook sums up its method of historical interpretation: "as we lay the facts of history alongside revealed truth in the Bible, we can often see God working through events."[13] Comparing biblical passages to historical events allows these textbooks to assert that their historical narrative is authoritative or even true.

What does the Bible tell the Christian about history? The form of the question is important because the non-Christian "is capable of intellectual but not spiritual perception."[14] Only Christians can truly understand the past. This claim allows these textbooks to apply biblical exegesis to confirm their judgment of past events with biblical citations. Citations, correlated to events, define historical analysis and sustain historical arguments. The earliest events are confirmed by the Bible; later historical events become comprehensible by applying Bible verses to them. Often the verse cited has no obvious connection to the event, but it nonetheless confirms the specific interpretation of the event to which it purportedly refers. This method evokes "proof texting" as used by evangelicals. The Bible is simply cited, using a concordance without comment or attention to context. As the evangelical historian George Marsden notes, this use makes the Bible an encyclopedia where words have no textual or historical context.[15] This method came to great prominence after the Scofield Reference Bible was published in the 1920s when evangelicals were splintering off from other denominations into fundamentalist congregations. The Scofield Reference Bible gave them the ammunition to support their defection. Proof texting thus has a long history in religious disputation. It plays a decisive role in establishing the authority of many historical arguments of evangelicals and these textbooks.[16] This method is particularly idiosyncratic in the ACE curriculum, which interjects biblical quotations, seemingly at random, with almost no attempt to integrate them into the narrative.

In using biblical quotations as corroboration, these histories deploy a strikingly narrow range of citations. They rely almost entirely on the Old Testament, especially the prophets' dire warnings. The gospels are strangely missing from the application of the Bible to historical analysis. Paul is the only New Testament figure consistently cited. Jesus plays an astonishingly small role, although His death redeemed man.[17] Jesus is never presented as a model of Christian conduct, nor is the gospel cited as the heart of the Christian message. He simply saved sinful man.

History shows how God expected human beings to behave: it records those He punished or rewarded. These curricula use their narrative to both point this out and explain why. The course of history documents the errors of peoples who failed to understand "biblical truth."[18] These educational materials present themselves to students as the litmus test for the true understanding of the past. They share a belief that historians' faith profoundly shapes their narratives. According to the BJU textbook, historians make key decisions by faith about what to emphasize in their respective histories. This curriculum isolates fundamental premises as essential for any Christian history: (1) God made the world and everything in it; (2) the world is in a broken state because of sin; (3) "God is working to redeem men and women to Him"; (4) the task of historians is to interpret present events in light of the Bible, because "God has written a completely accurate and ultimately useful history."[19]

Not surprisingly, with these underlying premises, history documents the role of sin in the world. History is a battle between good and evil, a conflict between the "seed of woman and the seed of Satan."[20] A key lesson these textbooks convey is that the preponderance of sin entails the futility of human efforts unless motivated by the pursuit of biblical truth. Other human undertakings are mired in the sin of "humanism." The Abeka curriculum defines humanism as "the worship of man" and as rebellion against God and asserts that "like evolution, humanism is destructive."[21] Guenter Salter, Dean of Arts and Sciences at Bob Jones University from 1971 to 1998, maintained this fundamental distinction: the Word of God alone gives students the truth. Humanism "embraces the doctrine of evolution; declares heredity and environment to be responsible for a person's value system; dismisses all absolutes, [and] makes man the measure of all things."[22] The Christian's study of history reveals truth and exposes its antithesis—the malign influence of humanism. As sin defines human history, students will come to understand that any political, literary, or intellectual endeavor not grounded in biblical truth is futile, frequently meaningless, and, in these curricula, deplored as humanism. Most importantly, sin is responsible for the ills of the world: "not scarcity, disease, social inequality, or poor education that is to blame for pain in the world."[23] Sin makes social ills impervious to human attempts to remediate them. Such efforts reflect the sin of humanism. Only proselytizing biblical Christianity provides relief for the human condition. Other attempts are at best misguided and at worst sinful—a case of men making themselves gods. ACE lays out these premises most starkly: "We have witnessed throughout history that man in his own wisdom and counsel, can never solve the problems of the world as stated in Psalm 33:10 'the Lord bringeth the counsel of the heathen [the nations] to naught: he maketh the devices of the people of none effect.'"[24]

Such a stance seems to urge Christians to disengage from society. Such alienation contrasts strikingly with the social engagement of early Christians, firmly committed to the poor and the dispossessed, or to the industry of the much later Calvinists, motivated by their willingness to serve God's purpose, or to the commitment of nineteenth-century evangelicals to the Social Gospel. Nor does this disengagement seem in accord with the current political involvement of the Christian right. This apparent contradiction may be resolved, however, by distinguishing the individual from society and a Christian government from a secular one. This seeming paradox is further developed throughout these textbooks' historical narrative as they define specific political and economic views that distinguish between Christian social activism and the political engagement of the Christian right. As the BJU history contends, the study of history will "produce graduates sound both in their theology and in their devotion to a Protestant-based social order."[25]

Despite their emphasis on sin, these textbooks are confident that American Christians are part of providential history. American providentialism evolved from a general appreciation of God's providence toward His creation into a thoroughly articulated notion of Divine Providence as God's active intervention on behalf of His new chosen people—American Christians.[26] This view has a long history in the United States, but it was explicitly articulated for Christian educational circles by Rosalie Slater in the 1960s. After she defined "America's historical Christian method of Biblical reasoning as the basis of every subject" and trademarked her "principles approach" to education, it was widely taught in Christian schools and promoted for homeschooling.[27]

This amplified notion of Divine Providence also reads Scripture as harmonious; there can be no contradiction, as all elements of Scripture are reconcilable. This understanding has been common to Christianity, but it became a blunter method as promoted by the Scofield Reference Bible and its concordance of biblical citations. This position is commonly cited as axioms: "Scripture interprets Scripture," or the "Bible is its own best commentary." Such claims are loosely connected to the fundamental Lutheran principle of *sola scriptura,* or Scripture as the sole source of religious truth. The current sense further entails that any obscure biblical passage should be understood in light of other passages or the entire Bible. These curricula apply this method even more expansively to correlate Scripture and historical events: textual corroboration becomes the key to understanding history. Armed with this allegedly correct approach, they treat each historical period according to principles confirmed by the Bible and demonstrated by the historical events they highlight.[28]

These Christian curricula, like Slater, see God's relationship to man as determined by a series of successive relationships with His chosen people from ancient Israel to the Christian United States. While the Abeka website condemns a host of religious beliefs, including "extreme Calvinism," its world history clearly invokes the Calvinist understanding of God's role in human history. It, like Calvin, explicitly believes that God works through human history to fulfill His plan through a sequence of "chosen peoples." They are the Jews, early Christians, Protestant reformers, and, finally, American Christians.

The sense that Divine Providence has now settled on the United States makes its history of vital importance. Students must, ACE notes, "recognize the moving of the hand of God in guiding our country's direction."[29] The BJU textbook insists that, as historical memory shapes national identity, it is imperative that this Christian narrative be taught. Not only does "the study of history help us to understand our identity as Christians," but it also endorses a more expansive history, as "we cannot simply study our own identity, because we are also human beings."[30] Thus the study of non-Christians is warranted.

The historian's task is to detail God's actions and intentions as he surveys the past. As committed Christians, the authors of these textbooks have a unique vantage point for judging where God's favor and wrath have fallen. Every period of history offers examples, allowing students to judge how past civilizations accorded with "biblical truth." The exegetical method of treating historical events and the status accorded believers as the new chosen allow these educational materials to define what is true and who can make any claim to it. They have unfailing confidence that they present the truth that must be spread.

These textbooks reflect the centrality of religion in America, from those who came to the New World to find a more hospitable place to practice their religion to the present. But they also reveal the opposition to mainline culture that has long been a feature of reactionary forms of American Protestantism. In recounting world history, these curricula echo several causes, which have defined evangelicals, fundamentalists, and other, more recent offshoots of Protestantism. Some of their distinctive approaches to social and religious issues include the construction of the myth of the Christian founding in the nineteenth century, the invocation of the Bible on both sides in the Civil War, the fundamentalist-modernist split within Protestantism in the early twentieth century, anti-immigrant and states' rights political positions, the anti-communism of the 1940s and 1950s, the rejection of the civil rights movement and feminism during the 1960s, and the alliance of the religious right and corporate capitalism in contemporary Christian culture.[31] The Christian right has been shaped by these past battles, all of which reverberate in current political debates and are reenacted in these world histories.[32] When they look to the remote past, these curricula seek prior intimations of current views of the Christian right. When they treat the periods since the American founding, they tell the story of battles evangelicals fought and the positions they took.

Thus, if these curricula begin with a statement of faith, they also tell a fascinating story of the development of evangelicals' views and of the political right; they read world history largely in terms of American history and their own political and religious views. They single out American Protestants as the divinely favored "winners" of the historical process. Their histories not only confirm Americans' status as God's favored but also neglect or disparage other peoples and civilizations as less worthy and of less interest.

This understanding of the United States reflects early nineteenth-century histories, which articulated myths of national origin and American exceptionalism. Those myths remain salient, undergirding contemporary, conservative political discourse. With this understanding of history, these curricula read modern political, religious, and economic positions back through God's history to identify His intentions. Their juxtaposition of historical events to Bible verses gives them the means to endorse quite specific political and economic policies. As they move into modern times, they use the historical past more explicitly to connect Christianity, modern capitalism, and right-wing politics.

Proponents of the narrative these curricula advance often contend that they are simply countering the left-wing slant of the academy with more balanced views, suggesting that the differences between these textbooks and others should be considered merely political. This argument is frequently made at State Board of Education of Texas hearings, for example. But this claim discounts the radical arguments these curricula make. Indeed, objections to history textbooks have been traditionally and vehemently directed from the right against the left in the belief that histories written since the 1960s reflect a left-wing or even anti-American perspective on America's past. For example, when the National History Standards of 1994 attempted to include nonwhites, women, or less-than-heroic events and individuals into history textbooks, they provoked vociferous criticism. Much of it was directed against professional historians in the misguided sense that they, like these curricula, cherry-pick bits of information to support their political views. As the political and religious right sees the historical profession as promoting positions antithetical to theirs, it identifies historians as the enemy—left-wing, Marxist, feminist, or anti-American. Despite these inflammatory charges, those who make them are right to note that history as practiced by historians bears little resemblance to the polemical stances of these textbooks or those advanced by some state legislators and school boards.

The conventional view of historians as left leaning is supported by polling that shows that humanities professors are liberal. But the attack on professional historians developed largely in response to the kinds of questions historians have asked since the 1960s. Those questions responded to the profession's changing demographic composition. In the wake of World War II, many Americans gained access to higher education through the G.I. Bill. With the subsequent phenomenal increase in university enrollments, more working-class and minority students as well as women of all social classes and races pursued advanced degrees and ultimately became professors producing scholarly work. Some works of social and economic history produced in that period were influenced both by Marx's model of economics as the driver of history and Marxist class-conflict analyses of the historical past. But when these newly minted PhDs looked at the past, they also wondered, Where were the women? What were the lives of immigrants or slaves like? Where were their stories? What about the Spanish colonies in the United States? Why have the Hispanic roots of the United States been so neglected? Unquestionably, contemporary preoccupations shape historians' investigations. While their research may challenge some cherished myths, historians rarely intend to produce left-wing polemics. They instead ask new questions and uncover new evidence to address concerns of their own times, as historians have done since of Herodotus.

It should not be surprising that many or even most of those who spend their careers in academia support progressive causes, as polls of university humanities and social science faculty reveal (unlike conservative faculty in business schools and economics departments). Many in such disciplines defer earnings for nearly a decade in graduate study and face difficult economic prospects. Over their entire careers, they earn far less than other professionals, even if they secure much-prized tenure-track positions. Their study of the humanities and social sciences may also make them more sympathetic to liberal values.

When historians personally support progressive causes or when their professional research focuses on topical issues, conservatives frequently condemn their work as advancing a leftist agenda. Just as historians educated in the 1960s asked questions made central by the cultural changes they experienced, so too some conservatives, discomfited by those same changes, found historians' attempts to study those changes objectionable and maintained instead that the retrograde history of elites is "real" history. Conservative commentators who fill prominent think tanks may bemoan the greater attention of professional historians to women, workers, or minorities than to powerful elites. However, their own work is rarely indicted for advancing the right-wing positions of the think tanks to which they are attached, even though they are often required to hew to the party line.[33]

Disparaging academic historians as left-leaning suggests that they, like these textbooks' authors, begin with fundamental preconceptions they intend to corroborate. Quite the contrary. Historians instead gather relevant evidence to address the questions they ask to better understand the past. They begin from a base of knowledge derived from prior study of a topic or field. Historical inquiry changes as new scholarship adds to our knowledge, as new sources are discovered, and as historians ask new questions both about historical materials and the past more generally. New inquiries open historical debates, but new interpretations do not become accepted until they meet standards of historical analysis and criticism.[34]

Historians do not begin from tenets of faith. They both understand and acknowledge the interests that that led them to pursue their research. They rely on evidence that can be documented and on interpretation of that evidence. But historical interpretation is not and has never been static; there is no *one, invariable* way to understand the past, and historians make claims neither to single truth nor objectivity. They use history to make sense of the past and the present by raising questions about the compelling issues of their times. For example, after 9/11, when Americans recognized how little they knew about the Middle East, that field of historical study grew exponentially. The financial crisis of 2008 intensified the study of the Great Depression. Awareness of global interconnections has led to studies placing nations, including the United States, in a global context. Concerns about the changing climate have led historians to examine data about the environment of the past and its effects on historical events and developments. Surely the COVID-19 virus will elicit re-examinations of the impact of diseases in history.

The public, unlike professional historians, often sees history as the command of facts or the reiteration of familiar narratives or national myths. The public also remains attracted to older, more conventional types of historical writings—sagas of military successes or biographies of famous figures, for example. The public appreciates histories written to attract broad readership. They are not as readily engaged by questions historians typically pursue or the products of their research.

Despite this gap between what the public expects and professional historians produce, history and how it is taught have a prominent role in debates engaging both historians and the public. Education, as a means of transmitting ideas and values from one generation to the next, has always been both of intense interest and greatly contested. To cite two examples central to these curricula: the American adoption of the scientific discipline of history that German universities developed in the nineteenth century raised alarm about the decline of educational support for Christian morality.[35] Evangelical colleges and universities formed to combat these changes. These Christian curricula assert the legitimacy of this earlier model. Much later, widespread opposition mobilized to contest the 1994 National History Standards and their presumed leftist influence on the teaching of American history. Professional historians were both surprised by the opposition and unpersuaded by its insistence on a heroic narrative. Once the furor had died down, some prominent historians assumed that the National History Standards uproar had been a mere tempest in a teapot or even that its end presaged popular appreciation of the narrative that historians endorsed.[36] That optimism seems too sanguine in light of contemporary attacks on the teaching of history by state legislatures and school boards. Such attacks often intend to impose some of the polemical points these curricula assert, including fervent support for American exceptionalism and capitalism, commitment to the "Christian nation" thesis and to Protestant Christianity, and the inaccurate understanding of the Civil War previously discussed.[37]

Such positions are more polemical than historically accurate; they almost defy historical criticism. As these histories provide a religiously inflected narrative confirmed by biblical citations, they are impervious to the evidence or analysis of historians. Only competing Bible verses can contest them. These textbooks presume to tell "God's history" and encourage students to see historical events from God's perspective. What does that perspective entail? The "right" answer is unquestionable; there is no room for discussion or analysis. History does not open debate but rather forecloses it. It advances religious proselytizing.

Fundamentally, these curricula assert an understanding of history that completely subverts the study and teaching of history. They rely on a singular notion of historical causation: God determines all history, which is the story of His action in the world, and divine favor or punishment explains historical events; although the devil sometimes plays a crucial role, God is the ultimate actor in human history; human beings advance His plan when they act for identifiably religious motives; evildoers, and especially bad ideas, show Satan abroad in the world. As a result, these histories are strangely devoid of human actors. Prominent figures are mentioned, but only God, the devil, some religious figures, and missionaries act. There are rare mentions of social or economic aspects of history; they play no causal role. Ideas, most often bad ideas—Catholicism, Darwinism, socialism, communism—propel history. Ideas are rarely attributed to specific human beings; they seem analogous to a virus infecting mankind. As a result, the analysis of this book focuses on the ideas that shape these curricula. In them, religious faith wars with other ideas, which are clearly sinful and direct man away from God.

This good-versus-evil play of ideas does not allow students to understand events or give them tools of historical analysis.[38] Instruction with these histories makes them witnesses to this religious contest.

These textbooks differ profoundly from historical scholarship. For their authors, the writing of history is fundamentally a statement of faith or, as they might put it, "I write my history based on my faith, which is the true narrative as confirmed by the Bible." The BJU textbook asserts that history written by a Muslim or a Hindu would be different from one written by a Christian.[39] While Christian textbooks faithfully relate God's history, other histories are misleading or false. History is thus a high-stakes discipline: an erroneous narrative misrepresents God's revelation, misconstrues His actions and intentions, or does not recognize God as the force behind all history. An improper understanding of history could jeopardize man's role in God's plan or even the firmness of God's relationship with modern Americans. The promulgation of this historical narrative becomes a moral imperative and makes heated history wars inevitable.

The historical method these educational materials consider most authoritative is extremely idiosyncratic. Historical study is biblical commentary or a kind of "proof texting," examining both events and the Bible.[40] These curricula's premises sanction an exegetical reading of all human history to identify those God rewarded and punished.

The underlying premise that historians write accounts of the past according to their faith is completely at odds with the modern understanding of the historical profession. (In earlier periods, American historians wrote to assert a Protestant perspective, as these curricula explicitly still do; it is one reason our historiography has been shaped by Protestant Anglophilia.) No historian would claim to write "the truth." Historians are aware of how understanding of the past evolves in response to new evidence, scholarship, and the changing questions they ask. Every period elicits different questions. For historians, "taken on faith" is not comparable to grounded in evidence. Historians recognize that a narrative established by biblical citations is impervious to contradictory evidence or analysis and interpretation. Comparing a biblical quotation to a later event would carry no weight in historical debates. Nor would historians cherry-pick events, texts, and quotations to connect them to the Bible or religious beliefs. For these Christian curricula, that method is not only desirable but rather the way to determine a true understanding. Their histories offer religious education, not about a specific creed but rather a distinctive understanding of Christianity rooted in American evangelicalism.

What are some implications of history as these curricula teach it? Christians have a unique power to interpret history. These curricula assert a singular notion of causation: God determines all history, and divine favor or punishment explains historical events. History becomes a way to know God. Being able to identify what God has done and, in many cases, why He has done it, gives the authors of these curricula a kind of moral hindsight about the past and an authority to forecast the future. Like the prophets of old, the authors warn of coming punishment. They introduce as a fundamental corollary that disastrous events are the work of the devil or God's punishment and rooted in human sinfulness. Evils in the world are impervious to human beings' attempts to rectify them.[41] These ways of defining the discipline of history are unconventional and sharply at odds with the historical consensus on the practice and nature of history, to say the least.

4

The Beginning of History

For these Christian curricula, the Bible is not only the authoritative text for interpreting history but also *the only* truly credible source for understanding the earliest human history. What does using the Bible as the key to understand the ancient world entail? It allows these textbooks to correlate their histories of early civilizations directly with the Bible, treat other accounts of them skeptically, disparage other civilizations by comparisons to the Israelites, and dismiss evidence challenging biblical accounts. With the Bible as its authoritative foundation, these educational materials can articulate fundamental positions on religion, politics, and society they emphasize in their subsequent historical analysis. First, as the Bible is inerrant, they can draw firm conclusions about the earth's age from the Book of Genesis. Second, they define the biblical foundation for society, race, and the establishment of government. Third, they emphasize two fundamental examples as defining the Christian's appropriate relationship to society—the Tower of Babel and the Creation Mandate. Fourth, they differentiate biblical Israel and Mosaic Law from other laws and societies. Finally, the Bible reveals God's covenant with the first chosen people. The history of biblical times thus lays out crucial parameters of historical interpretation.

Pensacola Christian College, publisher of Abeka Books, stipulates the Bible's authority as a fundamental article of faith: "We believe that the Bible is the verbally inspired and infallible, authoritative Word of God and that God gave the words of Scripture by inspiration without error in the original autographs." God's word is infallible in the Greek and Hebrew manuscripts, and "the Authorized Version (KJV) is an accurate English translation of the preserved Word of God."[1]

A commitment to the King James Version's authority does not recognize it as the product of its time, with debate over its history and language, shaped by centuries of philological, theological, and historical study, or as a collaboration with contested translations, to say nothing of its multiple printings and editions with various wordings. Furthermore, although these

Hijacking History. Kathleen Wellman, Oxford University Press. © Oxford University Press 2021.
DOI: 10.1093/oso/9780197579237.003.0005

curricula consider inerrancy unquestionable, they do not acknowledge that it is a recent position in the history of Christianity—a response to religious modernism.

When the Princeton Theological Seminary faculty defined biblical inerrancy in the late nineteenth century, they applied it only to the "original autographs" of the Bible and, as none existed, the claim was irrefutable and thus inconsequential.[2] The subtleties of that interpretation have disappeared from contemporary notions of inerrancy, which are more rigid and more widely accepted. The authority of KJV even divides the institutions that publish these curricula: Pensacola Christian College takes the extreme view that it is inerrant; Bob Jones University denounces that position as heretical, because only the Hebrew and Greek manuscripts are inerrant.

Despite these disagreements, the Bible's authority as a source of historical interpretation is indisputable for these curricula. The history the Bible tells not only supersedes any other history of the period but also must be true in its particulars. As a result, these textbooks' treatment of the earliest historical periods is the most dubious. The Abeka curriculum praises the Bible as "the only completely reliable source," and, as the Word of God, it "therefore contains no mistakes." Thus these curricula concur that the world begins with Genesis and is, as Young Earth creationists maintain, less than 10,000 years old. Other histories that begin with prehistory or claim that the earth is older than biblical dating these curricula condemn as false or even godless.[3]

In his *Annalium pars posterior* of 1654, Bishop James Ussher first asserted Young Earth creationism, although it was neither so called then nor generally accepted. On the basis of his extensive study of chronology and the Church Fathers, Ussher determined that Creation occurred on October 22, 4004 BC. How did the work of a seventeenth-century Irish Anglican bishop establish a crucial belief for many American evangelicals, reflected still in these twenty-first-century textbooks?

Several early twentieth-century developments brought this view into prominence. The popular Scofield Reference Bible (1909) promoted Ussher's view.[4] In 1925, the Scopes trial also revived it when Clarence Darrow, in cross-examining William Jennings Bryan, used Ussher against him. These uses gave Ussher modern currency and privileged his chronology of the Bible.

One might think that the current divide between creationists and evolutionists was rooted in Young Earth creationism or biblical inerrancy, but these theological positions did not define anti-evolutionary views. Although evangelicals initially objected to the theory of evolution because it seemed to degrade man's position in nature, they were, however, more horrified by the threat that higher biblical criticism posed to inerrancy. Their antipathy to evolution developed later, largely because of a deliberate propaganda campaign to mobilize American support for entering World War I on the side of the Allies, propaganda that united evolution and biblical criticism. When that campaign demonized German barbarism, evangelicals singled out evolution and Friedrich Nietzsche (both, these curricula presume, products of biblical criticism) as sources of the decline of German civilization, reflected in its much-publicized wartime atrocities.[5] Prior to that time, evangelicals had been divided in their response to Darwin, with many seeing nothing objectionable in his views.[6] Even Bryan, who argued against the introduction of Darwin into public schools in the Scopes trial, thought evolution could be combined with biblical inerrancy.[7]

When some evangelicals took a more rigid view in the early twentieth century and became fundamentalists, they influenced the culture at large through popular media. Throughout the 1920s and 1930s, they cultivated local churches and established radio networks. By 1940, Charles Fuller's *Old-Fashioned Revival Hour* had the largest audience in America. Fundamentalists founded universities in reaction to both evolution and biblical modernism, but not until the 1960s did they insist on Young Earth creationism or even a literal flood. They took this more rigid position only after some faculty at the evangelical Wheaton College in Illinois urged them to recognize mainstream science. Fundamentalists repudiated Wheaton's recommendation and insisted that belief in Genesis 1–3 as literally true defined orthodoxy. In the 1970s, Liberty Baptist College (now Liberty University) cited Young Earth creationism as attesting to its unquestionable commitment to truth: Young Earth creationism distinguished true fundamentalism from mere or false evangelicalism.[8] Commitment to this view now characterizes more of the evangelical community and is more widely held by Americans, although polling on such issues is frustratingly ambiguous and inconclusive.

There is also a range of understandings of what "inerrancy" means among those who hold to it. Some insist on literal interpretation, but many do not. For example, the seven days of creation could be construed less literally as seven periods of time rather than as seven twenty-four-hour days. Biblical literalism, the extreme form of biblical inerrancy, was not always inextricably tied to creationism and anti-evolution as it often is now. It was initially promoted by the Seventh-Day Adventist George McCready Price. When Seventh-Day Adventists asserted a literal six-day creation account, their views were accepted by a small minority but have become more widely held.[9] According to the Pew Religious Landscape Study of 2014 some 33% of Americans currently believe that their particular Bible is word-for-word true.

Just as evolution had initially been relatively uncontested by evangelicals, so too most had reconciled their religious beliefs with the age of the universe agreed upon by scientists. Those who did not were increasingly marginalized within the religious community. As late as 1954, Bernard Ramm, an evangelical theologian, published *The Christian View of Science and Scripture*, which refuted the Bible as a reliable source of scientific information. He made evolution acceptable for most Christians, even fundamentalists.[10]

Thus the scientific understanding of the age of the earth was generally accepted by evangelicals until the 1960s. The use of biblical literalism to deny evolution became more mainstream with the publication of *The Genesis Flood* by John C. Whitcomb and Henry M. Morris in 1960. Opposition to the geological dating of the earth with its corollary acceptance of evolution became "creation science" when Morris promulgated a pseudoscience, which claimed that the recent, supernatural creation of the earth was supported by geological evidence, including that fossil-laden strata were the result of the biblical flood. He juxtaposed the biblical account of the flood with the evidence of mainstream science to argue that Christians could subscribe only to the former. He reasserted that the Bible was *the* source for science. While the scientific community either ignored or vehemently rejected Whitcomb and Morris's work, many evangelicals eagerly embraced it. Read by hundreds of thousands, the book ultimately had an outsized impact on Americans' understanding of the natural world.[11]

This view received a stronger theological underpinning when the Christian Reconstructionist Rushdoony published *The Mythology of Science* in 1967, arguing that creationism rejected not only Darwin but also any evolutionary idea as an attack on God's authority. The Institute for Creation Research (ICR), founded in 1970 in San Diego by Henry Morris (and later moved to Dallas), established graduate degree programs, giving Young Earth creationists academic credentials and intellectual credibility in some circles. Another founder of the Institute was Tim La Haye, who made creationism an educational cause for the political and religious right.

Young Earth creationists have been astonishingly successful in promoting their pseudoscientific claims as a legitimate form of "intelligent design." As state after state has positively insisted that these ideas or the "strengths and weaknesses" of evolution be taught, the commitment of Americans to creationism has grown, despite the consensus of the scientific community, based on overwhelming scientific evidence, that the universe is approximately 13.7 billion years old, the earth at least 4.5 billion years old, and life on earth occurred at least 3.5 billion years ago.

Significantly more Americans now subscribe to the Young Earth creationist dating of the world than did so in the nineteenth century, although polls show considerable confusion about what Americans believe. Between 1982 and 2014, successive Gallup surveys found that between 40% and 47% of adults in the United States were inclined to the believe that "God created humans in their present form at one time within the last 10,000 years." A 2009 Harris Interactive poll found that 39% of Americans agreed with the statement that "God created the universe, the earth, the sun, moon, stars, plants, animals, and the first two people within the past 10,000 years." A 2014 Gallup survey documented that 42% of American agreed that the earth is less than 10,000 years old. According to a Pew poll, two thirds of Americans want creationism to be taught with evolution; 48%, including 27% of college graduates, believe that humans have existed in their present form since the beginning of time. According to a University of Texas study, one of four biology teachers believes that dinosaurs and men roamed the earth together. In response to these confusing results, Pew intends to ask broader questions in hopes of eliciting more nuanced answers.[12]

Just as for Whitcomb and Morris and many Americans polled, the belief that the earth is 10,000 years old has become a test of Christian orthodoxy. For these educational materials, that belief is *the* Christian perspective, unquestionably endorsed by the Bible. They attempt to forestall some questions or evidence that might challenge a Young Earth creationist chronology. The Abeka history takes an aggressive stance, claiming that the theory of evolution has logical failures; it cannot explain the development of language, reason, or society, all of which Adam had at the moment of creation.[13] The BJU textbook explains the extraordinary longevity of biblical figures by their godliness. That longevity ended when Seth's descendants intermarried with Cain's. Tainted by "the seed of the serpent," they were then no better than Cain and their life spans shortened accordingly.[14]

The literal use of Genesis to explain the earliest human beings has further ramifications: the claim that Noah cursed Canaan, a son of Ham, but blessed Ham's brothers Shem and Japheth intimates that God established a racial hierarchy and prohibited racial mixing.[15] The Abeka textbook explicitly claims that the sons of Noah are the originators of the various races of human beings.[16] In Canaan, God's land, the descendants of Ham worked for the descendants of Shem—the Israelites.[17] Curiously, the Abeka history tries to integrate some quasi-scientific information to support racial hierarchy. After God created man, He divided them into different "kinds of people" called races. But "Adam and Eve, as the parents of all humanity, had within their genes potential for the subsequent development of the different races." This textbook uses the Bible to support outdated and discredited notions of race as real rather than as socially constructed and then tries to use gene theory to sustain it. Thus the Bible gives a prescient account of genetics and explains the development of different races. This edition of this textbook also draws sharply racialist conclusions about the distinctive racial characteristics and uses them to explain the diverse accomplishments of different civilizations. Ham's descendants remain less accomplished.[18] The most recent edition of this textbook no longer makes this argument, but it emphasizes that Ham's descendant Nimrod defied God by building the Tower of Babel.[19]

The Abeka curriculum uses the dispersion of biblical people and Genesis 9's confirmation of God's covenant with Noah to suggest that God favors the white race. This verse has been frequently cited in the Christian West to justify slavery. Such arguments were especially emphatic in the antebellum rhetoric in the American South.[20] In response to religious claims about race, evangelicals and mainline Protestants fragmented first into Northern and Southern denominations and communities during the Civil War and then again in the 1960s over civil rights. As late as 1979, W. A. Criswell, a prominent pastor of the First Baptist Church in Dallas, subscribed to this interpretation of Genesis 9 and featured it in the *Criswell Study Bible*.[21] For these curricula, this verse underscores Africa's backwardness from earliest times to the present.

Bob Jones University has an especially problematic history on race. Only in 2008, after it reversed its discriminatory policies toward African Americans, did Bob Jones University issue an apology for having maintained policies that were "racially hurtful."[22] Nonetheless, its textbook remains tinged with white racial superiority, especially, as we will see, in treating the American Civil War, correlated to the presumed favor of God toward that race. Some fundamentalist clergymen use these purported biblical foundations of race to make more extreme denunciations of other races. For example, Pastor Mark Downey of the Fellowship of God's Chosen People claims that, from the time of Cain, the Bible reveals the disastrous result and divine punishment for race mixing, including the Flood "from which Noah and his unpolluted descendants were saved (Gen. 6:11)."[23] Only the Bible's prohibition on racial mixing will preserve Christian identity. The iteration of such extreme claims in the present-day context of American religious opinion might have seemed unthinkable until their current, prominent exposure, largely on uncensored Internet sites. The reemergence of the alt-right in American political culture also has been supported in extremist circles with biblical citations legitimating racial differences. These textbooks do not follow racial claims to their most extreme ramifications. Nonetheless, biblically supported claims of white racial superiority allow any student exposed to more extreme views to see these textbooks as corroborating them.[24]

As these textbooks attempt to establish biblical antecedents for the social policies they advocate, they make other, equally problematic uses of the Bible. They contend that the first thousand years between Adam and Eve's sin and Noah's story demonstrated the need for government as human beings proved incapable of regulating themselves. God then established limited civil government as the history of ancient Israel confirms: once the Hebrews had conquered Palestine, the land was divided between the twelve tribes. They had no central government, and God thus sanctioned only limited government. "The Bible states that God has ordained civil government and that the state is a divine institution but not itself divine," the Abeka textbook contends. God also specifically ordained the death penalty and thus established a moral imperative for its current use.[25]

Like many of the central, political claims these curricula make, it is not entirely clear what they mean by limited government or civil government, although they consistently use the term to criticize governments and their policies. The espousal of limited government seems to imply that a return to decentralized government will lead to the restoration of biblical law, as indeed Christian Reconstructionists explicitly claim. For its most extreme proponents, biblical law entails a literal application of any punishment spelled out in the Old Testament, including extensive use of the death penalty for homosexuals and adulterers, among many other transgressors. Although proponents of these extreme views, notably Reconstructionists Rushdoony and Schaeffer, were challenged on these points by leading evangelical scholars, including Marsden and Noll, arguments for the restoration of biblical law have emerged in contemporary antigovernment rhetoric.[26]

The divine origin of government seems strikingly at odds with these curricula's harsh criticism of modern governments. This seeming contradiction disappears when one realizes that these textbooks ultimately favor the restoration of a Christian nation, to which their criticisms would presumably not apply. They do not specify what kind of government they would endorse once a Christian nation has been re-established. How far they might go in establishing a theocracy is never entirely clear in either these textbooks or in popular discourse. It may simply require Christian control of civil government to ensure that society conforms to Christian moral standards or perhaps, as recent Supreme Court decisions suggest, that religious liberty sanctions discrimination in the marketplace or exemptions from laws governing civil society.[27] These textbooks oppose a state church as antithetical to religious fervor, much as the earliest evangelicals opposed established churches in colonial New England, but they seem to want a government controlled by Christians and imposing Christian laws. The claim that only biblical Christianity can be the foundation of legitimate government has disturbing ramifications, which these curricula develop in their analyses of later periods.

For many evangelicals, the fact that God established government and that Paul's *Epistle to the Romans* enjoins obedience to political authority leads them to argue that one must unfailingly support the government, although they apply this claim selectively and idiosyncratically. Romans 13:1-2 is the Bible verse most often cited to buttress this point. "Let every soul be subject unto the higher powers. For there is no power but of God: the powers that be are ordained of God. Whosoever therefore resisteth the power, resisteth the ordinance of God: and they that resist shall receive to themselves damnation." This citation resonates in the public sphere; many evangelicals cited it to explain their support for President Trump.[28] These textbooks extend the requirement of obedience to established social hierarchies: children must obey their parents, wives their husbands, citizens the government.[29]

A definitive biblical event for these curricula was the building of the Tower of Babel. It epitomizes humans' desire to develop one civilization, as opposed to the many God intended—a ramification of God's endorsement of limited government. The Tower of Babel offers a dire warning against united political action among nations or political unification under a central government. Their narratives of the subsequent history of the world will condemn all such attempts. This specific example indicts the sinfulness of human beings and their willingness to construct a society on their own initiative rather than according to God's plan—a striking case of "humanism." The Tower of Babel represents an effort to implement specific goals BJU condemns: "religious ecumenism, globalism, one-world economy, one-world police force, unisex, etc."[30]

The Tower of Babel was directly relevant to Bob Jones University. Bob Jones Sr. condemned humanism as the effort of people "seeking a man-glorifying unity," when he defended the university's segregationist policies as resisting it. Segregation, he claimed, was as an effort of "one-worlders," misbegotten or even sinful because only Jesus's return will establish unity.[31] The connection between the Tower of Babel and the power of the state and one-world government worries Christian Reconstructionists as well. According to Rushdoony, the destruction of the Tower of Babel, which attempted to make mankind its "own Messiah," confirmed that all legitimate political authority comes only from God.[32]

These histories set the evil efforts of the Tower of Babel's builders against the commendable, God-given rationale for building a society: civilizations exist to fulfill the Creation Mandate as stipulated by Genesis 1:28: "Be fruitful and multiply, and fill the earth and subdue it; and have dominion over the fish of the sea and over the birds of the air and over every living thing that moves upon the earth." As this injunction "reveals mankind's reason for being," all human activities must conform to it as God's expressed intention for man.[33] In other words, the Creation Mandate requires that culture conform to biblical teaching.

For the BJU history, the Tower of Babel presents human beings who were "seeking to enjoy the blessings of the Creation Mandate, while refusing to obey God's command to fill the earth." The Creation Mandate directs human beings as stipulated in Genesis. This textbook claims that "toward the end of our race's first day, the first man spontaneously authored a poem (Gen. 2:23)." As this passage attests, all human culture was apparent on the first day and implicitly there has been no evolution and explicitly Genesis guides how God intends human to interact in civilization.[34] It is never entirely clear how or to what these various textbooks apply the Creation Mandate or what determines compliance with it, but it is unquestionably a litmus test for identifying good social actions and public policies.

This invocation of the Creation Mandate, as intended to bring civilization into conformity with the Bible, is a recent interpretation of its meaning. While this verse had some currency in the Reformation, the Creation Mandate was cited somewhat more frequently during the Scientific Revolution to justify investigation and manipulation of nature.[35] Contemporary conservative politicians have focused explicitly on this understanding of the passage as granting license to exploit the earth in any way human beings choose and prohibiting any limitation of that right.[36] For these curricula, concerns about global warming thus contravene God's Creation Mandate and constrain man's ability to use nature. Objections to birth control and reproductive science are significant exceptions to this general rule, perhaps because their use limits patriarchal authority, which these histories affirm as the foundation of society. The Creation Mandate is sometimes expanded to support extreme, pro-natalist views. The Quiverfull movement's adherents believe they are submitting to God's will by not practicing birth control because God controls how many children a woman bears. They cite a biblical "opening of the womb"—a phrase chillingly reminiscent of Margaret Atwood's *The Handmaid's Tale*.[37] This movement has become more tightly connected to Christian homeschooling through the advocacy of the biblical, patriarchal family by Doug Phillips, an attorney for the Home School Legal Defense Association (HSLDA), founder of Vision Forum, and a leader of the Quiverfull movement.[38] While the views of the movement are a distinct minority, the popular reality television program featuring the Duggar family, *19 Kids and Counting*, brought them into greater public prominence.[39]

While many Christians would recognize the Creation Mandate quotation from Genesis and find it unobjectionable, some on the religious right have more recently expanded the mandate into a requirement to bring a sinful culture under Christian control. The radical ramifications of this quotation characterize Christian Reconstructionists, for whom modern culture should conform directly to biblical law. They have brought this sense of the Creation Mandate into common parlance, as many on the right now assert that the United States must return to biblical law.

The Book of Genesis, as the beginning of human history, provides a foundation for fundamental social parameters about race, government, and science, and crucial ways to assess ancient civilizations. But early civilizations generally provide negative models. ACE is the most neutral with statements such as "a short people of unknown origins came to Mesopotamia sometime after the Flood. They invented the wheel, the arch, and the dome but, where they got those ideas, 'only God really knows.' "[40] As the cradle of human civilization, perhaps even of the Garden of Eden, the Middle East must be discussed, but its peoples must also be emphatically denounced for failing to accept the true God. In earliest human history, only Israel is commendable. The verses "And so all Israel shall be saved. . . . For this is my covenant unto them" (Rom. 11:26–27) confirm its distinct status. The quotation is also important for these curricula's political positions, as here the apostle Paul announced the future conversion of the Jews. Paul, the disciple with the most profound influence on Christianity's spread, made clear that the Christian gospel was not intended just for Jews.

Israel was privileged among ancient civilizations because of its biblical role as "the 'light of the nations,' leading other peoples to the knowledge of the one true God and His salvation." For ACE, students must learn about ancient civilizations so "you will be able to explain how God brought the Hebrews into existence and blessed them through the centuries."[41] But Israel's importance extends to the modern state as well.

Since its founding in 1948, Israel has fueled evangelicals' millennial expectations.[42] They believe that its existence foretells imminent fulfillment of prophecies that the return of Jews to Israel will prepare the way for Christ's return. Then the Jews will either accept Jesus or be lost. Sixty-three percent of white evangelicals share this belief according to a Pew survey.[43] In these curricula, comparisons between the biblical Jews and modern Israelis and Americans make the current political policies of the nation of Israel as legitimate as those of the United States. The identification with modern Israel connects the old and the new chosen people as part of the frequently invoked "Judeo-Christian" tradition.

As end times prophecies suggest that Israel must possess its land, evangelicals have engaged politically to broaden American support for Israel.[44] Israel's occupation of the West Bank in 1967 heightened millennial hopes. Hal Lindsay's the *Late Great Planet Earth* (1970), which sold 30 million copies, recast modern Israel's millennial import for modern readers and for college students through his work with Campus Crusade for Christ.[45] In contrast to many American Jews who support a Palestinian state, many evangelical Christians believe that all of Israel, including the West Bank, must be under Jewish control to fulfill Old Testament prophecies.[46] Benjamin Netanyahu has courted American evangelicals assiduously since the 1980s, and evangelicals now support Israel to a far greater degree than American Jews currently do.[47] In 1985, when the first Christian Congress for Biblical Zionism was held, it proclaimed, "We affirm that the restoration of Israel will usher in the coming of the Messiah."[48] The International Fellowship of Christians and Jews currently has 330,000 Christian donors supporting projects in Israel and Jewish settlements. When the Fellowship surveyed their Christian donors, 28% supported the Christian Congress because of their beliefs about end times and 58% because God has blessed Israel. The

Christians' Israel Public Action Campaign lobbies Capitol Hill to advocate "policies that support Israel on Biblical grounds."[49] The support of the
Christian right for Israel has become increasingly significant, as their leaders
have direct access to influential members of Congress and some presidents.

As this chapter attests, the Book of Genesis gives contemporary Christians
critical interpretive tools to understand science, government, civil society,
and even the modern Middle East. But it also emphasizes another, essential element of the unfolding of history. Genesis reveals the power of evil.
Whether called "sin" or "Satan," evil plays a leading role in human history.
Because of sin, there are two dominions: the seed of the woman and the seed
of the serpent. These two seeds were destined for conflict: "Throughout the
long centuries ahead, Satan's offspring would wound the followers of Jehovah
many times." With this thesis statement, history becomes a battle between the
people of God and others. The story of Cain and Abel offers a salient lesson
as Cain's descendants predict the future course of human history. When
they built cities, they were asserting their independence from God. Cain's
descendants were the "seed of Satan," and Seth's were the "seed of woman," as
the BJU textbook defines this fundamental battle throughout history.[50]

For these curricula, conflict between nations is almost inevitable as one
nation tries to create a man-centered world and another rises to thwart it,
particularly as God uses one nation to destroy another. The BJU textbook's
definition of a nation as a large group of people with the same land, customs, and language suggests a tribal sense common to some elements of
the Christian right in the United States and nationalist political parties in
Europe. "Nation" so identified can be undermined by immigrants.[51] Equally
significant, the Abeka textbook describes a culture "as the way of life of a
group of people" defined by "how people relate to God."[52]

The fundamental test of any ancient civilization is whether it accepted the
One True God. Any civilization that did not is entirely culpable: "False religion . . . is an attempt to hide from the testimony to this God found everywhere in this world."[53] These textbooks condemn, as did John Calvin,
the failures of individuals or groups to accept the one true God no matter
where or when they lived. Calvin contended that He was accessible to all.[54]
And, of course, Luther excoriated the Jews at the time of the Reformation
for not accepting Christ, although, for him, believers in other gods simply
had not received the gift of faith and were not saved.[55] For these histories, no
early civilization is credible unless it accepted either the Jewish or Christian
God. Presumably, Israel's role in the Judeo-Christian tradition and end times

prophecies allows it to escape the indictment of other ancient civilizations for failing to accept the Messiah.

Biblical history allows these Christian curricula to assert that Mosaic Law is the fundamental and only credible source of morality and law. This claim reinforces Calvin's argument: "There are some who deny that a commonwealth is duly framed which neglects the political system of Moses. . . . Let other men consider how perilous and seditious this notion is; it will be enough for me to have proved it false and foolish."[56] It is never entirely clear what Mosaic Law entails in concrete terms in its recent invocations. It could simply refer to the Ten Commandments or have much more expansive implications. Moses, "Mosaic Law," and "biblical law" are terms identifiable within some quarters of the Christian community as signaling the Christian nation argument.[57] Many on the religious right advocate a return to "biblical law" in the United States, as they assert that it founded the new nation. These terms, although widely used, remain unspecified but sufficiently malleable to advocate various positions, from the loosest sense that our laws must enshrine Christian values, to a staunch claim that our laws and institutions are based on the Ten Commandments, to the promotion of a re-established Christian nation, or even to the imposition of the legal strictures of Leviticus and Deuteronomy. The fact that the Ten Commandments are not a system of government and the Constitution does not punish infractions of religious laws does not deter supporters of this argument, nor does the fact that many of our Ten Commandments monuments, particularly in state parks, were donated by the Fraternal Order of Eagles as part of publicity promoting Cecil B. DeMille's 1956 film, *The Ten Commandments*. Such monuments do not attest to Americans' understanding of the foundation of the nation's laws.

To establish Mosaic Law as the foundation of every credible legal or moral system, these histories compare it to the Code of Hammurabi to the latter's disadvantage.[58] "The higher class paid less in penalties for the same offense than the lower classes," as ACE criticizes the code's inequity. For Abeka, "God always makes the punishment fit the crime, but Hammurabi did not."[59] These curricula sharply distinguish Moses, who had God's law, from Hammurabi, who simply had man's. Whether or not a government is predicated on Mosaic Law becomes a crucial means to evaluate subsequent civilizations and to disparage other law codes. This view underlies the current emphasis on Moses in the American founding and in some state standards, notably those of Texas.[60]

A more balanced account of Hammurabi's Law would recognize not only how impressive a legal code it was but also, as a record of 282 cases dealing with commerce, family relations, criminality, and civil laws, how rich a source it is about life in Mesopotamia, replete with information about business contracts, professional requirements, and landholding. This law code gave women extensive legal protections, suggesting that spouses acted more as partners than within a patriarchal hierarchy. It might thus be more apt to compare Hammurabi's Laws to Jewish law, with its complex strictures on diet and custom.

Several features of the treatment of ancient civilizations in these Christian histories are especially noteworthy. They first distinguish those who accepted the God of the Bible from those who set up false gods and then denounce them for their godlessness. Such civilizations also undertook cultural activities for the wrong reasons, and thus their accomplishments came to naught.

A decisive event in these world histories was God's calling Abraham out of the polytheistic idolatry of Mesopotamia to establish His chosen people through the "Abrahamic Covenant."[61] This phrase summarizes God's promise to Abraham of land and descendants to form a great nation in an eternal and unconditional covenant. These promises lead the BJU textbook to conclude that "the story of our race is the story of how God is working to make the disobedient kingdoms of this world the kingdom of his Messiah." The use of "race" and "our race" is disconcerting, as these educational materials see the sons of Noah divided into races, associated with Caucasian, Asian, and African races. (Given the historical uses of racial claims, it is unfortunate that the textbook does not use "human beings" or the "human race.") The term "Abrahamic Covenant" emphasizes that God established Israel as a theocracy and gave the Jews His law, which "provides for all time a perfect moral standard by which men can distinguish right from wrong."[62] Or, as the Abeka history puts it, in the biblical history of Israel "a permanent record had been made of the general principles of morality, the basic beliefs for a nation under God."[63] The significance of this point for these Christian curricula cannot be overstated. Every time they praise or blame a law code, an idea, a nation, or a moral position, they reinforce that no other moral code is legitimate. The relationship of God to the ancient Israelites is the template of "a nation under God."

God's relationship to peoples in biblical times shows how He directs history. For example, although God initially used the Assyrians to punish other nations for their pride in their conquests, He sent an angel to kill 185,000 of them. God also used Nebuchadnezzar to punish the Israelites, but later "God's judgment fell upon Nebuchadnezzar . . . [for] the folly of his pride." God's use of one nation to punish another is an important key to understanding ancient history, as, for example, "God used the Assyrians and Chaldeans as His instruments of judgment upon the Hebrews. . . . God used the Persians as His instrument for preserving the Jews."[64]

Whenever disasters or misfortunes occur to ancient peoples, these curricula interpret them as punishments for sinfulness or God's disfavor. However, they construe both boons and disasters for the Israelites as signs of God's favor. In the first instance He shows they are His chosen people; in the second He brings them back to Him. When, for example, Solomon allows false gods in Israel, God punishes them with Solomon's oppressive taxation, a frequently cited divine punishment.

The failure of the Jews to recognize Jesus as the Messiah was due to their expectation that He would remediate their temporal condition, saving them from Roman oppression. This claim allows the BJU history to emphasize, as it will do frequently, that the Christian message is not intended to alleviate political or social problems. Human attempts to remediate social ills are so illegitimate that God might reject his people as a result. For these curricula, the destruction of Jerusalem in 70 AD and Titus's victory over the Jews revealed that "God had judged the Jews for their rejection of Jesus Christ and their persecution of the early church."[65] Although this event signaled God's definitive repudiation of His chosen people, the Jews retain a privileged status in these curricula because of their predicted role in end times and because they were the first of successive covenants.

Other peoples in the ancient world merit condemnation for the evils of their religions, with the notable exception of Egypt, where God preserved His people. Its history interests these curricula when it corroborates the Bible. For example, the twelfth dynasty may have been when Abram sought food in Egypt, as described in Genesis 12:15–20; Joseph may have been the prime minister during the Middle Kingdom; and Egypt was the greatest power in the world at the time of the Book of Exodus. The Abeka history appreciates that its "government, ruler, and religion all represented a single divine order"—a disconcerting acceptance of theocracy. But it condemns Egyptians as humanists who worshipped man. When God sent plagues to punish the Egyptians, He "turned their worship of nature against them" and showed "the ridiculousness of the Egyptian religion." While these curricula acknowledge Egyptian advances in science, they denounce Egyptians for attempting to set themselves up as gods. The BJU textbook concludes that "the greatness of Egypt is no more."[66]

These curricula offer a limited treatment of the ancient world beyond the Bible's history. When they consider parts of the world beyond the narrative of successive chosen people, they do so in a cursory fashion and as ancillary to the central narrative. For example, the Abeka history's 2013 edition expends only twenty-six pages on the rest of the world before Europeans evangelized, explored, or conquered it and does so in largely negative terms. Its 2016 edition further reduces its coverage of the non-Judeo-Christian ancient world to fourteen pages and does not discuss it until after the sixteenth-century Protestant Reformation. India, the New World, and Asia are each featured in a few paragraphs with a concluding condemnation of their adherence to false gods in each case. Neglect of the rest of the world is even more striking as it announces it as a matter of principle: "Because so many events of history have, in one way or another, been a response to Christ, we now focus on the relatively small part of the world."[67]

In both the Abeka and BJU curricula, pre-nineteenth-century India warrants only three pages, primarily about its geography and rulers. It has remained economically backward and mired in poverty because of its "superstitious religions." But despite their idolatry, Indians contributed to mathematics and the development of cotton and steel. Subject to "the darkness of pagan religions," Asia has been kept "in spiritual darkness," but much later it will be "blessed by the efforts of evangelization."[68]

In contrast to their appreciation of Egypt, limited as it is, these textbooks label Africa the Dark Continent. They describe its geography and begin its history from the arrival of Ham's sons—Misraim, Phut, and Cush—who give their names to its kingdoms. Their history too intersects with biblical accounts. A Cushite helped Jeremiah, and a Cushite eunuch was the first African converted to Christianity, according to Acts 8:26–40, for example. Although Africa's coastal cities had extensive trade, the "fear, idolatry, and witchcraft associated with animism" prevented African economic and cultural development. Failure to embrace the one true God doomed the continent to backwardness.[69]

The history of the ancient world these textbooks provide differs markedly from the historical consensus or what students might learn in more standard curricula. World histories begin with the origin of human civilization in Africa. They appreciate the development of distinctive human accomplishments and correlate them to human evolution during the conventionally accepted historical ages of the earth, drawing evidence from paleography, archeology, and anthropology. They acknowledge the categories of human development from the Paleolithic age, from 1 million to 10,000 BCE, when humans developed tools, fire, language, and cave art. As the textbooks treated here insist that creation occurred no more than 10,000 years ago, they reject such evidence or point to it as what non-Christians believe. If students educated with these curricula become familiar with the evidence of the earliest human activities, particularly from the study of bones of human ancestors dating back many thousands of years, their relationship to us corroborated by DNA and other scientific studies, they may well reject it as simply impossible—as these publishers doubtless hope.[70]

Historians place ancient civilizations in more complex relations with one another, not simply in relation to the Israelites or the Bible, and they more thoroughly appreciate their accomplishments. They highlight other prominent cultures, especially those with long histories or extensive written records. They recognize that Egypt, with 3,000 years of cultural preeminence as a powerful civilization before its decline, deserves more than a footnote to the history of the Israelites. Other textbooks treat ancient civilizations on their own terms, rather than as merely non-Christian and of interest only for their interactions with the biblical Jews.

While historians recognize flood stories as common to other cultures, they do not invoke them in the contradictory way these curricula do. The Epic of Gilgamesh, recorded some thousand years before Genesis was written, describes not only a flood story but also an angry god and a favored human, who released birds to look for land. For these curricula, such stories confirm the validity of the biblical account. Only the story of Noah is historically accurate, confirming the authority of the Bible over all other sources.[71]

History textbooks that do not rely on the Bible as the authority are careful to indicate what we do not know about earlier periods. They acknowledge other laws and ethical codes. They might, for example, discuss Zarathustra's religious reforms and ethical mandates, which recognized Ahuramazda as the only god and thus rejected polytheism but included demons, who represented good at war with evil, with the reward of glory for goodness and punishment for evil. Students educated with more standard textbooks might be fascinated by stories of the gods and religious beliefs of other civilizations. Those educated with these Christian curricula will see them as mired in error and sin.

These curricula unreservedly appreciate the Bible, but they circumscribe that appreciation by considering it only as inerrant and literal. Their understanding is very much at odds with a long tradition of how the Bible has been studied and understood. Already in the seventeenth century, both Protestants and Catholics studied the Bible not only philologically but also historically. These scholars recognized that the Bible needed to be amplified by other accounts, unlike these textbooks. Some of those early studies of the Bible led scholars to conclude that the Pentateuch, the first five books of the Bible, was not written by a single author called Moses but by several over a prolonged period. For those seventeenth-century scholars, those conclusions enhanced their appreciation of the Bible, although these Christian textbooks find such claims anathema.[72]

Historians place Israel's history within the context of large, contemporary empires. When the Bible is studied as a historical text, it details a broad history in which Abraham came from Ur and went to Egypt. When the Israelites were led out of Egypt by Moses, they conquered Canaan and forged a united kingdom under David and Solomon. But when Solomon's sons could not keep the kingdom united, it was divided into Israel and Judah. Israel was conquered by the Assyrians; its ten lost tribes were scattered and never found. Judah was defeated by Babylonians under Nebuchadnezzar II, who destroyed the temple and took the Israelites into captivity.

Historians recognize the Hebrew Bible as the most extensive source for understanding the history of the Jews, especially because they were rarely mentioned by their contemporaries. They would point out as well that it is fragmentary and much about the history of the Jews cannot be known from it. It was recorded in such a variety of literary genres—law, poetry, narrative—that its richness has led to many "Bible as Literature" college courses.

Historians considered the Israelites as of great interest as the first to adopt monotheism, perhaps as early as the eighth century BCE and as the seedbed for two other world religions—Christianity and Islam. As the historian Donald Kagan notes, "the Jews' belief in an all-powerful creator (who is righteous himself and demands righteousness and obedience from a human king) and a universal God (who is the father and ruler of all peoples) is a critical part of the Western tradition."[73]

In standard world history courses, students would likely learn enough about early civilizations to distinguish them from more recognizable models offered by the Greeks and the Romans. Early civilizations required cultural conformity, their governments were monarchies sustained by a belief that they represented the divine, and the civilizations made few distinctions between animate and in-animate. The pervasive role religion played in these ancient societies would be obvious to students: rulers claimed to speak for god; nature and the gods were unpredictable, required propitiating sacrifices, but, when angered, unleashed natural disasters. These aspects of ancient civilizations often intrigue students because they seem so foreign to modern sensibilities. Students educated with more standard curricula would appreciate ancient history as much richer and more complex than the narratives of these Christian curricula allow.

If what is missing from these Christian curricula seems a loss for student's education, what students using them might well absorb is disturbing. First, the biblical inerrancy these histories insist upon has crucial ramifications, as students are encouraged to mistrust all scientific findings about earlier human beings or societies. The rejection of anthropological, geological, and biological evidence must surely play some role in our culture's declining be-lief in science or facts. Second, with the Bible as the unquestionable source of historical knowledge, these Christian curricula either reject or denigrate other cultures. They take it as a given that all other civilizations had an op-portunity to accept the God of the Jews but chose instead to reject truth and espouse error. Third, these textbooks also derive a notion of race from Noah's sons, even though "race" is not a biblical notion. They map those sons and their offspring onto world history in a racialized way. Different races have dis-tinct intellectual capacities, destined to different levels of accomplishment. The superiority of the white race is, at least implicitly, biblically ordained and endorses a divinely established separation of the races. Finally, God is the source of government. As previously noted, the Abeka history pronounces that "the state is a divine institution but not divine in itself."[74] This pronounce-ment has two different but equally problematic implications. First, whatever state exists is ordained by God. In other words, no matter how disturbing any manifestation of a political state is, God intends it. This stricture might explain the disequilibrium the election of Barack Obama created for many evangelicals as well as their acceptance of Donald Trump. The second and equally unsettling conclusion is that the legitimacy of the state inheres in its divine establishment. As these narratives of world history unfold, it becomes clear that the United States is sanctioned by God, although England has had its moments. The claim that the state is a divine institution implies that gov-ernmental legitimacy rests on its being sanctioned by religion, specifically Christianity. The strongest implication of this view, although it is never stated directly, is that government should be theocratic or at least that the law and the community should enforce biblical law and morality.

In their treatment of the biblical beginnings of history, these textbooks introduce several features crucial to the Christian interpretation of history. The Tower of Babel will be a constant trope, cited as the first example of "humanism." Moses gave to the world the only acceptable morality. However they invoke it—"Mosaic Law," the Ten Commandments, or simply Moses himself—it becomes an unassailable source of legitimate government, law, and morality.

These textbooks analyze early civilizations to condemn specific government policies and to describe the contest between the godly and godless. The policies they praise become features of God's plan for human beings; those they deplore become signs of divine disfavor. Thus the stakes in political debates become much higher than policymakers might imagine and explain some of the righteous indignation fueling contemporary discussions. That the history of the world documents a battle between the "seed of woman" and the "seed of Satan," in which God uses one nation to punish another, has crucial implications for international relations. Victories can be construed as signs of divine favor. If other civilizations are godless and should be subject to the legitimate control of the godly, is a godly nation limited in the actions it can justifiably take? Can there be any reason to work toward international agreements, since defeat in war is divine punishment and efforts to unify peoples smack of the humanism of the Tower of Babel?

These histories condemn other early civilizations for failing to accept the God of the Jews: they had the opportunity but rejected Him. Although this premise seems to raise a crucial theological question about who chooses, God or those who accept Him, or about how these curricula understand election, it allows Christians to repudiate all civilizations that failed to take the right path. When they disparage ancient civilizations as failures or reduce them to footnotes to biblical history, these educational materials narrow historical inquiry about ancient history in crucial ways: (1) the Bible is the only inherently legitimate history of the ancient world; (2) the Israelites are the only commendable ancient civilization; (3) divinely established government is the only legitimate government. The first two points challenge the understanding of the history of the ancient world. The final point undermines liberal democracy as established by "we the people."

5

Misguided Ancients

In company with Sallust, Cicero, Tacitus, and Livy, you will learn
Wisdom and Virtue. . . . You will even remember that all the End of
study is to make you a good Man and a useful Citizen.
                                        —John Adams to John Quincy Adams
                                                               May 18, 1781

This chapter's epigraph is one of many acknowledgments by a founder
of the American republic of the centrality of Roman texts and rhetoric to
the moral and cultural underpinnings of the new nation.[1] While this quotation recognizes a debt to the Romans, the Greeks too were significant to
American political and cultural traditions. Not surprisingly, important
writers and leaders of the founding generation invoked them as models, but
the Christian world histories we are examining largely repudiate this foundational legacy of the ancient world to us.

Historians traditionally emphasize the crucial significance of the Greeks
and the Romans to the development of a distinctly Western civilization,
not simply for their political legacy but also for their cultural contributions.
The Greco-Roman intellectual influence has been enduring and profound
in many spheres but particularly in science and philosophy. No less significant is the contribution of these two ancient civilizations to the arts, notably
sculpture and architecture. Indeed, revivals of Greek arts have occurred regularly to the present day, inspiring artistic and cultural reinvigoration. The
Greeks developed a variety of literary forms, including lyric poetry and the
dramatic forms of tragedy and comedy. They inaugurated democracy.

Through their conquest of Greece, the Romans not only brought much
of what we appreciate about Greek culture into the West but also made their
own distinctive contributions to Western civilization. Even the Abeka history, which makes many critical comments about the Greeks, considers

Hijacking History. Kathleen Wellman, Oxford University Press. © Oxford University Press 2021.
DOI: 10.1093/oso/9780197579237.003.0006

that "Western Civilization as we know it today is largely a mixture of Greco-Roman culture and Judeo-Christian religion and morality."[2]

Mainstream historians frequently single out the Romans for the forms of government they inaugurated—the republic and the empire. The Roman Republic resounded with public debate, fueled by the inspiring rhetoric of orators such as Cicero. The Roman Empire unified and administered an expansive territory, including continental Europe, the Mediterranean world, the Middle East, and beyond. The organizational genius of the Romans allowed them to conquer vast territory and sustain their conquests over a long history. Extant remains of their buildings and aqueducts crisscross their former empire, attesting to their skill as builders and engineers. Their contributions to culture, while in part derived from the Greeks, continued the development of what we now identify as a distinctive Western civilization. The accomplishments and failures of the Greeks and Romans have provoked analysis of subsequent political regimes, as they continue to do, although these curricula are too dismissive of ancient models to accord them such significance.

The classics have long been a staple of Western education. Elites of every generation in Europe and the Americas were educated with them, at least until the early twentieth century. The classics provided a foundation and models of thought, action, and accomplishment for them. In the recent past, education in the classics has declined. In the university, that decline is due, in part, to the association of elites with Western civilization, provoking charges of ethnocentrism.[3] Classical studies have waned as universities increasingly narrow education to professional training. Neither are the classics prominent in secondary education in the United States. Classical texts challenge current expectations of secondary students and have little place in curricula geared toward skills acquisition and immediate practical relevance. The history of the classical world is less prominent in high school and university curricula as Western civilization courses have been replaced by world history courses, which consider a broader range of ancient civilizations but treat the Greco-Roman world more cursorily.

As previously noted, the Christian textbooks treated in this book focus primarily on Western civilization. One might then expect them to appreciate its classical legacy. Instead, the Greeks and the Romans provide compelling examples of how humans went astray. In part, these textbooks' disparagement of the classical period reflects a deep distrust of education and an underlying anti-intellectualism. That distrust has a long history in the United

States, frequently tied to evangelicalism and its nineteenth-century attacks on secular education. With their advent in the early twentieth century, some fundamentalists denounced the classics during the Gilded Age as causing American culture to descend into decadence, just as Greece and Rome had. In discussing the ancients, these curricula introduce many crucial religious, social, political, and economic arguments they subsequently develop more thoroughly. Their limited appreciation of the classical tradition foreshadows their later arguments about the Christian American nation: discredited classics can have influenced it only as mediated by Christianity.

The ancient world advances these curricula's narrative: classical civilizations did not accept the one true God, but they can function as negative examples to make explicit polemical points. Many examples are immediately politically relevant—from taxes to government regulations to social practices like birth control, euthanasia, and homosexuality. Ancient civilizations failed to promote the correct public policies or family values. They offer warnings for contemporary Americans.

Classical texts provide especially rich material, enabling these textbooks to condemn humanism as the defining feature of civilizations.[4] Early Latin scholars traced the derivation of the term "humanism" from the Greek word for philanthropy. Subsequent Latin scholars, particularly Cicero, used it to describe humane learning. The Renaissance, greatly indebted to Cicero, emphasized the *studia humanitatis*, or the study of the humanities—philosophy, history, literature, and the arts. By the nineteenth century, humanism was widely recognized as an ethical philosophy rooted in the appreciation of human abilities, particularly reason. Religiously driven opponents, who objected to rationalism and condemned its adherents as deists or Unitarians, construed it as a pejorative term. In contrast, a conference at the University of Chicago in 1933 produced A *Humanist Manifesto*. Many of the supporting signatories were religious figures themselves who, nonetheless, appreciated humanism, advocated reason and social justice, and argued for science to replace appeals to the supernatural as the basis for public policy. For evangelicals and fundamentalists, the fact that religious figures acceded to humanism as a legitimate ethical philosophy revealed just how formidable an enemy humanism had become and how emphatically the Christian had to resist it. For these textbooks' authors and publishers, humanism is anathema: its roots are traced not to humane letters but rather to resistance to God as the Tower of Babel first revealed.

These histories deploy the term "humanism" as a broad brush of denunciation, condemning virtually any human accomplishment not rooted in Christianity. Greek philosophy provokes special ire. For the Abeka textbook, the Greeks followed "an arrogant, humanistic way of thinking." The BJU curriculum quotes the apostle Paul to condemn Greek philosophy for glorifying "the creature more than the Creator." For example, the Sophists "taught young men of Athens that since the gods were not real and therefore could not punish them, they should do whatever they thought they could get away with." Although Aristotle concluded that the universe came from God, ultimately, he, Socrates, Plato, and all Greek philosophy "erred and placed man at the center of all things." These philosophers "put themselves in bondage to sin by rebelling against the one true God Who is clearly revealed in nature." The Greeks could have "turned to the one true God," but "instead they began to think of themselves as gods," the Abeka textbook charges. Failing to recognize man's responsibility to God, these philosophers and their followers fell into "gross immorality."[5]

This term, implicitly understood but never explicitly stated as homosexuality, connects Greek philosophy to a major cultural issue for the Christian right. Both evangelicals and fundamentalists mobilized to attack homosexuality after the American Psychiatric Association in 1974 repudiated its former designation of homosexuality as a mental illness. On the basis of Leviticus 18:22, "Thou shall not lie with mankind as with womankind; it is an abomination," some religious communities condemned homosexuality as a sin. Same-sex relations had become more controversial and more rigidly defined during the nineteenth century, when scientists and social scientists focused on defining sexual difference and identity. While acceptance of gay rights, particularly the right to marry, is much more pronounced among young evangelicals than among their elders, denial of such rights and efforts to "reeducate" homosexuals into heterosexuality still mobilize some in the ongoing culture wars.[6] The rationale for including homosexuality in a discussion of the Greeks, if only obliquely, is that the Greeks idealized relationships of older men with younger ones. Such relationships were to prepare young men for public life; relationships with women, excluded from the public sphere, could offer no such guidance. Ironically, these textbooks advocate a similar gendered division of public male roles from the private female sphere.

Although the injunction from Leviticus is frequently cited, other biblical prohibitions, including Exodus 22:18, "Thou shalt not suffer a witch to live," or Leviticus 20:27, "A man also or woman that hath a familiar spirit, or is a wizard, shall surely be put to death," are not, even though the Plymouth witch trials and an American colonial law code of 1641 both did so. In early America, those biblical quotations defined capital offenses. Fortunately, they no longer inform legal proceedings against transgressive women. The point here, of course, is that the biblical stipulations of Leviticus, as well as other frequently cited Old Testament verses, are used highly selectively even by the most rigid of fundamentalists; only extremists argue for restoring them completely.

According to these curricula, Greek philosophy rested on a fundamental misapprehension—belief in the "basic goodness of man." Greek philosophers also failed to recognize that the "wisdom of this world is foolishness with God," as the BJU history cites Paul.[7] ACE mocks the futile efforts of Greek philosophers to discover what made up the universe, for the only answer is to be found in Genesis 1:1: "In the beginning God created heaven and earth."[8]

Although generally negative, these educational materials include some mixed messages about Greek accomplishments, occasionally praising and denouncing the very same thing. The BJU history singles out the Parthenon as a symbol of both "the cultural achievement" and "the spiritual blindness of the Greek people."[9] Some aspects are described neutrally—the acropolis, gymnasium, and theater as features of Greek cities and Greek military successes against the Persians, for example. The Battle of Salamis is recognized as crucial to Western civilization because it halted the westward expansion of the Persian Empire.[10]

These textbooks do not generally appreciate the Greeks, but some of their denunciations are astonishing. The Abeka curriculum claims the Greeks made no progress in science, even though Greek scientific works set the standard for virtually every science for over fifteen hundred years. It makes this claim, in part, because it sees evolutionary ideas and modern psychology as derived from them. Another crucial point is that the Greeks were so completely deluded that they modeled their gods on human beings, who were "immoral, impatient, whimsical, unjust and deceitful."[11] As a result, their civilization was fundamentally flawed, and their efforts ultimately produced no benefits. Even Alexander the Great experienced no satisfaction from his accomplishments, or, as the Abeka textbook claims, "He did not realize that God permitted his conquests only to serve His own purpose."[12] The BJU history wonders, "How often men have tried to satisfy their soul's desire by seeking the fleeting pleasures of this world."[13] This critical assessment applies to many aspects of Greek culture. The Greeks' pursuit of wisdom, under-standing of nature, and political ideas were illegitimate because they were not motivated by a quest for "biblical truth." Nonetheless, these curricula do acknowledge some Greek literary and artistic achievements, including those of Homer, Aesop, Sophocles, Aristophanes, and Herodotus, the last of whom interestingly, as Abeka puts it, "often embellish[ed] the fact with fiction and attribute[d] the outcome of events to the whims of the gods"[14]—an unrecognized irony.

ACE takes an idiosyncratic stance toward the Greeks to emphasize their deviation from Christian beliefs. While the Minoans had a notion of the afterlife as "a happy place," the Bible stipulates "a Hell for the unright-eous." As the Minoans "seem not to have believed in any type of Hell," they are dismissed. The Greeks sacrificed to their gods, but not appropriately "as a sacrifice for sin." ACE frequently inserts biblical quotations into the historical narrative to indict other civilizations as misguided. After discussing the Golden Age of Pericles, ACE advises, "Be ye steadfast, unmovable, always abounding in the work of the Lord" (1 Corinthians 15:58), amplified by the more colloquial advice that "in the matter of sal-vation, he who hesitates is often lost." ACE is filled with random, hor-tatory injunctions. A discussion of the Roman army invites students to "put on the whole armour of God, that ye may be able to stand against the wiles of the devil." Similarly, after discussing the Roman Emperor Nero, this curriculum warns, "Remember, the pleasures of sin are 'for a season,' but its wages are for eternity."[15]

These histories' accounts of the Greeks offer dire warnings for high school students. They suggest direct correlations between the failures of these an-cient regimes and current policies. For the Abeka textbook, Sparta's demise offers a sobering example that "extensive governmental regimentation of a people results in intellectual stagnation." So too Greek civilization failed be-cause the Greeks did not prohibit abortion and euthanasia.[16]

Ancient civilizations offer rarer positive models: the Greeks believed in private, parental education, and thus educated women solely for house-hold management; they were "held in high esteem within the household."[17] These specific social policies elicit praise whenever these curricula see them in the past. The Romans, to their credit, built strong patriarchal households in which an authoritarian father exercised control. Caesar Augustus estab-lished the crucial moral values of "duty, discipline, and hard work," passed laws favoring those with many children, and punished immorality—another implicit condemnation of birth control and homosexuality. The Roman *paterfamilias* "ruled his family without interference from the state." And "parents instilled into their children the values of loyalty, *submission to authority*, self-control, and duty. Romans epitomized patriotism and hard work."[18] The traditional family—a strong father as head of the household and a mother largely restricted to it—makes the Roman family admirable. Roman education appropriately reinforced this rigid gendered division with boys benefiting from a classical education while girls learned the domestic arts.[19] These claims invoke "family values" rhetoric central to modern conservatives.

These curricula insist that the Romans' acceptance of divorce led to the disintegration of the family and the end of its civilization.[20] One cannot help wondering how students respond to attacks on divorced historical figures as immoral. Evangelicals have a divorce rate higher than the national average, so one might think it problematic to condemn it in twenty-first-century textbooks. While the evangelical community has long harshly condemned divorce because of explicit biblical prohibitions and some evangelical churches still exclude the divorced, divorce is now more accepted.

For these textbooks, any repudiation of the "family values" they assume are rooted in the Bible leads either to a civilization's precipitous decline or divine retribution. Their biblical foundation seems tenuous, given the unorthodox family relations of biblical figures. As Andrew Klumpp and James Levison have noted, biblical examples expose clearly dysfunctional families and the family devalued: the biblical family was polygamous; wives sometimes dominated husbands or tricked them, as Rebecca did Isaac; men fathered children by many women as with Jacob's twelve sons by four women; the family of David was the stuff of salacious miniseries—no models for touted family values. And Jesus required his disciples to repudiate their families to follow Him. Biblical figures may have been models of fidelity to God but not positive models of fathers in families; they instead exemplify "faithless families, faithful God."[21]

When James Dobson began Focus on the Family in 1977, he emphasized patriarchal families as biblical, asserting the father's unquestioned authority. The originators of these curricula share that view. The vice president of ACE, Ronald Johnson, insists that education must to be rooted in obedience: "A student obtains freedom by obedience and subjection to parents," as confirmed by Galatians 4:2.[22] These histories privilege social relationships they wish to extol; they subscribe to a rigid and reactionary system of "family values"—enforcing patriarchy, condemning divorce, and damning homosexuality—and promote that view as Christian.

Contemporary cultural issues resonate so strongly because these curricula long for an idealized past when the authority and status of the male head of the family was unquestioned, when men controlled women and children, and when male hegemony in the public sphere was inviolable. These curricula and contemporary "values voters" hearken back with nostalgia to a notion of the family dynamic characteristic of the 1950s, a highly anomalous and frequently mythologized family structure made possible by the postwar economic boom and the need to reintegrate returning soldiers into the workplace by excluding women from it. It shapes these textbooks' analysis of the ancient world. In contrast, recent scholarship on the family in the classical period is more nuanced, noting that, while Greek women were largely restricted to the private realm, with the notable exception of well-educated courtesans, women had greater autonomy under the Romans.[23]

These histories use their discussions of the ancient world to initiate several other central arguments. The Abeka textbook notes that, in Rome, "the government tried to appease the people with 'bread and circuses'—free food and entertainment," with devastating results. "Handouts of bread squelched what little remained of the traditional Roman ideals of personal initiative and self-respect." Rome's social welfare policies debilitated its citizens and destroyed its civilization.[24] Social policies directed to poor relief are disastrous, both for those given aid and for civilizations providing it. This argument becomes increasingly prominent when these curricula consider how more modern governments address the needs of their citizens, but the groundwork is laid in classical antiquity. With every election cycle, this argument becomes more central to the Republican Party's core contention, derived from many sources—from Ayn Rand to libertarianism. For these curricula, these social and political views are simply "Christian."[25] The negative effect of government funding was an argument thoroughly developed by Christian Reconstructionists. It became a crucial tenet of the political right and its attacks on the social safety net. These curricula do not acknowledge the essential role that early Christians played in establishing a welfare system for public charity as integral to their faith. The reasons for that glaring omission will become clearer as these textbooks develop a political, social, and economic agenda antithetical to that of the earliest Christians.

For these educational materials, the decline of Rome offers sober lessons, as "inefficiency and waste had accompanied the sharp rise in the size of the government. It attempted to solve its economic problems by raising taxes." The BJU history acknowledges other economic aspects of Rome's decline— the expense of maintaining a large bureaucracy (and an army), an excessive tax burden on the people, and inflation, central tenets of Republican economic orthodoxy. When the Emperor Diocletian tried to inaugurate economic reforms, they proved to be completely ineffective because they "involved greater government control and regulation." Along with these economic signs of decline were moral failings: whereas Roman republicans had been self-reliant, the citizens of the Empire "looked to the government to supply free grain and public amusements . . . a hard-working patriotic citizen was hard to find."[26] Another key to Rome's decline is clear: Rome could not survive "the dissolution of its families; the decay of its traditional moral values of hard work, self-discipline, and patriotism; and the adherence to its pagan religions."[27] The lessons for contemporary America are clear: only these family and moral values can save America from the disastrous decline Rome experienced. Jarringly anachronistic claims that civilizations declined as much for their failures to adopt current American ideological positions as for their failure to adhere to correct religious views are prominent throughout these textbooks. The BJU textbook directs students to this crucial comparison, asking, "Do you think some of the reasons for Rome's decline can be found in our culture as well?"[28]

Conventional histories often praise Rome's practice of peacefully incorporating the gods of conquered peoples into the Roman pantheon as an effective way to reconcile them to Roman rule. In the BJU account, this practice signals Rome's failure, as it "readily embraced the pagan gods and false teaching of her many conquered peoples."[29] Despite their criticisms, these textbooks recognize "limited, representative government and her reverence for rule of law" as Rome's distinctive gifts to Western civilization.[30]

These textbooks' understanding of ancient history is overtly teleological: history fulfills God's plan. Thus the Pax Romana occurred so that Christianity would spread easily:[31] "God directed the affairs of men and civilizations in ancient times to make the world ready for the coming of His Son and the spread of the gospel."[32] Specifically, "God's plan of salvation" required the common language, transportation, and communication network of the Roman Empire.[33] The story of early Christianity in the Roman Empire is primarily about Christian persecution because Satan "always attacks God by persecuting God's people." The Romans saw Christians as social misfits and "made them scapegoats for problems in the Empire."[34] The early Christians' virtue contrasts with the Romans' depravity. Persecutions broke out as "Satan hurled his venom against the Christians in a vain attempt to squelch their witness for Jesus Christ."[35] Christians refused to worship the emperors as the state demanded.

The Abeka textbook praises the early Church Fathers, their definition of doctrine, and their church councils, but after the Council of Nicaea in 325 CE, which defined the divinity of Christ, the church became pagan. Members were no longer true believers but were instead forcibly converted. Their rituals evolved from the "simple meeting of believers on the Lord's Day to hear Scriptures read" to become instead "sacrificial rites of body and blood offered by priests."[36] Or, as any good Protestant will understand, these examples reveal that the early Christians were Protestants until they became paganized Catholics.

Constantine's conversion in 312 CE at the Battle of the Milvian Bridge, followed by the Edict of Milan proclaiming equal rights for all citizens, was a noteworthy event. It led many to abandon Rome's " 'imaginary gods' who provided no meaning or purpose" and to "turn instead to Christianity's 'hope of salvation.' " Although Constantine's conversion allowed Christianity to flourish, it gave rise to an evil form of Christianity—that is to say, "Romanism" or Roman Catholicism or Christianity as tainted by paganism. Christianity became paganism when presbyters become *sacerdotes* or, in other words, when ministers became priests "who offer the Lord's body and blood as a sacrifice for the living and the dead." In articulating the theology of the Mass, the early Christians became pagans, and so they remain until the arrival of Luther, as these errors "grew and developed into the false teachings and practices of the medieval church."[37] These curricula describe the organization of the early church in Calvinist terms with pastors and presbyters so that, with its institutional structure, the Roman Catholic Church immediately revealed that it was no longer Christian.

While persecuting Christians was Satan's work, the end to those persecutions under Constantine presents a quandary for these thoroughly Protestant histories. The church Constantine sanctioned cannot be considered legitimate. The adoption of Christianity by the Roman Empire as an official religion led to the "worldliness of many Christians, the adoption of pagan ideas and religious hierarchy"—the end of true Christianity. Constantine's support allowed the introduction of paganism into Christianity. As the church divided into Eastern Orthodox and Roman Catholic, both were tainted by pagan practices. In the West, the church incorporated practices of ancient Rome and the Germanic tribes, while Greek and Oriental ideas strongly influenced the Eastern Church. Whether Eastern or Western, for these curricula, Christianity became pagan.

These Christian curricula spend surprisingly little time on the early Christians: They are victims of persecution rather than models of Christian life. Early Christians were committed to poor relief and social justice and thus do not epitomize the contemporary prosperity gospel. More importantly, these histories assert, there were essentially no Christians from the time of Constantine to Luther. Although the earliest Christians had a mission to proselytize, conditions would not again be propitious until the missionary efforts of nineteenth-century Protestants. Pointing to Protestant proselytizing signals that Christianity did not flourish after its earliest years and that Roman Catholic missionary efforts were illegitimate. Just as the persecution of the early Christians reflects Satan's combat with God, so too the "seeds of error" this battle planted subsequently bore fruit as the Roman Catholic Church. Events inexplicable in a "God-centered" history these textbooks ascribe to Satan, a powerful historical actor and the ultimate explanation for evil in the world. Satan is so powerful that their account sometimes seems Manichean—a dualist religious view of the battle between the equally strong forces of good and evil.

The collapse of the Western Roman Empire and the rise of Byzantium and Islam document the role of evil. Such developments demonstrate Christ's revelation that the world is like a field of wheat in which weeds are sown; the Byzantine Empire and Islam are insidious examples of weeds sown among Christians. Although "God is at work in the earth growing the kingdom of his Son," as the BJU textbook notes, "He also raises up rival civilizations." While some ancient Asian civilizations are exotic enough to be interesting, Islam is a heretical threat to be defeated. Mohammed was inspired by Satan, and God allowed the creation of the Muslim and Byzantine Empires to test Christians' faith.[38] According to the Abeka textbook, Islam poses a dire threat: "The Koran corrupted Judaism and distorted Christianity."[39] Mohammed claimed to worship the same God as the Christians: "But the god of the Koran is not the God of the Bible, for Mohammed rejected the doctrine of the Trinity and denied that Christ is the Son of God." Islam encouraged believers to practice a fanatical religion. It misled them into believing that they could attain salvation through their works even though "such external practices do nothing to relieve the guilt of a conscience smitten with sin." In other words, Muslims contest the fundamental Protestant tenet of justification by faith alone. Islam warrants harsh repudiation because Muslims rejected Jesus as the son of God even though the New Testament was available when Mohammed promulgated his errors. Muslims claimed Allah is just and forgiving, but Allah cannot be forgiving "if Jesus never died to pay the penalty of sin."[40]

These Christian textbooks are unable to consider other religions and the cultures that practice them as anything but aberrant and abhorrent. Willfully ignorant, Muslims delude their fellow believers with a false gospel: "while Muhammad [the BJU spelling] used many biblical terms in his teaching, he distorted biblical truth." Satan often uses this tactic to deceive people— he "dresses error in the clothes of truth."[41] Such claims resonate powerfully among some contemporary American evangelicals, particularly in the aftermath of 9/11, when Islamic terrorists could be condemned as tools Satan sent to wage war on Christian America.[42] Similarly, the "birther" lie signaled that President Obama was a secret Muslim born in Kenya, undermining both Christianity and white national identity.[43]

As the BJU textbook points out, Islam spread fast and widely because of (1) the need of people for land, (2) the weakness of the Byzantine Empire, and (3) its mission of jihad, or "holy war." Jihad generated fanatical zeal because Muslims who died in battle were assured paradise.[44] While Christianity spread because it was true and through peace, Islam advanced only for economic and political reasons and through violence. The Abeka history warns that the Middle East has posed challenges for missionaries and will remain the "center of international conflict as the world nears history's last great battle, the battle of Armageddon."[45]

Why should these textbooks' histories of ancient civilizations matter to us? They are not simply inadequate as histories but also treat those civilizations negatively because they are not Christian. Acknowledgment of their contributions to the West is muted. Their civilizations are distorted to advance the social and political views previously discussed. As negative models, these civilizations are explicitly denied an influence on the American founding. Although it has long been conventional to see in the American Constitution the influence of the Roman Republic, mediated by both the civic humanists of the Renaissance and political thinkers of the Enlightenment, that influence must be tempered because the ancients were not Christians. Eighteenth-century thinkers, worried about how a government might avoid corruption or the concentration of power in the hands of an individual or branch of government, looked to Rome. For these curricula, such concerns are negligible compared to the founders' purportedly deep, biblical (essentially Calvinist) understanding of sin.

Historians credit the Greeks and Romans with the invention of citizenship and notions of representative government. They recognize the Roman Republic as a government of citizens governed by law with limits on political authority. In contrast, these curricula slight the social and political innovations of the Greeks and the Romans; they emphasize failings rather than their accomplishments in developing government, cities, trade, the arts, and literature. The Abeka textbook describes democracy as "rule by the many or the common people," but contends that in fact this means "ruling by the poor," which "did not mean *rule* at all."[46] In contrast, the BJU textbook recognizes Greek democracy as "a remarkable achievement for this period in history."[47]

These textbooks do not acknowledge the adaptability of either the Greeks or the Romans to other cultures as positive. They do not mention Homer's aristocratic code of behavior or the Greek notion of *aretê*, extolling manliness and courage, because Christianity is the only possible foundation for ethics or morality. The Roman philosophy Stoicism might seem an appealing morality, but, since it is not Christian, it cannot be good or moral. As the BJU textbook concludes, "Moral behavior without love for God is not true morality."[48] These curricula do not recognize as positives Roman multiculturalism, their globalism, or their ecumenical incorporation of the religious beliefs of conquered peoples. None of these are commendable values for these textbooks, even though the Romans fostered the subsequent promulgation of Christianity. That good outcome occurred because God used the Romans.

These textbooks are unsparingly critical of Greek philosophy. Although it introduced an entirely new way of thinking, it was misguided. When the earliest Greek philosophers asked questions about the world, they gave naturalistic answers: Xenophanes suggested that men posited that gods resembled them, as, of course, the Greek gods did. The famous historian Thucydides explained history in terms of human nature and chance, with no place for the supernatural. Rational skepticism was an important feature of Hippocrates's medicine. The Greeks inaugurated innovative ways of thinking that defined philosophy and science in the Western world for centuries, but these curricula do not appreciate them.

These educational materials thus largely reject the long historical tradition that has recognized the genius of the Greeks and the Romans. Each age has selected what was useful to it from these civilizations. The various forms politics took in the classical age have been cited ever since, even though not in the same way. For example, until the nineteenth century, the Spartans, with their effective military and political organization, were more often praised than the Athenians with their contentious and untidy democracy.[49] The clergymen who preached in the English colonies were educated at Oxford and Cambridge, where the curriculum was steeped both in Reformation theology and the Greco-Roman classics; they considered these educational traditions complementary and valuable as models of the virtuous life.[50] The classic texts of ancient Greece and Rome were central to education in the early American Republic and much appreciated for providing inspiring models of governance and personal and political morality. Members of the founding generation frequently acknowledged their influence in forming the character and political ethos of the new nation. John Witherspoon claimed that the study of the classics made men fit for public service. For James Madison, the classics were crucial in inculcating fear of monarchs and demagogues.

Classical texts inspired the new nation's political oratory. Those who wanted to praise founders compared them to classical figures. Washington's contemporaries proclaimed him as a new Cincinnatus, the Roman model of civic virtue. During the American Revolution, the Roman historian Tacitus offered an inspiring model of political opposition. As Carl Richard notes in his study of the influence of the classical tradition on the Founding Fathers, "the classics taught a love of liberty, an understanding of human motivation, an appreciation for the written and spoken word." Roman Stoicism shaped "the theory of natural law on which they based the bill of rights." It is hard to overemphasize the classical influence on the founders, on "their theories of government form, social responsibility, human nature, and virtue."[51]

The curricula examined here revert instead to a long tradition of American anti-intellectualism to which disparagement of the classics has been integral. This tradition mistrusted education and saw the classics as fostering elitism. Rejecting the intellectual accomplishments of these ancient civilizations fits evangelical anti-intellectualism, pervasive ever since the First Great Awakening's repudiation of the elitism of New England Congregationalists in the 1740s. Itinerant preachers adopted populist language and introduced anti-intellectualism into this new strain of Protestantism; it rejected knowledge that conflicted with the Bible. As Frances FitzGerald notes, some early Baptists even called learning one of the "frivolities of the unsaved."[52] Some nineteenth-century Southerners feared education's potential to challenge the slave-owning status quo, although others could look to the slave-owning ancients as models of appropriate social hierarchy.

Religious fundamentalism, Susan Jacoby argues, remains the most pronounced strain of anti-intellectualism in the United States.[53] Fundamentalism has been deeply skeptical or even fearful of learning not controlled by the church. Religiously grounded anti-intellectualism undergirds these twenty-first-century textbooks as well. They praise only those ideas and cultural developments they can correlate to the pursuit of biblical truth and repudiate any they see as a threat to ideas they hold. In these respects, they share the more general desire to curtail education deemed untrustworthy and to cement ties between the dominant church (invariably Protestant) and local values. Such concerns have kept public education firmly under local control and still fuel attacks on national educational standards. A well-rooted anti-intellectual conviction that learning is antithetical to traditional values and religion often reverberates in the halls of state legislatures as they debate educational issues.

These curricula lay out important premises that shape their narrative of later history: (1) historical events reveal God's plan; (2) the earliest Christians were "true" Christians, as distinct from Roman Catholics; (3) only Christianity is a basis for morality; (4) Satan is a historical actor who allowed the persecution of early Christians and the flourishing of Islam. These textbooks are especially intolerant and inaccurate on Islam; they condemn rather than inform. They categorically denounce ancient civilizations for failing to accept genuine Christianity. If the earliest civilizations should have accepted monotheism, after the coming of Jesus Christ, they should have become Christian. In treating classical Western civilizations, these curricula begin to articulate the stronger claim that all human actions must be grounded in religion and that all education, be it historical, scientific, or literary, should be religious and reinforce biblical Christianity. As such, the pagan world of the Greeks and the Romans is of scant interest. Particularly disturbing for citizens of modern Western democracies are these curricula's unwillingness to appreciate the engaged citizens of Athens and the Roman Republic.

6

Medieval Darkness, a Dim Renaissance

If these curricula are to be believed, between the Old Testament and the Reformation lies a deplorable hiatus when Christianity was perverted into Catholicism—the Middle Ages. The BJU history insists that "unlike the early Christians, Europeans conceived of the church solely as an outward, visible institution." They did not experience a genuine conversion of spirit. The textbook further insists that "the true universal church and the Roman Catholic Church are not synonymous." The Abeka account is even more stringently critical of medieval Catholicism: it does not capitalize the word "church" and refuses to call the church "catholic." Medieval Catholicism is not "Christian." Roman Catholics are "Romanists" practicing "Romanism."[1] (Luther used the term "Romanist" to challenge the Catholic Church's claims to be universal.)[2] For these curricula, the Middle Ages offers a sobering saga of the errors of a heretical sect.

The ideas and practices of medieval Catholicism contrast with "true" Christianity, the unacknowledged pastiche of Protestant theological tenets and social and political concerns these curricula present. When they identify central heretical beliefs of medieval Catholicism, they single out errors Protestant reformers condemned during the sixteenth-century Reformation. The history of early Christianity is a series of misbegotten decisions, which led the church away from "true" Christianity. But the textbooks never mention the Reformation context or theological sources of their "truths." Instead, as the Abeka account asserts, Scripture conforms to the central theological beliefs of the Protestant Reformation. The BJU history first claims that the theology of the Mass distorted Christianity and then criticizes the penitential system of the Catholic Church just as Luther did. It dismisses the sacraments of the Catholic Church as rooted in error.[3] While these claims were central Protestant criticisms of Catholicism during the Reformation, presenting them as unchanging and uncontested Christian truths is not only historically inaccurate, but it also reads the Reformation backward in time. The Middle Ages tells the story of how the church rejected Lutheran theological tenets centuries before him or how proto-Protestants adopted them before his time.

Hijacking History. Kathleen Wellman, Oxford University Press. © Oxford University Press 2021.
DOI: 10.1093/oso/9780197579237.003.0007

The Middle Ages also tells a tale of admirable Anglo-Saxons. Their praise-worthy qualities of military valor differentiate them from the deplorable and heretical French. More importantly, these examples also suggest the Anglo-Saxons as fitting antecedents of the American Christian warrior, an ideal espoused by evangelicals in the Cold War period and promoted to this day, particularly in the American Air Force.[4] The Magna Carta signals Anglo-Saxons' regard for liberty and their affinity with the founding of America.

This treatment of the Middle Ages has immediate topical resonance. Appreciation of the Anglo-Saxons reverts to several white-racist tropes, used widely since the nineteenth century. The identification of Catholics as "other" has a long and disturbing history in the United States. More consequentially, identifying Catholics as heretics, privileging Protestant Christians at the expense of others on the basis of religion, and going to far as to see Islam as the work of Satan undermine religious and cultural pluralism and promote intolerance.

According to these curricula, the Roman Catholic Church from Constantine to the sixteenth-century Protestant Reformation deliberately promulgated errors. Only the very earliest Christians had the "truth," the correct understanding of Scripture. The malign efforts of the institutional church produced a nearly 1500-year gap between the teachings of Christ and the Reformation restoration of Christianity. Christianity's plunge into the errors of the "Romanists" allows the Abeka textbook to identify Satan as a prime agent in the post-Constantine world.[5] This textbook sees Satan as key to the history of the Catholic Church, with some help from bad popes and bad kings.

When these textbooks look at the institutional church, they see a structure explicitly intended to cultivate its wealth and power and to mislead the people. The Abeka history dismisses as nonsense the scriptural source the Catholic Church has traditionally cited as the basis for its foundation and for Peter's status as the bishop of Rome and founder of the papacy: "Thou art Peter and upon this rock, I will build my church" (Matthew 16:18). It asserts instead that the statement meant that Christ was the rock of ages that the church was built upon. This textbook also uses Luther's terms to denounce the early church's establishment of the papacy, clerical hierarchy, and Petrine succession.[6]

The BJU history concurs that the history of the medieval church demonstrates the accretion of error and concentration of papal power. As a result, people lived in "spiritual ignorance and darkness." It uses quotation marks to discredit Catholic claims, for example, "saint" and "conversion." Indeed, it cites the church's creation of saints as one of the greatest errors, promulgated to mislead the people. Furthermore, all church reform efforts were misguided; Catholic reformers "failed to see that genuine reform is possible only when hearts have been regenerated."[7]

The contest between kings and popes over the issue of lay investiture (the question of who should appoint the holders of church offices) indicts the Catholic Church as corrupt, according to these curricula. Most histories would challenge this one-sided description of the late medieval battle between church and state, noting instead that strong monarchs attempted to diminish the power of the church and strong popes contested them. Ironically, the papacy's claims to invest officeholders is now cited, rather improbably, in current legal cases to endorse the intervention of religion into modern American law.[8]

These curricula see those who pursued the monastic life as seriously misled by the Catholic Church. The BJU history contends that monastic life misdirected people from their true mission of evangelization, and monasteries simply fostered their own wealth. Christ, the Abeka account insists, never intended monasteries to exist, invoking implicitly Luther's priesthood of all believers and his attack on monasteries. At the apogee of church hierarchy was the papacy, which these curricula condemn for its dedication to the accretion of wealth. "The people wanted eternal life, so they did whatever the church leaders told them. They confessed their sins to priests . . . and filled the church treasury with gold." Catholic practices during the Middle Ages were the superstitions of the credulous, including veneration of the Virgin Mary and relics, which the BJU textbook describes as good-luck charms.[9] To preserve its power, the medieval church kept the people ignorant of the fact that salvation was a free gift; it failed to inform the people of this fundamental tenet of Lutheran theology.

Although these curricula condemn greed as the moral failing of the Catholic Church, their subsequent discussion of the acquisition of wealth is inconsistent. They condemn the pursuit of wealth before the Reformation as directing human beings away from God. After the Reformation, however, wealth becomes a sign of God's favor, as financial success rewards virtuous industry.

The true heroes of the Middle Ages in these accounts were the church's critics, especially those it condemned as heretics. Before the Reformation, the light of the gospel shone only through men such as Peter Waldo, John

Wycliffe, and John Hus. These histories praise Waldo's courage in claiming Scripture as the sole authority. They assign to Wycliffe fundamental Protestant positions. He denied confession and transubstantiation, began to translate the Bible into English, and espoused predestination.[10] He saw the Bible as the only authority and knew "that salvation is through simple trust in Jesus Christ and not through works of any kind." Hus was excommunicated for criticizing the sale of indulgences, another crucial foreshadowing of Luther. When Hus appealed to the Council of Constance, he was arrested and then executed even though he had been granted safe conduct. "This betrayal," ACE charges, "was entirely within the rules of the Roman Catholic Church. To deceive and betray accused heretics was considered to be a meritorious act."[11] Despite their commitment to the biblical truth, neither Wycliffe nor Hus had a major impact, because, the BJU history remarks, "in the providence of God, the time was not yet ripe."[12]

The political and social arguments of these proto-Protestant heroes are not discussed, even though they were central to them and crucial in attracting their followers. Wycliffe not only challenged the authority of the pope and some Roman Catholic tenets, but he also criticized the church's wealth and favored seizure of its property. His attack on wealth went further: only the good were entitled to property, including that of the immoral. This argument threatened the social hierarchy of England as well as the Catholic Church. When Wycliffe's followers, the Lollards, seized church property, Lollardy became not simply a heresy but also a capital offense. Hus's followers used his ideas to advocate a social utopia under a military leader.

One might imagine that these textbooks would appreciate the crusades of the Middle Ages for their role in spreading Christianity; instead, they use the crusades to compare heretical Catholicism to heretical Islam. The Abeka textbook presents a derogatory account: Urban II motivated crusaders with tales of gory atrocities; "Disciplined Turks" defeated "unruly mobs of Europeans"; the capture of Jerusalem yielded little territory and only temporarily; over time, "crusades became more and more ridiculous."[13] Ultimately, the crusades were a battle between two heresies in which a destructive stalemate was a good outcome: neither heresy prevailed. Crusaders traveled to the Holy Land in the mistaken belief that this was what God wanted, but the Catholic Church deliberately deceived them, assuring crusaders "that anyone who died while on Crusade would be granted eternal life . . . a false assurance, given by church leaders who manipulated the credulous people."[14]

These curricula see the Middle Ages as dominated by the church until secular states with strong kings challenged papal power. Strong monarchies would enable the subsequent acceptance of the Reformation. The Holy Roman Empire was therefore problematic; its decentralized states prevented the Reformation from taking root in that "unnatural union of Germany and Italy and of the emperor and pope" as firmly as it might have in a more centralized state.[15] Blame for the inability of the Reformation to thrive in the Holy Roman Empire rests squarely on medieval popes whose political interests thwarted centralization.

This remark is the first indication of these textbooks' overt hostility toward Germany. That hostility sharpens in treating later periods, largely because they associate Germany chiefly with nineteenth-century theological modernism. Nonetheless, given their consistent attacks on central government, it is surprising that these curricula see centralized government as a necessary precondition for the Reformation's success. However, that appreciation underscores the state's legitimate role in furthering true religion.

Discussing the Middle Ages provides an opportunity for these histories to advance other arguments that shape their subsequent narrative. England and the English point the way to the Reformation, and the English Reformation prepares the way for the chosen people of America.[16] For these textbooks, the Anglo-Saxons were remarkable, even though their association with the American founding seems to belong to the realm of wishful thinking or even racist imaginings. The Abeka history claims that, although the Anglo-Saxons "worshipped many gods, they had a deep love of freedom and independence and a firm sense of Justice." In other words, they warrant less criticism than other pagans. So too, although England accepted "Romanism" in 664, their appreciation of "true" Christianity was somehow better; they had more of the Bible and were more influenced by Scripture than other medieval peoples—claims for which there is no evidence. The Abeka history cites Patrick, an early Christian convert in Ireland and later as a missionary to its pagan population, but insists, "Patrick had no connection with the Roman church or pope."[17] This is a peculiar claim, given fifth-century accounts of his ordination as bishop and his time in the monastery at Auxerre. But, for these curricula, the English were quasi-Protestants before the fact or, at the very least, predisposed to assume the admirable traits later attributed to both Protestants and Americans.

Alfred the Great demonstrated this affinity between medieval England and the future United States in Anglo-Saxon military power when he laid the foundation for the army and the navy. In the BJU textbook, Alfred's character also contrasts sharply with that of William the Conqueror. The positive trajectory of English history was derailed by the Norman Conquest, which brought "French" feudalism to England. Nonetheless, Henry II later restored the heroic stature of English kings when he challenged the pope and established common law.[18] To note that traveling circuit judges, inaugurated by the Norman William, regularized legal procedures in what we now call common law would mar this heroic English story.[19] Instead, these textbooks emphasize that, when the English barons challenged King John, the Magna Carta established the principle of limited government.[20]

Although the Magna Carta has attained a mythic status as a foundation for crucial features of modern democracy, including constitutional government and individual rights, it was intended to limit the king's power over his barons, especially his ability to coerce money from them, and did not refer to the people. Only much later, as the king's advisors evolved into a quasi-permanent group called Parliament, did they claim the right to approve the king's decrees and taxes. Nonetheless, the mythical status of the Magna Carta reinforces the English link to American exceptionalism.

In treating the virtuous English, these narratives develop an argument about the nature of government. Government, beyond local government, exists to provide justice and defense. A strong military, at least as developed by the Anglo-Saxons, is a sign of incipient Protestant virtue. England thus had distinctive praiseworthy qualities—freedom, justice, and a military culture. Admittedly Romanist, England was nonetheless more skeptical about Romanism, more tied to the Bible, and more rooted in military valor than other countries during the Middle Ages. A proto-Protestant England paves the way to the Reformation and is thus a fitting progenitor of the United States.

This narrative advances a historical association, demonstrated by the direct lineage drawn from medieval England to the United State through staunch Protestantism. Nonetheless, English virtue is so pronounced that students taught with these materials can scarcely be aware that England was a monarchy or that its later history documents contested succession crises and the civil wars they produced.

ACE is somewhat less committed to English exceptionalism, although it points to England as "the first example of a nation-state rising." It recognizes that the Magna Carta was the result of a baronial tax revolt, which limited the king's power and gave rights only to certain groups—nobles, churchmen, and townspeople—and was thus much more limited in intent and impact than the US Constitution.[21] ACE also acknowledges the War of the Roses: in other words, England's political history was not entirely strifeless.

Maintaining its teleological thrust, the Abeka textbook heralds England's defeat in the Hundred Years War as allowing it to focus on its own development rather than on pursuit of French territory and cites the denouement of the War of the Roses as producing the strong king Henry Tudor. It concludes, "Englishmen could look with pride not only upon their independent, powerful nation state but also upon their individual rights and liberties."[22]

Anglo-Saxon England is now frequently cited in a direct line of descent to American political virtue despite the dubious historical credibility of this connection. ACE claims that Virginia's "Great Charter" of 1619 laid the "foundations of political liberty" and originated in ideas "deeply seated in the evolving traditions of the Anglo-Saxon peoples of England."[23] English virtues become the virtues of the American founding. Both documents, the Magna Carta and the US Constitution, place everyone under God and were based, so the argument goes, on a staunch commitment to biblical moral absolutes. This connection is unequivocal in the Abeka history: "The basis for constitutional government in a civil society is the existence of a higher law—a body of principles created by God."[24] These two documents have joined the Ten Commandments as America's founding trinity, a claim central to both these Christian curricula and many on the political right.

When these curricula invoke America's Anglo-Saxon roots, they foster the explicitly racist usage found in extreme-right circles today, even though they discuss them in the context of the Middle Ages.[25] Appreciation of the Anglo-Saxons has long resonated in disturbing ways in both England and the United States, particularly when preceded by the adjective "pure," which none of these textbooks, to their credit, use. During the nineteenth century, the Victorians invoked "pure Anglo-Saxon" to justify their colonial mission. That term, a commonplace in the South after the Civil War, asserted the white, Anglo-Saxon foundation of the United States and is frequently found in Neo-Confederate texts after the Civil War. A pamphlet circulated by the Sons of Confederate Veterans not only called for the preservation of Anglo-Saxon culture and the deportation of African Americans, but also begged with its title, "Give us back the Constitution of our Fathers."[26] "Give us back our Constitution" retains currency as a conservative rallying cry.[27] In nineteenth-century America, antipathy to Catholic immigrants meant that they were considered neither white nor Christian, and the Irish were sharply differentiated from Anglo-Saxons as uncivilized "Celts."[28]

Such hypothesized racial distinctions were exploited in even more disturbing ways on the eve of World War II, when some archeologists deduced the earliest antecedents of known ethnic groups from their discoveries. The German archeologist Gustaf Kossinna (1858–1931) argued that Germans were the founders of Indo-European civilization. His assertion fostered Nazi claims of antiquity and racial purity of the German people.[29] Other contemporary archeologists contested these conclusions, but the term "Anglo-Saxon" remained politically salient. In the 1940s and 1950s, the term was used to support blatant antisemitism, particularly in Southern California. "British Israelism," a philosophy of Anglo-Saxon superiority derived from a claim that the English were the heirs of the Lost Ten Tribes of Israel, featured in sermons of the day.[30] When this completely unsubstantiated belief took hold, it became a crucial component of the Christian identity argument that Jews cannot be saved.

In the postwar period, when evangelicals moved to California from the South, they frequently objected to restrictions on redlining as attacks on "pure Anglo-Saxons." The term was also used in the South to object to desegregation as elected officials reacted with horror to the prospect of the "mongrelization" of the Anglo-Saxon race.[31] In current parlance, the term Anglo-Saxon functions as a convenient way to make white, racist rhetoric seem historically grounded.

The appreciation of a direct filiation between medieval England and America relies in part on a Calvinist notion of a covenant that implicitly undergirds these curricula.[32] Eventually, God will move from favoring England to its heir, the United States. The Anglo-Saxon legacy, the Magna Carta, and the proto-Protestant virtues of medieval England all foretell the distinctive, fundamental link these curricula assert between England and the United States: "God alone is above the law; in British and American government, therefore, all earthly rulers and subjects are under the law. A constitution places the government and the people under this higher law."[33]

To better signal England's extraordinary role, these textbooks disparage France as its antithesis. France had no rudimentary sense of freedom or justice and no intimation of limited government, and it remained mired in religious error. The motives of France's leaders who first adopted Christianity were reprehensible. Clovis converted to Christianity as a canny political move; his was not a spiritual conversion but rather a mere "outward

conversion for his followers." Subsequently, the rulers of France did not behave as Christians. Clovis united the Franks, "not hesitating to double-cross,
trick, or murder." The kings of the Merovingian dynasty "committed many
savage and violent crimes" and were undone by "drunkenness, immorality,
and family strife."[34] The French benefited when the Carolingian king Charles
Martel took over from the "do-nothing" Merovingians. Martel's victory over
the Arabs and Berbers at the Battle of Tours saved the Christian West from
conquest by a Muslim empire. (Indeed, anti-Muslim websites currently identify Martel as their hero.[35]) But the Carolingian kings immediately forfeit ap-
probation when Martel's son Pepin, whom the pope endorsed, bestowed the
Papal States upon the Catholic Church. That document, formerly believed to
date from Constantine's time and thus called "The Donation of Constantine,"
was, after carbon dating, renamed the "Donation of Pepin." Ironically,
these histories dismiss such dating of the fossil record but accept its evidence to discredit a prior claim of the Catholic Church. The Abeka textbook
cites the Donation to indict a diabolical alliance of France and the papacy.
Charlemagne, like his French predecessors, endorsed this alliance and recognized the political expediency of religion, which defined the corrupt relationship between the French and the Romanists.[36]

Although conceding that Charlemagne had some accomplishments—
notably, his interest in educational reform, which led to a greater appreciation
of the Bible—the BJU textbook condemns his personal life as sinful. "He had
little regard for the sanctity of marriage; he married, divorced, and remarried
many times."[37] Such charges could be applied as well to many early medieval
kings whose notion of marriage was not necessarily monogamous, but moral
opprobrium applies distinctly to the French. When these curricula make in-
vidious comparisons between the un-Christian, immoral French and the virtuous, proto-Protestant English, they are further developing their argument
that good government and the good order of society depend on a Protestant
moral code, which will be actualized in post-Reformation England and more
fully realized in the United States.

These textbooks also use the Middle Ages to initiate economic arguments
that run through them. The Abeka history heralds the emergence of entrepreneurial spirit from the ashes of the failed crusade of 1290, leading directly
to the economic successes of the Reformation. The BJU textbook asserts that
the rise of the middle class occurred in the year 1000, even though such an
early dating is ahistorical. The Abeka history cites the development of towns
during the High Middle Ages as a challenge to the church's power, although

they undermined feudal hierarchy more directly. Market development was generally impeded by the church's prohibition of business practices such as usury, but eventually "social business practices" prevailed, the BJU history asserts. This curriculum connects the serf's lack of freedom to his lack of access to the Bible, pointing toward Luther's religious but apolitical notion of "the freedom of a Christian." With the advent of the middle class, commerce developed with an inevitable association between freedom and Protestantism—even though the relationship could only be presaged in the Middle Ages.[38] From this point on, commercial developments universally signify the rise of Protestant Christianity.

The Abeka history sees the economy of the Middle Ages as inaugurating a free-market era before government regulations hampered entrepreneurial spirit—an egregious misunderstanding of the guild system. While this textbook sees guilds as analogous to trade unions, it hastens to add that their association was completely voluntary. Presumably, medieval guildsmen operated within a "right to work" environment.[39]

When these curricula consider the secular culture of the Middle Ages, they appreciate chivalry for its honor code and for putting women on a pedestal. None of these textbooks take cognizance of recent scholarship on medieval social history, particularly on women's roles and agency. ACE warrants special criticism for frequently praising gender inequality in the past; it approves of the historical restriction of women to the domestic sphere to reinforce it in the present. During the Middle Ages, ACE claims, a wife was "cooking and making clothing," while her husband worked in the field.[40] In fact, both men and women worked in the fields; rural labor was much less gendered than this curriculum suggests.

These textbooks are highly suspicious of scholasticism, the philosophical tradition of the Middle Ages, largely because of its appreciation of reason and ancient philosophy. The Abeka history derides it as a form of "humanism" and as the product of the "Roman church."[41] The church found it "useful for making distorted Christianity seem reasonable."[42] Reason can, nonetheless, be well deployed to undermine Catholicism. Both Roger Bacon and William of Ockham win praise for challenging scholasticism, even though historians recognize that Ockham worked firmly within the scholastic tradition.[43] Ockham becomes a proto-Protestant who "used scriptural logic to argue that man is totally depraved and in absolute need of divine revelation and saving grace." He, like all such heroes, refuted Catholic theological authority and saw that "the Holy Scriptures were the only true authority."[44]

A more conventional account of the Middle Ages would recognize it as a period of great social, political, and cultural innovation. Historians place the accretion of the central power of the papacy in its late medieval context rather than treat it as an evil of "Romanism." They do not condemn every action of the Catholic Church, praise every anti-papal position, or dismiss reform movements. They recognize that church and state were in a complex relationship of negotiation and conflict as each made claims to political and moral authority. They do not place free-market capitalism in the Middle Ages or dismiss human endeavors as sinful humanism. They instead appreciate the Middle Ages on its own terms rather than as a prefiguration of the Reformation or capitalism.

The Renaissance, traditionally associated with the rebirth of the classics and tremendous cultural flourishing, poses an even greater quandary than the Middle Ages for these curricula: it extolled human achievement. The problem is particularly acute for the Abeka account. It dismisses Renaissance humanists as "hardly more than playful children imitating the past" who had "nothing much to say." It charges that the Renaissance "began to ignore God and exalt man instead," as Machiavelli did in *The Prince*. Nonetheless, it deems Machiavelli's work "the only book of lasting importance produced by the Italian Renaissance."[45] But, even though he recognized the "hypocrisy of the age," Machiavelli did not turn to God's word. Similarly, Abeka praises both Chaucer and Dante for recognizing "the religious hypocrisy of their age."[46] More generally, the Renaissance is both Italian and Catholic; neither can be appreciated—its philosophy is even called "humanism."

For ACE, the interest of the Renaissance in the classics brought to the fore "non-religious" writers, who "made man the center of all things." It dismisses Dante's *Inferno*: "Note: Purgatory is consistent with good Roman Catholic theology. . . . As we know, the Bible has nothing to say about Purgatory." It praises Lorenzo Valla's scholarship because it led to re-dating the Donation of Constantine to the eighth or ninth century and thus invalidated papal claims to supreme authority in the West. In this instance, humanist scholarship was used commendably to contest Roman Catholic authority.[47]

The BJU history presents a view of the Renaissance that is more nuanced and better informed by recent scholarship than the other two curricula. It distinguishes Renaissance humanism from secular humanism, a distinction rarely made by those who denounce humanism. Nonetheless, it immediately uses the prophet Isaiah's denunciation of the "proud and lofty" to castigate Renaissance humanism for putting man above God. When the textbook distinguishes Machiavelli's *Discourses* from the *Prince,* it condemns the latter but appreciates the former for its discussion of republics, likely because it influenced America's founders.[48] Nonetheless, the overriding message to students is to be wary of the Renaissance.

Renaissance arts elicit a mixed response. The BJU textbook values them, noting that some men wanted to honor the Lord. It praises artists' innovative techniques but denounces their emphasis on classical subjects. In the historical scorecard these curricula keep of those God brought low, Renaissance artists' efforts to advance their careers provide potent negative illustrations. Brunelleschi received the commission for the dome of the Duomo in Florence because of Ghiberti's pride, for example. The BJU history does not entirely condemn the Renaissance cultivation of the individual, because it also fostered individual responsibility. It also explicitly (and accurately) underscores the ways in which the Renaissance prepared the way for the Reformation, including that Renaissance inquiry extended to critiques of the church and that humanists studied Christian sources as well as classical ones. The Renaissance made education more widely available and saw the invention of movable type. Nonetheless, in this curriculum's view, the church was too corrupt to be reformed by humanist critiques and its secular culture loosened morals. Humanists sometimes supported the evils of the church or even succumbed to heathenism, meaning the influence of the classics.[49] ACE has an even harsher view of Renaissance Italy: "the cultural life was corrupt and immoral even though material and artistic progress was great."[50] Ultimately, this period sets the stage for the Reformation. Only then will a proper balance of the concerns of this life and the next be possible.[51]

The dissonance between the way these curricula see the Renaissance and the way it is usually discussed is striking. These textbooks cannot place this great spur to human progress in Italy: Catholic Italy is no part of their narrative of human progress. The ethical dimensions of Renaissance humanism, including its appeals to the common good and its emphasis on the family and the community as a focus for Christian virtue and moral suasion through rhetoric, cannot be recognized. The only morality is "biblical Christianity." The Middle Ages experienced a "distorted form of Christianity," and the Renaissance merely created beautiful art while promoting pagan philosophies. Only the Reformation would free Europe from Catholicism and revive biblical Christianity, "which had been suppressed though never destroyed by leaders of the Roman church through the Middle Ages."[52] By seeing the Middle Ages as a period mired in error, these educational materials essentially dismiss 1500 years of history as little more than a waiting period between the earliest Christianity and the coming Reformation.

Some topics these textbooks focus on have immediate contemporary relevance. Their negative depiction of France begins with the Middle Ages, but it is essential to the political and religious arguments they develop about subsequent historical periods. Denunciations of everything French even provided a point of reference for attacks on John Kerry's ability to speak French or the renaming of French fries as "Freedom Fries" when the French opted not to join "the coalition of the willing" in invading Iraq because they found the evidence for weapons of mass destruction unpersuasive. When President Trump repudiated the Paris Climate Accord, he invoked anti-French sentiment with a "Pittsburgh not Paris" rally but chose a bizarre place to do so— Lafayette Square, named, of course, for the famous marquis who fought the British in the American Revolution.[53] France remains an ideological enemy for some conservatives.

Since the US invasion of Iraq in 2003, the crusades too have a new currency in American political discussion. Both the Christian right and groups within the American military sometimes point to the recent wars in the Middle East as a new crusade.[54] This crusade, however, will be conducted by Christians, not Catholic heretics, and motivated by religious fervor to destroy Islam. If the medieval crusades produced a stalemate between two forces of evil, a new crusade could see the forces of God unseat those of Satan.

Ostensibly focused on the Middle Ages, these curricula draw on a tradition of singling out Catholics as other. In condemning Roman Catholicism as a heresy, they revisit the history of anti-Catholicism in the United States. The Abeka curriculum is most committed to this negative view of Catholicism, but Bob Jones University has a long history of denouncing Roman Catholicism as unchristian or even as the work of the devil. Despite the contemporary political alliance between conservative Catholics and evangelicals, particularly over abortion, some evangelicals do not recognize Catholics as Christians. Remnants of anti-Catholicism persist.

Anti-Catholicism arrived in North America with the Puritans who had fled to the colonies during the English Civil War, a time when England itself was vehemently anti-Catholic. Those settlers brought to the colonies, most notably Massachusetts, deeply ingrained beliefs that Catholics were both politically and religiously corrupt. Their fellow Puritans, who remained in England, would subsequently contest any English king who evinced Catholic sympathies. On the eve of the American Revolution, views about Catholics

were conflicted: Sam Adams condemned both king and pope in his inflammatory petition, The Suffolk Resolves, written to object to British tolerance
of Catholics in its Quebec colony. But the French were also crucial allies in
the War for Independence.[55]

In the post-Revolutionary era, because of the influence of the
Enlightenment, Americans were presumed to be English, Protestant, and
enlightened. Unlike such Americans, Catholic immigrants subscribed to a
hierarchical church, accepted absolutist government, and were committed
to religious superstition. In the nineteenth century, Protestants mobilized
these arguments to identify Catholics as "other" with respect to fundamental
American commitments to democracy, science, reason, and the separation
of church and state. Their otherness became ever more apparent as waves of
immigrants arrived from Ireland, Germany, and Italy. Catholics then became
the targets of scurrilous literature and active discrimination. Lyman Beecher,
the well-known Presbyterian revivalist minister, saw Catholic schools as an
immigrant plot to convert Protestant schoolchildren. Mainline Protestants
embraced their obligation to assert an American ethos to contest the foreign influence of Catholics through institutions such as the Order of the
Star-Spangled Banner. Founded in 1849, this secret society opposed Catholic
immigration on nativist and racist grounds.[56] In the 1920s, Catholics were
targeted by the Ku Klux Klan as both unchristian and anti-American. From
the 1920s through the 1940s, Fort Worth Baptist minister J. Frank Norris was
a key figure in mobilizing Southern fundamentalists as anti-Catholic anti-
modernists.[57] As late as 1947, the fundamentalist Carl F. H. Henry worried
that Catholic dominion would wipe out fundamentalism.[58]

In treating medieval Catholicism, these curricula revive a sense of
Catholic otherness that seemed to dissipate in the 1950s when Catholics and
Jews joined the mainstream and shared with Protestants a belief in the value
of education, fair play, and equality.[59] As the Catholic sociologist Andrew
Greeley documented, Catholics were phenomenally successful in integrating
the professions in the postwar decades.[60] But the election of John F. Kennedy
brought anti-Catholicism, especially among evangelicals, into renewed
prominence. They feared that Kennedy would use public funds to support
religious schools—an irony, given that the religious right is now eager to
do so.[61]

These textbooks follow just one of two strains prominent in historical scholarship tying American Protestantism to national identity. One
strand contended that evangelical Protestantism defined a distinctive

American ethos. The more prominent interpretative strand saw that ethos as fused to the crucial influence of the Enlightenment in establishing American commitments to egalitarianism, rationalism, and anti-authoritarianism.[62] Catholicism was seen as antithetical to both elements of that fundamental fusion—Protestantism and Enlightenment.[63] Ironically, these textbooks repudiate the Enlightenment, as we will see, and criticize Catholicism, particularly scholasticism, as unacceptably committed to reason. For them, Protestantism is by definition anti-rationalist and neither egalitarian nor anti-authoritarian, as their treatments of later periods amply develop.

These world histories recast the anti-Catholic tradition in American history for the present moment. They place Catholics firmly in the category of un-American and unacceptable "other." Since these textbooks disparage any appreciation of the Enlightenment by their Protestant forebears, they cannot use Enlightenment values to differentiate Catholics from Protestant Americans. Instead, only their religious beliefs set Catholics apart from the "true" beliefs of Protestants—the touchstone of American identity. Indeed, a Pew poll taken in February 2017 reported that 32% of Americans but 57% of white evangelicals believe that it is "very important" to be a Christian to be a true American.[64] These curricula suggest that to be American is to be "Christian," but only in the Protestant sense they define. "Christian" becomes a narrower designation than one might imagine.

Some modern evangelicals, including Jerry Falwell and Jimmy Swaggart, emphasized, as these curricula do, that Catholicism, like Islam, is a heresy. Swaggart, whose telecast in the 1980s was regularly viewed by over 2.5 million viewers, cited the book of Revelation to exhort Catholics to separate from their heretical church.[65] Robert Jeffress of First Baptist Church in Dallas and a prominent religious advisor to Donald Trump proclaimed Catholicism a cult-like pagan religion and the work of Satan in 2010, a position he refuses to repudiate.[66] Even though the issues of abortion and gay marriage have made evangelicals and conservative Catholics political allies, evangelical college students are often still surprised to hear that Catholics are Christians. Despite the political expediency of that relatively recent alliance, these textbooks suggest that, for some evangelicals, Catholics remain unredeemable heretics and entirely "other." They are, in a fundamental sense, neither American nor Christian. If this exclusion applies to Catholics, how much more thoroughly must it apply to believers in other religious creeds, particularly Muslims?

White evangelicals often identify as "other" heretics and Muslims in particular but non-Christians and immigrants in general. These views are reflected in their loyalty to Donald Trump. They, more than any other group, adamantly favored construction of the border wall with Mexico. A Public Religion Research Institute poll of September 2018 documented that 67% of white evangelicals support it. They saw the wall as an important symbol of Christian culture under threat by immigrants who do not share white ethnicity or Protestant religion.[67] The film *The Trump Prophecy* (2018) presented Trump as a savior who would redress the fact that "America has become a nation without walls" and "restore the crumbling wall that separates us from cultural collapse."[68] Walls thus protect national sovereignty and Christian racial, religious, and cultural identity. These curricula use the Middle Ages to establish a historical foundation for that identity. They give students the means to identity the other, onto which they may well graft more extreme views.

In the Middle Ages, as these curricula present it, students find no colorful history filled with valiant knights, castles, formidable crusaders, or intriguing male and female rulers that they might expect from their previous acquaintance with the period in stories, video games, or popular television series, like *Game of Thrones*. Instead, the Middle Ages presents a grim account of error and evil, brightened only by foreshadowings of the Reformation in medieval England. These histories warn high school students not to be misled by heresies. They define negative attitudes students should adopt toward other cultures and religions. Most disturbingly and immediately relevant, these educational materials use their discussion of the Middle Ages to promote religious intolerance, and, admittedly quite subtly, they revert to the racist trope of an Anglo-Saxon America.

The last is especially disturbing, given the current polarization of political discussion and the emergence of the alt-right as a political force in contemporary America. These curricula revive ways the Middle Ages have previously been used to support white racism and fascism, particularly in idealizing the Anglo-Saxons.[69] In these textbooks, Anglo-Saxons are heroic crypto-Protestants, but they have also been used as code for white racism. The Middle Ages have frequently attracted conservatives, harkening back to a lost world tinged with cultural nostalgia. But looking back to the Anglo-Saxons more explicitly invokes a culture presumed to be white, tied to traditional values, and sustained by hierarchies both political and gendered.

The emphasis of the alt-right on the "whiteness" and supposed ethnic and cultural cohesion of the Middle Ages derives in large part from myths Victorians constructed first to justify colonialism and then to cope with the loss of the British Empire.[70] Medieval crusades have continuing but distinctive appeal as images of Western culture resisting an inferior, even diabolical culture of the East. After the Civil War, some Southerners proposed a second Anglo-Saxon secession. Right-wing dictators such as Francisco Franco and Adolf Hitler claimed the ethnic and cultural superiority of the white Middle Ages as a racist, nationalist narrative. Christian Identity, an extreme right-wing religious movement, claims that Anglo-Saxons are the true children of Israel, Blacks are "mud people," and Jews the "spawn of Satan."[71] In 2017 neo-Nazi demonstrators in Charlottesville, Virginia, used symbols and replicas of artifacts associated with the Middle Ages, including shields with Anglo-Saxon emblems and double axes, to identify with a white nation. (Ironically, some months later archeologists discovered that the first residents of the British Isles were blue-eyed but also very dark skinned.[72])

Historians of the Middle Ages have been quick to point out how inaccurate this nostalgic understanding is and, even more vehemently, how incongruous the appropriations of the Middle Ages are for white nationalist narratives. Historians document the racial, ethnic, and cultural diversity of the Middle Ages in blogs, bibliographies, and teaching guides.[73] Historical scholarship has vastly expanded our understanding of the Middle Ages, particularly its connections beyond continental Europe, beyond the emphasis of these curricula on an imagined England peopled by proto-Protestants and poised for greatness with New World exploration inspired by the coming Reformation.

7

The Triumph of Protestant Truth

Human history awaits the Protestant Reformation as the decisive watershed. It was the definitive beginning of "the Modern Age" when "Europe experienced a great spiritual reawakening," according to the Abeka history. Any discussion of the Protestant Reformation "would likely observe the Lord's propitious ordering of events on the eve of that century, making possible the success of that movement," as the BJU faculty wrote in *The Christian Teaching of History*. It would reveal God's "own purposes in destroying the European ecclesiastical monopoly of Rome, reasserting individual responsibility, and restoring individual liberty, both spiritual and political."[1] Indeed, these world histories more than thoroughly fulfill this agenda as they see the Reformation as the restoration of biblical truth and the establishment of a renewed covenant between God and man. The rejection of Catholicism enabled the proper relationship of human beings to God and society: only biblical truth allowed liberty.

These textbooks enshrine an explicitly English Protestant historiography, which saw the Reformation as liberating the Christian people from the tyranny of the Catholic Church. Catholicism had kept people in ignorance and servitude, while Protestantism allowed Englishmen the freedom they relished because of their ancient traditions. This historiography fails to recognize that many Englishmen, whether Protestant or Catholic, were committed to religious reform: only Protestant religious reforms are genuine; those of Catholics are disingenuous. It also relies on the erroneous claim that Englishmen readily adopted Protestantism.[2]

These textbooks distort even the Reformation (which they unequivocally endorse) to serve ideological purposes. Until now, their history has been a tale of past error and failure with glimmers of light cast only by those who, against the conventions of their time, prepared the way for the Reformation. History now becomes more edifying with the emergence of "biblical truth," even if some history of the Reformation period has to be altered or "scrubbed" to support this triumphalist narrative. These curricula's treatment of the

Hijacking History. Kathleen Wellman, Oxford University Press. © Oxford University Press 2021.
DOI: 10.1093/oso/9780197579237.003.0008

Reformation develops crucial features of the much later alliance of the political and religious right.

According to these textbooks, the momentous transformation wrought by the Reformation bore productive fruit in the sciences, arts, and politics. Protestants were rewarded for their adherence to "biblical Christianity" with, as the Abeka history proclaims, "tremendous progress, the fruit of freedom, in every field of human endeavor." Making the filiation unquestionable, it asserts, "the biblical truths set loose by the Protestant Reformation gave the Modern Age more potential for progress than any previous era."[3]

The Reformation began with Martin Luther in what is now Germany, because he "was willing to step out and stand alone for what is right against the Church of Rome." Luther rediscovered biblical truth, which had been subverted by heresy since the earliest Christian times. "The reformers reasserted biblical truth and the authority of the word of God," as the Abeka textbook puts it. "Luther said nothing new; he simply revealed that the walls the Roman church had erected between man and Christ were a distortion of the Word of God."[4] As Protestants worked to root out the errors that perverted Christianity, "God's initiative" began the Protestant Reformation as Luther "and other Protestant reformers exposed the false doctrines of Catholicism," including "the equal authority of tradition and Scripture, papal authority, and indulgences," according to the BJU history.[5] There is simply the "truth," and Protestants have it. They are the only Christians.

None of these curricula place Martin Luther in the context of outspoken criticism of the Catholic Church from within by Francis of Assisi, Catherine of Siena, and Desiderius Erasmus, among many others. They recognize only those persecuted by the Catholic Church whom they deem Protestants before the fact. They do, however, place Luther and his theological evolution in context. ACE notes that Martin Luther's father "was a miner who worked hard, saved his money, and had become wealthy." Luther's family thus epitomized the Protestant work ethic before the fact. These curricula note Luther's crisis of faith and its resolution in his reading of Paul's *Epistle to the Romans*. This reading inspired his central understanding of Scripture; he was saved "by faith in the finished work of Christ on the cross." Both the Abeka and BJU textbooks recount the evolution of Luther's theological views, his conflicts with the papacy, and his debates with Catholic theologians, in which Luther was "guided by the spirit of God." After his break with Rome, Luther dedicated himself to defining doctrinal positions, as in his *Augsburg Confession* of 1530. He emphasized education, particularly parents' role in educating their children, instituted new religious practices, and made music central to Protestant practice. His emphasis on music "caused the whole Western world to 'break forth into singing.'" Furthermore, "Luther renounced his monastic vows as unbiblical, married, and had a fine Christian family."[6]

Because Protestantism is true, the intra-Protestant disputes of the Reformation can scarcely be mentioned. The BJU curriculum acknowledges relatively slight disagreements among Protestants about how to interpret Scripture. Luther and Zwingli disagreed about the Lord's Supper—a distinction between consubstantiation and commemoration. ACE, which seems more aware that Protestant doctrines changed over time and that the Reformation occurred in different political and social contexts, recognizes that Luther and Zwingli "violently disagreed with each other on the meaning of the Lord's Supper." It notes that Anabaptists were persecuted by both Protestants and Catholics for their rejection of infant baptism and for their adherence to the separation of church and state. The BJU curriculum chides the Anabaptists for failing to understand that justification by faith alone inevitably leads to good works. In other words, it takes a Lutheran position on the relationship between works and faith without acknowledging it as such. That is to say, the Christian will be moved to perform good works but is not required to do them to win salvation. Despite these minor disagreements, the BJU textbook insists, Protestants were unanimous on the essentials of "Scripture alone, faith alone, grace alone."[7]

Because they present Protestantism as quite uniform, these textbooks blur the differences between Luther's and Calvin's theological positions or social and political views; they mention some but without discussing their implications. Even though the BJU history is Calvinist in theological orientation, it does not recognize Calvin's support for theocratic government. Instead, it asserts that Calvin agreed that church and state should be separate, but that the law should enforce a Christian life.[8] This position seems to describe a distinction without a difference, as the government of Calvin's Geneva essentially functioned as a theocracy, enforcing Calvin's harsh prescriptions. If these textbooks endorse a form of government, it might be what we might call a "theocratic republic." Government would enforce religious beliefs and compel citizens' moral behavior as in Calvin's Geneva. Thus church and state do not have to be one, if laws constrain all to live as Christians. The commitment of the state to Christian law allows these curricula to use American Puritans' Calvinism to later assert that the new nation was founded as just such a Christian republic.

Clearest in differentiating Protestant creeds, ACE notes that Calvin "laid heavy stress upon the sovereignty of God," by which he meant "God's control of everything in the universe." Nor does it flinch from Calvin's stringent view of predestination: "God predestined some to be saved and some to be lost." It asserts Calvin's conclusion that individuals could not change their eternal destiny: God had already chosen the saved and the damned; human merit played no role in determining either. ACE emphasizes that "the work of Christ on the cross was limited to those elected to salvation."[9] The notion of "work" invoked in this quotation is common to these textbooks. Christ is "working" for salvation on the cross; God continues to "work" to bring about His plan. Evangelization furthers God's work.

These curricula acknowledge Luther's and Calvin's roles in advancing what they deem the "true" understanding of the Bible, but they suggest that early Protestants simply uncovered the truth. While they consider Luther significant as the first to recover biblical truth, these histories rarely make human agency central to their narratives. (Protestant missionaries are the most significant exception.) This absence is especially striking when these histories treat this pivotal period; even during the Reformation, there are no heroic human beings, except Luther, who stood up to the Catholic Church.

These histories espouse Luther's repudiation of political resistance as the legitimate political position of the Christian. ACE notes that Luther was dedicated to "safeguarding the Reformation from going to extremes (such as Luther's opposition to the Peasant's [sic] Revolt in 1525)."[10] The Abeka history briefly mentions the Peasants' War but disassociates it from the Reformation by saying that peasants had revolted five times before the Reformation. It insists that religion does not justify political action, just as Luther made clear: "Christianity must not be thought of as a revolutionary political movement." Instead, these curricula counsel acceptance of the status quo: "Spiritual freedom does not always guarantee political or economic freedom." The BJU textbook claims that only Anabaptists resisted; they had "revolutionary ideas or advocated heresy." Nonetheless, only the "biblical truth" of the Reformation allows freedom. That claim is essential to their understanding of government. But what does it mean? It is likely, though not explicitly, informed by Luther's notion of Christian freedom as spiritual. Ultimately, these curricula insist that Protestantism does not entail political or social reform. Equally importantly, it prohibits resistance to a government.

None of these textbooks acknowledge political discord, often to the point of war, between Protestants who disagreed about theological tenets. Religious conflicts had significant political ramifications: Calvinism defined profoundly revolutionary political positions. Calvinist writers such as Philippe de Mornay used Calvin's theology to sanction political revolution, if carried out by duly constituted magistrates, and even recognized that God occasionally raised up an assassin to remove a ruler who countered His law.[11] None of these curricula acknowledge that Calvinism empowered and inspired many to overthrow their governments in the name of religion. Quite understandably, the crowned heads of Europe were discomfited by calls to revolt as well as by this overtly theocratic message. Every country in which Calvinism made inroads experienced civil war in the name of religion—England, Scotland, the Netherlands, France, among them. These textbooks do not acknowledge that politics played a role in the spread of the Reformation, even in England, Scandinavia, and the Holy Roman Empire, where rulers imposed new creeds.

When forced to recognize political developments, these curricula take inconsistent positions. The Abeka history blames the chaotic political uprisings in the German territories for the uneven success of Protestantism there but praises Dutch Protestantism as "encouraging thought and action, and causing the Dutch to rise up and continue their fight for independence."[12] The contradiction is obvious: Protestantism has no political implications; Christians have no right to revolt; yet Protestants win praise for revolting against Spanish Catholic rule in the Netherlands. It notes too that in Germany "government control of religion was necessary for law and order.[13]

If, as these curricula insist, great benefits accrue only with the Protestant Reformation, recognizing the religious wars unleashed in its aftermath from 1517 until 1648 becomes problematic. In the Holy Roman Empire, Lutheranism and its various offshoots led to political warfare for nearly forty years. Warfare ended only with the agreement that the ruler could impose his religious creed on his people. For those who refused to follow the ruler's confessional lead, their only recourse was relocation, a virtual impossibility for peasants whose economic well-being was tied to the land. For these Christian curricula, the political, social, and economic issues involved in the coming of the Reformation and its aftermath are largely irrelevant. Instances in which Protestants fought against or persecuted those of other Protestant creeds are largely overlooked.

Nor can Catholic reform efforts be recognized. These curricula see the Catholic Reformation, like previous Catholic reform movements, as disingenuous or even duplicitous attempts to redress external issues instead of "doctrinal errors." The Inquisition and Index were ineffective and misguided; the Jesuits ascribed their own faults to others; and the Catholic Reformation intended only to halt further Protestant inroads. At root, Catholic reformers failed to see biblical truth. When the Catholic Church convened the Council of Trent to restore unity to Christendom, the outcome was predetermined by the predominance of Italians. The council "rejected the doctrines of justification by faith alone and the sole authority of the Scripture," established adherence to its positions as binding, and made no doctrinal or moral changes (the latter a historically inaccurate claim).[14] These textbooks thus underscore that the Catholic Church did not accept biblical truth: it remained wedded to error.

These histories single out the English Reformation as *the* Reformation—the "best" or the "right" Reformation. It made the English "a people of the book and that book was the Bible," as the Abeka history puts it.[15] (In fact, *The Book of Common Prayer* unified English Protestants.) The impact of the Reformation was completely transformative: "Because of the Bible, a great moral change came over the people of England. Greediness was replaced by kindness; laziness by industry; ignorance by a great desire to learn to read." Not only were the English people fundamentally changed, but they also first enjoyed the social and political benefits of the Reformation. "The liberties of the English people, the prosperity of their businesses, the growth of education, and the justice that prevailed in the land were all the result of obedience to the Word of God."[16] Abeka argues emphatically that without biblical truth there can be no political freedom.[17] These benefits accrued to England as the direct result of the Protestant Reformation.

No other event in human history has proved as significant for these curricula, with the probable exception of the birth of Christ, even though it is treated less extensively and dramatically than the Reformation. Nonetheless, the specifics of the English Reformation prove something of a challenge. England had no central figure or theologian who brought the truth to light. The BJU history explains the absence of heroes by the fact that the English already had greater familiarity with the Bible.

Far from being a model of the easy acceptance of biblical truth these Christian world histories describe, the Reformation in England imposed Henry VIII's new model of religion on the English people. It entailed acceptance of a generally Catholic theology with the king rather than the pope as head of the church. This model satisfied neither Lutherans nor Calvinists. As a result, England experienced more dissent over religious issues than these textbooks acknowledge. But to discuss the diversity of English theological views would introduce unwanted complexity into this narrative of simple acceptance of biblical truth. Thus the conservative character of the English Reformation, which initially remained Catholic in theology and ritual, is scarcely noted, and the sharp divisions between Anglicans and Puritans remain unstated. Henry VIII had even declared Lutherans heretics. Nonetheless, for these textbooks, England remains an idealized model because of its eager adoption of "biblical truth," while France stubbornly persists in heresy.

The political rationale for the English Reformation, that is to say, Henry VIII's desire to divorce his wife Catherine of Aragon and marry Anne Boleyn, cannot be entirely overlooked. ACE admits that "in England, the Reformation was more closely tied to the monarchy and English nationalism." While it blames the pope who would not grant Henry's divorce, it concedes, "Henry was more Catholic in his opinions or more Protestant as his mood or political necessity changed. He really seems to have had no consistent principles." But eventually "political motives gave way to spiritual concerns."[18] When Henry's young son Edward VI succeeded him, the crucial tenets of Protestantism were confirmed in the *Book of Common Prayer* he promulgated. This account obscures more than a decade of religious division.

The death of Edward VI, after a six-year reign, brought Mary Tudor to the throne. She is the ideal Catholic villainess: "She had about three hundred [Protestants] killed and many others were forced to flee for their lives. . . . Her rampages against Protestants earned her the title of 'Bloody Mary.' She died from a tumor in 1558 amid great rejoicing by the persecuted Protestants." While Mary's death reveals God's favor for English Protestants, these textbooks point out only events that foster the Reformation: "in God's Providence, Mary died childless."[19] No curriculum suggests that the early death of the staunchly Protestant Edward VI, which brought the Catholic Mary Tudor to the throne, revealed God's intentions. Only events with negative ramifications for enemies these curricula identify—Catholics, pagans, or heretics thus far—reveal God's punishment.

The late sixteenth-century battle between Catholic Spain and Protestant England, which led to the defeat of the Spanish Armada, is the most decisive example of divine providence, as the "Protestant wind" came from God.

Accordingly, when Mary Tudor's widower husband, Philip II, "intent on restoring unity to the Roman Catholic Church," meddled in England, he was defeated. This defeat became the decisive battle for Europe's soul with stunning results: "Spain began to decline in nearly every matter that determines the greatness of a nation." Divine support meant that England was preserved from Catholic Spain, and Spain's decline opened the New World to the English.[20]

In contrast, Elizabeth I provides a model of virtuous Protestantism. She "replaced Mary's bloody persecution with toleration," enacted a religious settlement, making the Church of England Protestant, based on Thirty-Nine Articles. She compromised with Catholics, retaining elements of their traditional rituals. As the BJU textbook notes, many Protestants were unsatisfied by the compromise, including Puritans who wanted to purify the Anglican Church and Separatists who seceded. Elizabeth, who executed dozens of Jesuits and some Separatists, was "bloodier" or less tolerant than these curricula acknowledge.[21]

In treating the English Reformation, the Abeka history relies on thoroughly outdated scholarship. It takes the romanticized and moralizing *A Short History of the English People* of 1874 by clergyman-historian John Richard Green as authoritative. About the English Reformation, Green contends "the whole temper of the nation felt the change. A new conception of life and of man superseded the old. A new moral and religious impulse spread through every class." In Green's history, English exceptionalism points the way to American exceptionalism, as the Bible "would also find its way to new worlds across the sea."[22]

France again offers a thoroughly deplorable counterexample to the eager English acceptance of the Reformation. During the sixteenth century, the French, unlike the English, had no established rights, and thus French Protestants could not practice their religion.[23] The French monarchy viewed opposition to the Catholic Church as a threat to its own power and authority. (These textbooks are notably silent on the fact that English rulers felt the same way whether the dissenters were Catholic or, later, Puritan.) The French monarchy's response was, these curricula suggest, entirely unreasonable, for the French Wars of Religion—civil wars largely over religious division—were simply the repression of virtuous Protestants by reprehensible Catholics, as these histories portray them. As a result, Huguenot (French Calvinist) unrest is never described as revolt, even when it extended to armed resistance. The revolutionary impetus of Protestants becomes more benign "unrest."

These educational materials praise the Huguenots, who violently resisted the French crown, even though other cases of resistance are condemned. Perhaps those of the Huguenots are acceptable because these curricula construe them as a quest for religious liberty. The Wars of Religion were not a political revolution, and the Huguenots made no political demands—claims any historian of France would dispute. In fact, Calvinism attracted a sizeable proportion of the French nobility, many eager to regain political power previously lost to the crown by launching a religious challenge to its authority. Political opposition to the monarchy as much as religious conviction fueled the French Wars of Religion.

The Abeka history singles out Catherine de' Medici, queen mother and regent for her minor son Charles IX, for the strongest indictment. Even when she was tolerant, expediency rather than conviction motivated her: she was duplicitous. Thus her edicts granting toleration to Protestants are particularly suspect. She is blamed for the St. Bartholomew's Day Massacre, "one of the most brutal acts in history." The BJU textbook claims that she "planned this attack and lured many Huguenot leaders to Paris under the guise of attending a marriage."[24] Current historical consensus suggests that Charles IX, likely advised by his mother and his brother the future Henry III, among others, sanctioned an assassination of a few Huguenot leaders considered threats to the crown. The zeal of some Parisians to kill their enemies transformed the planned assassination of a few enemies of state into a shocking massacre, leading to the deaths of as many as 3,000 Parisians and 10,000 Frenchmen throughout the country. The massacre and its extent horrified Protestant Europe and caused some self-congratulation in Catholic circles that the Protestant threat had been eliminated. Certainly, its denouement was appalling, but historians recognize it as a desperate act of a beleaguered monarch and threatened kingdom. Some consider it an act of political expediency or *raison d'état*—a strategic strike against enemies of the state that is shocking in the early modern period but sometimes even condoned in contemporary politics.[25]

For these Christian textbooks, France's refusal to accept the Reformation sealed its fate. It was "headed for ruin. . . . In forcing the Christian Huguenots out of the country, the monarch emptied France of the 'righteousness that exalteth a nation' (Prov. 14: 34). As scores of Frenchmen turned from Christianity to the humanism of the Enlightenment, France approached its darkest hour."[26] This claim foreshadows coming disasters—the Enlightenment and the French Revolution—even though it telescopes

200 years of history. There is no equivocation in these histories: the French remain Catholic and thus accept humanism. As a result, they will suffer the Enlightenment and its punishment in the French Revolution. Post-Reformation Catholics are unquestionably beyond the pale.

Many histories of this period see the relationship between the Protestant Reformation and the Enlightenment quite differently, drawing a positive or even causal connection between the two movements: the Reformation fostered individualism and the critical analysis of established institutions as well as religious beliefs.[27] Luther's probably apocryphal statement "Here I Stand" before the Diet of Worms is frequently cited as the beginning of modern individualism and freedom of conscience.[28] The Reformation is thus thought to have directly paved the way for the later Enlightenment.[29] In these Christian curricula, there can be no connection between the virtuous Reformation and the diabolical Enlightenment. As a result, the freedom the Reformation gives is "individual responsibility," which both narrows the term to self-sufficiency and connects the Reformation to current antigovernment stances.[30]

These curricula present the Reformation almost entirely divorced from its context, apart from the exceptional English and Luther's biographical details. The story they tell is of the simple displacement of error by "biblical truth." The specific national, regional, and local contexts, which shaped both the articulation of Reformation challenges to Catholicism and the ways in which such challenges were understood, are completely absent. The situation on the eve of the Reformation was much more complex than these curricula's account of error displaced by truth. They do not acknowledge the significance of the social and political motives that influenced the conversion of individuals, groups, or nations to Protestantism. The fact that the Reformation occurred in a period of political conflict between centralizing nation states and more independent towns, crucial sites of emerging Protestantism, is not recognized. Similarly, the ways the religious message of Protestant reformers ignited political revolts is not discussed, because for these histories, Protestantism has neither social nor political ramifications. As a result, these curricula cannot treat the profound social, political, and economic changes, including civil wars rooted in confessional divides, that the Reformation produced.

These textbooks do not appreciate Luther within the context of German culture. His message resonated deeply with his compatriots hostile to foreign influences, especially that of the papacy. The German states had been too weak to negotiate greater autonomy in appointing clerical offices and

in arranging their financial relations with Rome. (More powerful monarchies made advantageous agreements.) None of these curricula recognize
the political and economic reasons German princes responded so eagerly to
Luther's message, particularly their desire to control church lands. Nor do
the curricula acknowledge growing national identity as a force behind the
Reformation, especially in Germany. Germany is strikingly insignificant to
the Reformation in these curricula, likely because biblical modernism later
developed there.

None of these histories directly address the issues raised by the Peasants'
War in Germany or Luther's condemnation of both the peasants and
those who attacked them: "there is nothing Christian on either side."[31]
He denounced the powerful and the wealthy and their exploitation of the
poor: "You do nothing but flay and rob your subjects in order that you may
lead a life of splendor and pride, until the poor folk can bear it no longer."
Luther also condemned the *Robbing and Murdering Peasants,* as he titled
his pamphlet in response. The peasants misconstrued the message of the
gospel as politically relevant, whereas Luther pointed out, "The kingdom
of this world is nothing else than the servant of God's wrath upon the
wicked and it is a real precursor of hell and everlasting death."[32] Luther saw
this world and its significance in a dramatically different way than Calvin
later did.

While these textbooks generally accept Luther's argument that that
Reformation had no political ramifications, they do not discuss Calvin's religious authorization of political resistance. His theology emphasized an all-
powerful God whose ways are unknown to men but who acts through human
history with His chosen people. Calvin's understanding of God's plan required a dramatic remaking of society. Since these textbooks offer a relatively
undifferentiated "Christianity," they leave unexplored crucial differences in
theology and in the social and political context and impact of these two fundamental Protestant creeds. They do not acknowledge the distinctive characteristics of the coherent Protestant theology Calvin developed. To do so
would undermine Protestant uniformity and complicate the narrative of the
Reformation as a simple rediscovery of biblical truth. In Calvin's Geneva, religious reform produced a firm alliance of religion and politics, enforcing a
strict moral order. But Calvinists also advocated political revolutions in the
name of religion. Do Calvin's stringent codes of behavior support current
calls for the restoration of "Mosaic Law," which stipulates some of the same
constraints on behavior?

These curricula note some Protestants' discontent with the incomplete character, theologically and socially, of the Reformation. For them, the Reformation did not go far enough. Anabaptists challenged Luther's acceptance of infant baptism because there was no biblical source for the practice. More critically, they separated themselves from society to form communities more in keeping with early Christianity. The biblical literalism of the Anabaptists was completely unacceptable to other Protestants, and rebaptism became a capital offense. The BJU history claims that they "twisted Scripture to support their false doctrines."[33] The Anabaptists are just one example of how some forms of Protestantism threatened the political and social status quo in Protestant countries, much as Catholic powers saw themselves endangered by Protestantism.

Another striking omission in these textbooks is their failure to recognize that leaders of emerging Protestant movement were committed to neither biblical inerrancy nor literalism. Both Luther and Calvin considered deleting some books of the New Testament from the Bible and winnowed the Roman Catholic Old Testament down to thirty-nine books. The BJU textbook simply declares that God's history is the sixty-six books of the Old and the New Testament that Luther stipulated.[34] Luther accepted only those he believed had been written originally in Hebrew and before the exile in the 500s BCE. Although later scholarship determined that some books he accepted did not actually meet his criteria, all Protestants accept the books of the Bible he deemed authentic. More importantly, Protestant reformers did not subscribe to biblical inerrancy. Luther acknowledged that the Bible was full of contradictions and errors of fact and that the prophets made erroneous predictions. He recognized too that the gospel was oral so not equivalent in authority to a scriptural text. Calvin understood that the writers of books of the Bible were not concerned with factual accuracy and that their ideas about nature were based on the ancients and therefore inaccurate. For these Protestant reformers, truth was not found in the details but the overall message of the Bible.[35] Both Luther and Calvin studied biblical texts with the skills of Renaissance humanists. By American evangelicals' standards, they might well be considered the Biblical modernists of their day, but, of course, any such claim would be anathema.

Beyond omissions of a social, political, and religiously diverse Reformation, why is the distinctive way these textbooks present the Reformation and its impact problematic? First, they use the Reformation to reinforce their extraordinary claim that divine favor rests on England and rejects much of the rest of Europe, especially France. Their Reformation encapsulates a central theme of these curricula: God favors some nations and punishes others. His newly chosen people were biblical Christians, primarily the English. Second, biblical truth is without political or social ramifications. The zeal with which Protestants, particularly Calvinists, pursued political ends to the point of civil war in virtually every country in which adherents of this creed struggled to advance their beliefs becomes incomprehensible. Activism is untenable and political revolt anathema. Events that might tar the reputation of heroic Protestants, such as the Protestant persecution of Catholics or other Protestants, or Luther's antisemitism, are not raised. Finally, the Reformation inaugurates these curricula's overtly triumphalist narrative: biblical truth is the foundation of a "righteous" nation. The stakes were lower before the Reformation, although arguments about earlier periods laid the groundwork for central claims the Reformation fulfilled. With the Reformation, the issue is truth. It must be made clearer who has espoused it and who has repudiated it. The errors of those who have either not accepted truth or who have misconstrued it as having a social or political message must be denounced.

Ironically, by reducing the Reformation to the simple recognition of obvious truth, these textbooks cannot convey the fervor of conversion or the commitment of the converted to their creed. As is generally true of these curricula, they do not offer compelling accounts of individuals and their actions. Even in recounting the Reformation, there are few models of courage, perhaps because these curricula do not encourage any action but proselytizing. History, both as it unfolds and as they write it, is explicit proselytizing.

This chapter sets the foundation for subsequent political analysis. It invokes familiar phrases used by the political right to call for a Christian nation, most notably that "without religious freedom, there can be no political freedom." The citation of the "righteousness that exalteth a nation" (Prov. 14: 34) is a clarion call for the restoration of a Christian nation and an endorsement of the actions of such nations and their leaders. These curricula address the pre- and post-Reformation periods in strikingly different ways: they critique human endeavors before the Reformation as humanist but recognize some achievements after it. The Reformation thus inaugurates the first era of commendable human accomplishment. But its impact, spiritual and political, is unquestionable: "The Protestant Reformation set loose the true spirit of individual spiritual liberty. It fostered respect for the dignity of every man and a sense of personal responsibility."[36]

8

The Fruits of the Reformation

It was not until the Peace of Westphalia of 1648 that more than a century of religious wars in Europe ended. The peace recognized that intractable theological issues divided Catholics from Protestants and Protestants from one another. The way to peace was to move religious belief from the public to the private sphere. No nation in Europe would again attempt to impose uniformity of belief. Most countries adopted an official or state religion in which those of other faiths frequently suffered social and professional discrimination, whether the official religion was Catholicism or a Protestant creed. But Europe would no longer go to war in the name of religion. Ultimately, the prolonged period of religious warfare produced "negative toleration," or "a willingness to accept the continuing existence of those you know to be wrong," as Anthony Pagden described it.[1]

This is not the story these curricula tell. Instead, they see the immediate impact of the Reformation as decisive, entirely positive, and largely uncontested. The restoration of true Christianity in the Protestant Reformation bore rich fruit in science, art, New World exploration, and political liberty. The integral connection between the Reformation and these developments is unquestionable. But to make this argument, these educational materials must, in each instance, advance an idiosyncratic and selective narrative.

Protestantism led to scientific innovation; biblical truth both motivated scientists and produced scientific discoveries, these curricula insist. Medieval science had been stymied because it relied on the Catholic Church and venerated ancient philosophy (presumably Aristotle). By the sixteenth century, both these authorities had been called into question. The Renaissance played a positive role in undermining them, but the Reformation reasserted the Bible as *the* trustworthy authority for man's understanding.[2] Recognition that the Catholic Church could not be trusted to interpret the Bible and that the pagan ancients could not give a true understanding of God's universe propelled the Scientific Revolution.

Hijacking History. Kathleen Wellman, Oxford University Press. © Oxford University Press 2021.
DOI: 10.1093/oso/9780197579237.003.0009

The claim that the Reformation fueled the Scientific Revolution was a truism or historical convention of an earlier era. The connection between these two movements was generally accepted until the history of science became less positivist and more rigorous. More recent historical research has made abundantly clear that scientists of the Reformation era were as likely to be Catholic as Protestant. In fact, the Jesuits, the Catholic Reformation religious order, were especially noteworthy practitioners of science.[3] That is not to say that the exposure of Europeans to new scientific texts in the Renaissance and Reformation did not bear fruit. Both movements studied and critiqued earlier sources and traditions and thus fostered new investigations of nature. Nonetheless, historians of science would certainly contest the unquestionable claim of these curricula that scientific achievement derives from adherence to biblical truth.

ACE gives Bob Jones Sr. the final word: "The Bible was not written to teach men sciences; but the Bible is scientifically correct." The Abeka textbook makes the association firmer: "Without the Bible, men would never have discovered the foundational truths upon which modern science is based." Before human beings turned to the Bible, they were misled by superstition, worship of nature, and "trial and error"—a rather strange denunciation, as much modern science relies on trial and error. Only since the Reformation have humans "begun to earnestly fulfill God's command to subdue the earth." Protestants, whose faith gave them the means, made scientific advances. When they turned to the Bible, they understood that God "established reasonable, orderly laws which nature obeys" or "because they believed the Bible, they had a good understanding of basic truths about the universe." In either formulation, scientific understanding depends on the Bible. The latest edition of the Abeka textbook is even more adamant: "only God's direct revelation, the Bible, could show man the true nature of the universe and give him the foundational truths necessary for science."[4] It baldly advances an ahistorical notion: "modern medical care has generally ebbed and or waned with Christianity." The BJU history recognizes that science was a religious quest, as indeed it was for many, whether Protestant or Catholic: "Many of these men saw science as a means of glorifying God; they could examine the handiwork of His creation and find practical knowledge to help their fellow men."[5]

Protestant beliefs were central to early modern scientists, these textbooks claim.[6] For example, after Copernicus questioned Ptolemy's geocentric understanding of astronomy, Johannes Kepler improved on that understanding because he was a Lutheran who did not fear the Catholic Church. Galileo discovered the laws of motion because he understood that "the universe is unified because it is created by one God, the God of the Scriptures." These curricula appreciate Galileo most for his disagreement with the church because, as a Catholic, he does not serve the narrative of the Protestant foundation of scientific discoveries. Ironically, these curricula insist on biblical literalism, but Galileo fell afoul of the church because the heliocentrism he asserted could raise doubts in the minds of the literal about the account in Joshua 10:13 that the sun stood still. It is completely inaccurate to proclaim, as the Abeka textbook does, that Isaac Newton was "a devout Christian" who tried "to imitate in his mind the divine simplicity by which God governs the universe."[7] Newton, an avid practitioner of alchemy, numerology, and other occult sciences, held heterodox religious views at the very least.[8] While the BJU history treats the Scientific Revolution more thoroughly, it emphasizes the religious foundation of every scientist's work, so that the Scientific Revolution becomes a story of Protestants' successful quests to "search for a truth about God's universe."[9]

The notable scientific societies of the period, the Abeka history claims, were composed of devout Protestants. In England, the Puritan clergyman John Wilkins founded both the Philosophical College and the Royal Society. Even the accomplishments of the French Academy of Science, which, one might suppose, would be condemned as Catholic, are instead the products of Huguenots (French Calvinists) and Jansenists (Catholics who held some quasi-Calvinist views). They, rather than the Catholic majority, were central to French scientific accomplishments, because they "followed several Calvinist teachings."[10]

Most historians of science no longer uncritically accept the so-called Merton Thesis, advanced by Robert Merton in 1936, which connected the scientific work of the Royal Society explicitly to Puritanism. That claim has been contested by much subsequent scholarship. Unquestionably, historians of science would reject the French Academy of Sciences as a bastion of Protestantism.[11]

These Christian textbooks also limit scientific investigation to a religiously circumscribed sphere. Although they see science as producing an understanding of God's universe, they hasten to constrain it. The Abeka history insists that science "can explain how something happens, but it cannot explain why." This curriculum severely restricts the questions scientists can productively address: "Science is limited to what men observe about the physical world; it cannot, for example, deal with the origin of the universe."[12] The student is also encouraged to be highly skeptical about scientific claims: scientific findings change, and scientific "facts" often prove incorrect. Science, like other human endeavors, remains dubious, even in the aftermath of the Reformation. It cannot challenge biblical truth.

The Reformation also bore fruit in the arts, according to these educational materials. Unlike Renaissance arts, for which these textbooks offer very muted appreciation, post-Reformation arts are commendable. Artists, including Albrecht Dürer, Hans Holbein, and Rembrandt van Rijn, reveal the Reformation's impact. For the Abeka history, the cause of this artistic flourishing is clear: "The return to the Bible . . . sparked an outburst of individual creativity such as the world had never known."[13] Artwork must be evaluated in light of "the work of God." The BJU textbook similarly considers the artist's faith and choice of subject matter crucial in assessing his work. It accurately describes the characteristic features of Baroque arts but does not recognize the centrality of the Catholic Reformation to them. (Ironically, Bob Jones University has such an impressive collection of the Baroque arts of the Catholic Reformation that it provokes concern about BJU's commitment to fundamentalism.[14]) What distinguishes an artist is whether he was Protestant. Religious subjects elevated Rembrandt's art and Handel's and Bach's music, for example. Post-Reformation hymns replaced "the droning of monks." If the arts must be products of Protestant religious conviction, secular arts and the works of great Catholic masters—Titian, Tintoretto, Velasquez, among others—who defy the exclusively Protestant narrative, cannot be included. Most importantly, as the Abeka textbook insists, "all human works should be evaluated in light of *the greatest classic of all, the Word of God.*"[15]

Just as the Scientific Revolution could occur only after the Reformation, so too exploration of the New World depended on true religious faith and zeal. "In God's plan, the lands of the New World remained virtually unknown to Europe until the sixteenth century—a time when Europe was also rediscovering the truth of God's Word."[16] While the former argument is suspect, the supposed connections between the Reformation and New World exploration these curricula present defy chronology and evidence. To establish a causal connection, these textbooks make strikingly dubious claims to assert "Christian" motivations for exploration.

Since exploration of the New World began before the Reformation, these textbooks go to considerable lengths to establish the "Christianity" of explorers. ACE discusses a wide variety of theories about the first North

American explorers, even though, it concedes, they have been advanced by "scholars and crackpots." Nonetheless, it presents these theories and tests students on them as if they were all equally credible. It points to Japanese, Chinese, Roman, and Greek artifacts in many locations on the North American continent and to megalithic structures in North Salem, New Hampshire, as likely built by Irish Culdee monks or Phoenicians. Advancing views that most people and virtually all historians would dispute or consign to the crackpot category, ACE credits tenth-century Culdee settlements of "Great Ireland" in North America and asserts that the Culdee monks were not Roman Catholics; they did not accept the pope. The monks thus implicitly serve as fitting, proto-Protestant explorers of the New World. When Eric the Red reached Greenland about 990, he entered the Western Hemisphere as "the first European who can positively be said to have crossed the Atlantic Ocean." His son Leif Erickson was a Christian, and "Norse expeditions were sent out to Vinland with the charge from their king 'to proclaim Christianity' wherever they made landfall." Erickson was thus a Christian missionary to the New World.[17] Since "Christian" means before-the-fact Protestant, no mention is made that if he were a Christian, Erickson would have been a Catholic. Even as ACE presents many questionable expeditions to the New World as credible, it asserts that explorers were motivated by their desire to spread true Christianity. Such an ecumenical inclusion of every possible exploration, no matter how dubious, also makes Spanish exploration of the New World less significant.

Christopher Columbus is an exception, but he too becomes part of a heroic effort to proselytize proto-Protestant Christianity. ACE supposes that Columbus's family had fled Italy because of Catholic persecutions of Sephardic Jews and cites his suffering at the Inquisition's hand. This idiosyncratic presentation of Columbus's possible religious antecedents endows a key explorer of the New World with a commendable religious pedigree and a firm link to a Judeo-Christian founding of the United States. ACE concludes, "In spite of his lip service to Roman Catholicism and his probably Jewish background, Christopher Columbus was very possibly a secret Christian." He lived up to his name "Christ-bearer," intending to bring Christ's teachings to the lands he explored. Columbus thus becomes a proto-Protestant missionary to the New World.[18]

ACE continues to teach the patently false claim that Columbus was one of the few who believed that the world was round. To signal Columbus's heroic stature, it relies on the old canard that Columbus's contemporaries believed the world was flat, but "because he believed the world was round," Columbus sought passage to the East.[19] This belief, putatively held only by Columbus, was, of course, understood by the educated.

This claim modifies the completely erroneous story promulgated widely in American history textbooks after it appeared in Washington Irving's *The Life and Voyages of Christopher Columbus* in 1828. This account extols the intrepid Columbus and his crew, who courageously set out, believing they were in imminent danger of sailing off the flat plane of the earth. (Students occasionally still come to college committed to this legend!) Irving intended to expose the scientific ignorance of Catholics, reflecting the nineteenth-century view that Catholics rejected science in the name of religion.[20] Irving's legend thus condemned Columbus's contemporaries whose religious faith led them to reject science.

ACE uses this story entirely differently. It contends that Columbus came to believe that the earth was round by understanding the biblical passage in Isaiah 40:22, "it is God that sitteth upon the circle of the earth." The Bible gave Columbus privileged knowledge unavailable to his contemporaries, particularly heretical Catholics. The other curricula contend that Columbus explored the New World to recapture the Holy Land, lead a crusade against the Muslims, and convert them. The BJU textbooks bemoans that Catholic explorers "won converts to the Roman Church rather than to Christ."[21]

These Christian textbooks treat European explorers and colonizers in diverse ways, depending on whether they were Catholic or Protestant. They are most critical of the Spanish explorers who, except for Columbus, were intent only on the acquisition of wealth. When Francisco Pizarro was urged to spread the gospel to the Incas, "he responded: 'I have not come for any such reasons; I have come to take away their gold.'" ACE heaps vituperation on Spanish colonization, particularly their missionary efforts; "thousands of unbelieving Indians were forced to accept the Catholic baptism of sprinkled 'holy water.' The result was not converted Indians, but merely thousands upon thousands of slightly damp but still unbelieving natives."[22] To further tar them, ACE claims the Spanish believed that some were destined by God and nature to be slaves. This claim obviously fails to note the existence of slaves in early civilizations, including in Israel in biblical times or ancient sources defining natural slaves. These Christian curricula attribute the arrival of slavery in the New World to the Spanish, who brought Africans to the New World, implying that it came to the virtuous Anglo-Protestant colonies because of the evil Spanish. Although the BJU history concedes that Columbus opened the slave trade in the New World, it condemns the Spanish rather than Columbus. As a result of their despicable and heretical practices, "God turned his back on them with the Armada's defeat" in 1588.[23]

The BJU textbook concedes that the French at least had good relations with Native Americans, although it considers their dealings with indigenous populations fatally flawed by Old World institutions: the French lived under a monarchy, and they lacked self-government, freedom of religion, and economic freedom, suggesting anachronistically that early seventeenth-century England enjoyed those benefits and, as a result, treated native populations better. Indigenous peoples of the New World can be integrated into biblical history only as the probable result of the "dispersion from the Tower of Babel." But they pose a problem for these textbooks. Ripe for conversion to Christianity, they should have been more amenable to it, but too many of them converted to heresy.

ACE focuses on French explorers' quest for wealth in searching for a northwest passage. Two early French explorers, Giovanni Verrazano and Jacques Cartier, were pirates or privateers, for example. While the expeditions of Samuel de Champlain established a fur trade in New France, Marquette and Joliet failed to find a northwest passage. Notably, these curricula do not acknowledge the religious motives of Jesuit explorers. However, as the Abeka history points out, the French colonial enterprise did not attract entrepreneurs, because of "tight political, economic, and religious restrictions set by the mother country."[24]

English colonial ventures offer a dramatic contrast to those of continental Europeans. The BJU history places the English colonization of the New World firmly in the context of the Reformation. While acknowledging that the motives for colonization were not entirely religious, it charges that historians fail to acknowledge religious motives sufficiently. Even though the English too were looking for gold, they wanted to develop colonies rather than exploit them. English exploration brought God to the New World and, these curricula emphatically insist, American freedoms derived from these earliest Protestant explorers.

These educational materials do not acknowledge that religious dissent threatened kings or that the Reformation inspired demands for political and social change, often revolutionary change. Nor do they recognize that many debates about the nature of government or arguments for liberty were articulated in secular terms, because for them liberation is religious. They insist that biblical truth had no social or political ramifications but that the

Reformation brought political liberty. They consider attacks on power illegitimate and attempts at social reform misdirected. Yet, throughout the early modern period, Protestants fought to overturn Catholic monarchs, advocated for both political power and social reform, and often attempted to advance their cause by violent dissent and warfare. Thus, navigating the political terrain of the seventeenth century while maintaining their narrative's trajectory proves difficult for these textbooks.

England, as the Protestant nation par excellence, poses acute challenges. How can they treat the outbreak of civil war complete with a regicide in virtuous England? How can England, enmeshed in civil war, demonstrate the association between biblical truth, economic prosperity, and cultural advance these textbooks assert? Finally, how can an England in turmoil and a stable France with growing political power and cultural preeminence show God's favor toward the former and rejection of the latter?

Seventeenth-century England experienced a protracted period of civil war fought to address political and religious dissent. While its immediate provocation was Parliamentary resistance to the Stuart kings' claims to power, religious conflict underlay political issues. The religious divisions in England were not simply between Protestant and Catholic but rather between warring Protestant sects, primarily Anglicans versus Puritans. These histories cannot address the English Civil War accurately or make sense of an England in which Protestants divided over fundamental questions of religious belief and practice. Instead, they condemn the crypto-Romanism of English kings that made them suspect as heretics.

The BJU history exposes a crucial dilemma these textbooks face. The seventeenth century was a period characterized by the pursuit of power by monarchies, usually called absolutism.[25] Monarchs' power was God given, as Romans 13 confirms. This textbook concedes that kings often used "their authority to satisfy their own pleasures and to increase their personal power."[26] Bad kings warrant criticism for using their power in ways that harm their people, but, with their political power given by God, they cannot be legitimately resisted.

Hard-pressed to make sense of the English Civil War, these curricula make short work of it. In essence, they treat the English Civil War as opposition to Romanist heresy as exemplified by Romanist kings, who were either clearly so, like Charles II and James II, or inclined to persecute some Protestants, notably the Puritans and Separatists, like James I and Charles I.[27] The Puritans were forced to turn to Parliament for protection and thus the cause of the two was united. Thus Protestant challenges to Catholic monarchs were legitimate rejections of heresy as, indeed, Calvin sanctioned resistance by duly constituted magistrates to a king who did not allow his people to follow God's laws.

ACE presents a more straightforward account of the early seventeenth century. It contends that, unlike the French, who accepted absolutism, the English challenged James I's claims to political power. "Parliament reminded him of the *Magna Carta* and the traditional rights of Parliament to a voice in the government." His son Charles I behaved as an absolute ruler, forcing loans and imposing taxes without Parliamentary consent.[28]

These curricula appreciate James I, despite his persecution of Puritans and Separatists, because he produced the King James Bible. For the most conservative of fundamentalists, the King James Bible is their preferred version and, for a small minority, the only authentic English Bible.[29] James I is also important for the colonies founded under his aegis—Jamestown and Plymouth; the latter, these curricula insist, transmitted both political and religious liberty to the New World.[30] As neither characterized seventeenth-century England, this argument is difficult to sustain.

England avoided absolutism because, according to the BJU account, Parliament was empowered to deny a king's request to raise taxes (no doubt the most appropriate role for the US Congress as well). When Charles I not only repressed Protestants but also tried to raise taxes, Parliament produced the Petition of Rights, which demanded no taxes without its consent and no arbitrary imprisonment. The BJU textbook cites the Book of Solomon, which advises kings to seek wisdom, to condemn the Stuarts for seeking power and wealth instead.[31] Monarchs can thus be criticized for failing to rule according to biblical injunctions. It condemns James I's desire to have Englishmen conform to Anglicanism as reprehensible and his private life as scandalous. (He had male favorites.) Anglicanism poses problems for these histories: should it be treated as genuine Protestantism or repudiated as crypto-Catholicism? The Abeka textbook takes the tack of praising Anglican Protestantism when it is at odds with Catholicism but condemning it when it contests Puritanism. For the Abeka textbook, the English Civil War is a battle between the Cavaliers supporting the divine right of kings and the Roundheads supporting "government by consent." Puritans joined Cromwell's Roundheads because they were "confident they knew the mind and purpose of God."[32]

Despite Puritan sympathies, the BJU history denounces Cromwell's fervent supporters even more vehemently. They "envisioned a republic where every man would have equal opportunity and privileges. Supporters of the Rump Parliament saw nothing wrong with boldly experimenting with England's longstanding political traditions to attain that end."[33] Conservative members of Parliament, who opposed the Rump Parliament, understood that things had gone too far before they were excluded from Parliament. Had those conservatives remained, this textbook suggests, they would have resisted attempts to create equality. This account objects to both the social aspirations of Puritan revolutionaries and the political action of their representatives in the Rump Parliament. These histories ignore the regicide of Charles I almost entirely. Instead, Charles I was simply forced from the throne and executed to allow truth to emerge. Religious controversy is generally missing in these histories but its absence from a period of civil war, in which armies could be differentiated by creed, is especially disconcerting.

Oliver Cromwell's Puritan Protectorate also raises certain problems. The Abeka history concedes that Cromwell exercised even greater power than the absolutist Stuart kings, but, according to this highly polemical account, Cromwell "rarely exercised these powers. Instead, he concentrated on maintaining peace and order in England, promoting religious toleration, and defending the country from foreign powers."[34] In other words, despite his absolutist tendencies, Cromwell was a virtuous ruler committed to admirable goals. His vision of himself as a Puritan Moses, acting with the blessings of Divine Providence, likely makes him a sympathetic figure as well. As a result, these textbooks overlook his extreme policies and downplay opposition to him. He was more controversial than they acknowledge.

Conventional histories point to Cromwell's extreme repression of Irish Catholics, his concentration of political power, and his imposition of Puritan standards of behavior on a resistant population. They condemn Cromwell's army's brutal conquest of Scotland and Ireland. They do not concur that he "rarely exercised" his absolutist policies, which led him to refuse to disband his army but to disband Parliament. Cromwell and his theocratic government proved no more willing than Stuart kings or monarchists to deal with Parliament. But the Puritans are godly and Cromwell's theocracy admirable. These textbooks give little sense of how disastrous the period of Cromwell's reign was, or how disgruntled the English were with Cromwell's attempts to impose theocratic government or rigid Calvinism, or how thoroughly the English people repudiated these policies when they spurned his son Richard in favor of the restored monarchy.

A thorough discussion of the period of the English Civil War or its complexity is not possible within the history of Protestant triumph these curricula tell.

Only ACE explains the restoration of the Stuarts with Charles II by pointing to the inability of Richard to maintain control and English repudiation of the Puritans and their measures. However, all these curricula consider the Restoration in religious terms. Thus, when Charles II "agreed to obtain tolerance for English Catholics and to join the Roman church himself," he was beyond the pale. When Charles's brother, James II, wanted to "reimpose Romanism," he provoked hostility.[35] With his wife's pregnancy, the disquieting possibility of a Catholic heir led the English to repudiate him.

For these textbooks, the Glorious Revolution, which ended the Restoration and brought William and Mary to the throne, is unquestionably praiseworthy and in no sense revolutionary: It is a conservative reversion to England's "struggle for rights and liberties which go back to the *Magna Carta* and end with the invitation to William and Mary and the Bill of Rights."[36] ACE points to the English Bill of Rights as a profound influence on the US Constitution. It is more usually compared to the American Bill of Rights, although neither comparison is entirely apt. The English bill gave landowners (only) the right to keep their guns, stipulated that elections should be free and Parliament be called into session, and prohibited the raising of a standing army. As historians recognize, the English Bill of Rights was less innovative than its American counterpart, as it was intended to both preserve royal prerogative and to appeal to both Tories and Whigs.[37]

Only ACE acknowledges that the Glorious Revolution was, in fact, an uprising. The others accept the Whig account of it, most clearly articulated by Lord Macauley in his *History of England*, which maintained that England had not suffered a bloody revolution like France. Its first two volumes, published in 1849, heralded the Glorious Revolution as the key to English constitutionalism, parliamentary monarchy, and political and religious liberty. This account is rather rosy: there was bloodshed in Scotland and Ireland, there was no tolerance for Catholics, and the fruits of the revolution were oligarchic rather than democratic.[38] Nonetheless, for these curricula, the Glorious Revolution fulfilled England's destiny as the purveyor of religious and political liberty and established beyond question the integral connection between them. As the Abeka textbook puts it, "The Englishmen established their liberties on the solid foundation of biblical truths revealed by the Protestant Reformation."[39]

The history of English Protestantism during the seventeenth century must be largely scrubbed of religious and political conflict to foster these textbooks' narrative. Ironically, seventeenth-century France experienced political stability when England was still wracked by war. France emerged from the chaos of its forty years of war between Catholics and Huguenots, the latter of whom resisted the crown for both religious and political reasons, with the Catholic monarchy as the only political entity able to assert control and provide a foundation for hard-won political stability. At the end of the Wars of Religion, France began an extended period of rebuilding under the first three Bourbon kings—Henry IV, Louis XIII, and Louis XIV. For these textbooks, the emergence and empowerment of the French state under the Bourbon kings signal their illegitimate concentration of political power.

The Revocation of the Edict of Nantes (the famous 1598 edict of toleration for French Protestants) by Louis XIV in 1685 signals the full realization of France's evil tendencies. Louis XIII's prime minister, Cardinal Richelieu, had targeted Huguenots with discriminatory practices and surveillance. When Louis XIV assumed the throne, he believed stability required religious uniformity and, with greater royal control, took repressive actions against both Protestants and dissident Catholics.[40] While these curricula criticize Louis XIV for his repression of Protestants, they fail to recognize that he was intent on enforcing religious uniformity—a goal they might admire had he been Protestant.

The Revocation was disastrous for France, because, as the Abeka textbook claims, Huguenots "made up the spiritual, moral, and economic backbone of the country." The BJU curriculum cites Psalm 34:21: "Evil shall slay the wicked: they that hate the righteous shall be desolate," to predict France's imminent decline, less than a hundred years later, in "a violent and bloody revolution."[41] The Revocation and the French Revolution present a clear-cut case of cause and effect.

While historians certainly see Louis XIV's repudiation of toleration of the Huguenots as one of the most destructive acts of his reign, they are unlikely to see the departure of the Huguenots as sufficient explanation for the French Revolution. Instead, they see the Revocation as contributing to the economic development of nations to which Huguenots emigrated, especially the Netherlands. Historians, unlike these textbooks, critique the highly speculative economic policies of the duke of Orleans, the regent for the young Louis XV. The duke was a gambler, who turned fiscal management over to John Law. The bursting of Law's speculative Mississippi Bubble wreaked havoc on the French economy. Since capitalism is an unquestionable good in these textbooks, they do not acknowledge the boom-and-bust cycles of rampant speculative schemes such as Law's. The complexities of early nation-states, particularly as they developed intense economic and political rivalries over trade in their quest to establish and cultivate national wealth through overseas empires, do not much feature in these histories. Government policies simply offer sober warnings. In this case, France was on the brink of economic collapse because of "extravagant government spending and excessive taxation"—policies it deplores.[42]

When these curricula condemn Louis XIV as an absolute monarch, they revert to an outmoded historiography and fail to recognize more nuanced assessments of French political structure. Historians now recognize the many limits on the French monarchy's control. While Louis XIII benefited from Richelieu's efforts to impose bureaucratic order, a strong nobility and Protestant resistance challenged him. After the Fronde (1648–1653), the noble revolt against royal authority that became a popular revolt and spread to the provinces, Louis XIV resolved to build on his predecessors' successes and make such rebellion inconceivable.

These Christian curricula generally see the centralizing power of any government as reprehensible, even though this stance seems to contradict their sense that God sanctions those who rule. They invoke the Bible for their claim that God favors limited, local government. They single out France under Louis XIV for concerted criticism, as it both centralized political power and manipulated the economy in its interests. Restrictions and regulations impeded French colonial development and the functioning of the market. Louis XIV's policies thus violated conservative economic orthodoxy as well.

Historians too assess Louis XIV critically, but they neither distinguish evil France from godly England nor use such a distinction to assert an antigovernment, anti-tax, anti-political resistance argument. They attribute France's eighteenth-century economic crisis largely to the indebtedness incurred by Louis XIV's and Louis XV's many wars. They recognize that, despite their different subsequent trajectories, France and England pursued the same economic policies—mercantilism—in the same markets—India, West Africa, North America, and the West Indies. Seventeenth-century centralizing states developed economic plans on a national scale, generally called mercantilism, based on the notion that a strong economy depended on a favorable balance of trade. This quest epitomized the government's desire to increase its tax base. The similarity of French and English economic policies makes it difficult to argue that only godly England followed God's economic plan. Nonetheless, for these curricula, the fiscal policies of French kings identified them as bad rulers: Louis XV (1715–1774) was capable but loved luxury and continued wasting France's resources lavishly; Louis XVI (1774–1793) was wasteful and inefficient. He refused to implement the reforms his ministers advocated.[43] No English king, even the mad King George III or the Catholic James II, elicits similar criticism. But England remains largely exempt from criticism as the Protestant progenitor of America.

The Abeka history even more explicitly reduces the history of seventeenth-century France to evil policies: raising taxes and persecuting Protestants. When Cardinal Mazarin, prime minister until Louis XIV assumed power in 1661, raised taxes, France experienced unrest. Louis XIV is first praised for regularizing French finances but then condemned for bankrupting France. It "was spending money faster than it took it in"—another sobering lesson for modern Americans. Louis XIV persecuted Huguenots because he "viewed their business skill, growing political power, and Christian testimony as a threat to his power." He failed to appreciate Protestant entrepreneurship. The central role of France in funding the Americans in their rebellion against England is downplayed even though France's support led to its subsequent bankruptcy. Instead, Louis XVI simply "aided the Americans in hopes of weakening Britain."[44]

Moral opprobrium falls particularly heavily on the French court: Versailles was the center of all that was base and immoral; adultery on the part of the king was expected; members of the court practiced homosexuality; gambling was commonplace. Every sort of vice could be found in the king's palace. Even though the reign of Louis XIV enjoyed seeming prosperity, "God, however, warns that 'it is an abomination to kings to commit wickedness: for the throne is established by righteousness.'"[45] The BJU textbook describes both Louis XV and Louis XVI as "indifferent to the affairs of government" and instead "interested in the frivolous pleasures of life at Versailles." They followed "the capricious advice of their mistresses or fell prey to the intriguing schemes of nobles."[46]

The court of Louis XIV was certainly the most significant and lavish in Europe. It not only brought the frequently rebellious nobility from their estates under its surveillance but also set the highest model of cultural sophistication. As for the moral behavior of the king and the members of the court, it is not clear whether, while better known, the court at Versailles was more dissolute than that of English kings—Charles II, for example. Other courts were perhaps not as obviously on display or as opulent.

The Thirty Years War (1618–1648), for these curricula, was the last great persecution of Protestants by Catholics: Protestants do not resist, but Catholics act against them. This is a highly unorthodox understanding of the Thirty Years War, especially since Richelieu, the French Prime Minister, allied with the Protestants—a shocking exercise in *raison d'état* or political expediency without respect for religion. If such wars are simply reduced to Catholic persecution of true Christians, no accurate understanding of the complexity of seventeenth-century religious, political, and international issues is possible.

These curricula are unstinting in detailing the benefits the Reformation brought to the world. Human efforts, inspired by biblical truth, produced scientific discoveries and great art, and were admirable rather than humanist. New World explorations are best understood as the desire to spread true Christianity, despite the problems for chronology that argument entails. And England experienced the benefits of religious and political liberty.

Why does this ahistorical narrative matter? An important ramification of the discussion of the Scientific Revolution is the discounting of science. These textbooks are more interested in scientists' faith than in their scientific work: science is possible only if the scientist is a Protestant. The argument is stretched beyond credibility and evidence. These curricula ostensibly praise science in the aftermath of the Reformation, but only the Protestant understanding of "biblical truth" allowed the scientist to understand nature and be rewarded with pathbreaking discoveries. Despite an appreciation of science thus far uncharacteristic of these world histories, without Protestant religious belief, no scientist can attain scientific distinction. Even the Protestant scientist must not seek to understand certain questions and must accept the transitory and ephemeral nature of scientific findings as compared to the certainty of the Bible. Ultimately, science can only be sectarian and based on biblical truth.

In these textbooks, only England thoroughly embraced the Reformation and thus received all the benefits of the sciences, the arts, and its New World colonies. England experienced a civil war with dramatic events, outsized personalities, and a whirlwind of political change, but these histories are largely unable to treat these developments. They see history as driven by ideas, particularly religious ideas. As a result, complexity and contingency and human agency are largely absent from them.

Standard world histories trace the development of both parliamentary monarchy and political absolutism in the seventeenth century, but they do not, as these curricula typically do, consider this evolution predetermined. They instead see it as the result of specific events and responses to them. Standard histories might well extol the introduction of constitutional monarchy in Britain, especially as a step toward more representative government, as opposed to the concentration of royal power in France. But they do not differentiate the virtuous English from the decadent and depraved French.

This treatment of the seventeenth century in these educational materials confirms that their ideological purpose is paramount, as, despite evidence to the contrary, this period documents English success and French failure. This narrative is an extreme version of the Anglophilia that has long informed a historiographical tradition that focused almost exclusively on the English roots of the United States. For these curricula, that interpretive strand is reinforced by England's status as the crucial conduit of biblical truth to the New World. Its history is Whiggish, meaning it considers history an inevitable march toward progress, and Anglophilic, as England remains the positive model. The Abeka textbook puts it most baldly: "the spirit of individual freedom and responsibility . . . grew as more Englishmen read the Bible." As a result, "a flood of blessings came to seventeenth-century England."[47] Ironically, their accounts also implement the seventeenth-century Act of Oblivion, which put a veil of forgetfulness over the period of the English Civil War during the Restoration of the Stuart monarchy.

The English Reformation is crucial in setting the stage for the American story. When these histories later consider the English colonies in the New World, they cannot accurately place them in the seventeenth-century English context they have so thoroughly distorted. But that distortion is crucial to the connections these textbooks later make between Protestant England and Protestant North America. As the Abeka textbook asserts, "freedom-loving, 17th-century Englishmen were the true discoverers of America."[48] Only the British colonies had the proper religious motives and the right approach to economics: there, where "considerable political and religious freedom gave every man a chance to prosper," history took a dramatic turn. "The English came to America in God's perfect timing, for by then England had become a

Protestant nation in which the Bible was freely available to all." The English were the crucial purveyors to the New World of biblical truth as well of America's fundamental values: "All of the ideas about morality, justice, individual responsibility, and freedom that have made America great came from the Bible," and they came by way of the English.[49]

9

What Reason Wrought

Historians are well aware that much recent scholarship has questioned the Enlightenment's idealism and exposed its inconsistencies and blind spots. They recognize that Enlightenment thinkers did not sufficiently recognize racism and sexism or repudiate slavery or colonialism and other eighteenth-century ills. If recent scholarship exposes the Enlightenment as a less unequivocally positive movement but a more nuanced one, historians also have found many of the same failings in works and actions of American Founding Fathers, who were both indebted to the Enlightenment and shared some of its myopia.[1] The confidence of proponents of Enlightenment in human progress now seems somewhat unwarranted or naive in the aftermath of the revolutions and the wars that have beset the modern world. Ironically, some scholars find Enlightenment roots of both the Terror during the French Revolution and National Socialism in Hitler's Germany, while others see it as providing a foundation for repudiating the excesses of both the French Revolution and fascism.[2] Scholars also recognize that the Enlightenment should be appreciated for acknowledging, as no previous period had, both the prospect and limits of human knowledge and for its unflinching indictment of prejudice and superstition. It developed and promoted the social sciences and religious tolerance. No matter how one approaches this movement, the Enlightenment, as the pivot point between the early modern and the modern periods, occupies a contested position and is tied, for good and ill, to all subsequent developments.

But these curricula's rejection of the Enlightenment is not a response to recent scholarly debates. Their antipathy focuses on the Enlightenment's appreciation of reason and science. Their attack undermines the conventional, formerly positive view of the Enlightenment's presumed influence on the American founding. The belief that the Enlightenment was anti-religious is the primary cause of modern hostility to it from the political and religious right. That sentiment, long a feature of American anti-intellectualism, seems to be ever more influential as alternative and Christian schools and state standards actively promote it. The fact that some American college students

Hijacking History. Kathleen Wellman, Oxford University Press. © Oxford University Press 2021.
DOI: 10.1093/oso/9780197579237.003.0010

now arrive on campus with an obvious hostility toward the Enlightenment reflects a new iteration of this sentiment. If they know anything about the Enlightenment, their views are often negative, seeing it as a period full of dangerous ideas.[3] Liberal political commentators remark, perhaps not entirely facetiously, that the goal of the Republican Party is to undo the Enlightenment.[4] Indeed, as these textbooks document, the Enlightenment has emerged as a target in the culture wars in the United States, especially over school curricula.

These educational materials recognize the Enlightenment as a crucial turn toward the evils of the modern world. What values does their denunciation of the Enlightenment call into question? Secularism, tolerance, political and social criticism, the social sciences, the commitment to social reform, internationalism—all defined the Enlightenment and are antithetical to these world histories' notion of progress.

If these curricula rejoiced in the coming of the Reformation and its spread to the New World, the Enlightenment undermines any possibility that human beings or society remained on the right track. "The rise of a new brand of humanism in France—the Enlightenment—proved to be the greatest threat to the survival of traditional French society. Hastened by the influence of these destructive, anti-Christian philosophies, France continued its downward slide toward revolution," one textbook warns.[5] The fruition of the Enlightenment in the French Revolution only confirms such dire prophecies. Since the reign of Clovis, France has been tied to "humanism"—a synonym for sin, foreshadowing doom for any country or civilization. Students are thus led to expect France's demise since its earliest espousal of Roman Catholicism.

Historians generally connect the Enlightenment to the Scientific Revolution but see them as independent movements. Jean d'Alembert's *Preliminary Discourse,* an introduction to the *Encyclopédie,* the massive publishing enterprise intended to disseminate knowledge, identified the roots of the eighteenth-century Enlightenment in seventeenth-century scientific and philosophical works. These textbooks, as we have seen, evaluate key thinkers of the earlier movement by assessing their Protestant orthodoxy. The Abeka textbook brooks no possible connection between the two movements: the Scientific Revolution was the fruit of the Reformation and thus religiously grounded. To acknowledge the Enlightenment as a product of the Scientific Revolution would sever the firm correlation between Protestant virtue and science. While the BJU history finds roots of the Enlightenment in the

Scientific Revolution, it carefully distinguishes reputable forerunners from those it condemns. It rescues Francis Bacon and brings him into the orthodox fold. His skepticism led some to believe he was questioning religion, but he also asserted that "natural philosophy is, after the word of God . . . the most approved nourishment for faith."[6] Scientists are admirable only if they did not use their new understanding of nature to question the Bible.

Some key figures of the Scientific Revolution who influenced the Enlightenment prove difficult for the BJU history to integrate into its religious narrative. While Descartes commendably admitted spiritual truths, such as the existence of God, John "Locke rejected the ideas that God had implanted certain truths within each person from birth." When Locke thus refuted Descartes's innate ideas, he thereby rejected original sin. This textbook condemns him for believing that, although revelation was necessary, it could not contradict human reason.[7] Such ideas gave scientists and philosophers false confidence, and they used those ideas to analyze society and define hopes for reform. Most damning, "men exalted reason as the highest authority, placing it above faith in God and His Word." Enlightenment thinkers rejected the supernatural and questioned miracles. They saw man as "basically good." Most reprehensible, they made reason "their standard of truth: it was their guide to understanding the universe and the proper way to worship God. This new religion was called deism."[8]

After describing the notion of a clockmaker God, this world history concludes that "Deism had little use for a personal God or His salvation" and cites Voltaire:

> The great name of Deist, which is not sufficiently revered, is the only name one ought to take. The only gospel one ought to read is the great book of Nature, written by the hand of God and sealed with his seal. The only religion that ought to be professed is the religion of worshipping God and being a good man.[9]

Although the BJU textbook uses this passage to condemn Voltaire as irreligious, his broader purpose should be noted. In this passage, Voltaire not only defined fundamental tenets of deism but also praised its moderation and tolerance in contrast to the wars and strife produced by religious fanaticism. This quotation comes from Voltaire's description in his *Treatise on Tolerance* of the horrific miscarriage of justice committed in the name of religion in the trial of Jean Calas. Needless to say, this textbook highlights none of these points but instead warns that deism was built on mere human wisdom and sets the previous quotation against a string of expurgated quotations from Corinthians, notably that "your faith should not stand in the wisdom of men, but in the power of God."[10]

These curricula are intent on condemning the Enlightenment, specifically the French Enlightenment, as the source of the depredations of the modern world. As Voltaire's quotation attests, French thinkers attacked the practices of the Catholic Church (as do these textbooks) and the status quo. They shared new currents of thought across Europe and the New World, applying new methods to the study of other cultures and religions. Those investigations sometimes questioned beliefs fundamentalists hold dear, especially biblical inerrancy, which, as we have seen, was not nearly as universally held by Christians as these textbooks suggest—not even by Protestant reformers. It did not even become a tenet of evangelical faith until the late nineteenth century.

Like all secondary-school materials, these curricula must simplify this complex period in intellectual and cultural history, but they do so with an explicit end: to trace a trajectory of evil from the Enlightenment through the French Revolution, to Darwin, to Hitler, to communism, as their treatment of modern history will document. To denounce the Enlightenment, they identify its key figures as enemies to be vanquished. Some of their characterizations of Enlightenment *philosophes* (as French Enlightenment figures defined themselves) are strikingly inaccurate. For example, the Abeka history identifies Voltaire as a political revolutionary, a view that would certainly have surprised him.[11] In fact, Voltaire's political stance was among the more conservative of eighteenth-century French *philosophes*; he supported reform of the monarchy or governance by an "enlightened despot." Voltaire was, however, a wickedly effective satirist, ridiculing myriad targets, including many these textbooks defend. His effective, scathing critique of religion would be cause enough for these textbooks to condemn the Enlightenment, despite Voltaire's focus on the Catholic Church.

Jean-Jacques Rousseau is dismissed as one who abandoned his children and "believed that man is born free and that he should be able to do whatever he wants to do. He believed in the basic goodness of man."[12] This statement grossly distorts Rousseau's *Social Contract*, which begins with the statement "Man is born free, and everywhere he is in chains," introducing his discussion of the ill effects of society on human beings, which constrained the freedom they had enjoyed in the state of nature. Rousseau argued for a direct democracy that reflected the General Will. He is nowhere near as unsubtle as the textbook quotation suggests. These histories likely single out Voltaire and Rousseau for explicit condemnation to discredit the two Enlightenment figures with whom Americans might be most familiar.

For these world histories, what was important about the eighteenth century was not the Enlightenment but rather its religious revivals. The BJU textbook gives this fulsome appreciation: "true Enlightenment came as men discovered the truth of God's Word." The social reforms that Enlightenment *philosophes* sought were in vain: only religious revivals are efficacious and religious conversion is the only worthy goal. It points to German pietism as a counterweight to the Enlightenment, as men like August Francke trained missionaries and established institutions "that emphasized godliness and Christian wisdom." However, pietism was destined to fail because it "emphasized experience over doctrine."[13] Although these curricula rarely discuss Protestant theology or acknowledge differences between Protestants, they condemn any significant manifestation of Protestantism that challenges Calvinist theology, even though pietists, like contemporary evangelicals, emphasize religious experience more than theology. These curricula consistently disparage German theologians after Luther, probably because they developed biblical criticism.

The real "Enlightenment" is the religious reinvigoration that occurred in a variety of manifestations—the Wesleyan revival in England and the First Great Awakening in America, the rise of pietism and the Moravian Brethren in Germany.[14] Particularly important was the "mighty spiritual awakening [that] shook England as God blessed the preaching of faithful men." Among those men was John Wesley, whom the BJU textbook credits with preventing a revolution from occurring in England. (In a rare highlighting of a woman, a block of text presents Wesley's mother as a "dedicated Christian mother."[15]) When the Great Awakening spread to America, Jonathan Edwards delivered his noteworthy sermon "Sinners in the Hands of an Angry God." These curricula thus rewrite the Enlightenment to make its central figures Protestant revivalists. Religious movements, not Enlightenment ideas or reforms, signal that "the people's hearts were prepared for religious and political freedom."[16] England remains the model of virtue and France its antithesis.

In treating this period of high intellectual and cultural achievement dominated by new ideas, these histories see human reason as negative. As a result, "the Age of Enlightenment proved to be almost a new 'Dark Age' for France." While the Abeka textbook distinguishes reason from truth and uses the distinction to repudiate reason, the BJU chapter on the Age of Reason begins by recognizing that God gave man reason, although it is darkened by sin. "Only by the entrance of God's Word into the heart can a person receive light and understanding." Enlightenment thinkers, however, failed to use reason appropriately. They "refused to acknowledge the authority of Scripture and instead exalted their reason to a place of supreme authority." This textbook distinguishes between good and evil uses of reason. For example, rejecting Roman Catholicism or its vestiges in Anglicanism was an appropriate use of reason, but using reason to examine religion critically was not. These curricula find particularly worrisome that human beings could deploy reason to address social problems: "Philosophers of the Enlightenment looked to human reason as the solution to all of life's problems."[17]

These histories are in a quandary in considering Enlightenment social analyses. They consider social criticism acceptable only if it fosters religion or the economic and social ideas they endorse. One might expect them to appreciate Enlightenment attacks on the Roman Catholic Church or the monarchy, but instead they condemn Enlightenment attacks on "the traditional institutions of home, church, and government."[18] Enlightenment attacks on absolutism are illegitimate, even though they resemble their own, perhaps because they were made on rational rather than religious grounds. Of course, when Enlightenment thinkers pointed out the absurdities of Catholic religious practices and beliefs, some of those criticisms could just as readily apply to Protestantism. It is irrefutable that no Enlightenment thinker would advocate theocracy or the enforcement of religious mores, or counsel resignation to social ills as punishment for sin, as these curricula do.

The BJU history grapples with Enlightenment political thought probably because of its generally accepted connection to the early United States. Enlightenment thinkers, like the founders of the new nation, were influenced by Locke's claim that men had natural and inalienable rights. Even though these curricula accept Locke as influential, for them, only God gives rights, and government is His prerogative; human beings do not form governments. Enlightenment thinkers were thus mistaken in believing that men were empowered to form or change governments.

For these curricula, the greatest problem of the Enlightenment was irreligion, which would lead France to perdition, otherwise known as the French Revolution. The Abeka history contends that "atheistic ideas of the Enlightenment laid the foundation for the French Revolution and all the turmoil and horrors that it brought the French people."[19] And the Revolution will lead, apparently inevitably, to the evils of socialism. The ties between the Enlightenment, the Revolution, the Terror, and socialism are firm. France has always and definitively been on the wrong side of history.

The Abeka history reduces the French Revolution to the Terror, which is the result of bad Enlightenment ideas. To describe the Terror, it simply cites a passage from Isaiah 39:7–8: "And of thy sons that shall issue from thee, which thou shalt beget, shall they take away; and they shall be eunuchs in the palace of the king of Babylon," even though its relevance to the revolution is unclear. It objects too that the French Revolution "abolished the divinely established seven-day week" in favor of ten-day decades instead, citing Genesis 2:2–3, that God rested on the seventh day of creation and the injunction of the Book of Exodus to do no work on the Sabbath. In this account, there is no possibility that the Bible was simply describing a conventional marking of time. Instead, Genesis established an immutable calendar. Ultimately, the French Revolution illustrates the saying "that a revolution devours its own," and Proverbs 11:5, "the wicked shall fall by his own wickedness," condemns the French collectively.[20] The French Revolution provides such a negative example that these curricula will easily differentiate it from the virtuous, nonrevolutionary American Revolution they assert.

A text box labeled "through the eyes of Faith" in the BJU history points to a host of Bible verses as relevant to the ensuing discussion of the French Revolution. It begins with the premise that "God permitted different results to occur in the American and French Revolutions" and asks students to consider this question: "How could the French Revolution have brought about the glory of God?" After describing Napoleon's brilliance as a military strategist, this textbook asks, "How does the rise and fall of Napoleon illustrate the truth of Daniel 4:17, 25, 37?" And "Why should this truth give believers a positive outlook on world events?" Verse 4:17 states, "This matter is by the decree of the watchers, and the demand by the word of the holy ones: to the intent that the living may know that the most High ruleth in the kingdom of men, and giveth it to whomsoever he will, and setteth up over it the basest of men." The other two verses reiterate the right of the Most High to give kingdoms to whomever He chooses. These verses, especially significant in contemporary evangelical rhetoric, are frequently cited to sanction deeply flawed political figures.[21] It is noteworthy that the most effective way to analyze the Revolution is with Bible verses. In conclusion, this textbook asks, "Is civil disobedience ever biblically justifiable?" It refers the reader to Romans 13:1–27 and 1 Samuel 15:23 to confirm that that resistance is prohibited by God.[22] This biblical ammunition confirms not simply that the French Revolution was a disaster to be denounced but also that citizens have no right to challenge those God put in power. The stance of these curricula on the eighteenth century could not be clearer: the BJU history concludes its chapter by ridiculing the "age of reason" for its irrational fashions; the Abeka textbook declares unequivocally, "The Enlightenment was a new Dark Ages."[23]

That claim of a "new Dark Ages" is more common and more insidious than one might assume, as its current use among white supremacists attests.[24] It rests on the supposition that all modern-day problems derive from the end of the Middle Ages with its presumably white, homogeneous society in the West, as promoted in white nationalist myths. While the extreme right lionizes the Middle Ages as a period of unquestionable white cultural superiority, much like Victorian mythmakers of an earlier era, these curricula do not extol the Middle Ages, because it is too overtly Catholic, with the important exception of the Anglo-Saxons. Instead, they focus on Reformation Europe as the high point of Western civilization, and they will later praise the Victorians in part for their recognition of the "White Man's Burden." However, they concur with the more radical right that the Enlightenment's espousal of equality and humanism was destructive. They reject the Enlightenment's tolerance, openness, and cosmopolitan internationalism. Instead of Enlightenment, these curricula propose a return to a patriarchal hierarchy and Christian hegemony—goals they share with the contemporary political right.

While ACE neglects the Enlightenment entirely, it discusses the French Revolution as a political movement rather than as divine punishment for the Enlightenment. It describes the background to the Revolution as "a violent and bloody time in France." Like the other Christian textbooks, it largely blames the moral failings of French monarchs. However, it also recognizes poverty and lack of access to political power as causes of the French Revolution.[25] It acknowledges that the people both supported the Revolution and gained political power from it, that the National Assembly corrected abuses and overturned feudal laws, and that Louis XVI lost even more credibility when he refused to sign the Declaration of the Rights of Man. It pays attention to the successive political developments of the Revolution and describes them neutrally. When a new assembly was elected, it split into factions, one of them led by Robespierre. The radicals began executing their enemies, and their circle of enemies expanded until, finally, the committee executed Robespierre himself. After four years under the Directory, France turned to a strong leader in Napoleon, who codified law, established an empire, and invaded Russia. After that defeat, the European powers allied to defeat him at the Battle of the Nations in 1813. ACE notes the role of the Revolution in bringing a new political order into being with an emphasis on civic equality and popular sovereignty. The other Christian curricula do not approach the accuracy or dispassion of ACE, but none of them recognize the way the French Revolution spread democracy and challenged the political and social institutions of Europe, giving ordinary citizens greater political influence.

Just in case this contrast between virtuous, Protestant, capitalist England and decadent, immoral France has not been entirely apparent, the Abeka textbook sets the scene of the Revolution: "there was one fundamental difference between England and France—the influence of Biblical Christianity. France rejected Christianity and embraced the Enlightenment in its place, reaping a bloody revolution." The contrast with England could not be more marked: "in England, spiritual revivals in the eighteenth century strengthened the Christian heritage of the people and made peaceful reforms possible."[26] Political freedom is thus firmly tied to biblical Christianity. Although, these curricula concede, England flirted with Enlightenment ideas, as exemplified by John Locke and David Hume, it was ultimately saved by the founder of Methodism, John Wesley, and the English jurist William Blackstone.[27]

The rejection of the Enlightenment and French Revolution allow these curricula to advance fundamental religious and political views: civil society can have no legitimate foundation except for Protestant Christianity; citizens can cite no acceptable rationale to take social or political action except to advance Christianity; human beings should neither expect nor attempt an amelioration of the human condition. Any improvement depends on God's implementation of His plan for individuals and nations. The negative answer to the question of whether human beings can or should act in the social and political sphere in hopes of improving their conditions dramatically differentiates these textbooks from others. Their views on these questions are also diametrically opposed to those of Enlightenment thinkers.

Conventional histories generally appreciate the optimism and belief in progress central to the Enlightenment as well as its confidence that the human condition could be improved through education, philosophy, economic growth, and political reform. It empowered human beings to challenge tradition and authority through critical analysis and appeals to public opinion. Science gave human beings the sense that they could rationally master nature and use it to improve human health and well-being, particularly through improvements in medicine and technology—an important legacy of the Enlightenment to the modern world.

Some history textbooks might, as recent scholarship does, criticize the Enlightenment for its sense that the West was "civilized" or more advanced than other parts of the world. But these Christian curricula, unlike scholarly critiques of the Enlightenment, appreciate that the West both civilized and Christianized the non-Christian world. But they do not appreciate such efforts until the advent of nineteenth-century Protestant missionaries.

The Enlightenment advocated the use of reason to bring about social, economic, and political reform. No other ideas have shaped the modern world as thoroughly. Deism emphasized reason and advocated religious tolerance as a positive good and as a means to end religious war and fanaticism. But for the Abeka and BJU histories, criticism is legitimate only when directed against impediments to Christianity or capitalism. The willingness of the Enlightenment to examine critically traditional society, politics, and economics sharply differentiates it from the complacency or passivity these curricula endorse. The Enlightenment criticism of royal absolutism, the inequities of the French social structure, the role of privilege, and the impermeability of social hierarchy are not discussed in the context of the Revolution. It is not clear that these textbooks see progress as conceivable before the nineteenth-century alliance of missionary efforts and capitalism. If so, it can be produced only by God and the godly, not through Enlightenment and its goals.

The German philosopher Immanuel Kant's assessment of the Enlightenment was positive as "man's emergence from his self-imposed immaturity."[28] In contrast, these textbooks see the exercise of reason as permissible only if it serves religion. Kant challenged orthodox religion with his claim that human beings could use reason to understand the world and define moral values; they did not need to rely on the authority of religion. These curricula denounce Kant for trying to solve the question of knowledge "apart from God"; these issues later embroiled American Protestantism as it wrestled with critical biblical scholarship. More extreme Protestant fundamentalists still single out Kant for explicit condemnation. Christian Reconstructionist Rushdoony proclaimed Kant's view as a satanic solution, as "man seeks to solve 'the problem of God' by becoming God in his own eyes." Rushdoony also condemned Kant's morality as "the triumph of natural

law philosophy," because Kant accepted human autonomy within God's ordered universe as a key to responsible moral action.[29]

When these curricula reduce the Enlightenment to an appreciation of human
reason and a rejection of religion, they rob the movement of its rich context of
social and political ideas. Thinkers advocated a variety of forms of government
from enlightened despotism, to republics, democracies, socialist societies, or
even forms of communism. They adopted no specific or coherent political ideology or agenda but were interested in whatever political configurations might
best advance humanity and increase freedom. But these Christian textbooks
treat the Enlightenment as a wicked intellectual movement without social or
political context or ramifications except for its inevitable connection to the
Revolution. None of them can appreciate the culture of the Enlightenment.
It was a movement that appealed to the public and attempted to disseminate knowledge. *Philosophes* deployed print culture to spread Enlightenment
ideas and ideals, applied science to society, and appreciated the passions and
sentiments as part of human nature. More than any other group, they opposed the authority of established churches and many religious doctrines and
practices, and advocated religious toleration. They wanted a science of man and
society, thus inaugurating the social sciences, which they hoped would produce
knowledge to maximize human happiness and productivity.

In its final assessment of the period, the BJU narrative both narrows how
students are to understand the achievements of the past and encourages a
religious meditation. It notes, "As in all periods, human beings made a
choice: some sought self-aggrandizement; others served God. Some decided to confine all of reality to their finite reasoning abilities, while others
looked to the God of the Bible to guide their thinking." It includes a sober
warning: "As countries must learn from history or be doomed to repeat its
mistakes, so also must people."[30]

The religious right sees the Enlightenment as a direct challenge. The
Enlightenment must be defeated, because its emphasis on reason, humanity,
science, freedom, and political reform led inevitably to revolution, socialism,
and the evils of the twentieth century. It is not surprising that these textbooks
criticize the movement so vehemently as the precursor of their twentieth-
century nemesis—secular humanism. More extreme sectors of the religious
right demonize the Enlightenment as creating a rival religion and enshrining
democracy as a "state religion." As Rushdoony put it, "the democratization of

society goes hand in hand with the divinization of the state. Power and right are withdrawn from God and given to the people."[31]

What is lost if the Enlightenment is rejected as these curricula do? Discounted is a culture of the "public sphere," of lively public debate and epistemological modesty about claims to ultimate reality. Lost is the ability to appreciate an intellectual culture shaped by optimism about human beings and what they might accomplish. Dismissed is the role of education in cultivating talent and meritocracy. Denied is the ability of human beings to both understand and ameliorate social ills. Disallowing the Enlightenment calls into question the value of tolerance, unfettered political and intellectual debate, popular political action, the social sciences, social reform, and internationalism. The Enlightenment advocated for all of them. Instead, for these curricula as for some of its critics, the Enlightenment sowed the seeds of evil modern ideas and political events. What are the implications for Americans of repudiating our roots in the European Enlightenment? The next chapter will explore the distinctive history of America relayed in these textbooks in which the Enlightenment could have no significant influence.

10

"As a City on a Hill"

In their world histories, these curricula treat American history briefly—a short chapter or course pack—at least until the mid-twentieth century, when the world in their view largely narrows to the United States and its interests. Nonetheless, they assert categorically the Christian character of the original Americans, by which they mean English settlers, and their intent to establish a Christian nation. English colonists to the New World inaugurate a new stage in human history, offer a model of human conduct and society, and shape the subsequent history of the world. The Abeka history sets the tone by objecting vociferously to other accounts: "American history is usually presented as a series of conflicts—rich vs. poor, black vs. white, North vs. South, labor vs. management, male vs. female, etc." Rejecting this narrative, it offers "positive, uplifting history texts that give students a historical perspective and its [America's] traditional values." This initial statement suggests that historical interpretation is largely a question of attitude. Professional historians focus on the negative, while the Abeka history tells a heroic tale, promoting pride in our history and inculcating "traditional values."[1]

How could one possibly quarrel with this reading of our nation's past? It presents a fairy tale rather than a history. The narrative these textbooks promote is not returning to "true" history or merely presenting an optimistic account instead of the supposedly cranky pessimism of professional historians. Instead, it endorses early-nineteenth-century myths. Are such myths the best we can do in the twenty-first century to understand our past? These curricula do not acknowledge the limits of the story they tell or indicate the distinctive and peculiar sources that inform them. Their history is not only "true" but will also impel a return to the traditional values of Christian America.

Implicitly, these world histories are committed to providential history based on a Calvinist notion of a covenant between God and His chosen people. Divine Providence shapes American history and thus is prominent in this chapter and the next. The first differentiates English colonization in North America from that by other nations. The second appreciates the founding of the United States as a unique historical moment supported by

Hijacking History. Kathleen Wellman, Oxford University Press. © Oxford University Press 2021.
DOI: 10.1093/oso/9780197579237.003.0011

God. As Bob Jones Sr. explicitly mandated, US history textbooks published by Bob Jones University Press "emphasize the providential circumstances of its [the US] founding and associate its prosperity with obedience to God."[2]

While there is no doubt that religion has always been significant in American public life, these Christian curricula claim that the United States was founded as a Christian (Protestant) nation. They leave little doubt that the nation should be Christian and that Christian values should be promoted and perhaps enforced, but by whom, to what degree, and in what manner is unspecified. As the nature of this "Christian nation" is not spelled out in doctrine or institutional forms, readers of these textbooks might assume that this designation simply refers to the religious motives and sentiments of the English colonists or to the Christian moral values early Americans held. But it is by no means certain that their agenda and that of others who make these claims are benign. And it is unquestionable in these textbooks that every aspect of American success is due to its adherence to biblical Christianity.

This chapter assesses these curricula's contentions about the settling of colonial America, contentions that home in on some essential points of the Christian nation thesis.[3] In contrast to America's demonstrable, well-documented religious history, these textbooks cite early American myths, which confirmed mythmakers' own religious experiences during the Second Great Awakening. Their arguments are doubtless compelling to modern evangelicals: the mythmakers were their forefathers, writing at the height of American evangelicalism.

Modern iterations of this argument build on similar claims developed in the fervent anti-communism of the 1950s. The works of Rosalie Slater and Verna Hall spread this claim through Christian schools.[4] Reinvigorated when the religious right engaged in politics and the culture wars in the 1970s, this claim is integrally connected to the argument that, as the US Constitution does not mention the separation of church and state, Supreme Court decisions affirming it are erroneous.[5] The current insistence on the Constitution's "original intent" reflects commitment to that view and hopes for a Christian restoration despite the founders' sense, particularly Madison's "living constitution" or Jefferson's insistence on "a wall of separation" between church and state.[6]

While historians appreciate the role of religion in early America, they do not espouse the Christian nation argument.[7] These curricula invoke central elements of that argument, but even they do not go as far as many popular discussions do. They may be less insistent because they credit America's positive development to God's intervention rather than human agency. In other words, because early Americans had biblical truth, God acted through American history and favored the new Christian nation. These textbooks thus do not present the founders as Christian actors in a heroic age, as many popular works do. They distill some tenets of the Christian nation position but do not subscribe to some of the most exaggerated iterations, common in popular media or even in the TEKS.[8] Nonetheless, these curricula lay a foundation for more expansive claims, which students educated with them may readily adopt.

Historians are acutely aware that defining a phenomenon as diffuse and diverse as religion in early America is complicated. The issues involved have generated rich historical debates, but, in these curricula, they are settled articles of faith. Core beliefs include the following: colonists intended to establish a Christian nation; if church and state were not one, both reflected and were committed to advancing Christianity. These textbooks narrow the story of the American colonies to one of religion and virtue. The English settlers came to the New World to promote religion and found a Christian nation based on the Bible.[9]

Unquestionably, one can find countless compelling examples of the religious impetus for the earliest English settlers to come to the New World, and seventeenth-century sources are invariably suffused with religious language and allusions. But that is just as true of heretical Frenchmen as biblically virtuous Englishmen. And the founding generation considered the relationship between church and state too contentious to settle, as we will see.

It is worth noting that the Pilgrims came to the New World after they proved to be especially problematic immigrants in the Netherlands. They refused to assimilate and neither learned the language nor accepted the notable religious tolerance of their hosts. As the Abeka textbook points out, they rejected the Netherlands as "too worldly."[10] Many English Protestants who came to this country to purify the Reformation planned to return to England, as some did in the 1640s and 1650s. Some seventeenth-century biblical interpretations asserted that the New World belonged to Satan. When colonists consulted Joseph Mede, an important interpreter of biblical prophecy, he warned that the continent would be a site for recruiting Satan's soldiers for the battle of Armageddon. Mede even considered Native Americans Gog and Magog of the Book of Revelation. Even after they settled in the New World, some colonists looked back to England and wondered about their place. Events of the English Civil War seemed to fulfill end times prophecies. Puritan victories led some to consider returning to engage on the right side of history. Others saw signs of their Christianization mission's efficacy in the decimation of Native Americans, a goal that they saw as intended by God to root Christianity in the New World. Others, notably Roger Williams, advanced more unorthodox views that Native Americans could be a lost tribe of Israel, and John Eliot received support from England for his efforts to convert them. Only Anglican triumphs, first with the restoration of Stuart monarchy and then definitively with the Glorious Revolution, made the return to England of New World dissenters unimaginable. Only then did they articulate a new and separate covenant as a rationale for their settlement of America. The First Great Awakening of the 1740s again revived prophetic expectations, imagining America's role in inaugurating a new millennium.[11]

To further distinguish the English colonies, these educational materials disassociate the "un-American" model of Jamestown from virtuous models of English colonialism.[12] ACE provides a moralistic narrative: under the Stuarts, "there were many idle men in England who could not or would not find employment. These social misfits were the very types sent to Jamestown." This colony was destined to fail because of its settlers' character flaws; they refused to work and thus most perished. When John Smith took over the leadership of the colony, ACE points out, he "abolished the system of primitive communism under which the colony had attempted to function. The socialist experiment had enabled the lazy to do nothing." It ended when Smith decreed, "He that will not work shall not eat, except by sickness he be disabled."[13] (Many Americans apparently believe that statement is a guiding principle of Christianity, even though it misconstrues Paul's injunction in 2 Thessalonians 3:10, which rebuked Jesus's followers for ceasing to work as they awaited the Second Coming.) This early, thoroughly unsatisfactory colony experienced another turning point in 1619 when women arrived from England and the Dutch brought twenty enslaved people to the colony.[14]

Jamestown is anomalous, a negative counterexample of English colonization. It warns that any consolidation or redistribution of community goods is communist and anathema. This point must be vehemently made because some early colonies did just that. But "God never sanctioned communism. The early church practiced a limited form of socialism, but it was 1) voluntary, 2) short-lived and 3) for a specific situation. Socialism promotes laziness which is definitely contrary to Scripture." ACE further insists, "Private property and individual labor are parts of God's plan for our lives." This argument is supported with a host of biblical quotations, which are, at best, opaque.[15] One of those cited, Micah 4:4, "But they shall sit every man under his vine and under his fig tree; and none shall make them afraid: for the mouth of the LORD of hosts hath spoken it," seems a somewhat less than straightforward divine endorsement of private property.

ACE acknowledges that even the admirable Plymouth colony erred. As William Bradford's memoirs attest, settlers in Plymouth set up a joint-stock company, establishing a common fund to be dispersed after seven years, holding land in common, and sharing the products of their labor. Although this practice allowed the settlers to survive, it ultimately failed because "there was no incentive to work, build, and prosper."[16] That sharing or redistributing goods is anathema to God is a crucial argument these curricula make and even more vehemently assert in their US histories. American exceptionalism is as much economic as religious. Furthermore, when the Massachusetts colony benefited from English strengths, those strengths did not derive from its government. Instead, it was "private initiative, not government, that prompted the founding of English colonies in America."[17] Colonies failed when they tried communism and succeeded only when free enterprise prevailed. American economic distinctiveness was evident in these earliest colonies.

While Jamestown's example reinforces this point, the account of the colony is idiosyncratic. Probably because Jamestown was neither admirable nor successful, these textbooks do not use it to illustrate the Christian founding of America, even when it could strengthen their case. The charter James I issued affirmed the London Company's intent to bring "Christian religion to such People as yet live in Darkness and Miserable Ignorance of Knowledge and Worship of God."[18] Jamestown thus had an explicit missionary purpose with an Anglican chaplain, churches, and compulsory church attendance. But for these Christian curricula, Anglicanism was the wrong kind of Protestantism; the staunchly Anglican colony decreed in 1643 that Puritans could not hold religious services there.

Despite injunctions intended to foster Christian behavior, colonists came to Jamestown for economic opportunity. They might best be described, as John Fea, the historian of American religion, has done, as "individualist, greedy, and selfish," and so lazy and inept that James I had to abrogate the original charter and make it a royal colony. Jamestown's tobacco-growing economy was fueled first by indentured servant labor and then by African slave labor. The wealth and stability of Virginia depended on slave labor. As Fea notes, the very founders who would later espouse Enlightenment liberalism benefited most directly from slave labor.[19] Even though the Jamestown colonists are no model, their economic practices resemble those these textbooks usually praise as serving capitalism. ACE does point to Jamestown's Great Charter of 1619 as a foundation for individual freedom, rooted in "traditions of Anglo-Saxon peoples of England."[20]

These Christian curricula disparage Jamestown to better highlight the inspiring models of the Pilgrims and Puritans. These Calvinist colonists were seeking a purer form of Protestantism, as they considered the Church of England corrupt. Ironically, given the argument these curricula assert, they were, essentially, fleeing the English Reformation. They believed that they were bound by a covenant in a Calvinist faith to create the kingdom of God in hopes that Christ would return to establish a millennium of peace. Or, as the BJU history puts it, the Puritans "had been sent on a divine mission . . . to establish an ideal state based on biblical principles." When this curriculum insists both that government "was to promote piety and restrain evildoers" and that "the state was to assist (not interfere) with the church in molding godly character in the community," its ambiguity about the role of government becomes obvious.[21]

In the new Massachusetts colony, political participation was tied to demonstration of religious conversion; only church members had political rights. Even if the colonists did not want the church constrained by the state and ministers could not hold government positions, religious behavior and orthodoxy were required for leadership in either sphere. John Winthrop's efforts in the Boston colony were especially admirable. The sermon he delivered on the colonists' voyage to the New World, "A Model of Christian Charity," urged the establishment of "a city on the hill" and proclaimed that the colonies' religious mission was to "work out our salvation under the power and purity of His [God's] holy ordinance."[22] As the Abeka US history textbook notes, the Puritans "intended to build a society that would fully embody what they understood to be God's truth . . . to offer the world a complete example of Christian civilization."[23]

The common amplification of Winthrop's sermon to argue that he intended the new colony to exercise moral leadership in the world is a myth, according to Daniel Rogers. Winthrop was exhorting his fellow colonists to live under public scrutiny to constrain their behavior—a Calvinist notion. Only in the nineteenth century was the phrase "as a city on a hill" used to endorse American exceptionalism and sanction imperialism. Winthrop's sermon plays a prominent role in contemporary American politics, in which its use reinforces the myth.[24] Not until the Cold War did any political figure cite it. Reagan used it to endorse attacks on communism and college students. It became coded language directed to evangelicals in his 1980 campaign. Frequently cited by the political right, it remains a clarion call to return the nation to its founding as a Christian nation and is enshrined as such in the current TEKS.[25] Under Winthrop's leadership, educational institutions from elementary schools to universities "were founded primarily to impart knowledge of God and the Bible," ACE claims.[26] For many on the Christian right, this model should be emulated in present-day America. Many current educational initiatives are directed to that end.[27]

These curricula overlook any aspect of Massachusetts history that does not support their religious or economic arguments. Winthrop opposed materialism and commercialism, a point they ignore.[28] Nor do they acknowledge the religious dissension among Puritans or the social radicalism of some Protestant sects. Quarrels over theology and church discipline led to the breakaway colonies of Connecticut, New Hampshire, and Rhode Island.[29] Nor do these histories detail the religious intolerance of those who persecuted dissenters like Anne Hutchison and drove Roger Williams out of the colony.[30]

In their US history textbooks, these curricula are more critical of the subsequent development of religion in the Massachusetts colony. (They presumably do not have time to address it in their world histories.) They note that, although the goal of a Christian society was admirable, the state church became a community not of the faithful but of the coerced. They denounce these state churches as responsible for a decline of religious fervor, just as the earliest evangelicals chafed against the constraints of official churches and inaugurated evangelicalism to revitalize religion.

Native inhabitants of the New World are scarcely mentioned. The BJU textbook merely notes the five tribal regions with "no knowledge of the one true God."[31] The Abeka history claims that Native Americans had been dispersed in the aftermath of the Tower of Babel and "forsook the things they knew about God."[32] Certainly, the colonists' harsh treatment of Native Americans has no part of this heroic tale. These textbooks largely ignore that relations between colonists and Native Americans were hostile primarily because colonists appropriated Native American lands. Instead, they present settlers as inspiring models; colonists insisted that public behavior conform to Christian moral dictates and brought Christianity to Native Americans. As Frances Paterson noted, ACE describes Native Americans as "savages," "primitive pagans," and "worshipers of demons" and mentions them only for their assistance to colonists and their conversion to Christianity.[33]

These curricula treat the relationship between settlers and Native Americans highly selectively. According to these histories, Native Americans were grateful for Christianity. For example, when peace between Jamestown colonists and Native Americans broke down, a Christian convert warned the settlers of an impending attack. ACE concludes without irony, "350 of the colonists were killed; but had it not been for the warning they received, probably all would have met their deaths. The Christians at Jamestown were more than rewarded for their missionary efforts among the natives."[34]

White Trash, Nancy Isenberg's recent book, offers a striking counternarrative of the social dynamic of the Massachusetts colony. Dependent on indentured servant labor, the Massachusetts colony forced others into servitude for crimes, debts, or outsider status, using captured Indians, Africans, or indentured servants from outside the colony. Families were required to supervise their children's work, and households purchased children from other households for labor. Nonetheless, these curricula might appreciate even the less savory aspects Isenberg describes as signs of the Massachusetts colonists' virtue; the colony's practices maintained parents' authority over children, men's over women, and employers' over employees. Governor Winthrop established a form of government whereby magistrates enforced both moral codes and the colony's religious distinctions.[35] A hierarchy of the elect enforcing Christian morality as conforming to "biblical law" describes not simply these colonies but also goals of some twenty-first-century Christians.

These Christian histories privilege the Mayflower Compact of the settlement at Plymouth. It announced that the Pilgrims' voyage was undertaken "for the glory of God, and advancement of the Christian faith" and that the colonists agreed to the compact "in the presence of God." It thus grounds crucial religious claims these curricula make. It acknowledges that (1) God's Providence grounded the Christian nation; (2) fundamental religious concerns informed the nation's subsequent documents; and (3) an alliance of religion and politics defined the model of government for the colonies. For Christian conservatives, the Mayflower Compact confirms the religious foundation of the new nation's government.

Claims about the Mayflower Compact and its influence are problematic, as Steven Green thoroughly documents.[36] Its author, William Bradford, described it as his attempt to quell dissent before the group landed, "observing," as he put it, "some not well affected to unity and concord." Less an idealistic statement than an attempt to defuse a crisis by excluding the "non-elect," the Compact divided the group and imposed the will of some on others.[37]

Bradford insisted that they agree to "submit to such government and governors as we should by common consent agree to make and choose." In other words, they collectively formed a government. This document reflects the belief that human beings could contract themselves to a form of government of their own devising. Although this American contribution to a social contract theory of government could be emphasized, instead its religious phrasing gives it renewed salience. These curricula overlook the Mayflower Compact's expressions of loyalty "to King James, by the grace of God both the king and defender of the faith" and that the voyage was undertaken for the "honor of our king and country" rather than for the glory of God. The document bound its signatories into a "civil body politic" to form laws "as shall be thought most meet and convenient for the general good of the colony." That the explicit foundation for the compact was the "general good," without reference to God, these curricula do not note.

Even though the Mayflower Compact seems a thin reed on which to ground the religious foundation of America, the Christian nation argument heralds it as the foundation of the religious significance of late eighteenth-century texts, including the Declaration of Independence and the Constitution. Connecting these documents telescopes more than 150 years of history and disassociates them from their context but does reflect later appreciations of them. Although these textbooks privilege the document, they do not go so far as to insist on this connection: they merely insist that the Bible is the foundation of all central founding documents.

The assertion that the Mayflower Compact explicitly laid the foundation for the Declaration of Independence probably rests on John Quincy Adams's oration in 1821 on the forty-fifth anniversary of the Declaration, which first cited the compact as a source of civil society in the new nation. There is no evidence that the Mayflower Compact was read before the 1790s, so its influence on the Declaration and the Constitution is completely improbable. It was not even called the Mayflower Compact until 1793. In the 1790s, those eager to disassociate the fledging American nation from revolutionary France cited it.[38]

The BJU textbook follows this line of argumentation. It uses the Mayflower Compact to distinguish colonial liberty from the unconstrained liberty of the French Revolution: "Pilgrim leaders realized the need for discipline to maintain order. They knew unrestrained liberty led to anarchy."[39] The Mayflower Compact defined the limits of freedom, the religious purpose of society, and the fundamental authority of religion in society. It became central to nineteenth-century national origin mythmaking as Plymouth and the Pilgrims attained iconic status in the nation's story. Insistence on the Mayflower Compact's importance is ahistorical but understandable, given its subsequent use and current utility in undergirding the Christian nation thesis, not simply in these explicitly Christian curricula but also in more standard textbooks.

The Massachusetts colony offered *the* model of political life in the New World, as the Pilgrims and the Puritans present the most compelling example of an attempt to base a nation on biblical law. For the Abeka history, the Puritans unified a nation because "the American colonists shared a common European background and a Protestant heritage" and all colonists shared "a common respect for English law and *a love for local government*." "Good" colonists recognized government as limited, founded in English law; they were certainly Protestant, and understood legitimate government as local—fundamental political arguments these textbooks make. They were, in fact, able to have "representative self-government because they were dominated by Scriptural concepts."[40]

In developing the myth of the Massachusetts colony, Noah Webster's conversion to evangelicalism was particularly significant. His 1832 *History of the United States* contended that Puritans founded the first real republic based on the Bible and that the laws of Moses laid the foundation for American institutions.[41] About Webster's history, the Abeka textbook makes the stunning claim, "God's timing is breathtaking! Could any reasonable man doubt that history is a story written by the finger of God?"[42] It cites Webster's assertion that it is to "genuine Christianity . . . we owe our free constitutions of government."[43] Rosalie Slater revived Webster's work as the most authentic history of the United States in her influential *Providential History,* in which the new nation explicitly begins a new covenant. Many Christian conservative popularizers revert to Webster and Slater's dissemination of that history as key sources.

By the mid-nineteenth century, through works such as Webster's, the Pilgrims and Puritans were enshrined as the source of religious liberty, civic virtues, and republican values. New Englanders, who predominated among the nation's schoolteachers, eagerly promoted this narrative as *the* story of the nation in the common school movement. Their continuity with these early religious communities made their past the source of national moral and civic virtue. Some nineteenth-century historians even found the religious intolerance of the Puritans commendable. The Congregationalist preacher Leonard Bacon, for example, praised the Puritans for using biblical codes to enforce religious uniformity and moral behavior.[44] The most extreme present-day Christian Reconstructionists endorse similar measures.[45]

These Christian curricula, like nineteenth-century histories and many subsequent textbooks, make the Puritans a substitute for the entire nation. This narrow understanding of American antecedents privileges Calvinism and its understanding of governments as a constraint on the evils of human nature. These premises have been vastly expanded in the public sphere by proponents of Christian nationalism. Reinforced by an echo chamber of books, blogs, videos, and radio shows, they insist that America was founded as a Christian nation on biblical principles that must be reclaimed as its history and current practice.

What will students take away from this brief though pivotal exposition of American colonial history in these Christian world histories? (1) America is exceptional; its true settlers, the worthy Pilgrims, established a Christian nation, confirmed by the Mayflower Compact. (2) They should take little note of the Native Americans, the Spanish, the French, the Dutch, or other groups found in seventeenth-century America; they were irrelevant to the founding of the new nation. (3) Neither God nor any virtuous American has ever sanctioned any form of socialism or the holding of goods in common; a short-lived expedient, it always failed. The distinction between the old world, mired in error, and the new nation with its privileged status is stark. These educational materials present American history as a narrow but crucial set of events and documents to indicate the fundamental Christian character of the United States and God's protection of the new nation. This view of history has important ramifications. God elected the American Christians, who, according to these texts, founded America on biblical principles as a Christian republic with, at the very least, theocratic implications. Students who learn this history are encouraged to adopt an attitude of what might be called Christian sanctimony. They can identify themselves as among the winners of history, God's chosen, the elect.

What about the story of early America these textbooks tell should be qualified? While religion led Puritans to come to America, they also wanted to create a staunchly Calvinist society, emphasizing sin and damnation and stringently restricting and policing occasions of sin and temporal pleasures—singing, dancing, card playing, swearing, and a host of other prohibited activities. If Puritan society was exclusionary, punitive, and intolerant, American society in the late eighteenth century was much less so. A Puritanical society does not correspond to what those writing or endorsing the Declaration of Independence or the Constitution would have sought for the new nation. It is highly questionable to attribute to the Puritans, with their notions of a powerful church and a punitive society, a definitive impact on more liberal founding documents written 150 years later. Making the Puritans the sum of early America not only misrepresents the period but also neglects a flood of recent historical scholarship focusing on the broad array of peoples of early America.[46]

There is another, more disturbing ramification: these histories of the early nation, in laying the foundation for a Christian nation, contravene the broadly held understanding during the seventeenth and eighteenth centuries that the people were empowered to form governments collectively, as William Bradford recognized in the Mayflower Compact. The Puritans were sufficiently imbued with the developing political ideas of the seventeenth century to see governments as constructed by men who came together to form them.

11

The Christian Nation

In 1775, John Adams described the theory of popular sovereignty underlying resistance to the British: "They are the principles of Aristotle and Plato, of Livy and Cicero, or Sidney, Harrington, and Lock [sic]—the principles of nature and eternal reason."[1]

The government of the United States is not, in any sense, founded on the Christian religion.[2]

—Treaty of Tripoli, 1797

In May 2016, a puzzled professional historian posed the question to the American Historical Association Forum, an online discussion among members: Why do our students think America was founded as a Christian nation? Historians responded by noting (1) many who arrived in this country in the early seventeenth century were looking to escape restrictions on their religious practice in England; (2) early nineteenth-century writers conducted a concerted propaganda effort to make this claim; (3) Americans wanted a national origin myth to support American exceptionalism. The American Historical Association Forum discussion might well have added that these Christian curricula and many other sources explicitly lead students to believe that the founders intended to establish a Christian nation. This chapter explores how and why these textbooks give an unequivocally affirmative answer to the question, Was America founded as a Christian nation?

The resounding "yes" that these curricula echo is a brief but crucial component of their accounts. They highlight pivotal historical moments as revealing God's hand in the providential unfolding of American history, affirming its exceptionalism and making it a model for the rest of human history. The Abeka history is unabashed in asserting American exceptionalism: "Because of the faith of the early citizens of the United States and because of the biblical foundation of its government and laws, God blessed the United States;

Hijacking History. Kathleen Wellman, Oxford University Press. © Oxford University Press 2021.
DOI: 10.1093/oso/9780197579237.003.0012

and it became the strongest and most prosperous nation on Earth."[3] Current debates about the relationship between religion and government at the time of the founding are even more contested than those about the colonial period; issues are more complicated, and the stakes are higher. How one defines the founding is a key to what the country should look like now.

The Enlightenment and its long-accepted influence on the United States is an obstacle to this Christian narrative, which requires the denigration or exclusion of the Enlightenment, as we have seen. These Christian curricula focus on the First and Second Great Awakenings to define the new nation as grounded in religion. This Christian nation then, they argue, broke with Britain as a religious cause, fought by the religious George Washington. The founders then produced the Declaration of Independence as a statement of their religious creed implemented in the nation's Constitution, or so proponents of the Christian nation argument assert. In their US histories, these publishers focus more extensively on the history of religion, in which evangelicalism defines the story of America. They extol the two religious revival movements that bookend the actual founding as defining the nation.

Christian America built on its Puritan heritage in the First Great Awakening of the 1740s. This momentous event, these curricula contend, was decisive in the new nation's history: it defined its religious character. Modern evangelicals doubtless still appreciate that this revivalist movement emphasized an intense personal conversion experience as the foundation of spiritual life, just as they do. However, this movement also took positions many of them would find objectionable. It repudiated mainline denominations, not only theologically but also socially, as the clergy had become wealthy, elitist pillars of their communities. This critique of established churches was especially strong in the South, where churches were most firmly tied to elites.[4] By circumventing established churches, the First Great Awakening eroded social and economic hierarchies, advancing egalitarianism—a position the contemporary alliance of the political and religious right rejects. This religious revivalist movement objected to tax support for religion and demanded the right to dissent. It fueled demands for the separation of church and state by Baptists as a necessary precondition for dissident religious sects to flourish. A state religion or "Christian nation" was thus impossible. By the era of the founding, evangelicalism had faded from the public sphere, but it had laid down roots and would flourish again.

To contend that the First Great Awakening exerted the greatest influence on the new nation, these textbooks draw connections between the movement and the views of those who resisted the British and shaped the nation's founding documents. To do so, they neglect the period between the arrival of the first English settlers and the American Revolution. These textbooks rarely treat social or economic changes as historically significant, but here the omission creates significant distortions. Late eighteenth-century culture was far different from that of the early seventeenth century. Population increased dramatically. Land was sold rather than allocated by towns, leading to increased wealth for the few and the development of a consumer culture. The early decades of the eighteenth century saw movement West with greater concentrations of wealth among landholders and merchants, espousal of Enlightenment appreciations of human reason, and the erosion of adherence to Calvinist beliefs in predestination and human depravity. Enlightenment ideas explicitly challenged the grim Calvinism of mainline Protestant churches.[5] Tying the Puritans to the Americans of the Revolution also neglects the arrival of significant numbers of German, Scots, Dutch, and Irish immigrants, to say nothing of enslaved Africans—all of whom make the assumed essential "Puritan" character of the revolutionaries untenable. As these curricula move seamlessly from the earliest colonies to the American Revolution, they overlook the diversity of religious creeds and the variety of institutional, social, and economic arrangements the different colonies developed.[6]

These curricula see the Great Awakening as essentially defining America and contest what was a conventional understanding of the Enlightenment's influence on America. The Enlightenment is so prominent in debates about religion in America because the founding took place between the First Great Awakening of the 1740s and the Second Great Awakening early in the nineteenth century. The debate, both scholarly and popular, revolves around the question of the degree to which ideas and ideals of the First Great Awakening shaped the nation and whether they were displaced by the secular ideas of the Enlightenment. It is a battle for the soul of America, playing out in educational and political venues.

Henry Steele Commager boldly stated a long-held view in *The Empire of Reason: How Europe Imagined and America Realized the Enlightenment*: "it was Americans who not only embraced the body of Enlightenment principles, but wrote them into law, crystallized them into institutions, and put them to work." Commager described the new nation's founders, who, like their European progenitors, strained "at the bonds of orthodox Christianity" and "rejected the rationalization of Biblical mirages to study man in his natural environment, even entertaining pre-evolutionary ideas."[7] This narrative too idealizes America but in an entirely different way—as a model of rationality. Other standard works of American history of that era, such as Henry May's *The Enlightenment in America*, saw the new nation as influenced by two distinctive European strands—Protestantism and the Enlightenment.[8] Historians have frequently seen these two traditions in balance, but the new narrative of the political right rejects the latter.

Much ink has been expended by members of conservative think tanks, school boards, and state legislatures to deny the Enlightenment's influence and to claim that the founders were Christians, who intended to establish a Christian nation on unspecified "biblical law" without a separation of church and state. They and the authors of these textbooks, whether deliberately or unintentionally, revisit critiques of the Enlightenment made in the early nineteenth-century Second Great Awakening, a mere generation or so after the founding.

Scholars of American religion continue to reappraise the long-held, presumed connection between the Enlightenment and the American founding. Revisionists argued that the First Great Awakening of the 1740s had lasting political ramifications and thus corroborated some claims of the Christian nation argument. The religious movement's challenge to authority fostered democracy and empowered some to later support the revolution, they claimed. Scholars noted the religious rhetoric clergymen used to mobilize support for the American Revolution, and conversely that political dissidents used the rhetoric Baptists directed against mainline religion to define their political arguments. After the revolution, clergymen attributed its success to God's favor. Such rhetoric cloaked the revolution with higher purpose and subsequently fueled American millennialism.[9]

These scholarly reassessments are examples of how historians continue to examine our nation's history. The history they tell is nuanced and complex. When historians subsequently reappraised twentieth-century assertions that the First Great Awakening led to the revolution, they qualified initial revisionist claims. They noted that the Great Awakening was a *deep* but not *wide* movement. It affected only a small percentage of the American population, and its influence had largely dissipated by the 1750s. Most importantly, colonists understood their political battles with England during the 1760s and 1770s as attacks on their rights. They made their arguments with the discourse of the Enlightenment, not the Great Awakening. Noted historian of the period John Murrin concluded that, even without the Great Awakening, colonial resistance to British rule would have taken the same form.[10] Evangelical scholar Noll noted that even ministers relied more on Enlightenment political ideas than religious arguments to support the revolutionary cause.[11] As Green documents, by the 1760s, Puritan clergymen reveal clear debts to secular English texts. Writers of the political tracts that most vehemently denounced the British relied on the secular texts of John Locke, Charles Secondat de Montesquieu, and, most notably, Thomas Paine's *Common Sense* of 1776.[12] Donald Lutz, who carefully analyzed the use of citations during this period, found that those involved were twice as likely to cite Enlightenment and classical authors as religious ones, although they cited the Bible more often than any other single source. Lutz's seminal article thus fuels both sides of the argument about whether the revolution was inspired by religion.[13] It is worth noting, however, that, because many sources Lutz examined were reprints of sermons and so biblical citations would have been entirely expected, the prominence of Enlightenment references is even more significant.

Christian nation proponents accepted with alacrity the initial connection that historians posited between the First Great Awakening and the revolution because it supported their claim that the revolution was religiously inspired. Subsequent revisions of this causal connection have not impacted central claims of a religiously grounded revolution.[14] What is crucial, however, is that historians' reexaminations asserted the irrefutable centrality of Enlightenment ideas to the revolution. Nonetheless, for these curricula, the revolution was, in large part, a religious cause; Americans' religious liberty was the crucial foundation for their political liberty.

Historians concur that the Enlightenment dramatically affected political discourse and attracted many elites to less conventional religious beliefs, like deism and freemasonry, but these curricula reject such influences on American history. Nonetheless, it is irrefutable that calls to revolution, such as Thomas Paine's *Common Sense*, challenged British authority and mobilized resistance to it with Enlightenment rhetoric. As John Adams put it, "Without the pen of the author of *Common Sense*, the sword of Washington would have been raised in vain."[15] But Paine epitomizes many ideas these curricula deplore and their evangelical forebears began to expunge from our history—deism, science, international cooperation, and openness to multicultural immigration. Paine condemned "mother country applied to England only, as being false, selfish, narrow, and ungenerous."[16] He also explicitly cited inspiring classical models of resistance to authority. Other calls to revolution compared George III to the cruel, autocratic Roman emperors

Nero and Caligula. George Washington and Thomas Jefferson were compared to virtuous Roman statesmen and orators, Cato and Cicero.[17] Classical
allusions were doubtless compelling to a generation thoroughly immersed in
ancient discussions of political virtue.

Some modern evangelical scholars also challenge the current evangelical
rejection of the Enlightenment. They appreciate the positive historical relationship between the Enlightenment and early evangelicalism. Noll argues,
for example, that, because evangelicals saw the Enlightenment's immense
utility to the developing nation, they forged a powerful synthesis between
the two movements. Even the authoritative evangelical theologian Jonathan
Edwards accepted many tenets of eighteenth-century secular faith—matter
in motion, knowledge gleaned from secular sources, and the pursuit of happiness, for example. This fusion of Enlightenment ideas and evangelicalism
put early evangelicals into the American mainstream. They too were interested in science, accepted Locke and Newton, and used the language of
the Enlightenment to express their ideas. They, unlike many present-day
evangelicals, relied on science and privileged it as rational and objective. Noll
contends this former alliance allowed Protestantism to triumph in the new
nation.[18] Nonetheless, modern evangelicalism repudiates the Enlightenment
and its values as a threat to the evangelical narrative of America's fundamental Christianity.

The period of the founding itself was not, however, according to historical
consensus, a conspicuously religious period. Scholar of Protestantism Martin
Marty documented that, immediately following the American Revolution,
church affiliation was only 4 to 7%, and many church members did not attend. As he noted, "The dominant faith overall was religious indifference."[19]
The belief that the founding of America occurred in a Christian golden age
is more mythic than real.[20] Virtually all mainstream historians recognize the
American founding as strikingly influenced by Enlightenment philosophers,
Locke in particular, and the new nation's ideas of government as decisively
and profoundly shaped by secular natural law, applied to all, regardless of
creed.[21]

Some proponents of the Christian nation thesis use other tactics to
neutralize Enlightenment influences on the American founding: (1)
Locke, with his notion of a social contract as a purely secular foundation
for government and his ties to the Enlightenment entirely too clear, is acceptable only because of *The Reasonableness of Christianity*; or (2) Locke
can be mediated through William Blackstone, giving conservatives

an Enlightenment influence expunged of its dangerous elements. Blackstone's frequently cited legal textbooks provide a Christian antecedent, even if his fervent support for monarchy must be overlooked as well as his respect for the authority of Parliament as the colonies resisted its impositions.[22] As the Abeka US history textbook puts it, "The law of nature is not reason, as Locke decreed, but the law of God." Blackstone, unlike Locke, understood that "man's reason is not sufficient for establishing laws to govern mankind and that only in Scripture are such divine laws revealed."[23] Blackstone then becomes a canonical figure in the conservative understanding of eighteenth-century America and in these curricula as well. The Founding Fathers were thus almost entirely untainted by the Enlightenment.

While the Christian nation argument privileges religion by denying the secular influence of the Enlightenment or of the pagan classical tradition, the leaders of the founding generation were especially indebted to the political ideas of the Roman Republic and the English Whigs. They did not base government on a biblical model. They believed that men could form a government by the consent of the governed. In contrast, these curricula insist that the founders rejected Enlightenment thinkers' optimism about human nature as, at least potentially, good. They "had a healthful fear of human nature and the power of government."[24] The Calvinist understanding of sin grounded the new nation.[25] This emphasis denies the founders' recognition of the political causes of the corruption they saw in Roman history, as they proposed a division of powers between the three branches of government to thwart it.

Although many Christian nation claims are dubious, others are more solid: the founders, like educated men of their age, knew the Bible, and their writings are peppered with religious references. Religious discourse was common, and many of the period's most prolific writers were clergymen. While most of the founders likely could not have conceived of a nation whose citizens did not believe in some form of Protestantism or, at the very least, in a Creator, they expressed various views on religion and even more disparate views on its role in the new nation, particularly its relationship to government.[26]

But these textbooks go further. They selectively interpret crucial events and documents to define the founding generation and new nation's fundamental Christian character. They connect seventeenth-century Puritans to religiously motivated leaders of the American Revolution. They rule out the influence of the Enlightenment, even though it defined the terms of eighteenth-century political discourse.

Another tack these textbooks take is redefining the "revolution" out of the American Revolution: they recognize no right to resist political authority and differentiate the American Revolution from the French Revolution. For the BJU curriculum, the success of the revolution was "due to its conservative nature, rather than a 'rebellious' nature." It further deradicalizes the revolution as a simple tax protest "not against government as such but against too much government and a government that had violated its own rules."[27] English relations with the colonies, according to ACE, were fine until it faced bankruptcy because of the Seven Years War: England had followed unsound fiscal policies.[28] The colonists did not object to paying taxes, but rather to England's "interference in local affairs." The greater threat to colonial liberty · was the Quebec Act, which "favored Roman Catholicism and French law, and the colonists feared for their religious and political liberty." The Abeka textbook praises the revolution's successful resistance to regulation and predicts, "The suppressing of American ingenuity through government regulation would prove to be a difficult and dangerous task for the mother country."[29]

This sense of the revolution as insignificant in cause and effect is a conservative truism strongly challenged by Gordon Wood in *The Radicalism of the American Revolution*, which documents the profound ideological transformation in the American colonies from monarchy, to aristocracy, to democracy.[30] In these textbooks, one would hardly know that a revolution against the British occurred. The Abeka textbook suggests that it was almost inadvertent: "George III proclaimed the colonists to be in rebellion. . . . In effect, the American colonies were thrust out of the British Empire." Those who participated did so extremely reluctantly: "biblical values guided the English colonists in their attempts at reconciliation, their decision to take a stand for individual liberty, and their eventual fight for liberty."[31] As the BJU history concludes, "the so-called American Revolution was a conservative movement tempered by the Protestant background of the colonists."[32]

Revolutionaries sought freedom, but, as the Abeka textbook underscores, freedom must be understood as religious freedom. Liberty becomes possible only with the Reformation. As a result, the revolutionaries enjoyed what Martin Luther famously described in (and as) *The Freedom of a Christian*. By Christ's sacrifice, Christians are freed of the many requirements of the Catholic faith, including the need to do good works; they will do them instead from a joyous rather than a constrained heart. Christians are thus "freed from the penalty and power of sin."[33] Luther's understanding of freedom is the legitimate one, in sharp distinction to secular claims that human beings were free by nature and could form governments and dissolve them to protect that liberty. In America, liberty is possible only within Protestant Christianity. A Christian's freedom, as Luther argued in response to the Peasants' War, does not sanction political resistance. With the American Revolution de-revolutionized, its advent becomes almost inexplicable.

The BJU textbook suggests that Americans on the eve of the revolution faced the difficult choice of which religiously sanctioned authorities to follow. They had no right to resist because political authority comes from God. However, when legitimate representatives of colonial political authority called for resistance to the British, then (and presumably only then) the colonists "were able to support the colonial cause in good conscience."[34] This justification of resistance again reflects a Calvinist political theory, which contended that duly constituted magistrates had the right to resist the king, if he did not rule according to God's law.[35]

In contrast, historians point out that, while revolutionaries admittedly sometimes used religious rhetoric, they argued their cause in political terms and took overtly political action. Their boycotts and demonstrations led to the "Boston Massacre" of five men by eight British soldiers and to the Boston Tea Party. The severity of the British response persuaded many that their actions violated colonial self-government and imposed an illegitimate military occupation.

These Christian curricula see nothing revolutionary about the revolution, because they construe the incipient revolutionaries' motives within acceptable religious terms.[36] As a result, they adamantly reject any comparison with France unlike historians who associate the two as "influenced by the Enlightenment ideas." The malign influence of France could not take root in the United States: "America had the benefit of righteousness, a characteristic that always brings God's blessing." America's Protestant-Puritan heritage protected the country from "the wanton destruction that took place in France." The two revolutions had entirely different understandings of liberty: "the American Revolution recognized the responsibility that accompanies liberty . . . the radicals who took control of the French Revolution, on the other hand, simply emphasized liberty itself." Americans understood that liberty entailed personal responsibility without changing the social order. Unlike the French, who were overthrowing tyranny, Americans were protecting "time-honored traditions of religious and political liberty."

The French Revolution "did not establish liberty or lead to greater freedom; it merely produced social upheaval and dictatorship." Most importantly, as the Abeka textbook insists, "we must also remember that true liberty does not come through revolution but through regeneration." It cites Paul (Gal. 5:1), "Stand fast therefore in the liberty wherewith Christ hath made us free," to claim that Protestants recognized that "true liberty is found only in Jesus Christ."[37]

These curricula extol the leader of the revolutionary forces, George Washington, as guided by Divine Providence to confirm the revolution's religious foundation.[38] Stories about Washington are particularly dear to advocates of the Christian founding. The famous story, frequently visually depicted, of Washington praying at Valley Forge is likely apocryphal, but it has pride of place in the ACE US history. Washington, it asserts, "probably would not have been able to perform his almost herculean task," save that he "was a man of God who had great faith in his Maker." Praying at Valley Forge "demonstrated James 5:16 . . . The effectual fervent prayer of a righteous man availeth much." Washington's prayers were decisive: "Without the hand of God intervening on their behalf, the Continentals would never have defeated the combined armies and navies of the empire of Great Britain."[39]

This famous story of Washington first appeared in Mason Locke Weems's *Life of Washington* (1800), source of the even more famous story of Washington as a boy who could not tell a lie about chopping down the cherry tree. Schoolbooks promoted both myths well into the twentieth century.[40] The myth of Valley Forge serves the Christian narrative of the revolution as a religious cause, largely because Washington was almost completely silent on religion. Given that silence, what can one conclude about Washington's beliefs? He was an Anglican whose religious practice as a biblically literate, once-a-month churchgoer conformed to that of his social peers. According to Fea, Washington believed in Providence in a general deist sense that God controlled the world. Green describes Washington as a humanistic latitudinarian, who abjured sectarian differences.[41] Ultimately, scholars conclude that Washington was not an orthodox Christian, even in the ecumenical terms of the late eighteenth century, and that his religious beliefs correlate most closely with those of eighteenth-century deists.[42] Nonetheless, Washington's *Farewell Address* of 1796, which claimed that religion was important to moral improvement and essential to republics, is often cited as testament to his faith.

As Green notes, the deification of Washington and, by association, the American founding began immediately after his death. Eulogies and biographies claimed that providence guided his actions and cloaked him in personal sanctity, making Washington a Christian who shared his biographers' evangelical faith.[43] Nineteenth-century millennialists saw the founding of the United States as inaugurating the thousand-year period before the Second Coming. The revolution and Washington's role in it became part of their millennial hopes.

Washington's alleged commitment to Christianity links a Christian Revolution to the Declaration of Independence, understood as the fundamental creed of the new, Christian nation.[44] The staunchest Christian reading of the document claims that the nation was subject to God's laws and that rights come from God. Several phrases of the Declaration, some claim, point to this intent, including "our Creator as a source of inalienable rights" and "separate and equal station to which the Laws of Nature and Nature's God entitle them," as well as the invocation of the "Supreme Judge of the world" and "firm reliance on the protection of Divine Providence." In popular writings, these quotations underscore the founders' theism and, for some, the theocratic foundation of the nation.

In contrast, David Armitage's study of the Declaration of Independence asserts that it more accurately attests to the new nation's desire to secure a place in the international community. It was thus a foreign policy document or, as Thomas Jefferson described it, "an appeal to the tribunal of the world." To make common cause with the international community, the Declaration explicitly used Enlightenment language. The phrase "Laws of Nature and Nature's God" connects the document to deist and Enlightenment views. Even the more religiously weighted phrase, "endowed by their Creator," added by Benjamin Franklin, contemporaries saw as neutral enough to be accepted by deists, Unitarians, and freethinkers, as Fea notes. "Supreme Judge of the World," added during the editing process, merely reflected the conventional belief that God protected the new nation.[45]

As these curricula oppose political resistance, they do not recognize the revolutionary language and intent of the Declaration, except for the BJU US history, which notes that every signer understood he was committing treason.[46] In John Locke's sense, signers were reverting to the state of nature ante-contract. People formed governments to secure natural rights, and the government derived its power from the consent of the governed. None of those fundamental suppositions support the notion that government was established by God. Nonetheless, the Abeka textbook signals the transform-ative import and religious significance of the Declaration of Independence as "the most important statement of political principles in the history of the world," as it recognized "that all men have a right to be treated with the dig-nity due God's special creation."[47]

To make the Declaration of Independence central to a Christian nation, some go so far as to portray its author, Thomas Jefferson, as a bona fide Christian—a goal of concerted revisionist efforts. They often cite, as the BJU narrative does, Jefferson's statement that "the God who gave us life gave us liberty at the same time; the hand of force may destroy but cannot dis-join them."[48] This quotation makes a much less compelling argument when placed in context. It appeared in the 1774 *A Summary View of the Rights of British America*, in which Jefferson condemned British taxation as unjust control of colonial markets:

> But let them not think to exclude us from going to other markets to dis-pose of those commodities which they cannot use, or to supply those wants which they cannot supply. Still less let it be proposed that our properties within our own territories shall be taxed or regulated by any power on earth but our own. *The God who gave us life gave us liberty at the same time; the hand of force may destroy but cannot disjoin them.*[49]

Like many quotations identifying Jefferson as an orthodox Christian, this one is less persuasive in context. It makes an economic argument without explicit Christian content.

Perhaps because evangelicals see the Christian nation argument as so es-sential, the dubious use of historical evidence by its proponents has been es-pecially pronounced. Some resort to the historically questionable practice of taking quotations completely out of context or combining phrases from several sources, as if they were a coherent expression of an author's religious views. This practice has become so common that a website at the University of Virginia is dedicated to the careful deconstruction of these frequently cited quotations, which undermines or completely refutes any notion that the speaker or writer intended to convey orthodox Christian views.

David Barton's books are some of the most egregious examples of these fundamentally flawed methods. A political activist, dedicated to "rebuilding the religious foundations of America," he argues that all fifty-five signers of the Declaration of Independence were orthodox Christians, even though he has frequently had to issue corrections about his citations. His book on Thomas Jefferson made such flagrant use of patched-together quotations or quotations that could not be documented that it was withdrawn from publication.[50] Barton misleads readers by claiming that he alone has primary sources revealing "truth" that academic historians have hidden to thwart the true, Christian history of America.[51] (Most are widely available in print.) Despite his questionable methods, Barton exerts an outsized influence as a popularizer of Christian nation argument in right-wing media.

Another frequent but perhaps more forgivable lapse of critical historical method is the practice of using a single quotation by a central founder to encapsulate the totality of his religious views, much in the way Bible verses are invoked as "proof texts." Those quotations have entered public debate as definitive. A deeply religious Franklin, Jefferson, and Washington feature in popular works such as those of Peter Marshall and Michael Novak.[52] The chief founders then become staunch Christians through selective citation, as we briefly saw with Jefferson's quotation. Thet practice of proof texting sets up dueling quotations between those asserting a religious foundation and those refuting it.[53]

The argument that Jefferson was an orthodox Christian is a difficult case to make. Jefferson was clearly a proponent of the Enlightenment, and, while he was interested in spiritual issues, he was a most unconventional believer. He pursued moral and religious understanding and admired the moral precepts of Jesus. But he was also deeply skeptical of the Bible, horrified by religious fanaticism, and intrigued by many religions. (Contemporary Muslim Congressmen are often sworn in with Jefferson's copy of the Quran.[54]) After the ratification of the Constitution, which prevented the establishment of a national religion, Jefferson was vigilant in rejecting any intrusion of religion into government, especially by Presbyterians, remarking, "the Presbyterian clergy are the loudest, the most tyrannical, and ambitious."[55] He considered himself a Christian but a member of "a sect by myself."[56] He would never have heralded Christian orthodoxy as grounding the nation.

In contrast to claims that the Declaration of Independence called for a Christian nation, scholars usually emphasize a secular, Enlightenment influence on the document, citing John Locke's *Second Treatise* as especially significant.[57] The Declaration is fundamentally framed by Enlightenment rationalism; the laws of nature were to be uncovered through reason.[58] The preamble, which emphasizes natural rights, equality, the right of revolution, and the consent of the governed as foundations of government, utilizes

Enlightenment language. The claim that the Declaration of Independence was rooted in a religious understanding of the nation reverts to nineteenth-century revisionists, who sought to give it iconic status. Abolitionists were empowered by the document; it became for them a theological foundation for rights. Abraham Lincoln made the Declaration an authoritative text, underscoring fundamental American values.[59]

Contemporary conservatives make many exaggerated claims about the founders' Christianity, designating anyone who believed in God a Christian. Some founders can be more easily cited to support that assertion: John Witherspoon was a Presbyterian minister; John Jay was a Christian Providentialist; and Samuel Adams was a devout Congregationalist. Even such arguments are undermined by the complexity of views, both religious and political, held simultaneously even by those individuals. Witherspoon was also influenced by the Scottish Enlightenment and Greek and Roman classics and expressed his enthusiasm for the French works pouring into the colonies.[60] Another devout Calvinist, Oliver Ellsworth, paraphrased Locke's treatise to argue for civil government. But proponents of a religious founding are unwilling to recognize that rationalism and religion were not necessarily at odds in the eighteenth century.[61] While the founders held a wide variety of religious views, none asserted that republican values arose from Christian thought or a biblical notion of government. Neither did their religious views require rejecting the Enlightenment.[62]

The desire of the religious right to make the founders' religion comparable to theirs contests the long-standing scholarly consensus that the founders were more free thinking than their contemporaries and that many of them were religious liberals or deists, casual about their own religious practice, and deeply suspicious of religious enthusiasm.[63] Nonetheless, many founders likely assumed that the new nation would be populated by Christians of a variety of Protestant denominations with the range of beliefs and degrees of religious adherence characteristic of eighteenth-century America. Regardless of how they appreciated religion, they did not generally suggest that the government should promote it.

For those who argue for the restoration of a Christian nation under biblical law, the Declaration announced the commitment of the new country to Christianity and the Constitution reaffirmed it.[64] As the Abeka history announces,

To Americans of the late eighteenth century, the hand of God was clearly visible in the framing of the Constitution. They realized, however, that, even with such a remarkable Constitution, a great nation could be built only upon the continued blessing of God, which comes from the righteousness which "exalteth a nation."[65]

This account distills America's success in forming a republic to adherence to biblical Christianity. It gave Americans "virtue and character." Other countries have not succeeded in forming such a government "because their people have not embraced a moral code based on the Bible." The Abeka US history textbook is even more expansive on the connection between the Bible and the nation: "The secret to America's success is the influence of Biblical Christianity." Only it makes possible a democratic republic, as "our system of government will only work in a nation where a majority of citizens are steeped in the virtues of Biblical Christianity. . . . The only hope for a democratic republic is constant Biblical evangelism. The only sure way to save a nation is to save the souls of its citizens." It cites Noah Webster, who maintained that "the principles of all genuine liberty and of wise laws and administrations are to be drawn from the Bible and sustained by its authority."[66]

While the BJU textbook concedes that the Constitution's notion of popular sovereignty was an Enlightenment legacy, it objects that the Enlightenment saw men as essentially good. In contrast, the founders' "Protestant-Puritan heritage taught them that man could not be trusted," and they incorporated their central understanding of sin into the Constitution. Their Protestant heritage thus provided a corrective to any Enlightenment influence.[67]

As Green amply documents, since the 1800s, Americans have wanted a creation myth of the providential founding of the United States to distinguish it from other nations.[68] But using the Constitution to support a Christian founding discounts the prominence of Enlightenment ideas and overlooks the absence of appeals to religion in the Constitution.

Historians recognize that the Constitution was deliberately silent on the issue of religion, unlike earlier colonial governing documents. Green sums up the more usual understanding of the Constitution:

> The Framers taught that eternal truth could be discovered through reason and common sense and that factions could be controlled through the mechanism of republican government. The decision to adopt a constitutional

government could not rely on moral virtue which in turn helped to bring about a detachment of religion from republican government.[69]

Those who instead see the Constitution through a religious lens inevitably point to James Madison, as the Abeka curriculum does. This " 'Father of the Constitution' . . . recognized . . . the need of a Christian moral base in government to restrain the inherent sinfulness of human beings."[70] Proponents of a Christian Constitution also usually cite Madison's statement in Federalist #51 that "if men were angels, no government would be necessary" as evidence. This quotation more accurately reflects a Whig fear of political corruption than a belief in human sinfulness. It combines Enlightenment idealism and pragmatism. In fact, Madison was skeptical about religion as a political restraint, writing in April 1787 that religion could be "kindled into enthusiasm . . . by the sympathy of a multitude," and, even in "its coolest state," religion could become "a motive to oppression as . . . a restraint from injustice."[71] As John Adams remarked, the Constitution was the "first example of governments erected on the simple principles of nature."[72]

As Green notes, even in the relatively brief period between the revolution and the adoption of the Constitution, the support of the colonial governments for religion declined precipitously. He points to a telling example of attitudes about the appropriate relationship between government and religion: In 1775, nine of the thirteen colonies maintained a religious establishment and provided funding for the preferred denomination, but by 1790, ten of fourteen colonies no longer did.[73]

There were compelling reasons for delegates to avoid religion altogether and instead base the government on natural rights of men. Even those founders who were staunch Christians recognized the dangers of religious involvement in government and the desirability of a secular foundation for political institutions. With such a foundation, the new nation might avoid the destructive religious wars of Europe. Even those who were uneasy because the Constitution did not spell out the relationship between church and state would have had conflicting ideas on how that relationship should be defined.[74]

If a religious Constitution is dubious, it is especially difficult to explain away the First Amendment, ratified in 1791, which prohibited Congress from making any law "respecting an establishment of religion, or prohibiting the free exercise thereof." Ironically, it was written because religious minorities, in this case Baptists, maintained that the Constitution alone did not sufficiently protect them from religious persecution.[75] Jefferson strongly supported the First Amendment as guaranteeing religious protection. As he reassured Danbury Baptists on January 1, 1802, "I contemplate with sovereign reverence that act of the whole American people which declared that their legislature should 'make no law respecting an establishment of religion, or prohibiting the free exercise thereof,' thus building a wall of separation between Church & State." Balmer notes that the First Amendment allowed all sorts of religious "entrepreneurs" to disseminate their ideas, and evangelicals at that time vehemently insisted on the separation of church and state.[76]

For modern conservatives, the founders were Christians who believed that legitimate government derived from the Bible.[77] They argue that the founders never intended such a wall. To cite just one example among many, D. James Kennedy, evangelical pastor and broadcaster of Coral Ridge Hour, a radio program featured on some 500 stations, asserted that any claim that the First Amendment intended to separate church and state was a lie. His 1996 book, *The Gates of Hell Shall Not Prevail*, proclaimed "our job is to reclaim America for Christ."[78]

At the time of its ratification, some denounced the document as irreligious. The Anti-Federalists opposed its ratification, attacking it as godless, especially for its failure to have a religious test for officeholding. In the election of 1800, John Adams supported the creation of a Christian state (although he was a Unitarian). When orthodox clergy supported Adams against Jefferson, they indicted Jefferson for irreligion and charged that the Constitution did not acknowledge God. Reverend Samuel Austin, president of the University of Vermont, proclaimed the Constitution was defective, because "it is entirely disconnected from Christianity. It is not founded upon the Christian religion."[79] In 1832, William Lloyd Garrison, who described the Constitution as an unholy bargain with slavery, saw it as entirely unchristian.[80]

While some regretted that the United States had not been founded as a Christian nation, others later claimed that it had been. They could do so largely because the religious terrain of the nineteenth century was so markedly different from that of the founding era. Protestant clergy asserted the biblical authority and spiritual foundation of the republic and the Constitution to argue for temperance and other social reform movements. They promulgated the myth that the Constitutional Congress came to a fundamental agreement only after stopping to pray. Evangelicals frequently invoked such myths. Early nineteenth-century biographies and histories embellished and disseminated them. In the 1830s and 1840s, the Whigs, most notably

Lyman Beecher, used them to argue for a Christian nation. By 1860, 85% of American congregations were evangelical, many of them doubtless informed by these myths.[81] On the eve of the Civil War, both sides used the notion of a Christian nation to bolster their positions. For the North, the religious character of the nation sanctified the Union. The Confederacy used biblical examples of slavery to sanction slaveholding and appealed to God in their constitution.[82]

Early American legal professionals played a prominent role in corroborating the religious founding by relying on British law to ground their rulings. William Blackstone's *Commentaries on the Laws of England* (1765–1769) were a fundamental source for legal procedures in the new nation. He asserted that natural law underlay other laws because "these are the external, immutable laws of good and evil to which the Creator Himself in all dispensations conforms."[83] Such a law could be discovered through reason but did not conflict with divine law. Both elements formed "part of the original law of nature." Nineteenth-century jurists appreciated this claim, as it seemed to endorse a Christian coercive sense to constitutional law: officials must be faithful to Christian law as Christianity was the source of all law. This relationship was reinforced by Joseph Story, whose 1833 *Commentaries on the Constitution of the United States* refuted both a social contract and Enlightenment natural law as sources of the Constitution and instead insisted that it came directly from God.[84] These nineteenth-century views underlie the understanding of a Christian constitution promoted in these Christian curricula.

These textbooks do not engage with the wealth of scholarship on religion in eighteenth-century America. Nor, to be fair, do their brief accounts allow them to do so. However, even in their brief remarks, they proselytize for a Christian nation by reducing the intellectual complexity of the period to a set of claims: (1) the founding of the nation was untainted by the Enlightenment except insofar as that movement can be Christianized; (2) the American Revolutionary War was a minor protest and not a revolution at all; (3) the leaders of the new nation were orthodox Christians who shared a vision of a Christian nation; (4) documents central to the nation's founding reflect this commitment.

For these Christian world histories, America's early history reveals Divine Providence in the New World. They see no appreciable difference between the English colonies of the early seventeenth century and those of the late eighteenth, particularly on questions of religious belief, practice, or fervor.

They do not recognize the wide variety of religious experience and practice in the early United States or consider the religion of non-English immigrants, Native Americans, or enslaved Africans. For them, it is inconceivable and would be anathema to acknowledge that many educated colonists, including many of the founders, were deists who saw God in nature rather than the Bible.

Even if some founders shared the Christian beliefs of their fellow citizens, such beliefs were largely tangential to how government should function. Instead of invoking the Bible as a desirable model of governance, the founders appreciated the ability of men to form a government, although they may also have seen their success as enabled by divine favor. But in their deliberations, they invoked examples from the ancient world and the constitutional monarchy of England and Enlightenment texts. They would have had no sense of the Bible as the foundation of the new nation. They did not favor a theocracy, a government by Christians or in accord with "biblical" or Mosaic Law.[85] The horrors of more than a century of European wars over sectarian differences would have made such a conjunction of religion and politics anathema rather than ideal: religious differences, they knew, divided and destroyed nations.

These textbooks influence homeschoolers and Christian schools, but their central claims are also widely disseminated in the Bible curriculum in use in thirty-seven states. While such courses have not been as heavily subscribed as the authors of the bills promoting them expected, nonetheless they promulgate crucial claims of these explicitly Christian curricula.[86] With wider diffusion of such views, not simply in educational materials but also in popular media, readers should no longer wonder, as some did in the American Historical Association Forum, "Why do some of our students think America was founded as a Christian nation?"

The positive claim that the United States was founded as a Christian nation resounds in the media, endlessly promoted as the way to assert the social agenda of the religious and political right. Such claims intend to revert to this imagined nation. What that means is not clear, but it is not benign. It has led to court cases asserting a positive right to have one's religious views sustained in the public sphere. The right to discriminate against others whose faith or sexual orientation offends a Christian in a commercial or professional setting is expanding from wedding services to health care. Baking wedding cakes for same-sex couples, renting wedding venues for mixed-race couples, or filling prescriptions for contraceptives infringe on religious liberty of the Christian, such cases claim.[87] Hospital workers can opt out of providing services on religious grounds. A Health and Human Services ruling, Protecting Statutory Conscience Rights in Health Care, of July 22, 2019, extends the right of religious objectors; they may withhold information about treatment options or abandon patients entirely without care.

The Christian Constitution argument was embodied in the proposed Constitution Restoration Act, introduced in the US House and Senate in both 2004 and 2005, where it languished in committee. It insisted that the First Amendment did not apply to state or local governments when those governments acknowledge "God as the sovereign source of law, liberty, and government." It contested federal laws, arguing that the Fourteenth Amendment did not apply when religion was involved.[88] While initial efforts to pass that bill failed, its ratification remains a goal of the religious right. The vehement promotion of such views reflects popular fears that the United States is no longer a Christian nation, reflected in hysteria over the "war on Christmas" and "Sharia Law." The Christian nation narrative is so prominent that it is routinely cited as a truism.

The urgency and the vehemence with which students are directed to understand human failures throughout history increase exponentially as these textbooks move into modern times. Their fervor seems to reflect a fear that God could reject America if it fails to remain a "righteous nation." In considering the modern world, these curricula are demonstrably more concerned; they see it succumbing to the blighted inheritance of the Enlightenment in all its deplorable variants from Darwinism to communism, as we will see. These curricula carry these claims forward in their narrative of later periods, in which the United States is the exceptional purveyor of Christianity. Elements of this narrative circulate widely and more vehemently in popular media. Such sources share with these educational materials the essentialist claim that what they say the nation was at its founding should define what it should be now.

12

Christian Colonialism and Capitalism

"It was the best of times; it was the worst of times." The first sentence of Charles Dicken's *A Tale of Two Cities*, cited by the BJU textbook, encapsulates the bifurcated characterization of the nineteenth century these curricula share. This chapter focuses on what they see as unquestionably positive in ascending order of importance: (1) the Industrial Revolution made Europe prosperous; (2) colonialism spread European culture and prosperity; (3) capitalism, the engine of industrialization and colonialism, is God's means to reward and punish; (4) missionaries spread Christianity. Not surprisingly, given these curricula's Anglocentrism, England provides the model of all four for the rest of the world. Its colonializing efforts brought prosperity to native people as "God used imperialism . . . to open foreign lands to the gospel."[1]

Under Queen Victoria, British virtue was rewarded with imperial glory and capitalist success. The Abeka history tells of an eleven-year-old future queen who resolved not to follow her immediate predecessors' bad example, "the Georges and her immoral uncle William." Instead, she "would be good." It reports that Victoria gave an Indian prince a Bible, saying, "Here is the secret of England's greatness." With her husband, Albert, Victoria modeled an ideal marriage for the English nation and, through its empire, the entire world. These curricula lionize Victoria for *the* role for women they extol—wife and mother. The mother of nine children, Victoria became the "grandmother of Europe," as her children married into many European dynasties. Her example allows these curricula to define the appropriate place for women as narrowly domestic and maternal; she and Albert "delighted in their 'domestic home.'"[2] This is a peculiar argument to make about a ruling queen, for she, not her husband, ruled England. While Victoria is an ideal woman restricted to the private sphere in these curricula, recent scholarship reveals a more complex and interesting woman, who was both powerful and sexual.[3] But what wins praise is that, as a heartbroken widow, she "lived in relative seclusion" for thirty-nine years and dedicated herself to preserving Albert's memory. Her policies revealed her rectitude: She banned alcohol and refused

Hijacking History. Kathleen Wellman, Oxford University Press. © Oxford University Press 2021.
DOI: 10.1093/oso/9780197579237.003.0013

to have the Crystal Palace open on Sundays. Its opening ceremonies, filled with prayers, indicated that "the leaders of Victorian England honored God and thanked Him for the great blessings the nation enjoyed."[4] England unquestionably exemplified that "righteousness exalteth a nation."[5]

These textbooks single out Victoria as an advocate for nineteenth-century evangelicals' galvanizing causes, namely temperance and the preservation of Sunday blue laws. She exemplified their focus on the hierarchical family and morality. Most importantly, under Victoria, England was a country with a public Christianity. Many, the BJU textbook contends, recognizing the Bible as the inspired word of God, advocated self-improvement, thrift, and hard work and supported missions abroad and evangelical efforts at home.[6] The Victorians' great benevolence revealed their virtue. "Never before had so many people done so much for others."[7] Victorian "righteousness" promoted private charity, which, for these histories, is the appropriate response to the needy, with the strong suggestion that only the "deserving" poor should be helped. To be deserving, the poor must be Christian and work.[8] The Victorians believed that social conditions improved only with true conversion, such as that religious revivals effected. "Many thousands or even millions of souls were snatched from eternal hell," the BJU textbook notes.[9]

Dwight Moody (1837–1899), a preacher who enjoyed phenomenal acclaim in the United States and England, is a central figure in evangelical history. He features prominently in these curricula because he preached that the deplorable conditions of the working class were due to their bad habits. Moody insisted that social inequities would not be redressed until Jesus returned to earth and that the solution to poverty was evangelization with the concomitant adoption of Protestant virtue. Moody's life story made him a Horatio Alger figure, who preached that conversion would bring prosperity—a resonant theme in American debates about public assistance.[10]

In the United States, Moody's message specifically addressed anxiety that the poor, especially the waves of Catholic immigrants, might be radicalized; they did not share Protestant virtues, which alone could protect them from dangerous political ideas. Moody warned that "either these people are to be evangelized or the leaven of communism will assume such enormous proportions that it will break out in a reign of terror such as this country has never known."[11] The Moody Bible Institute he founded became central to evangelicals' educational mission.[12] God used Moody, the Abeka textbook claims, to bring America back to "one nation under God."[13]

The benefits of science, industry, and the arts accrued to the Victorians, because they lived in accord with Scripture. This relationship, like many causal connections these curricula draw, seems supported by little more than wishful thinking. Before the religious revival, according to the Abeka history, England was mired in crime, drunkenness, and superstition. (It is not clear what happened to the virtuous Bible-reading English of the Reformation.) Religious revival made England's economic success possible but for a bizarre reason. Before John Wesley, the English depended on astrology to know when to plant their crops, but Wesleyanism eliminated superstition and thus completely altered the economic terrain and "work was given a new sense of nobility." It is likely telling that these curricula do not identify Wesleyanism with Methodism; to do so would single out a Protestant sect rather than "truth." Connecting Wesley to the Protestant work ethic also places it in England rather than in Calvin's Geneva or the Calvinist Netherlands. The Abeka history spells out this ethos: "the biblical teaching [is] that God expects all men to work and that all work is a noble duty to be performed toward God." The Wesleyan commitment to work "paid off in greater food production, new technology, and a generally more advanced civilization" and made the Industrial Revolution possible.[14]

Unlike the discoveries of the Scientific Revolution, which, for these curricula, required religious orthodoxy of the innovative scientist, the Industrial Revolution apparently does not. Perhaps attributing them to Protestants inspired by God proved more difficult.[15] Or, perhaps, Darwin was too striking a counterexample. Nonetheless, the Abeka history is fulsome in admiring inventors. It appreciates Thomas Edison's famously expressed sentiment: "Genius is one percent inspiration and ninety-nine percent perspiration."[16] The BJU textbook includes a conventional discussion of nineteenth-century innovations in agriculture, textile manufacturing, and transportation but asks students to consider this question: "How are the discoveries, inventions, research projects discussed in this section steps toward fulfilling God's mandate that man exercise dominion over the earth?"[17] Unquestionably, the answer is that industrial development empowers man to bring the earth's resources under his control. As coal mining indicates, "improvements in technology always improve upon or add to our natural resources," the Abeka curriculum contends, offering a bizarre view of fossil fuels.[18] Nineteenth-century economics is almost Panglossian; every cause had its effect in this the best of all possible worlds. "Great Britain was the country in which all the different elements that went into the Industrial Revolution fell into place," ACE explains.[19] By neglecting the causes of economic change, these curricula give economic developments, when tied to Christianity, an air of inevitability.

Another crucial feature of industrialization was "entrepreneurship," best exemplified by England and America. These two godly countries epitomized the fundamental connection between virtue and economic gain.[20] The Victorians explicitly suggest the positive economic ramifications of conforming to scriptural morality, much as the contemporary prosperity gospel does.[21] Nonetheless, the Abeka history warns, it would be a mistake to put one's trust in man, citing the *Titanic* crewmember who supposedly proclaimed, "God himself could not sink this ship."[22]

The Abeka history rarely recognizes economic factors but instead ascribes historical developments almost entirely to the unfolding of God's plan to reward and punish. In contrast, the BJU textbook notes that Britain experienced rapid industrialization because it had an adequate food supply, a large labor force, and expanding trade. Key British advantages were low taxes and lack of government regulation, always hallmarks of good government that these textbooks praise. But the BJU account concedes that industrialization had a negative impact on some segments of society, bringing miserable working conditions to many. Workers became wage laborers with less control of the means of producing their work, but "these changes were a necessary part of industrialization." Furthermore, those who see only industrialization's negatives overlook the jobs created and the deplorable conditions rural workers had left.[23]

The Abeka textbook doubts that working conditions were ever that bad and provides an example to clinch the point. A certain Mrs. Taylor confided to her diary a dinner-party discussion about the reputed, deplorable factory working conditions, when a guest proclaimed that "people, from starvation, oppression, and over-work, had almost lost the form of humanity" in Lancashire. When Mrs. Taylor went to Lancashire herself, she found "factory people . . . better clothed, better fed, and better conducted than many other classes of working people."[24] Concern about the working class is thus allayed. Mrs. Taylor's diary is reproduced in a collection edited by F. A. Hayek, the conservative Austrian economist who argued against John Maynard Keynes's view that government should invest in social programs and who continues to define many conservatives' economic positions.

These textbooks pay scant attention to the miserable conditions of some workers who lived in cramped, filthy, and disease-ridden urban slums; were worked to death in factories; and died young.[25] The BJU textbook urges students to "remember that the problems—both individual and collective—are the result of sin. In the Industrial Age, as in any time, greed and cruelty, discontent and immorality were to blame for poor conditions." The appropriate response to working-class ills was that of William Booth, who assuaged "the sinful hearts of the poor through the creation of the Salvation Army." Reform efforts cannot remediate sinfulness; evangelization is the only solution. ACE reports that workers lived in "centers of drunkenness and immorality" but concludes with the disconcerting remark that "God is more interested in making you what you ought to be than in giving you what you think you want."[26]

Failure to recognize that undesirable social conditions were the result of sin led even England to make misguided attempts to rectify them. While acknowledging the sincerity of reform-minded members of Parliament, the BJU history condemns them for failing "to realize that increased government involvement in these problems could easily lead to government control of industry and a decline in individual freedom." While conceding that workers lost control over their working conditions and other circumstances of their lives, these curricula do not see such developments as a loss of freedom. Instead, freedom is lost only with government involvement in society, which also produces economic disaster. Even if well-intentioned, reforms were inevitably a "change for the worse." This curriculum advises instead that reforms "should be measured only according to the standards of God's Word." It chides "ungodly man," who "has rejected his obligation to God and sought by his own efforts to correct the ills of society."[27]

The experience of American evangelicals shapes these analyses of the nineteenth century. They reflect the religious fervor of the Second Great Awakening as well as the split between Northern and Southern evangelicals in the antebellum period. The Second Great Awakening was anti-elite, adamantly Protestant, and vociferously opposed to Catholicism, but it was also socially reformist. It moderated the Calvinism of established churches by emphasizing positive rather than negative predestination—the saved rather than the damned. This fervent evangelical revival splintered as myriad theological views proliferated. Mainline churches and seminaries worried that charismatic revivalists, like Charles Finney, felt free to define their own theology. For Finney, revival was the work of man (not God, as for Jonathan Edwards and, of course, Calvin). Finney attracted many with his more optimistic theology as well as his belief that the righteous would soon inaugurate the millennium.[28] He advocated social reform, focusing on the evils of slavery. Many evangelical churches committed to social reform, building hospitals and orphanages, and working for temperance, education, and penal reform. Many were pacifists. But they divided into Northern and Southern congregations over slavery as early as 1845, with Southerners defending slavery and supporting African-American inferiority with biblical quotations. The immediate provocation for the split was the decision of the Baptist Convention not to seat slaveholders on the board of its Home Mission Society. Southern evangelicals rejected the social reform movement largely because it attacked slavery. Their expedient uses of the Bible hardened into the theological principle of the "spirituality of the Church," firmly repudiating any connection between social reform and evangelical Christianity.[29]

While these curricula appreciate industrialization quite uncritically, historical consensus about the nineteenth century is more nuanced. Historians discuss industrialization in economic terms as spurred by technological advances and human ingenuity. They are more cognizant of the social costs as well as economic benefits of new modes of production. In treating England, they emphasize its tremendous advantages with the largest free-trade areas, the best transport system, a mass press, and great social mobility as engines of its industrial growth. By the nineteenth century, London had become Europe's most populous city. Concentrated population in cities exacerbated problems of rapid urbanization, including slums, poverty, and urban riots. Industrialization depended on raw materials extracted from British colonies. Historians do not invoke the Bible to advise workers retrospectively to simply accept their deplorable conditions without complaint or credit the Wesleyan religious revival for producing industrialization. They do, however, recognize Methodists' commitment to the poor.

For these curricula, Britain's activities abroad are as remarkable as its industrial development. Britain's religion and virtue became available to other parts of the globe through colonialization. The BJU textbook recognizes that Britain's pursuit of empire benefited it, cultivating colonies for "gold, God, and glory," but also asserts that, even if gold was the primary motive for some, religion was a very close second. The Abeka curriculum even claims that, because of the social and institutional benefits British colonialization provided, none of her colonies wanted to leave Britain but hoped instead to become "Little Britains," which became "great nations" because of colonialization. Furthermore, "many of these colonies . . . came to enjoy the Christian influence that made Victorian England great."[30]

Just as their view of colonialization is entirely too uncritical, so too these Christian curricula wax lyrical about the benefits of British rule for India. Protestant missionaries' efforts were edifying. William Carey was an ideal missionary. In 1792, his influential work, *An Enquiry into the Obligations of Christians to Use Means for the Conversion of Heathens*, advanced the then novel claim that British Christians must carry the good news overseas. He not only translated the Bible into forty Indian languages but also "did much to discourage the Hindu practice of idols and suttee." He recruited others to fulfill the Biblical injunction "Go ye into all the world, and preach the gospel." The missionary Amy Carmichael worked to "rescue Indian girls from a life of prostitution in the pagan temples."[31] Agents of positive change are almost invariably and exclusively missionaries, and colonialism created opportunities for heroic missionaries to backward lands.

Although these textbooks see colonialization and Christianization as complementary endeavors, in fact, their diverse goals often brought them into conflict. Missionaries recognized that imperialism made their efforts possible and were often willing to serve the colonizers' political ends. But their work often conflicted with imperialism. When they advocated for native peoples, they ran afoul of colonial administrators. Missionary work, in these textbooks, is entirely and unquestionably positive: "With Christianity and the Bible came a written language, education, literature, and a more humane treatment of Indian people." The relationship between the Bible and the benefits of colonialization is causal, as an Indian prince recognized. "'Where did the English-speaking people get all their intelligence, and energy, and cleverness, and power?" he asked. "It is their Bible that gives it to them. And now they bring it to us and say, 'This is what raised us. Take it and raise yourselves.'"[32] The Abeka account uses this inspiring anecdote to sum up colonialism.

This focus on missionaries' efforts is not surprising, as missionary zeal fueled nineteenth-century American evangelicals' efforts abroad and at home. When they looked at their own nation, they saw a population in need of conversion. "Christianize the immigrant," evangelical leader Josiah Strong declared, "and he will be easily Americanized." Ironically, given the harsh anti-evolutionary stance these textbooks take, they view society in social Darwinist terms with survival of the fittest applied to human beings and to races. Britain's colonial outreach demonstrated the preeminence of Anglo-Saxons. Part of what would come to be called "the white man's burden" was the obligation to share the strengths of the Anglo-Saxon race, particularly

Protestant Christianity, with more benighted and less developed peoples.[33] For nineteenth-century Americans, Anglo-Saxon superiority was reflected in their commitment to Protestantism and democracy. These textbooks appreciate only the former, as they, like most modern conservatives, emphasize that the United States is a republic to discount democracy. They do not consider the greater democratization of nineteenth-century governments as positive: when governments became more representative, people began to make completely inappropriate demands on them. They "began to expect the government to be directly involved in establishing and funding various social programs."[34]

English political and economic involvement on the Indian subcontinent is incidental to its religious mission and treated rather perfunctorily in these textbooks. In discussing Robert Clive's victory over Indians who sided with the East India Company, these curricula give little indication of Indian resistance to British colonialism. They give no reason for the rebellion and do not mention its bloody suppression. They assess colonial institutions almost entirely for their impact on missionary efforts. Thus the political power of the British East India Company was reprehensible. It did not support missionaries' work, because it impeded the company's commercial relationship with Hindus and Muslims.

An unquestioned assumption these curricula share is that the non-Western world benefited from Western involvement. They give only occasional hints that the colonized were not entirely amenable to colonizers' efforts. An inkling is the Sepoy Revolt in India, when Indian troops rebelled against British rule. The BJU history notes in passing that some native people objected to "the 'superior' attitude of most Westerners" and to the disparagement and destruction of their cultures.[35] Despite minor criticisms, they portray the English colonies as both admirable and successful. Many South Asians, however, would quarrel with this rosy view of the colonial enterprise, as do contemporary scholars.

British colonialism faced more overt challenges elsewhere, these curricula concede. Australia, which had replaced the American colony of Georgia as Britain's penal colony, was in urgent need of moral regeneration. But "as biblical standards of morality were established under Britain's watchful eye, Australian society grew more stable." Britain's impact on New Zealand was far more negative. They exposed the Maoris to alcoholism, violence, and modern weapons. Christian missionaries had to overcome British settlers' bad influence on the native population. The BJU history acknowledges that occasionally greedy officials enriched themselves, some colonists abused natives, and colonizers sometimes ignored traditional boundaries and "downgraded native cultures."[36]

Such limited criticisms do not significantly temper these textbooks' enthusiasm for imperialism as the source of civil order, bureaucracy, and building programs in colonies. The religious benefits were the most significant. Along with the news of salvation, missionaries brought attitudes of political and social equality. The impetus to self-rule developed in India from exposure to "the political ideas of the eighteenth-century."[37] Again, this is an untenably positive view of colonialism, but it is worth noting the irony that Enlightenment ideas apparently were beneficial to India but had little impact on the United States or England itself.

The case of China poses some difficulties for the positive colonial narrative. ACE frankly acknowledges that European colonies intended "to promote European wealth and influence." It recognizes that Chinese resentments over foreign interference led to the Boxer Rebellions of 1899 and 1900. However, China does provide an example of an inspiring missionary, J. Hudson Taylor, who established the China Inland Mission. China's resistance to British trade, especially in opium, led to the Opium Wars—blurring the fundamental fact that Britain demanded that it be allowed to export opium to China! A British victory forced China to open its ports and to give them Hong Kong. The West's intervention in China and its insistence on "extraterritoriality," meaning that Western citizens accused of crimes in China would be tried in their own nations' courts, increased tensions. Secret societies, dedicated to rooting out Western influences, formed. The Boxer rebellion terrorized both Chinese and Western Christians, because, according to BJU, they considered Christianity merely a Western religion (presumably as opposed to the truth).[38] Both British and American troops intervened. These curricula do not question intervention in China, even when it fostered the drug trade and addiction.

Japan, a backward feudal society, resisted the beneficial influence of the West, according to these histories. Matthew Perry's arrival with a trade agreement that many Japanese did not want led to civil war. Once the emperor was back on the throne after the Shogunite (the bureaucrats who controlled foreign policy and the military) was overthrown, Perry declared, "The uncivilized customs of former years shall be abandoned." Japan developed rapidly once it sought guidance from Western ideas and institutions.[39] In these curricula, the West is thus the agent of cultural and religious salvation.

These textbooks treat African colonization more cursorily. Less clearly an explicitly English and religious endeavor, colonization there they see as competition among European nations to control territory and resources and thus report it uncritically. As the BJU textbook notes, before 1880, Europe controlled only 10% of Africa, but intense competition among European countries meant that, by 1914, only Liberia and Ethiopia were still independent. Britain, intent on controlling the Suez Canal, took control over the Egyptian economy and government to protect its trade in India and the Far East.[40] The French became involved in Africa, when Louis-Philippe established the elite army corps of the Foreign Legion in 1831 to control West Africa. Belgium gained control of the Congo in 1908. Germany, initially preoccupied by reunification, eventually secured Tanzania and Namibia.

These curricula describe the continent as the "White Man's Grave," because of the difficulties colonizers faced in penetrating it and surviving its climate. Missionary efforts were complicated by African suspicions that white men were slave traders. The Abeka textbook concedes that colonizers were divided in their approach to Africa: some wanted to exploit it and others wanted to save it. But even when their motives were not idealistic, the British brought civilization. For example, once the British had fought the Dutch settlers in the Boer War, the Union of South Africa became the most progressive and prosperous African country. Ultimately, these educational materials do not question the legitimacy of colonizing powers advancing their interests, no matter how exploitative those policies. Thus there can be no question but that British shipping interests had to be protected with the Suez Canal.[41]

Although "imperialism was an economic and political movement," the BJU history appreciates it as ushering in the greatest period of missionary activity since the early Christian era. As previously noted, these textbooks do not acknowledge earlier Catholic missionary efforts across the globe. In the nineteenth century, godly men and women dedicated their lives to carrying out the Great Commission.[42] Africa benefited from heroic Christian missionaries, most notably David Livingstone, best known as an explorer of Africa.[43]

While the BJU textbook notes nationalism and industrialism as other motives for imperialism, it insists that they pale in comparison to religious aims. Europeans, especially the virtuous English, responded to Rudyard Kipling's call to take up the "White Man's Burden" and "launched sincere efforts to improve education, abolish slavery, and stamp out disease and famine."[44] Ironically, social improvements in the colonies are extolled likely because they win converts, while those at home are deplored.

When these histories contend that colonization bestowed civilization and Christianity, they present an extremely limited and distorted history. They underreport the negative effects of colonization on the colonized, who faced massive dislocation of populations, dispossession of lands, and, in some cases, ethnic cleansing. The colonized lost wealth and became the exploited labor of the colonizers. Colonial rulers and administrators enhanced their power by cultivating or even creating ethnic and religious divisions; they often introduced authoritarian government. These curricula do not recognize the enormous financial benefits colonizers derived from goods and raw materials or the humanitarian disasters they produced. The exploitative and inhumane labor practices enforced by rubber companies in the Belgian colony of Congo were so egregious—slave labor, torture, mass murder, and mutilation, notably cutting off hands for minor infractions—that they generated international outrage. Scholars recognize the massive decline in population, as workers were worked to death and diseases spread, as genocide. In 1904, the Germans in South West Africa (present-day Namibia) violently repressed a rebellion by the Herero people. The men were executed; women and children were driven into the sea; prisoners were placed in camps—a grim foreshadowing of future German policies. Presenting resistance to colonialism as insignificant seriously misrepresents the realities of colonialism; resistance was a consistent feature of colonial interactions.

While these curricula see the influence of the West in only one direction as the colonized benefited from Western civilization and Christianity, recent historical studies recognize that both parties were transformed for good and ill by their interactions. Historians focus on the relationship between the two parties to detail their reciprocal influence and their ongoing impact on modern questions of identity and multiculturalism. The West learned about other civilizations. Napoleon's campaign in Egypt exerted a profound impact on the arts of the West, for example. Even missionaries' impacts were also less one-sided than these curricula would have one believe. When they brought Protestant Christianity, non-Christian religions were melded to Christianity, changing religious practices and beliefs of colonial Christians.[45]

These complexities of the colonial relationship do not feature in these curricula's discussion of the United States as a colonial power. It enjoyed the benefits of colonization after the Roosevelt Corollary (1904) to the Monroe Doctrine authorized US intervention in Latin America where its interests were threatened. The continent's immediate problems were rooted in the evil of political revolution imported from France and inspired by the Napoleonic Wars. Its long-term discontents focused on Spaniards, who used "their position selfishly to amass personal fortunes." To repudiate the Spanish and sanction US involvement in support of independence movements, these curricula see them as carried out by "educated people," that is to say, by elites who feared popular liberation movements.

The BJU textbook deplores the characteristic degeneration of liberation movements into popular rebellions: independence movements brought new leaders to power who were then overthrown by military dictators; nations then experienced sectional conflicts followed by civil wars. Unscrupulous leaders, the devastation of war, and racial division characterized Latin American liberation. These curricula blame the Spanish and the Catholic Church for this appalling pattern. In contrast, the actions of the United States in "policing of Latin America" are disinterested and commendable. The United States had to exercise greater control to redress prior Spanish involvement in Latin America.[46]

Nonetheless, America's laudatory efforts could not overcome Latin America's intractable problems. But, the BJU textbook insists, the United States understood that the problem was one of faith. President William McKinley claimed that, after "the Philippines had dropped into our laps," he sought God's guidance and determined that "they were unfit for self-government." He then concluded, "There was nothing left for us to do but to take them all . . . uplift and civilize and Christianize them."[47] Unmentioned is the ensuing three years of war with approximately 200,000 civilian deaths.[48]

The interests of those colonized in the Western hemisphere are not discussed. Colonies simply served US political and economic interests or Christianization efforts. These narratives do not acknowledge that colonial independence movements, apart from Brazil's, were reactionary. Creole elites fought to thwart the impact of reform movements that might jeopardize their privilege.

Not surprisingly, given that these curricula understand the United States as the beneficiary of divine favor, they focus on its great prosperity "primarily from God's blessing and provision." Throughout the nineteenth century—even during the Civil War—the American nation experienced a great spiritual revival, so "God allowed this young nation to enjoy material prosperity and to become a major world power."[49] These curricula overlook that slave labor fueled economic growth. For the Abeka textbook, the Civil War was "brought on by sectional differences between the North and the South."[50] The BJU account simply lists slavery as one of many irresolvable differences between North and South and describes the immediate cause of the Civil War as the question of whether Western states would join the Union as slave or free. Ultimately, "the Union was preserved, but the wounds of war were slow to heal." This textbook treats the Civil War as a mere sectional dispute and is almost mute on slavery.[51] The Abeka history goes further, insisting that most slave owners treated their slaves well. It acknowledges that the African slave trade complicates this rosy scenario but places it in a context that largely exculpates England and the United States. The Portuguese brought slaves to Europe in small numbers in the fifteenth century, and the Spanish first enslaved Native Americans. Once African slaves had proved to be better laborers than Native Americans, an extensive slave trade developed, ultimately bringing "thousands of black slaves to Brazilian plantations."[52] By emphasizing that the trade was carried out primarily by Africans against other Africans, the curricula diminish US involvement in the slave trade and relativize the evils of slavery.

These publishers' American history textbooks develop their analyses of slavery and the causes of the Civil War more extensively with deeply disturbing elements. In the Abeka account, slavery bestowed the benefits of evangelization, as "God gave Christian slaves the ability to combine the African heritage of song with . . . Christian praise." The spiritual cultivated the slaves' patience to "wait on the Lord" and to learn that "the truest freedom is freedom from the bondage of sin." Such patience was presumably necessary, because "by first giving them their spiritual freedom, God prepared the slaves for their coming physical freedom."[53] The BJU textbook uncritically describes slavery as integral to Southern culture. While noting the obvious disjuncture between slavery and "all men are created equal," it points out that, on the eve of the Civil War, "some even insisted the Southern slave culture cultivated the virtues of honor, courage, duty and dignity." It also comments, "Slavery also provided educated Southerners the time to better themselves intellectually." Both the BJU and Abeka textbooks present states' rights as the fundamental issue provoking secession and argue the constitutional justification for it. These textbooks idealize Confederate general Stonewall Jackson as a man of God and Robert E. Lee as a man of integrity, bound by duty.[54] The Abeka account features a curiously contemporary anecdote of a Northern abolitionist burning the American flag to impugn abolitionists' patriotism.[55] The BJU textbook acknowledges the Ku Klux Klan as racist but defends it as a force for moral improvement, "fighting the decline in morality and using the symbol of the cross to target bootleggers, wife beaters, and immoral movies."[56]

Narratives as sympathetic and exculpatory of the South as these do not, needless to say, reflect the historical consensus on this period. The neglect or positive treatment of slavery in these textbooks fits the narrative promoted by Southern evangelicals when they broke with their Northern brethren over that issue. They rallied to the Confederacy and cited biblical support for it.[57] In the aftermath of defeat, Southern evangelicals promoted the myth of the "Lost Cause" and the cult of heroes fallen in defense of a chivalrous, virtuous white culture. Significantly, Bob Jones Sr. was the son of a Confederate soldier, named for his father's fallen comrade, and a firm believer in the Lost Cause.[58] In the aftermath of the Civil War, many Southern preachers argued that the South alone was truly religious. Defeat was not a divine repudiation of their cause but rather a sign that evangelicals had to more rigorously espouse states' rights, white supremacy, and the economic status quo to retain God's favor.[59] Southern evangelicals rejected social reform as threatening and distinct from the "spirituality of the Church," just as these textbooks do.[60]

When Southern evangelicals supported slavery as divinely sanctioned, they insisted that their reading of the Bible was authoritative and condemned those who disagreed as non-Christian.[61] For them, the commitment to biblical literalism entailed acceptance of slavery and vice versa. Similarly, they focused on the threats Catholics and Jews posed to Christianity and supported nativist movements and the Ku Klux Klan. Southerners warned about immigration's dangerous impact on the white race, citing works such as Madison Grant's bestselling book, The Passing of the Great Race (1916).[62] Grant, a noteworthy eugenicist, asserted scientific racism and crafted harsh anti-immigration and anti-miscegenation laws.

The treatment of slavery in these Christian histories fits this rewriting of the Civil War.[63] That effort, as has recently become more obvious, was by no means restricted to the nineteenth and early twentieth centuries. The Lost Cause myth regained currency in response to the civil rights movement of the 1950s and 1960s. For Southern evangelicals, the movement explicitly raised fears of interracial marriage. The editor of the Baptist Bible Fellowship warned that the civil rights movement intended "to make intermarriage between Whites and Negroes as commonplace as black tomcats squalling in back alleys."[64] Rushdoony, the noted Christian Reconstructionist theologian, added other religious dimensions to this mythology by insisting that only Confederates had resisted the impact of humanism and maintained patriarchy—*the* Christian family value.[65] These textbooks, all produced in the South, may intend to appeal to Southern sensibilities by treating slavery obliquely or nonjudgmentally. The effort to scrub US history of slavery or downplay its negative impact is disturbing particularly because it resonates in the current national conversation about race and social welfare. Numerous cities, particularly in the South, remain conflicted over prominent monuments to Civil War leaders. The Lost Cause mythology, whether scrubbed of its most vehement racism or not, remains salient.

These textbooks use biblical slavery as injunctions to present-day employers and employees. The biblical master-slave relationship, spelled out in Leviticus 25:39–46, Ephesians 6:5–9, Genesis 1:27, Leviticus 19:18, and Luke 10:25–37, is invoked as a model for twentieth-century American labor relations.[66] The verses from Leviticus emphasize the obligations of the slave or servant to his master as well as the expansive power of the slaveholder over slaves who were not Jews; they could be bequeathed to one's heirs. The verses from Ephesians counsel "servants be obedient to your master . . . with fear and trembling as unto the Lord." Against this is set the tale of the Good Samaritan, and, for inexplicable reasons, the passage from Genesis that God made them male and female.

These passages have disquieting and immediately relevant implications. On the one hand, they sanctioned slavery when it involved those of other nations. Only then was a slave a possession to be passed on. The injunction to the slave or the servant to be obedient is used in some conservative circles as a "biblical law" model for the responsibilities of employee to employer and taken to require that employees demonstrate unquestioning obedience as a condition of employment.[67] The BJU history's citation of Paul's warning in 1 Timothy 6:1, "Let as many servants as are under the yoke count their own masters worthy of all honour," seems to place workers as "servants under the yoke." As interpreted through specific biblical passages, God thus mandates the subservience and obedience of worker to employer.[68]

Just as these textbooks insist that the US government was grounded in Christianity, so too was its economy. As Divine Providence fueled America's nineteenth-century industrial growth, the fact that its economy was founded on the slave trade and sustained by slave labor can scarcely be acknowledged. Instead, God's election of America supports the triumph of capitalism. Between 1850 and 1900, the United States outpaced Europe during this "great age of free enterprise capitalism."[69]

These textbooks fuse Christianity and capitalism just as it was vigorously propounded at that time.[70] God endorses capitalism, and, as a result, capitalism is the only basis for an economy and, by extension, morality. These curricula also argue that capitalism is the only economic system consistent with personal liberty and responsibility. In this mythology, capitalism becomes a moral system rather than simply an economic one.[71]

The BJU textbook defines capitalism as an economic system in which "there is private ownership of the means of production; investments are determined by private decision rather than by the state; and prices, production, and the distribution of goods are determined mainly in a free market rather than by state control."[72] The Abeka history's definition is more idiosyncratic: free enterprise "leaves the individual free to make something of himself, if he has the enterprise (energy and initiative) to do it." It allows individuals to follow their economic pursuits as they see fit. "Enterprise" becomes individual industry. Capitalism, as these textbooks define it, disallows any notion of the common good as a foundation for society. Government has no social role to play and, whenever it does, it destroys personal liberty: "A nation is free when its people accept the responsibility for their own welfare." Any demand for government services or regulation inevitably means that "the nation loses its freedom."[73]

In the narrative of God's relationship to His people, the new dispensation inaugurated by the American founding was as much economic as religious. It enjoyed a special blessing in its capitalist foundation, endowed with an economic success not accorded to others. "Since America had a unique blend—a people of high moral character with a will to work, the greatest degree of individual responsibility and freedom the world have yet seen . . . the blessings of capitalism were most bountiful in America." Capitalism allowed the United States to emerge as a world power and made the twentieth century "the greatest financial age mankind has ever seen."[74]

Even in its most rapacious form, American capitalism is unquestionably beneficial. The Abeka history identifies Andrew Carnegie as a hero who understood the benefits of capitalism in terms reminiscent of modern trickle-down economics: "the race is benefited thereby. The poor enjoy what the rich could not before afford." The efforts of robber barons "brought manifold benefits to others. . . . they not only provided thousands of jobs but also stimulated other industries." More usually excoriated for exploitative labor practices, the robber barons attain capitalist sanctity in these Christian textbooks as they "helped to provide the world with much-needed commodities to create better, safer, and more enjoyable living conditions for mankind."[75] Those who opposed them were envious or "wanted the government to help them succeed at the expense . . . of successful entrepreneurs."[76]

Robber barons too saw their economic practices as religiously sanctioned. As George Marsden notes, John D. Rockefeller Sr. claimed, "God gave me my money," and Andrew Carnegie propounded a secular "Gospel of Wealth." For both, the capitalist pursuit of wealth was moral and religious.[77] This idealization of nineteenth-century financiers likely finds ready acceptance among the many modern evangelicals who subscribe to the "prosperity gospel," which developed from early twentieth-century Pentecostals who maintained that God wanted people of faith to enjoy wealth. It was readily fused to notions of the American dream and individualism.[78] This is not a surprising position for modern American conservatives or Christians to take. It resonates loudly in many megachurches whose gospel seems to owe more to Dale Carnegie than to Jesus Christ. Christianity comes with an afterlife guarantee and a life-on-earth key to wealth.

When these textbooks make economic arguments, they cite Adam Smith as their heroic spokesman. According to the Abeka history, Smith believed that "most people are naturally concerned with improving their family's material wealth and well-being" and that "economic growth occurs when each family is free to make its own economic choices and decisions."[79] Government involvement in the economy saps families' interest in providing for themselves and produces "poverty and tyranny." Thus Smith supports these curricula's notion that the family is the primary and autonomous social unit. In fact, Smith's *Wealth of Nations* is silent on the family and more interested in the good of society than these curricula concede.[80] In his *A Theory of Moral Sentiments*, he characterized admiration of wealth as "the most universal cause of the corruption of our moral sentiments." He emphasized that people should seek real achievement or "praiseworthiness."[81] In contrast, these curricula subscribe uncritically to Smith's invisible hand or a simplistic version of it—if individuals are left to pursue their self-interest, economic benefits will accrue to all. The material welfare of everyone improves and growth produces a greater number of property holders—an obvious endorsement of trickle-down economics.[82] According to the BJU textbook, Smith advocated laissez-faire economics in which government must foster business interest and is restricted to providing an "adequate education system, road system, and defense."[83] These textbooks thus make Smith conform to their restrictions on government, although they question its involvement in education.

Fundamentally, Smith's economic views are more nuanced than either modern conservatives or these textbooks concede. Their conventional but rather crude understanding of Smith assumes that he advocated modern, completely unregulated capitalism. It neglects his pronouncements on the need for government involvement in crucial social issues, particularly education, urging "the first remedy [against the ruin of the common people] is the study of science and philosophy, which the state might render almost universal."[84] Notably, Smith argued that capitalism would advance the arts and men would become more sociable. They would converse, appreciate their common humanity, and foster one another's pleasure. Early twentieth-century economists too thought that capitalism could most effectively foster common interests.[85] In these curricula, capitalism is not about humanity, sociability, or community.

The BJU history does distinguish capitalism from personal greed, which it condemns: Loving money rather than God leads to great evil; the Christian will obey God by giving part of his wealth back to Him in tithes and charity. This textbook counsels charity, but only once and *only* at this juncture and to justify the pursuit of wealth. It praises John Wesley's advice to his followers: "Gain all you can; save all you can; give all you can."[86]

The economic arguments these curricula make repeat those nineteenth-century evangelicals made to repudiate the Social Gospel.[87] They are also indebted to central economic ideas of Christian Reconstructionists even though the latter are more emphatic in correlating democracy with evil "humanism," demonizing the state as a new divinity or "deep state," and seeing government as antithetical to freedom and Christianity. Those ideas are merely implicit in these curricula.[88] Nonetheless, for both Christian Reconstructionists and these textbooks, the "invisible hand" of the market becomes an incontrovertible manifestation of God's plan, and the Bible sustains these more extreme economic views. As the laws of the marketplace, like the laws of nature, are written by God, the market has a deeply religious import. As the rise and fall of empires are engineered by God, so too God rewards or punishes individuals.[89] As the Christian Reconstructionist Gary North expresses it, "the operation of the market, like the operations of the atom, are ultimately guided by and upheld by God."[90] The Christian right has developed other ramifications of this view: private property is part of stewardship, but government is profane and untrustworthy; the Creation Mandate entails private property and

repudiates government regulation;[91] God rewards work and economic success reveals His favor; and the responsibility of Christians to others is quite
limited.[92] To take any positive action on others' behalf is entirely presump-
tuous because it interferes with God's rewards and punishments. Casting
economic issues in terms of personal responsibility makes poverty an individual moral failure, just as many conservatives assert. Extreme arguments
of the Christian right have been elevated to political and religious orthodoxy.

How might a Christian curriculum without a right-wing agenda treat this
period? In her *World Empires, World Missions, World Wars,* Diane Waring
sees the Second Great Awakening as sent by God to help people cope with
the dislocations of industrialization. She appreciates circuit preachers but
also notes "there were excesses and odd behaviors among a few." She acknowledges that conservatives in Europe and Latin America at this time supported
both a state religion and the political interests of the elites and, as a result, the
poor rejected both. In many cases, "instead of Christians being the bearers
of the good news, they were identified with greed, repression, and heartless
cruelty," she notes.[93]

Needless to say, such critiques of either conservatives or Christians do
not characterize the curricula treated here. Instead, their narratives use
the nineteenth century to draw conclusions historians would contest or
qualify: among them, Western colonialism Christianized and civilized; colonial resistance occurred either because the colonized were "backward" or
would not accept "biblical truth"; capitalism is an unalloyed good. They tell
a story of nations rewarded with prosperity for being Christian or "righteous." The Protestant work ethic signaled Christian virtue rewarded with
industrial development. Social problems, including economic problems, are
due to sin. They cannot and should not be redressed. Britain, the model of
Christian virtue, spread Christianity and its values throughout its empire.
Despite some minor failings, imperialism was positive primarily because it
brought missionaries in its wake and it had a civilizing impact. The failings
of colonizers do not weigh against its laudable Christianizing mission.
Industrialization and imperialism depended on capitalism, which these curricula tie to biblical Christianity.

This saga of virtuous, Christian countries prevailing in the religious quest
to spread civilization and Christianity throughout the world deviates sharply
from the historical consensus about nineteenth-century colonialism. It
teaches a mythic British history of ' "drums and trumpets' in which Britannia

munificently scattered 'British values' around the globe," as Priyamvada Gopal put it.[94] It makes capitalism a moral, divinely ordained economic system. Nonetheless, the positions these curricula take about this period are fundamental to their purportedly Christian political, social, and economic views. Their treatment of the modern world allows them to make such connections much more explicit than in their discussions of earlier periods. Here they directly apply positions evangelicals took in the nineteenth century to define the historical narratives they advance. As these Christian textbooks begin to treat the modern era, they tell an ever more conservative and polemical story as they focus more directly on America. As the next chapter shows, Europe lost its way in the nineteenth century.

13

Bad Ideas and Deplorable Politics

Nineteenth-century American evangelicals were confident that the entire nation could and would be Christianized, and these textbooks relish their successes in advancing that end. Before the Civil War, slavery dampened Northern evangelicals' optimism about the nation's prospects, although Southern evangelicals argued that slavery was consonant with the Bible. But the end of the war held out great hope. This was when many Americans confidently propounded the Christian nation thesis. They believed Protestant Christianity provided its moral and civic foundation. The famous McGuffey Readers, popular in American schools from the mid-nineteenth to the mid-twentieth centuries, enshrined these views in public education. These curricula not only make the history of evangelicalism the central history of the world, but they also revert to history as it was taught during the nineteenth century to sustain a national myth.[1]

While nineteenth-century evangelicals were optimistic about the international spread of Christianity, they were deeply pessimistic about European developments. They looked at Europe through the lens of their emerging battles against theological liberalism and Darwinism. Evangelicals saw these ideas as threatening strings that could unravel the biblical truth they asserted. They saw perils in political revolutions in Europe and the measures governments adopted in response. For these curricula, which continue the battles of their evangelical predecessors, the dangerous ideas of the late nineteenth century made the horrors of the twentieth century inevitable.[2] In the *Christian Teaching of History* (1978), Bob Jones Sr. urged history teachers to recognize that in "the latter part of the nineteenth century, Christians found their society overwhelmed by materialism, secularism, big statism, humanism, and denominational apostasy."[3] The BJU history points to evangelicals' profound disquiet as "many intellectual and religious leaders began to question the authority of God's Word." This development "produced a secular humanism that abandoned belief in God for faith in human potential."[4]

Hijacking History. Kathleen Wellman, Oxford University Press. © Oxford University Press 2021.
DOI: 10.1093/oso/9780197579237.003.0014

This grim assessment of nineteenth-century culture might seem surprising. Many histories instead document the continuing, positive
Enlightenment influence on this period, fostering liberalism, toleration,
cosmopolitanism, and science. Romanticism fostered imagination, sentiment, and the artist as a cultural model, reacting against or moderating
Enlightenment rationalism. Science attained greater prestige in society at
large. It flourished in new professional societies and became more significant
in universities. Some countries became republics, more representative of
their peoples' interests and more responsive to their needs. In these Christian
histories, these developments are not much appreciated. They level stringent criticism against Romanticism, Darwinism, and, most of all, religious
modernism. They are wary of nineteenth-century intellectual and cultural
developments and see disastrous public policies and political events as fore-
telling the impending doom of the twentieth century.

Although these curricula condemn Enlightenment rationalism, they do not appreciate Romanticism even though it reacted against that movement. The BJU
history identifies key themes of Romantic literature as mysticism, nostalgia for
distant lands and times, and "an emphasis on nature, love of freedom, and pride
in one's nation." But, it insists, "the romantics went too far." They became rebels
against rules and therefore rebels against God. They made their feelings their
authority—"if it *felt* good, it must *be good*." This statement tars Romantics with
the charge usually made to indict the culture of the 1960s. When the Romantics
exchanged Enlightenment reason for Romantic emotion, they ignored the
Bible's warning that "the heart is deceitful above all things, and desperately
wicked" (Jer. 17:19). These histories thus reject both reason and emotion; neither is legitimate. The Bible offers the only hope. Leading Romantic poets offer
sobering examples of unsavory characters: "Byron's free lifestyle was full of
sin." Percy Bysshe Shelley, an even more despicable example, "sought to throw
off all restraint" and condemned "the Christian faith, the role of government,
and traditional customs" as forms of oppression. The BJU history tempers its
harsh disparagement of the nineteenth-century arts with recognition of Charles
Dickens's realism and the Impressionists' use of color and light.[5]
One might expect these curricula to appreciate the Romantics' emphasis
on individual experience and their criticism of the insufficiency of reason.
Romanticism identified the inner emotions as the foundation of religion as
evangelicals do and directly influenced John Wesley, a figure they admire.[6]
While Wesley is essential to the positive narrative of English virtue, these

curricula turn away from their prior, uncritical appreciation of England as a model. The elevated status it held from the reign of Alfred the Great through Queen Victoria declined. The degenerate personal morality of England's rulers epitomized its general decline. Victoria's son Edward VII did not share "his mother's resolution to 'be good.' When the morality of the monarchy fell, so did that of the nation."[7]

English moral integrity was even more seriously threatened by "the false philosophies of Darwinism, socialism, and modernism." Nonetheless, because the British people retained some of their exceptional integrity, they were less susceptible than others to "the pseudo-scientific ideas of Charles Darwin." After Darwin published *On the Origin of Species* (1859) and *The Descent of Man* (1871), "those who wanted to break away from the moral restraints of society and religion" espoused his ideas.[8]

Darwin advanced a humanist heresy when "he taught that man developed from animals. His theory opposed the Biblical doctrine of the special, direct creation of man by God," the BJU textbook asserts. The Abeka history has an identical message: "Darwin's theory of evolution is not consistent with what the Bible says in Genesis 1–2 that God created man, plants, and animals after their own kind." Students are asked, "Why would God permit an ungodly theory such as evolution to gain such widespread popularity when it is diametrically opposed to Christianity?"[9] Given the dialectic these histories present, students are most likely to see Darwinism as the work of Satan. Darwin's ideas are such a great threat that, for these curricula, the tragic events of the twentieth century are ultimately due to acceptance of them.

Many evangelicals and fundamentalists now perceive Darwinism as an evil to be challenged or refuted. But this was not always the case. Although some nineteenth-century evangelicals worried about the impact of Darwin's work on the authority of the Bible, mainline Protestants and many evangelicals accepted Darwin and evidence supporting his theories. They saw nothing in it antithetical to a divinely created and divinely controlled evolutionary process. The Christian theological tradition since Thomas Aquinas believed that the universe and reason were ways to know God and that science and religion were compatible because Truth was one. Protestant theologians, most notably Calvin, affirmed this understanding as well. Calvinists believed that science revealed God's laws for the universe and that science and religion would always accord. Initially Darwinism was seen to pose no threat to this central belief.[10] Even Benjamin B. Warfield of Princeton Theological

Seminary, promoter of the concept of biblical inerrancy, did not see creation and evolution as antithetical.[11]

Despite evangelicals' more nuanced earlier assessment of Darwinism, that moment has clearly passed with anti-evolution a firmer tenet of evangelical Christianity, differentiating the godly from the ungodly. Darwinism undermined the positive relationship between science and religion and still calls it into question. Opposition to Darwinism remains an important impetus for establishing alternatives to public schools.

Nonetheless, these textbooks appreciate some nineteenth-century scientific advances. ACE heralds Edward Jenner's smallpox vaccine, Louis Pasteur's germ theory, and Pierre and Marie Curie's identification of radioactivity.[12] The BJU history again ties scientists' accomplishments to their religion, pointing, for example, to the "English Quaker" John Dalton as the founder of modern atomic theory. Although these textbooks note technological innovations and improvements in the material conditions of life, they generally see the influence of nineteenth-century science as profoundly destructive. It became a new religion for many, who "rejected the authority of God's Word for the authority of scientific theory." This quotation reasserts three central points about how the Christian must understand science: (1) it must be grounded in the faith of the scientist; (2) his work must conform to the Bible; (3) science must otherwise be distrusted. Many scientists, according to the BJU history, drew unwarranted and unacceptable conclusions from their appreciation of Darwin's science. Others applied science to society with disastrous results. Einstein's theory of relativity led to moral relativity, as "sinful men demonstrated their rebellion against God and His word." In contrast, the Abeka narrative integrates Einstein into its claim that science is a religious quest. It cites his statement that "a conviction akin to a religious feeling, of the rationality or intelligibility of the world lies behind all scientific work of a higher order."[13] To construe this statement as a religious claim is a misrepresentation, but students would likely not discern the subtlety of Einstein's statement.

While science, particularly evolution, exerted a profoundly negative influence, the advent of biblical modernism posed the greatest threat. The Abeka history traces this dangerous idea to eighteenth-century German philosophers. When they read Locke and Rousseau, they began to believe that "all authority stems from the general will of the people (rather than from God)" and to support popularly constituted government. These Enlightenment ideas led them to foment discontent with their political rulers, question authority, and advocate resistance—none of which are legitimate for these curricula.

The Abeka textbook identifies three specific villains—Immanuel Kant, Georg Wilhelm Friedrich Hegel, and Friedrich Schleiermacher—and denounces them with the briefest of interpretations. Kant saw the senses and the mind as the only routes to knowledge and claimed that "man's conscience should be the starting point for religion." For him, the Bible was written by man and Jesus was "just a good example." Hegel's dialectic of thesis and antithesis valued conflict and fanned flames of revolution across Europe. Because he believed that truth was relative, Hegel challenged absolutes such as '"God created the world' or 'it is a sin to steal' . . . or '2 + 2 = 4.'" These simple-minded denunciations ridicule philosophers rather than grapple with their thought.[14]

Both the Abeka and the BJU histories single out the German philosopher Schleiermacher because he emphasized the experience of the divine. Ironically, religious modernism began in Germany to rescue religion from Enlightenment attacks. Schleiermacher responded to Enlightenment rationalism by describing religion as the awareness of God. These curricula denounce Schleiermacher's philosophy as a reprehensible "theology of feeling," in which "man's authority replaced God's authority in matters of theology."[15] Their denunciation seems ironic, given that modern evangelicals too accentuate the emotional experience of faith.[16] Although Schleiermacher accorded Christianity a higher status, he considered all religions a means to intuit the divine, a belief that may account for his singular villainy here.

These three dangerous German philosophers paved the way to Germany's destruction as their "rationalist and revolutionary ideas" took hold in German universities. Philosophical relativism led to "'higher criticism,' which, under the guise of scholarship, questioned the inspiration, authority, texts, and meaning of the Bible." The philosophical undermining of absolutes had devastating consequences. It "opened the door to humanistic views of history, education, morality, science, government, and mathematics that reject facts and authority and place the emphasis on changeableness and subjectivity (feelings)."[17] To the degree that a nation espouses these reprehensible philosophies, it will experience destruction, these curricula foretell.

These dire statements point to evangelicals' objections to late nineteenth-century changes in university education, particularly the understanding of the discipline of history as a social science. By the end of the eighteenth century, German universities were in the forefront of education, and German scholars dominated the study of antiquity. When they applied the tools of philology, archeology, and literary criticism to the Bible, they reached conclusions deeply disturbing to evangelicals. They did not begin with the premise that the Bible was inerrant; rather, they made claims these curricula indict: Judaism developed out of a Near Eastern civilization; Moses did not write the first five books of the Bible; and purported prophecies described events after they occurred, among other conclusions drawn from historical research. The Abeka textbook charges, "Modernism, or religious liberalism, began in Germany with faithless theologians who believed that the Bible was merely a beautiful myth and full of errors." It denounces higher criticism as "merely unbelief clothed in modern, pseudo-scientific garb."[18]

These textbooks' critiques rest on battles fought by their evangelical forebears who were adamant in defining theological positions against biblical modernism. Evangelicals even attacked traditional theological seminaries, including the venerable Princeton Theological Seminary, because it accepted both reason and experience as guides to knowledge.[19] They were uneasy about higher education's embrace of new disciplines taught by professionals in those disciplines, rather than by clergy, both symptomatic of greater secularization. Indeed, both higher criticism and Darwinism were accepted in America in the 1870s and 1880s, largely because graduate studies in theology in American universities followed a German model and thus adopted new methods of study.[20] These conclusions horrified many evangelicals. For them as for these textbooks, the Bible is a history, but a history like no other. As the transcription of God's word to man, it is not to be understood in context or subjected to historical analysis. The historical study of the Bible attacks most directly fundamental premises of these curricula and thus is the greatest danger they see to truth.

This vehement repudiation of nineteenth-century German Protestant scholarship, one of the strongest positions these Christian curricula take, likely explains why they appreciate the German Reformation so little, especially as compared to their entirely positive view of England's less thoroughgoing Reformation. Evidently, biblical truth did not become well enough established on German soil to resist the danger of religious modernism. The sins of German religious liberalism will come to the fore in its twentieth-century fate.

From its beginning, American fundamentalism adamantly rejected religious modernism and defined itself in opposition to it.[21] From this point on, the history of the world in these textbooks maps directly onto American evangelicals' own history. The causes they have espoused and the battles they have waged are etched clearly and directly onto the historical narrative. When some evangelicals emphatically rejected biblical modernism, they articulated their positions between 1910 and 1915 in pamphlets, most notably in the extremely influential *Fundamentals: A Testimony to the Truth*, which sold over three million copies. As is often the case, these curricula cite those who resist new ideas as heroic.

Nineteenth-century evangelicals responded to contemporary social challenges, some in ways these curricula deplore. For example, after executives in his congregation crushed a coalminers' strike, Washington Gladden focused on income inequality and insisted that Christians must work to perfect society. His argument owed much to Charles Finney's post-millennial sense that Christians should build the Kingdom of God on earth. The theologian Walter Rauschenbusch's study of the New Testament led him to reject Jewish apocalypticism and assert that the Kingdom of God could be created on earth. His view, referred to as New Theology, became popular with many Protestant denominations and was taught in many seminaries.[22] Rauschenbusch's international best seller, *A Theology for the Social Gospel*, also challenged evangelicals' understanding of sin and evil. He gave to both a social dimension: individuals had to combat sins such as religious bigotry, graft, and corruption; other evils were not personal but failures of society—militarism, nationalism, and capitalism.[23]

Such views provoked a conservative reaction from other evangelicals, which, as Frances FitzGerald notes, was a mirror image of the New Theology.[24] As conservatives focused on individual experience and super-naturalism, they refuted the New Theology's optimism about society and reform. And, of course, New Theology contests these textbooks' positions. The fact that they are more critical of religious liberalism than of Darwinism might seem surprising. It is worth remembering, however, that the battle against religious liberalism defined and created American fundamentalism. In treating the nineteenth century, these histories revisit the schism that divided evangelicals. That fundamentalist position has remained coherent, as these Christian textbooks still articulate 1880s objections to biblical modernism and identify them as "Christian."

For fundamentalists and many evangelicals, biblical modernism and the Social Gospel confirmed the increasing danger of humanism: humanists accepted both. The modern manifestation of humanism produced "the exaltation of man above God." Humanists "believed that they were responsible not to God but to society but did not believe in heaven or hell."[25] Popular preachers expounded on hellfire and brimstone, emphasizing end times prophecies of the coming Armageddon and challenging optimistic post-millennialism.[26] The influential preacher John Nelson Darby rejected mainstream religion, citing the corruption of the church, and urged his followers to withdraw from society. He added several significant dimensions to evangelical beliefs. He developed a theory of dispensationalism, the previously discussed theory of discrete periods of divine revelation, and the rapture, an idea he derived from passages in Paul's letters.[27]

In contrast to these presumed positive developments, Christianity took another misbegotten turn when churches focused on the Social Gospel rather than *the* gospel. The BJU textbook cites Paul to the Galatians 1:7–8, "preach any other gospel unto you than that which we have preached unto you, let him be accursed," to condemn this development. As we have seen, these curricula are unalterably opposed to any movement, including religious movements, that address social ills. The Social Gospel movement was especially disturbing: "Church leaders became more concerned with attacking social injustices and working toward establishing total democracy than with bringing people to personal salvation through Jesus Christ." Influenced by "higher criticism," they wanted social improvement even if it entailed government action. Some even promoted democratic socialism. Their appreciation of ecumenism was destructive, leading to pernicious alliances of churches with political liberals and social revolutionaries.[28] The strong stances these curricula take against evolution, higher criticism, and the Social Gospel were those Southern evangelicals took in the late nineteenth century and stipulated as Christian orthodoxy.[29]

"Ideas always have consequences," the BJU history announces portentously to explain nineteenth-century political events and to look ahead to the coming disaster of World War I. The late nineteenth century ushered in Europe's political decline, due not only to biblical modernism but also to new popular attitudes toward government, which these curricula see as dangerous and antithetical to Christianity. "Revolutionaries, spurred by ideas, hoped that their violent revolts would bring about change."[30] These textbooks generally limit government, without clearly defining its roles, but no government should attempt to remediate social ills.

With the advent of more democratic societies and the popular vote, citizens' expectations of their governments changed: they made demands. Such demands and the programs they produced were illegitimate, these textbooks contend. They are not condoned by God and contravene biblical injunctions because, as the BJU history notes, "man has responsibility to both God and society. Christ makes clear that man's first responsibility is to God and his second to his fellow man." However, "too often ungodly man has rejected his obligation to God and sought by his own efforts to correct the ills of society."[31] This is an interesting quotation because the latter point seems to undermine the former. This quotation acknowledges a Christian's responsibility to one's fellow men, but that is never emphasized in these curricula's understanding of Christianity. As Christians' responsibility can never be social, it is restricted to proselytizing or perhaps private charity, although charity scarcely features in these histories. They instead undercut a Christian imperative to charity with their economic arguments. God will respond to social ills. Society should, in good Calvinist fashion, enforce God's laws.

Even the government of admirable Britain extended its purview: "Parliament passed bills providing for unemployment insurance, health protection, workman's compensation, and old age pensions. In addition, it placed secondary education under state control." These programs fostered unacceptable roles for government and began the welfare state, which the Abeka textbook defines as "a state in which the government assumes the responsibility for the material and social well-being of every individual 'from the cradle to the grave.'"[32] To its credit, for these textbooks, Britain pursued gradual change rather than violent revolution.

But reformers often espoused socialism. Some were misled into believing that socialism embodied Christianity, but they "failed to see that the very basis of socialism, the perfectibility of man by man, is contrary to the teaching of Scripture."[33] In fact, socialism must be condemned; socialists believed that social ills could be remedied "by changing society." Reform efforts were entirely misguided because, as the Abeka history echoes the BJU account, they are premised on "the perfectibility of man and society and reject the fact that *sin* is the root of all social evils." Socialism not only misunderstands human beings and their relationship to society but also epitomizes erroneous economics. It advances "the idea that government should own or at least control a nation's economy . . . to provide for the needs of the people." Such goals are both illegitimate and economically unsound. Socialism undermined the British economy "by retarding personal initiative and interfering with the exercise of free enterprise capitalism." The Fabians, a British socialist society, advocated both democratic socialism and public education.[34] For these curricula, support for public education inevitably provokes criticism;

it introduces the state into the family. This fundamental tenet was emphatically insisted upon by Christian Reconstructionists, who were key to the successful legal case for homeschooling in the United States.[35]

At the same time that Southern evangelicals were rejecting the Social Gospel and other attempts to remediate social ills in the name of Christianity, the term "socialism" was used in the United States to repudiate attempts by the federal government during Reconstruction to make it possible for the formerly enslaved to benefit economically. In the 1930s, in response to the New Deal, the charge of socialism was expanded to attack any government role in the economy from providing a social safety net to funding infrastructure. The term again came into wide use in the late 1980s by right-wing media after the Fairness Doctrine of the Federal Communications Commission, which required that licensed radio and television stations present balanced coverage of contemporary issues, was eliminated. The current use of the term socialism incorporates not only all of its prior targets but is even more broadly applied to condemn any government policy and to stoke fears that minorities will have greater influence or power.

For these curricula, socialism leads inevitably to Karl Marx, unquestionably the great villain of nineteenth-century politics and economics, who brought evil ideas to their fullest fruition. Marx, according to the Abeka textbook, "associated with radical students and professors and came under the spell of the religious modernists of Germany," highlighting the dangers of education to religion and the connection of biblical modernism to Marxism. When he argued that wages did not reward workers for the value of their labor, Marx failed to appreciate capitalists' investments in factories and raw materials necessary to produce industrial goods, the BJU textbook objects.[36] Investors' interests must be recognized and prioritized over workers' contributions to economic productivity. Despite the social dislocation workers faced, only their immoral behavior required redress. Attempts to remediate social conditions reflect (1) man's belief in his own ability to effect change, (2) utopian and completely impractical idealism, or, worst of all, (3) an intent to interfere with God's plan to reward or punish through economic good or ill fortune.

For these textbooks, Marx epitomized a completely wrongheaded approach. In *Das Kapital*, he applied evolution to his political theories to give them a scientific basis, but neither evolution nor science is a legitimate foundation for belief or action. Socialist economic proposals were worthless because Marx's predictions about capitalism did not come to pass. Furthermore, "without private property, individuals have no incentive; therefore, they are motivated to 'get by' and consume all they can get."[37] Capitalism, without any pressure from governments or workers, redressed poor working conditions, these curricula contend. This glaring overstatement of capitalism's role in remediating labor conditions completely ignores the mobilization of workers and reformers in advocating for labor laws to ameliorate deplorable and dangerous working conditions and in gaining rights for workers.

Marxism is "the epitome of rebellion against God by Satan and by fallen humanity." Marxists are materialists who believe in matter and motion, have no absolutes, and seek to perfect human beings and society. The Abeka history argues that students must understand the horrors of Marxism to make sense of the modern world. The political philosophy developed by Marx and Friedrich Engels was the product of their "violent hatred for God and humanity." Marxism is thus best understood by Christians as the "beast-state of the book of Revelation, seeking to dominate man."[38]

These curricula distill Marx's political philosophy to several points. Marx opposed capitalism because he believed "capitalists who owned the means of production would continue to ruthlessly exploit the poor and grow rich from the labors of the proletariat." He saw economics, not religion, as the driver of history, and he opposed capitalism as favoring the bourgeoisie over workers. These last statements are generally accurate reflections of Marx's views. Most crucial for these textbooks, however, is that Marx's works reveal his godlessness. Marx claimed that one should "recognize as the highest divinity, the human self-consciousness itself," which the Abeka history deems "a concise summary on the religion of secular humanism." Marx called religion the opiate of the masses because it encouraged them to look to the next life rather than to live in this one. This textbook responds that the Christian "knows that God wants men to do their duty in this life to hold back the forces of evil, and only a person who is in the will of God can know true happiness is this life."[39]

It is noteworthy that this is the first occasion on which a Christian is urged to do something, although "his duty" is quite vague. What does it mean to "hold back the forces of evil"? Does it mean to resist biblical scholarship and Marxism? Nor is it clear what it means to be "in the will of God." Would those instructed by these curricula be able to reassure themselves that they were "in the will of God"? How much of this is coded language, clear to the initiated but unclear to those who are not? An entire page of the Abeka textbook, labeled "Communism: A Negative System," specifies its evils: communism has no God, no creation, no morality, no family ties, no individuality, no incentives, no hope.[40]

These curricula routinely use personal invective. Not surprisingly, Marx is a prime target. The Abeka history sums up his life: Marx was a personal failure; he failed to support his family; his children died in infancy due to lack of food and medical care; and "he sat in the library and spent all his money on travel, liquor, and tobacco." He thus flagrantly violated the proper role of *paterfamilias* by failing to provide for his family.[41]

Students exposed to these educational materials will understand that Marxism denies "all that is true, righteous, and good. In its suppression of the higher aspects of man's character, it unleashes the beastly aspect—the utterly sinful nature—of man." Because Marxism does not acknowledge biblical creation, it offers no foundation for morality and is thus completely relativistic, affirming these histories' consistent claim that without Christianity there can be no morality. As a result, "communists state that they intend to complete the 'perfect' course of evolution by remaking man's nature and society through social engineering, psychological conditioning, and genetic manipulation."[42] Thus, in their critiques of Marxism, these educational materials point to contemporary moral issues even though the developments they cite were, of course, not possible in the nineteenth century. Ironically, these developments do interest modern corporations, which of course are not Marxist. These textbooks denounce communism's negative impact on the family: Marx himself did not recognize families as promoting "economic, emotional, and social stability" and as preserving traditional values and customs. Marx's denial of sin produced dire results for the individual and society.

For these histories, the nineteenth century was not simply full of bad political ideas. The misbegotten forces unleashed by the French Revolution generated revolutions across Europe, but such attempts to contend with political crises were illegitimate. In the aftermath of the Napoleonic Wars, revolutionary ideals did not subside despite the reemergence of conservative support for the Catholic Church and absolute monarchy. The Abeka history describes the challenge the European continent faced in harsh terms: "Napoleon's empire . . . spread the ideas of the French Revolution, especially the ideas of trying to use government to make everyone equal"—an inaccurate assessment of the appeal of Napoleon's call for careers to be open to talent rather than birth and a crude sense of the revolutionary ideal of equality before the law.[43]

Historians emphasize the conservative response to Napoleon's defeat. The Congress of Vienna, under Prince Klemens von Metternich of Austria's leadership, tried to confine revolution to France, restore Europe to its pre-Revolutionary status quo, and establish an alliance system to preserve the peace. To that end, a revolution in Spain was quashed, but the ability of the European powers to suppress Latin American revolutions was thwarted by the Monroe Doctrine, by which the United States claimed Latin America as its sphere of influence "to look out for the interests of its neighbors," as ACE describes this sanguine view of US involvement.[44] Nonetheless, the Continental System of alliances was successful in preventing a European-wide war for a hundred years.

But these educational materials pay relatively little attention to concrete political events. Instead, the BJU curriculum focuses on liberalism as a disruptive idea. It notes that liberalism, supported by the middle classes, emphasized individual rights, democratic reforms, and representative government. The lower classes advocated for even more extensive social and economic protections of their interests. Individual rights were tied to nationalist demands for independence, unification, and appeals to ethnic identity.[45] The BJU textbook views all these demands with equal antipathy. This discussion does not distinguish clearly between liberalism and nationalism or between the interests of liberals and those of the working class. While it unusually mentions class interests in this instance, this curriculum does not recognize that governments implemented policies to keep the powerful in control, such as the Corn Laws, which England passed to keep the price of grain high, or the replacement of an income tax on the wealthy with a sales tax on everyone. It would be more accurate to see the political crises of the nineteenth century as due to a resurgence of conservatism and its resistance to reform. Even though these curricula ascribe nineteenth-century failures to liberal ideas, conservatives largely retained their power until World War I. Metternich was masterful in restraining these developments, insisting on monarchs' right to intervene in other states' domestic concerns to quell popular dissent. Conservatives made modest concessions to demands for reform but usually in response to popular violence.

For any discussion of nineteenth-century politics, it is important to distinguish the meanings of political terms, particularly those that are still used but that had different connotations in the past. Nineteenth-century conservatives represented the interests of monarchs, aristocrats, and the church. They were committed to the protection of their political and economic power and did not believe that any representative government would do so. They opposed written constitutions, as they might erode conservatives' power. They supported established churches because they opposed the influence of Enlightenment ideas, abhorred the French Revolution, and were committed to the status quo.

Nineteenth-century liberalism challenged these ideas. It developed from the Declaration of the Rights of Man of the French Revolution and thus was committed to equality before the law, religious toleration, and freedom of the press. It defined governments as based on the consent of the governed through elected representatives and stipulated a written constitution as a necessary protection of rights. Liberals tended to be educated and wealthy but excluded from positions in the existing political order conservatives held through birth and inherited, landed wealth. In their economic views, liberals subscribed to Adam Smith and advocated free enterprise and competition. Liberals across nations shared these political views after Napoleon had spread the ideas of the French Revolution through his conquests. Opponents of the established elites also appealed to national interest to undermine traditional hierarchies. In eastern and central Europe, for example, nationalism focused on ethnic identity to challenge the Austro-Hungarian Empire.

The BJU textbook traces the interplay of conservative power and liberal demands in nineteenth-century France. When the monarchy was restored after Napoleon's fall, Louis XVIII initially responded favorably to demands for greater liberty, but over the course of his reign (1814–1824), he reversed all such measures. When his successor, Charles X tried to reinstate an absolutist monarchy, he provoked the July Revolution of 1830. Louis-Philippe then came to the throne with a more liberal agenda but ultimately supported only upper-middle-class interests. (The BJU curriculum occasionally recognizes class interests in European countries but not in the United States, where battles are more clearly between good and evil.) News of the July Revolution also provoked the Belgians to revolt. After the revolts of 1830 were suppressed, the BJU history notes, the lower classes remained bitter against the upper classes. It does not recognize that neither liberals nor conservatives responded to working-class concerns. That failure would lead to widespread revolution in Europe in 1848.[46]

In France, the Revolution of 1848 overthrew Louis-Philippe and formed a government composed of revolutionaries who established national workshops to implement workers' demands. When a new constitution guaranteed universal manhood suffrage, elections returned a conservative assembly. When the assembly abolished the workshops, a rebellion, called "July Days," broke out and lasted three days until the army restored order. Louis-Napoleon, elected as a democratic leader, seized power in a coup d'état. Ultimately, the BJU textbook concludes, "French attempts to achieve democratic reforms through revolution led to widespread violence and to the establishment of a dictatorship."[47]

ACE treats the revolutions as challenges to the peace but also recognizes that they forced European rulers to accept that popular dissent could not simply be repressed: they had to make concessions "to combat desire for freedom and rising nationalism among the common people."[48] For the other curricula, both the reformists' cause and concessions made to it were illegitimate. Governments responded to political revolutionaries by implementing reformers' bad ideas. The accommodations made to French revolutionaries of 1848 were portentous: "Instead of providing useful jobs, the workshops became a public-relief program. It was one of the earliest modern examples of government-financed socialistic programs."[49] Similarly, the Abeka textbook condemns Otto von Bismarck for placating socialists with health and unemployment insurance, making Germany "the model welfare state."[50] The Revolutions of 1848 demonstrated the futility of both revolution and government policies adopted in response to them. No challenge to political authority is valid and only free-market capitalism, left to its own devices, is a legitimate economic policy. Being taxed to support others is also illegitimate. In this respect, these curricula espouse the views of more extreme libertarians and some on the Christian right who assert that taxation is theft.

ACE's treatment is again somewhat anomalous. It is generally not interested in ideas except as they concern Christianity. But it draws highly idiosyncratic conclusions, claiming that, in 1870 when France under the leadership of Emperor Napoleon III (Louis-Napoleon) lost its war with Prussia, it had to pay harsh reparations.[51] This grievance led directly to World War I and subsequently to the harsh terms France later demanded from Germany, leading directly to World War II.[52] In effect, ACE blames France for both the First and Second World Wars.

The political crises of the nineteenth century were due, according to the BJU history, to "the failure of governments and their citizens to fulfill their God-given responsibilities."[53] Those who rebelled against political authorities acted contrary to God's plan, as proclaimed in Romans 1:3. This frequently cited verse claims political authority is unquestionably legitimate, down to present-day leaders and government policies.

Rebellions, even for a good cause or against oppression, "have at their roots a rebellious spirit against God. God condemns such rebellion, whether it is directed against divine authority or human authority." Even more damning, the BJU textbook pronounces, "Rebellion is as the sin of witchcraft, and stubbornness is an iniquity and idolatry 1 Sam. 15:23," essentially categorizing rebellion as heresy. It asks students, "Through the eyes of Faith—Is civil disobedience ever biblically justifiable? If yes, what limits would such resistance have?" Given the way these curricula treat resistance, it is difficult to imagine a high school student answering "yes" or trying to determine what would allow an affirmative answer. Although this textbook concedes that revolutionaries were sometimes spurred by ideals, nonetheless, "those revolts often did more harm than good. Discontent led to rebellion, rebellion to strife, and strife to destruction." This indictment concludes, "How society thinks always determines how a society acts," which may essentially restate the earlier claim that "bad ideas have bad results."[54]

What are students to conclude from this treatment of the nineteenth century? They should unquestionably realize that the world was overtaken by sin. The most serious sins were ideas, including those these curricula still battle—Darwinism, socialism, Marxism, and religious modernism. The BJU history summarizes the evil ideas of the nineteenth century: "People rejected the Bible as their source of truth. They placed their faith in human ingenuity. Some people looked to the social theories of intellectuals who promised perfect society; others trusted in the 'cult of science.'" Most reprehensible of all were those "religious leaders, who departed from 'old time religion'" and interpreted God's word according to their preconceived ideas.[55] The severe assault on Christianity these curricula see in the late nineteenth century made the world ripe for disaster: "Acceptance of these ungodly philosophies would later have terrible consequences for both Europe and the entire world."[56]

The die was cast for Europe, as the continent accepted the "false philosophies" of Darwinism and socialism in conjunction with "the dangerous ideas of the French Revolution," all three of which connote belief in human beings' power to change their political, social, and economic conditions through revolt against political authority and to reconstitute a government in their interests. Attempts to apply innovative ideas or resolve social issues remain reprehensible no matter how serious the injustice or how desperate the circumstances any proposed reform might seek to redress. When states implemented social policies based on those ideas or revolutionaries were inspired to act on them, they become even more destructive. Efforts to ameliorate the ills of society were misguided, as modern Europeans "rejected biblical Christianity as the true cure for humanity's ills and instead accepted all sorts of ungodly philosophies as the solutions to man's problems." The textbook again quotes Proverbs 14:34: "Righteousness exalteth a nation: but sin is a reproach to any people."[57] This citation is almost a refrain.

The claims these narratives make about this period reflect the history of nineteenth-century evangelicals who criticized mainline Protestants for accepting Darwin and higher criticism. Evangelicals emphasized "self-reliance, strict moralism," supporting the temperance movement, for example. Some, primarily Southern evangelicals, feared immigrants and actively supported the extant social hierarchy, including segregation.[58]

This treatment of the nineteenth century, written against the backdrop of issues central to the development of American evangelicalism, raises issues of profound significance for modern America political life. Political resistance is never legitimate; God puts rulers in power and does not sanction the peoples' demands for reform. (The notion that Christians should insist that governments enforce God's law is merely implicit in these texts, although its connection to action is tenuous.) Political resistance is also ineffective; dictators inevitably seize power after any revolution. By rejecting reform movements, these textbooks narrow the role of government to enforcement of God's law. Any notion that government exists for the good of the people or to serve their needs is unpalatable. In calling into question the legitimacy of popular, political action, these curricula are at root profoundly undemocratic. Unable to make political demands, the people are powerless. Their lack of influence is not to be deplored, because rulers are sanctioned by God. As we will see, when the religious right later became involved in Republican Party politics, their views about the illegitimacy of social reform coincided.

14

The Wages of Sin

For these Christian histories, the twentieth century was a sobering period when humanity endured fitting punishment for its sins while embattled Christians fought against evil. This chapter explores how these textbooks assess that battle as bad ideas bore horrifying fruit from the beginning of the twentieth century through the end of the Second World War. Even if the causal correlation between ideas and political events remains vague, it is a given for these curricula that "how a society thinks *always* determines how a society acts," as the BJU history puts it. They use this period to define fundamental dichotomies—evil socialists versus godly capitalists, deplorable liberals versus admirable conservatives, wicked internationalists versus virtuous Americans. Two global wars and the rise of socialism and communism underscore this Manichean worldview. This period confirms that hopes for improving material conditions, maintaining peace, and cultivating international cooperation were and remain misguided and illustrates Paul's statement "In the last days perilous times shall come" (2 Tim. 3:1). Biblical quotations foretell coming wars and confirm the futility of peace efforts as "'wars and rumours of war' (Matt. 24:6) persist." As the epistle of James explains, wars "come, he says, from 'your lusts that war in your members' (James 4:1)."[1]

As the twentieth century begins, "spiritual decay erases hopes for peace." The Abeka history specifies, "As people rejected the Word of God and embraced the vain philosophies of men, they set the stage for the death and devastation of the world wars, 'reaping the whirlwind' of destruction sown by their unbelief." Germany's adoption of theological modernism destined it "for terror and destruction." Twentieth-century devastation is rooted in theological liberalism and religious decline even as "strong feelings of revolutionary nationalism, the result of spiritual decay, caused some European powers to seek to annex other territory."[2]

World histories typically begin discussions of this period by recognizing, as these curricula do, that European states promoted peace through a balance of power, dividing into the Triple Alliance and the Triple Entente. While

Hijacking History. Kathleen Wellman, Oxford University Press. © Oxford University Press 2021.
DOI: 10.1093/oso/9780197579237.003.0015

intended to create stability, such alliances, these textbooks contend, instead fostered mistrust. The curricula blame Germany most directly because its universities promoted biblical modernism and its government adopted reprehensible social welfare policies. In other respects, their narrative of the alliance system is factual and dispassionate. When Germany unified to prevent a French resurgence after its defeat in the Franco-Prussian War, Chancellor Otto von Bismarck exploited alliances to enhance Germany's power.[3] When Kaiser Wilhelm II took control, he allowed the treaty with Russia to lapse and antagonized Great Britain, critically weakening the alliance system. This action encouraged France, Great Britain, and Russia to ally against Germany. When the Balkan states sought independence from the Ottoman Empire, contested claims to the Balkans brought the two groups of allies into conflict. The immediate provocation for war was the assassination of Archduke Ferdinand by a Bosnian revolutionary. As Austrians believed that anti-Austrian propaganda in Serbia had provoked the attack, Austria declared war on Serbia.[4]

Conventional textbooks do not root World War I in either sinfulness or the theological disputes that roiled the evangelical community. Instead, they emphasize the complexity of the political situation on the eve of the war, including rivalries in the Balkans, the European arms race, Anglo-German tensions over naval superiority, the destabilization of the Ottoman Empire, and Austria's opposition to a Serbian Adriatic port, among other international complications. While some histories indict Germany's political ambitions as provoking the war, they do not condemn theological modernism as its cause.[5]

These curricula devote a disproportionate number of pages to the military campaigns of the world wars perhaps because military history engages students or perhaps because evangelicalism has been defined by strong support for American militarism since the 1940s.[6] The textbooks describe extensively the most significant and horrific battles of World War I—Ypres, Verdun—and Allied offensives to hold the Marne and Somme rivers; as well as innovations in chemical, trench, submarine, and air warfare. They treat the events of World War I on both the Eastern and Western fronts straightforwardly. They note the staggering losses of Russians fighting on the Eastern front and acknowledge that popular discontent over the war fueled the Russian Revolution.

After the Germans sank the luxury liner *Lusitania*, public opinion in America was roused against Germany, and the United States entered the war. These histories give several reasons for America's entry: it depended more on trade with the Allies; "the American people had a great respect for their English heritage"; and "historical gratitude to France for its role in the Revolution"—an unexpected appreciation considering these curricula's anti-French stance.[7]

American evangelicals were slow to support the war. Initially, they opposed intervention as pointless because war was the product of human sinfulness. The nations involved were being punished, and apocalyptic prophecies explained the war's events. But, by the time the United States entered the war, evangelicals described it as a holy war.[8] They became more fervent in supporting American intervention because they linked the German war effort to biblical criticism just as these curricula do.[9] A leading dispensationalist of the era, Arno Gaebelein, wrote that "the new theology has led Germany into barbarism, and it will lead any nation into the same demoralization."[10] The famous evangelical Billy Sunday supported the war, saying, "Christianity and Patriotism are synonymous" and "turn hell upside down, and you'll find the words 'made in Germany.'"[11] Foreshadowing their emerging political stances, evangelicals did not support the war to spread democracy. In fact, they feared that democracies could put the sinful in charge or be Satan's ruse. They looked instead to the war as a sign of the coming millennium.[12]

To understand the state of the world on the eve of this disastrous war, these textbooks expand their coverage of Europe to include Russia, not only because it plays a crucial role in World War I, but also because it delineates the battle between good and evil. Russia plays a unique role in the apocalyptic scenario these textbooks paint. For many evangelicals, Russia is the realization of the northern nation of Gog of end times prophecies. During World War I, some saw the Russian Revolution as a portent of a realignment of nations on the eve of Armageddon, presuming that end times would begin when Russia invaded Israel. That was a popular belief throughout the twentieth century and remains prominent in popular evangelical media.[13]

In the Abeka history, three pages summarize Russian history prior to the Russian Revolution. Peter the Great wins praise for westernizing Russia, but Catherine the Great warrants condemnation for her lack of spiritual discernment, likely obliquely referring to her reputed sexual exploits.[14] In the BJU narrative, Russian history offers sobering lessons. Czar Nicholas II lost prestige because of Russia's defeat in the Russo-Japanese War (1904–1905) over Manchuria. Even though he made concessions to popular opposition to avert revolution, he failed to modernize sufficiently. Defeat and mismanagement made Russia ripe for revolution. The populace turned against the czar after soldiers mowed down peaceful demonstrators on "Bloody Sunday."[15] Peasant uprisings and workers' strikes forced the government to create a representative body, the Duma, but that measure too proved insufficient to quell revolt. Russian involvement in World War I with its disastrous defeats, heavy casualties, and food shortages exacerbated popular discontent and ultimately led to revolution.

It is highly unusual for these curricula to criticize a government for not being responsive to the needs of its people or even to discuss non-religious causes of political events. They hold Russia to a different standard than other governments, perhaps because it will be central to evangelicals' anti-communist crusade and to their apocalyptic expectations. Their harsh denunciations of Russia are neither unusual nor surprising; the measures Russia adopted in response to the challenges it faced, many produced by its involvement in World War I, were often repressive and disastrous. However, it seems quite ironic that these textbooks disparage Russia for failing to implement a republican form of government and to address social and economic ills, given that they consistently counsel acceptance of such ills.

ACE analyzes the Russian Revolution quite simplistically. "When Lenin started telling the Russian soldiers about Communism, they began the Russian Revolution." Again, the impetus for disastrous events is a dangerous idea.[16] Lack of food fostered radical Bolshevik causes as Lenin "falsely promised peace, land, and bread to the Russian people" and as "urban labor organizations" made Russians "most susceptible to Bolshevik propaganda."[17] Bolsheviks' proclaimed goal of ameliorating social conditions misrepresented their true intent. War communism centralized the economy as Lenin inaugurated "his radical socialist program," creating economic disaster as millions died of starvation and disease," according to ACE.[18] Revolutionary Russia provides a horrifying economic and political model for these curricula.

The Abeka history condemns Lenin as a convert to the false religion of Marxism. He intended to establish "a Communist totalitarian state" and implement Marx's call to bring about "the bloody agony of the old society and the bloody birth-pangs of the new, only one means—*the revolutionary terror*."[19] The BJU textbook notes, more accurately, that Lenin saw the transition from capitalism to communism as potentially peaceful. While Marx believed in revolution from below, Lenin thought it could be imposed by strong leaders. Facing civil war, Lenin inaugurated "war communism" and later the New Economic Plan, and the Third International to advance worldwide communism. According to the BJU history, Lenin crushed all freedom because, for communists, human life has no value. He controlled education to influence the young and to destroy the family so that people would be submerged into the state. With no hint of irony, this account condemns Lenin's desire to control education. He "knew that by controlling the minds of students he could raise up a generation of loyal communists."[20] These curricula are, of course, similarly directed but to the laudable goal of producing capitalist Christians.

While any account of this period would certainly acknowledge the failures of Lenin, these Christian textbooks have a broader critical brush to wield. Their treatment of the Russian Revolution conveys to students that governmental economic planning creates a slippery slope to state control over all aspects of life. Political revolution and government control of the economy are both disastrous and evil. These critiques connect Russian history from the Revolution to Stalin to Western European political developments. These textbooks tie subsequent European political history to the Russian model, whether liberal, socialist, or Marxist. The equivalence they suggest between Stalinism and twentieth-century liberalism is a staggering misrepresentation.

The cataclysm of World War I allows these textbooks to emphasize sin as its cause and the need to return to God's favor. The Abeka history privileges Herbert Butterfield's *Steps to Christian Understanding* (1958) for three entire pages. Butterfield urged his contemporaries to understand World War I as "itself a judgment of God on certain evils of our civilizations." This curriculum concludes that World War I "showed how false the concept of 'continual human perfection'" was. It insists that "the only explanation for the horrors of World War I was the biblical doctrine of man's sinful, depraved nature, and the only solution was in Biblical Christianity."[21]

When, in the aftermath of World War I, the United States and the European powers sought to make and preserve peace, their efforts were misguided and based on foolhardy optimism, even as "standards of morality declined, and moral decay increased as a growing number of people abandoned belief in the authority of God's Word." International agreements and peace efforts "simply sowed more seeds of discontent and discord, which would eventually lead to World War II." War is intractable, rooted in human sin and impervious to human efforts to bring about peace. The BJU world history asks students to consider the following: "what is the real cause of war and international conflict? Can fallen man ever hope to have real peace?" Reiterated biblical citations, Matthew 24:6 and James 4:1, again point to the "right" answers. Students must realize that "lasting peace on earth will be possible only when the Lord Jesus Christ returns."[22] These curricula share the view of their evangelical progenitors that one could not expect progress. Instead, Europe remained mired in "spiritual blindness" as religious liberalism and "such false philosophies as Darwinism and socialism still gripped society." As a result, "many spiritually blind people became easy prey for dictators who promised better times."[23]

These textbooks reflect early twentieth-century evangelicals' certainty that they were uniquely positioned to understand these calamitous events and their ramifications. By pointing students to end times prophecies, they reflect historical millennialism as well as their current millennialist hopes. By the late nineteenth century, millennialism had become a significant dimension of evangelicalism. William E. Blackstone, an influential dispensationalist and Christian Zionist, published in 1908 a primer to John Darby's prophetic system of 1828. Blackstone's *Jesus Is Coming* highlighted new dispensations, and his *Blackstone Memorial* (1891) urged the United States to commit to the return of the Holy Land to Israel. Even more influential was the Scofield Reference Bible. Published by Oxford University Press in 1909, it featured an attractive format, identified biblical characters, and provided clear cross references. It disseminated several significant aspects of biblical interpretation essential to fundamentalists and many evangelicals: it claimed that God wrote the Bible and it introduced many readers to the literalism of Young Earth creationism.[24] It asserted that the Jews would return to Palestine in the last days and identified Russia as Magog of Ezekiel 38. It is significant that the Scofield Reference Bible was dispensationalist. This well-known biblical reference work took on the authority of Scripture itself.[25] Millennialists directed readers to explicit prophetic passages to highlight the futility of postwar peace efforts.

The religious crisis these textbooks identify in the post–World War I period reflects the battles American evangelicals fought against an array of enemies of Christianity on the home front—Catholics, Jews, and socialists. Evangelicals' view of the world was grim, especially as compared to progressive stances of mainline denominations, but it became overtly Manichean—good and evil were at war in the world.[26] Millennialism, these curricula suggest, was a more appropriate response to the war's end than the peace efforts of world powers.

ACE indicts the Paris Peace Conference explicitly for excluding the Central powers. Even more problematic was that Germany was forced to give up its colonies, demilitarize, and pay reparations for war, leaving it embittered and ripe for extremism as "the Treaty of Versailles helped sow the seeds for future strife."[27] Although these curricula blame Germany for the war, they sympathize with Germany in its aftermath. The Treaty of Versailles failed to correctly identify the problem—"the spiritual decay that was so prevalent in Germany before the war."[28] This failure made World War II inevitable.

For historians, World War I was not due to a decline in religious fervor or a failure to adhere to the correct religious beliefs. They do not castigate peacemakers for believing that their goals were attainable. They do, however, recognize that peace efforts were greatly encumbered by the postwar depression. They address the complexities of postwar politics, recognizing, among other factors, the crucial role the redistribution of former European colonies' mandates played.

The war had revealed to European powers how invaluable their colonies had been to their war efforts, but tensions between colonies and colonizers heightened the instability of the post–World War I world. The peace violated its own idealistic principles: victors promoted their interests rather than the principles of national self-determination they proclaimed. As treaties redrew the map of Europe and attempted to apply Wilsonian self-determination, these efforts too failed because the peace left significant minority populations outside the boundaries of their ethnic homelands.

The League of Nations, created by President Woodrow Wilson as an international institution dedicated to allowing nations to settle their differences without resorting to war, was, for these curricula, another misguided endeavor. While the League settled minor disagreements, it proved futile almost immediately as Japan, Italy, and Germany acted without regard for it. The failure of the League was, of course, guaranteed by the Senate's refusal to commit the United States to it. The Abeka history commends the rejection, because "many realized that the treaty would jeopardize American sovereignty in international affairs."[29]

These curricula reproduce the critiques of the League by early twentieth-century American evangelicals. They argued against internationalism because of their beliefs about end times. They denounced the League as a manifestation of a world empire rising to contest the church. The dispensationalist theologian Arno Gaebelein excoriated the League as a "god of this age, Satan, to lull a secure world to sleep." Evangelicals also objected to the

League as ecumenical—an unholy alliance with Catholics, Buddhists, and Muslims.[30]

The twentieth century unquestionably went awry but, for these curricula, liberalism had first unleashed the period's rampant political evils. The Abeka textbook defines liberalism as a retreat from authority and responsibility. It concedes that sometimes liberals support good things, like free enterprise, but deplores liberalism as "the desire to be free from absolute standards and morals, especially those of the Scriptures." Liberalism unequivocally leads to godless immorality and political disaster. This condemnation of liberalism exposes a crucial but contradictory element in the political philosophy these textbooks advance: one should submit to authority and yet take individual responsibility, best understood as economic self-sufficiency. Fundamentally, liberalism begins with the thoroughly objectionable proposition, which these curricula denounce, that man is basically good. It intends to "free man from authority, order, restraint, and responsibility." In practice, these curricula insist, liberalism imposes government control over many aspects of life and transfers responsibility from the individual to the state, and "leads inevitably to the totalitarian state" with "tragic consequences—war, tyranny, despair— for mankind."[31] This rejection of liberalism points to the very narrow sense of liberty, as these curricula understand it—religious freedom combined with economic libertarianism and social and political conformity.

For these curricula, liberalism is the gateway to evil governments. As we have seen, liberalism developed in the nineteenth century. But these textbooks are not associating liberalism with the moderate reforms and free-market economics of nineteenth-century liberals. Its blanket denunciation here is presumably directed at twentieth-century progressive governments, which espouse many positions these curricula abhor, including social welfare, humanitarianism, civil liberty, social justice, and a mixed economy— positions now condemned as "liberal." These curricula fear that these positions sanction a greater, illegitimate role for government in addressing social and economic issues. Government involvement is anathema. As a result, the textbooks do not acknowledge that liberalism is, by definition, opposed to communism and that liberal democrats formulated and implemented the US containment policy to thwart communism. They do not recognize the benefits of liberal governments and reject programs associated with them—social security, civil rights, public education, equality for women, and workers' rights. These advances, all tightly correlated with Western liberal democracies, came to fruition in the immediate aftermath of World War II as governments recognized that only liberal democracies would be able to thwart the rise of future right-wing dictatorships. For these curricula, these advances were illegitimate. Brought into being by collective action, they impeded unfettered capitalism and, more importantly, fostered moral relativism.

It is worth noting how fluid and nonspecific these curricula are in using political terminology. Lack of specificity allows them to elide Darwinism into socialism, Marxism, and totalitarianism. The first two are unrelated, but, in these textbooks, Darwinism functions as the gateway to all modern evils. Marxism is quite different from democratic socialism—a distinction these curricula do not respect. And totalitarianism has a distinct history. First used in the 1920s and 1930s by fascist political theorists, Giovanni Gentile in Italy and Carl Schmitt in Germany, the term "totalitarian" extolled the unifying benefits of fascism. Post–World War II, the term defined repressive state control over the individual's public and private life, so that the state and society became essentially the same. Stalin was the paradigmatic example. This relatively new term isolated these horrific events from other manifestations of government control and, more pragmatically, differentiated the United States' World War II ally from its postwar Soviet enemy. When these curricula apply the term, they use it to condemn communism and socialism. For them, the trajectory of evil governments moves from Darwinism to liberalism, to socialism, to communism, to totalitarianism.

Liberalism stands in sharp contrast to good conservatism, as these textbooks develop the distinction. The Abeka history defines conservatism as "the principle or practice of serving (preserving) established traditions or institutions and opposing changes in them." It points to two examples in which conservatism could be evil: A "conservative Communist" might try to preserve communism; a "conservative Muslim" might resist Christian missionaries. Religion is at the center of conservatism, which rests on God-given absolutes as the foundation of legitimate government and society. Conservatism recognizes a need for government because of man's fallen nature but also that "government alone cannot provide for man's needs." The "realities of human nature" mean that people are "happier and more productive" with private responsibility. Because "people differ from one another," any attempts at "equality" (in quotation marks) "will lead to discontent and, even, dictatorship." It concludes: *"the most powerful conservative force through the ages has been the Bible."* The Abeka history proclaims that conservatives "seek to preserve the Judeo-Christian heritage that has made Western civilization great."[32]

This citation of the greatness of Western civilization seems anomalous, since this textbook has consistently criticized its misdirection. Nonetheless, contemporary right-wing political rhetoric frequently invokes Western civilization as a great boon and as the antithesis of other malign cultures, notably Islam. "Western civilization" is also sometimes used now as code for white racial identity or even as a dog whistle to white supremacists, especially against nonwhite immigrants and more generally as a rallying cry in the political rhetoric of the clash of cultures.[33]

These curricula deplore the cultural impact of liberalism. It had deleterious effects on the social sciences, for example. The Abeka curriculum condemns "liberal pseudo-sciences"; Freud and psychology deny man's sinful nature, and behavioral psychology reduces humans to animals. Other, abhorrent "liberal philosophies" include pragmatism and positivism, both of which rely on empiricism rather than scriptural truth. So-called sciences contrast with "true science," which seeks to "understand the absolute order and harmony by which God designed and created the universe."[34]

Evil liberal or virtuous conservative also characterizes how these textbooks see twentieth-century artists. Authors whose themes are religious— G. K. Chesterton, J. R. R. Tolkien, and C. S. Lewis—are commendable. Impressionism and cubism are evil; Beatrix Potter and Norman Rockwell are good. Other arts reflect twentieth-century despair, which artists could have alleviated if they had looked to the Bible's discussion of end times.[35]

Liberalism also tainted economics as liberals seized on the fears the Great Depression engendered to condemn capitalism and free enterprise. As the Abeka textbook puts it, "Alarmed by socialist propaganda from the media and certain liberal politicians, many Americans blamed President Hoover."[36] While many twentieth-century evangelicals identified the Depression with sin, the Abeka curriculum offers a more simplistic explanation: some bankers and bureaucrats failed in their efforts to "create perpetual prosperity."[37] "Bad actors" have occasionally disrupted the "perpetual prosperity" guaranteed by unfettered capitalism. The blessings of the free market are irrefutable; it fulfills the utilitarian premise "the greatest good for the greatest number."[38] For these textbooks and many modern evangelicals, systemic failures of capitalism do not reflect sin, although individual economic failures do.

The economic crises of the postwar period led some European countries to adopt inappropriate solutions. Liberals, humanists, and modernists played on people's economic insecurities to propose a new economic and social order. The negative effects of the Depression and the Great War left Europeans vulnerable to reformers' agendas, because "their acceptance of religious liberalism leaves a void in their hearts."[39] To argue that religious liberalism caused the negative ramifications of the Depression is bizarre (unless as another effect of sin) but also a disturbing foretaste of these curricula's inability to understand populist responses to economic dislocations or to treat fascism in the interwar period accurately.

In fact, the Great Depression revealed that democracies required a governmental commitment to basic social needs. After the war, European countries came to believe that governments should enable economic sustenance and social security. Social insurance should mitigate against an unpredictable market economy. In part, this sense derived from the social solidarity the war effort produced. The successful implementation of social welfare programs also allied Social Democratic parties with Christian Democrats, preventing the success of communist parties in Europe, as did the New Deal in the United States. These Christian curricula are severely limited in addressing economic issues because, for them, the economy implements God's intentions, largely removing economics from the political sphere or historical analysis.

These histories' attacks on interwar economic and social policies reflect the beginnings of evangelical identification with Republican Party positions. They had not yet coalesced around a political party, but they identified with Republicans' concerns about the liberalization of culture and the rise of liberalism and revolution.[40] In attacking humanism, or what will later be called "secular humanism," these textbooks invoke battles evangelicals fought with proponents of theological modernism over education.

Evangelicals were especially concerned about John Dewey's ideas, which they saw as exerting a dangerous, liberal influence on education. The Abeka textbook condemns Dewey as an anti-Christian who believed in no absolutes but instead accepted both Darwinism and pragmatism. Dewey, it charges, asserted that "God is the work of human nature, imagination, and will." This denunciation of Dewey signals these textbooks' concern with the educational crisis evangelicals identified in the early twentieth century. For them, modern education rejected the predominant educational values since the Protestant Reformation.[41] Prior to the turn of the century, educational philosophy was rooted in Protestant theological seminaries. The Abeka US history adamantly insists that until then education "was basically the same as that followed by Martin Luther, John Calvin, John Wesley, the English and American Puritans. . . . It is called traditional education." But American universities instead adopted the social science seminar method of German universities and so introduced methods that had borne fruit in biblical modernism. Dewey's malign educational values fostered secular humanism, which, according to these critiques, is the belief that moral matters "should be based on consideration of the well-being of mankind in this present life, to the exclusion of all considerations drawn from belief in God or in a future existence."[42] Evangelicals deplored changes in the historical profession, as historians, such as Charles Beard, focused on economic history rather than on providential history or on history's moral lessons.[43] When the fundamentalist movement mobilized to root out Darwinian evolution from the schools, they believed they were fighting for the survival of Christian civilization.

Opposition to Dewey's educational ideas and liberalism, both political and theological, as well as horror that some Christians accepted these changes, led evangelicals to mount a direct counteroffensive with the publication *The Fundamentals* (1909–1915). These essays, which asserted specific tenets as defining Christian belief, ultimately divided some evangelicals from self-styled fundamentalists.[44] Financed by Lyman Stewart, an oil wildcatter who made a fortune with Standard Oil in California, and his brother Milton, three million copies of *The Fundamentals* were distributed to pastors and their flocks and professors and their students to spread this fundamentalist gospel.[45] As the Abeka textbook puts it, "God raised up a host of great preachers, Bible teachers, and Christian thinkers to defend the faith against the heresies of modernism and liberalism."[46] This alliance between theological and political conservatism, forged in the postwar period, advanced more extreme views as well. As fundamentalists rallied to defeat the pernicious intellectual and political developments of the early twentieth century, they reinvigorated their attacks on Catholics, Jews, Mormons, and Christian Scientists.[47] Bob Jones Sr. was concerned that university education was becoming secularized as science faculties accepted Darwin. The postwar world required the vigilant surveillance of education by true Christians.

Prominent fundamentalists recanted their prior acceptance of modernism. R. A Torrey rejected his education at the Yale Divinity School, and J. Gresham Machen critiqued modernism and fought against secularism in the universities and for fundamentalism with Old Calvinism grafted on to political libertarianism.[48] Most influential was Billy Sunday's media career, which brought fundamentalism to an audience of over 100 million.[49] Then, according to the Abeka history, "spiritual revivals and mass evangelism . . . helped preserve the world from collapsing into complete immorality and emptiness."[50]

Evangelicals found the post-World War I world profoundly disquieting. They saw any tinge of theological liberalism as undermining Christianity and the nation. Increasingly, many saw an acute need to restore a Christian nation in the face of threats to that identity from the influx of Jewish and Catholic immigrants and the introduction of evolution into the public schools.[51] The National Association of Evangelicals, founded in 1942, revived an idea, rejected in the nineteenth century, that there should be a "Christian amendment to recognize Jesus as Lord in the American Constitution." They opposed the New Deal and the teaching of Darwinism in public schools. Evangelicals' most zealous campaign was fought against communism, although some of them honed their economic arguments by inveighing against the social reforms of the interwar period.[52]

These curricula attribute the Depression to actions of bankers and modest failures of policy. It in no way indicted capitalism. This is how they construe its unfolding. While America became the leading industrial and financial center, Europe struggled to rebuild. Germany depended on American loans to pay reparations. The bankers injected easy money (not backed by gold) into the economy, distorting the balance of supply and demand. Prices then rose, leading to inflation. The Federal Reserve kept interest rates low, which encouraged people to take on debt and make risky investments. As industrial production slowed because of decreased demand, it became clear that stocks were overvalued, leading to the crash of October 29, 1929. According to the Abeka textbook, "government intervention by way of the Federal Reserve System only intensified the present problems and even deepened the Depression."[53] In other words, then as now, the Federal Reserve's monetary policy was destructive. These textbooks' assessments of the Depression replicate current attacks on Keynesian economics in general and the Federal Reserve in particular.

European countries, according to these curricula, responded inappropriately to these crises. Even Britain adopted deplorable socialist measures. In the aftermath of the war, the British economy suffered the effects of its war debt and loss of empire. (It granted Canada, Australia, New Zealand, and South Africa greater self-government.) The rise of the Labour Party demonstrated the influence of socialists. Although France recovered economically from World War I faster than England, socialists and communists became stronger there as well. "Socialist ideas crept into the economies" and "self-serving dictators took control of governments" in the interwar years. Both Britain and France began to experience economic and political crises—the causal connection implied rather than stated. But the greatest problem was that "religious liberals infiltrated the churches, turning many away from the truth of God's word." Ultimately, these forces of evil "led to the outbreak of World War II." The French constructed the Maginot Line to protect themselves. The BJU textbook notes its folly: "like so many other people throughout history, the French relied on human devices for their security."[54]

Interwar America too suffered "great decay in the moral life of the nation" during the Roaring Twenties. This decay is credited uncharacteristically to economic practices; "heavy advertising and credit purchases helped to weaken old ideas about thrift." The interwar period is full of foreboding, particularly about the US response to the economic crisis. Once the world economy was suffering a depression, Franklin Roosevelt introduced policies to redress it, called the New Deal. The BJU textbook insists unequivocally that the New Deal did more harm than good. It claims that, although it provided temporary relief, the New Deal was ineffective and failed to end the Depression or provide any real economic recovery. It increased government spending and power. In sum, Roosevelt's policies put the United States on the wrong path with "increased government involvement in economic and social matters, accelerating the trend in the United States toward a welfare state." It "introduced the United States to socialism."[55]

This claim is at odds with the virtually unanimous consensus of historians that the New Deal helped to thwart the emergence of strong communist and socialist movements in the United States. Socialism, as the career of labor organizer, member of the Indiana Assembly, and socialist presidential candidate Eugene Debs attests, was strongest just before New Deal measures were enacted.[56] Nonetheless, for these curricula the New Deal portends evil forms of government.

During the 1930s, evangelicals objected to the New Deal in part because they believed that the antichrist would be a totalitarian leader presiding over a one-world government. That belief is supported by Daniel 2:43 that government at the end times would be "a mix of iron and clay," the strong and the brittle, that cannot hold, which some evangelicals construe as a totalitarian leader who will be brought to power through democracy. These curricula thus consistently indict government plans to redress the economic devastation of the Depression as enhancing one-world government. Current attacks on New Deal programs by evangelicals are more tied to current Republican economic positions than to earlier fears of totalitarianism and one-world government.

The BJU textbook identifies characteristics common to totalitarian states—the use of propaganda and secret police, the emphasis on state goals rather than individual freedom, and government by force through one party. The term "totalitarian" was applied to the USSR, a former ally whose form of government presented a threat to Western liberal democracies, but these curricula apply it more indiscriminately. The BJU list of these characteristics gives students a better understanding of totalitarianism than the Abeka history, which cites socialism as the source of totalitarianism and defines fascism as "a form of socialism that is similar to Communism," except it allows some private property. It imposes control over society and "follows Darwinian ideas in its attempts to change society and bring in a new social order"; it exercises "totalitarian control."[57] In other words, fascism like socialism and communism derives from Darwin and liberalism. These curricula downplay fascism and its rise. Their treatment of this major modern political development is so cursory that students will likely understand fascism simply as an outgrowth of socialism.

The steps in Hitler's rise to power are treated more thoroughly. The BJU history provides a conventional account of the weaknesses of the Weimar Republic, recognizing that Germany had no prior tradition of republicanism and no majority party, and that Germans were politically apathetic. These factors enabled Hitler to exploit Germans' economic grievances and their opposition to communism. Storm troopers kept order at his party rallies, and the SS protected him. The Abeka curriculum describes Hitler's rise to power this way: He gave speeches, which persuaded people that he understood their economic plight. He came to power by first controlling public opinion—outlawing opposing parties and eliminating freedom of speech, the press, and assembly. He then attacked the churches.[58] Hitler quickly revealed his racist intent when German hospitals began to practice euthanasia and abortion. He blamed Jews for Germany's defeat in World War I and for degrading the Aryan race. He launched "his most nefarious scheme—the annihilation of the Jewish people and other groups he considered 'inferior.'"[59] Hitler doubtless provokes the question the BJU history poses: "What reason does the Bible give for the continued existence of the Jews despite the many attempts to destroy them? See Rom. 11:1, 5, 26–29."[60] Needless to say, none of these textbooks mention the inspiration for antisemitism Nazis found in some Christian sources, including the Gospel of John's denunciation of the Jews as children of the devil or Luther's harsh condemnation of them in On the Jews and Their Lies.[61]

These curricula treat Benito Mussolini quite gently. Mussolini came to power because of popular discontent with "the unrest caused by labor unions and Socialist political groups."[62] By manipulating democratic processes, Mussolini maintained the appearance of representative government. He negotiated an agreement with the Roman Catholic Church. Once the pope had recognized his government, the Vatican became a small state under his control. Implicitly, the Catholic Church and socialists are responsible for Mussolini's rise to power.[63] This discussion also suggests that fascism is an understandable response to government spending and economic policies that liberals pursue.

These curricula largely exculpate Europeans who supported fascist regimes. According to the BJU history, most Italians were not fascists; they were simply tired of the unrest caused by labor unions and socialists. Many Germans were simply distressed by the economic situation, due to high government spending and the resulting government debt.[64] The BJU textbook indicts "German Christians" as complicit in supporting Hitler, although the quotation marks allow it to differentiate them from other Christians. In fact, although some German pastors resisted, a significant proportion of German Protestants supported Hitler but, this textbook insists, they did so only because they rejected the Bible because it was written by Jews. "German Christians" claimed that Jesus was not a Jew and that He saved them from Jewish domination. Some even saw Hitler as a second messiah.[65] By pointing to such extreme views, the BJU history exculpates other Christians. It ignores the fact that many ordinary German Protestants and Catholics supported Hitler and that some American evangelicals used biblical prophecies to undergird their antisemitism during the 1930s.[66] None of these textbooks credit historian Fritz Stern's point: "It was the pseudo-religious transfiguration of politics that largely ensured [Hitler's] success, notably in Protestant areas."[67]

Students educated with these curricula would have little understanding of how a demagogue comes to power through democratic means or how that person might play on popular fears and resentments. Such students would likely believe that only socialists, communists, or "German Christians" could become fascists. In light of this treatment of fascism, it is worth citing Robert Paxton's warning in 2005, "fascism does not require a spectacular march on some capital to take root; seemingly anodyne decisions to tolerate lawless treatment of national 'enemies' is enough. [68]American fascism, he suggested, would not need Nazi symbols, only the flag and the cross.

The Abeka textbook details Hitler's attractions for Germans but draws idiosyncratic conclusions. The Germans wanted revenge for the Peace of Versailles, and "Germany looked for a leader who could deliver her from her enemies and from her disgrace." ACE notes that between the wars, Germany was governed by democratic parties, but the worldwide depression "opened the way for dictatorship." It describes the development of Hitler's dictator-ship in a curiously disconnected way: "Into that unstable situation came the National Socialist Party." National Socialism was based on two essen-tial ideas: Germans were the "master race," and Jews were responsible for Germany's problems.[69] Ultimately, although fascism develops in response to defeat in war or bad economic policies, it is the end product of Darwinism and socialism, according to these curricula. Students educated with them could reasonably conclude that those who believed in neither evolution nor socialism were and will remain untainted.

Except for the persecution of the Jews, these curricula focus little on the evils of National Socialism. They instead concentrate their critique on the evils of communism. They indict the United States for failing to recognize Russian communism's threat to Christianity. In 1933, the United States "offi-cially recognized the Communist government in Russia, making it possible for the Russians to acquire both loans and technology to develop their mili-tary might." In contrast, Francisco Franco took "the right position, fighting to keep Communists out of Spain."[70] The Abeka curriculum admires fascism's anti-communism, especially in Spain, and claims that Franco had to look to the Axis powers because the Soviets supported the Allies.

These curricula identify the West's policy of appeasement as its most telling interwar failure. When Germany invaded Czechoslovakia, only Winston Churchill recognized the danger. When Hitler wanted control of the Polish Corridor, Western resistance was hampered by Russia's nonaggression pact with Germany. Eager to expand German power, Hitler sent troops into the Rhineland, a demilitarized territory after World War I. He then seized Austria and claimed the Sudetenland for ethnic Germans. After the German invasion of Poland, Russia invaded from the East, a move "the British chose to ignore" with "far-reaching and tragic consequences." When Poland was partitioned between Nazi Germany and communist Russia in October 1939, "a reign of terror and oppression descended upon the freedom-loving Polish people."[71] Only when Germany would not withdraw from Poland did France and England finally declare war.

Other Axis powers are more readily condemned in these histories. They embraced false religions and were thus "destined for defeat." In Japan, "the militarists used Japan's ancient religious customs and long traditions of the samurai, or warrior class," to convince the people that they were invincible.[72] The war in the Pacific exposed a conflict between Hirohito, who "kept the Japanese in bondage to the religions of Buddhism and Shintoism," and General Douglas MacArthur, who recognized "that Japan's real needs were primarily moral and religious."[73]

These textbooks give a thorough account of the war's events. They cover the campaigns and battles in the Western theater, the Pacific, Africa, and the Mediterranean, as well as Hitler's invasion of the Soviet Union. They acknowledge the Soviets' central role in defeating Germany but condemn Western countries for supporting the Soviets' move into Eastern Europe. Not surprisingly, the US role in the war features prominently. The United States came out of an isolationist period with its Lend-Lease Program of providing materials for combatants fighting Axis powers, including lending the Soviet Union money and providing technology to develop its military power. This policy, these textbooks claim, made the spread of communism possible.[74] After the Japanese attacked Pearl Harbor, the United States entered the war. The Abeka textbook charges that the United States knew of the impending attack but did not inform the military base. This is a common anti-Roosevelt, anti–New Deal conspiracy theory. It was prominent in the 1940s, particularly among those who believed either that the United States should not get involved in the war or should support Germany.[75] The war itself, however, provides examples of divine intervention on the side of the Allies. The BJU history highlights "the miracle at Dunkirk" when "God used both human instruments and the forces of nature to answer the prayers of concerned but trusting British citizens."[76]

By 1945, when Axis defeat was imminent, Stalin, Churchill, and Roosevelt came together at Yalta to agree to conditions for peace. They recognized Soviet control of Eastern Europe, and, after Hitler's suicide, Germany surrendered unconditionally. The Abeka textbook condemns FDR. He gave Poland, Mongolia, and Manchuria to Stalin. More damning, he believed "that democratic socialism was the solution to the problems of the lesser-developed nations of the world."[77]

The Allies then discovered the horrors of the concentration camps—a claim that ahistorically whitewashes the Allies' prior knowledge. After the victors issued an ultimatum to Japan, the United States used incendiary bombs on Japanese cities. The United States dropped the atomic bomb on Hiroshima and Nagasaki in the belief that it would save American lives by making an invasion unnecessary. The BJU textbook sums up the war with the biblical quotation, "whatsoever a man soweth, that shall he reapeth." During the twentieth century, many "realized the vanity of life," but nonetheless trusted "ambitious, self-seeking human leaders but found them to be great oppressors."[78]

During the first half of the twentieth century, the world experienced two cataclysmic world wars. By contending that the cause of war is sin inherent to human lusts and that efforts to ensure or procure peace are both doomed and reprehensible, these curricula do not give students tools of historical analysis sufficient information to understand the complex causes of the wars or the complications of the peace. Instead, students are encouraged to judge as these curricula do. Calamitous events are due to the anti-biblical sentiments of others. These textbooks have no difficulty in assigning blame to any nation or civilization they consider deserving of divine retribution. Their unquestioned assumption is that Christians are always on the right side; those who do not identify with their views are not. They are either not Christian or do not adhere to the correct understanding of the Bible.

The ability of students to understand the complexity of this period is undermined by the indiscriminate critical brush these curricula wield to denounce political ideas—from liberalism to totalitarianism—without differentiating between them or, indeed, presenting them accurately. Liberalism is the root of dangerous modern political ideas. It led to the completely erroneous notion that government has a role to play in reforming society or in regulating the economy. It produced the welfare state and the New Deal.

The political ills these curricula identify inexorably flow from the rejection of biblical inerrancy. These histories retrace the alienation of evangelical Christians from the politics and culture of the early twentieth century. Evangelicals reacted with hostility toward domestic developments, including increased Jewish and Catholic immigration and the rise of the social sciences. In response, evangelicals insisted that only commitment to biblical Christianity could save the United States. The saving grace in this period of cultural decline was fundamentalism.

By identifying bad ideas as the cause of political disasters, these textbooks give students extremely limited means to understand them, particularly the rise of fascism in the 1930s. The ultimate explanation for modern dictators is their adherence to bad ideas, although this purported connection is neither explained nor developed. Students have almost no concrete context for the horrific events that unfolded or means to understand their political, economic, and social dimensions or their aftermath. The twentieth century's dire economic problems are due to government spending with attendant debt and inflation. These developments require neither regulation nor limits on capitalism.

Other world histories distinguish Western European socialism from fascism and National Socialism instead of inaccurately considering them as essentially identical. Indeed, some textbooks understand the battle against fascism as a defense of the values of Western liberal democracies, accepted since the eighteenth century, including constitutionalism, individual freedom, commercial capitalism, science and learning, and religious liberty. In other words, World War II was fought to maintain Enlightenment ideals these curricula deplore.[79]

These Christian histories categorically reject this understanding. Instead, two world wars were punishments for sin, especially the acceptance of biblical modernism. It led Germany astray and ended with divine repudiation of the Axis powers—Germany for its theological transgressions and Japan for its heretical religion. There is thus little reason to analyze Hitler's rise to power or to document the methods by which fascist dictators subverted democracy. This simplistic analysis leaves students ill prepared to understand this significant period as a historical phenomenon rather than a religious one or to understand the rise of similar movements in the current political moment.

15

Evil Abroad and at Home

These Christian textbooks see the period from the end of World War II to the 1980s through the lens of evangelicals' battles. The world was dangerous, and evangelicals felt beleaguered. Their values were under assault with the rise of communism and socialism abroad and, they feared, at home. Decolonization unleashed international communism, threatening their quest to spread Christianity throughout the world. In treating the post–World War II period, these curricula focus on essential campaigns of the American political and religious right: antipathy to the New Deal and support for Cold War anti-communism. These textbooks fight them with the virulence of the original battles.

At home, Supreme Court cases exacerbated evangelicals' sense that things were awry. In *Everson v. Board of Education of Ewing Township* (1947), the Supreme Court applied the Establishment Clause of the Bill of Rights ("Congress shall make no law respecting an establishment of religion or prohibiting free exercise thereof") to the states. When it ruled in *Engel v. Vitale* (1962) that prayer in the public schools was unconstitutional, many evangelicals did not initially object, because the prayer at issue was nonde-nominational. They were more concerned when the court ruled in *Abington v. Schempp* (1963) that Bible reading in public schools was a religious exercise. Reading the KJV version of the Bible had been common and was a central reason Catholics placed their children in parochial schools. Southern Baptists even supported the court decisions because they feared that arguing for religion in the public schools would give similar rights to Catholics and federal support to Catholic schools.[1] Despite disagreements about strategy, evangelicals agreed that the world was becoming increasingly secular, a development they abhorred. These rulings ultimately put many conservative Christians on the defensive and mobilized their attempts to reestablish a Christian America.

Like most Americans during the Cold War, evangelicals feared the spread of communism, but their response was more extreme and tied to their eschatology. They saw in the Cold War intimations of the coming

Hijacking History. Kathleen Wellman, Oxford University Press. © Oxford University Press 2021.
DOI: 10.1093/oso/9780197579237.003.0016

apocalypse; the battle between Christian and communist foreshadowed Armageddon.[2] Evangelical and fundamentalist universities deployed "political demonology," a polemical strategy characteristic of 1950s anti-communist crusades.[3] These textbooks, like the works of their evangelical forebears, raise the alarm about Satan's role in the world as they revert to the red-hot rhetoric of the Cold War. Communism was "a religion that is inspired, directed, and motivated by the Devil himself."[4] The battle against it required every Christian's commitment.

These textbooks also reflect the post–World War II alliance between evangelicals and Republicans who fused patriotism and religion to defeat communism.[5] Billy Graham emerged as a major force, proselytizing in a world divided between Christian and communist. He warned that communists were infiltrating universities and believed that Senator Joseph McCarthy was being persecuted by communist sympathizers in the United States.[6] The advance of communism in the East was a warning to the West. Only by defeating it could the West be saved.

Evangelicals were profoundly uneasy about cultural developments in America. These textbooks express that disquiet but also see American domestic history as continuing the saga of Christian virtue, inextricably tied to capitalism and confirmed by economic success. If business fostered the political right, particularly its effort to rescind the New Deal and attack communism, so much the better. If both the New Deal and communism could be tied to social progressives, the Democratic Party, or proponents of the Social Gospel, better still.

The extreme rhetoric of the Cold War shapes these textbooks' narrative. Communism more than fulfills their long-standing warning that human beings cannot improve social conditions and political revolutions cannot effect positive change. Those reprehensible ideas had disastrous ramifications in the twentieth century. Communism attacked the family, subsuming it under the state. "Communists' leaders could do whatever they felt was good for the whole of society without regard for individual human welfare," the Abeka textbook asserts.[7]

These textbooks' denunciations of communism entail a broad-brush critique of other cultural phenomena, just as they did in the 1950s. They offer dire warnings about phenomena that might seem benign but lead to perdition, including (1) social scientists, liberals, or closet Marxists, relying on "pseudo-sciences" like psychology; (2) public education, permeated with values of John

Dewey and democratic socialism; and (3) covert Marxism identifying the "haves" and "have nots." Such concern about the postwar period suggests worrisome comparisons to the present for any student who takes them to heart.

From the 1940s through the 1960s, anti-communism and perceived assaults on Protestant culture led religious conservatives to move to the Republican Party. Dwight Eisenhower fostered the Dixiecrat conversion from the Democratic Party to the Republican Party by supporting a public role for religion. He thought religion could exert a positive influence on democracy by moderating individual greed. Nonetheless, this period also saw the concerted use of religion to argue for the virtues of capitalism, giving greed a positive value as corporate leaders argued for capitalism against communism. They hoped to undo the New Deal by contending that it was communist, even though Eisenhower, in fact, consolidated it. During his administration, corporate capitalism and evangelicalism forged a firmer relationship. Capitalists, such as J. Howard Pew of Sun Oil, became major donors to the most prominent evangelical, Billy Graham. Pew believed that Scripture both endorsed laissez-faire capitalism and repudiated social reform, tying Christianity to the political goals of the Republican Party. Evangelicals' enthusiasm for Eisenhower waned after Graham criticized him for failing to win the Korean War and thus halt the spread of communism. Eisenhower also disappointed evangelicals by failing to support the Hungarian Revolution and Joseph McCarthy and by appointing Earl Warren to the Supreme Court.[8]

These curricula expose a stark dichotomy as they trace the steps the United States and the USSR took in defining their adversarial relationship. In 1946, Joseph Stalin and Vyacheslav Molotov proclaimed democracy a threat and imposed the so-called "Iron Curtain." The United States began a policy of "containment," supporting anti-communist regimes and underwriting their military expenditures. In 1947, the Truman Doctrine stipulated that the United States would "assist free people who are resisting attempted subjugation by armed minorities" or by outside pressures. The United States initiated an economic recovery plan for Europe called the Marshall Plan. "Her [America's] goal was to spread democracy and promote free trade through the world," the BJU textbook proclaims.[9] Stalin organized the Comintern to spread revolutionary communism and moved to control Eastern Europe. In February 1948, communists expelled a coalition government and brought Czechoslovakia under its control. The Soviets and their satellites ultimately agreed to the Warsaw Pact in 1955.

The Abeka textbook sounds an alarm about these developments: communism in Western Europe was "leading to Satan on earth," as "nations that fell to communism were locked into an atheistic dictatorship." In contrast, "the free world stood in opposition to the human slavery of international communism."[10] It cites the reactionary Whittaker Chambers, the former communist who recanted and then testified against Alger Hiss: "The Communist vision is the vision of man without God . . . of man's mind displacing God as the creative intelligence of the universe."[11] The Abeka textbook draws its characterization of communism directly from Schwarz's *Why Communism Kills* as (1) a form of socialism "which advocates the (2) violent overthrow of existing governments with (3) the goal of changing society and ultimately perfecting mankind," and finally that (4) "communism always leads to totalitarian dictatorship." Communism's goal is to transform society "into an atheistic, humanistic image of 'perfection.'"[12] The last point connects communism to illegitimate human aspirations going back to the Tower of Babel. ACE shares the grim sense of the period but contends that events of the twentieth century "point to His Second Coming, which is the very next event on God's calendar."[13]

In the contested relationship between East and West, Soviet Russia provides dire examples. These curricula point out that, since the Russian Revolution, relations between Russia and the West were fraught; even their wartime alliance was merely expedient. The Russian situation deteriorated after Lenin's death in 1924 and brought Stalin, one of "the most brutal rulers of all time," to power for more than twenty-five years. His five-year plans, intended to industrialize and modernize agriculture, rapidly "turned the country back toward socialism," and those who resisted were subject to severe repression.[14] Collectivization and the suppression of resistance to it led to five million deaths. Stalin purged opponents and, with communism secured at home, promoted international communism. From Russia's horrifying example, the BJU curriculum extracts an inspiring hero. Peter Vins, a missionary to Russia, was imprisoned for his anti-Soviet views. His example provokes the questions it asks: "How did God work to turn seemingly negative life experiences to His own glory?"[15] The correct response is Vin's proselytizing.

The BJU history acknowledges the geopolitical rationale behind the Soviets' creation of the Eastern bloc: They wanted a buffer zone in Eastern Europe. They had lost fifteen to twenty million as compared to 389,000 Americans killed in World War II, and it had reason to fear invasion. However, this textbook condemns the Soviets for failing to appreciate that "the Allies fought to free Eastern Europe from Nazi tyranny."[16] The contest between the two powers led to an arms race: once Russia had produced an atomic bomb, the United States began production of the hydrogen bomb. The Soviets expanded their control of Eastern Europe: In 1961, the East Germans, with Soviet support, constructed the Berlin Wall; 1962 was the year of a dramatic standoff—the Cuban missile crisis.

Subsequent developments moderated East-West tensions with, as ACE puts it, "cracks in the Iron Curtain."[17] In 1963, the nuclear test-ban treaty was signed. Leonid Brezhnev both maintained the USSR's right to intervene in the domestic politics of other communist countries and introduced a policy of détente with the West. The Prague Spring of 1968 briefly brought a more open form of communism to Czechoslovakia. To expand Soviet influence in Central Asia, Brezhnev invaded Afghanistan in 1979. That intervention sapped the Soviet economy and demoralized Soviet society. The BJU curriculum dedicates an entire page to Aleksandr Solzhenitsyn's warnings to the West about communism's dangers. By the end of the 1970s, it claims, the Soviets were violating agreements, but the United States was too weak to resist until Ronald Reagan's presidency.[18]

The conflict between the Soviet Union and the United States played out in the domestic sphere almost as intensely as in the international arena. These curricula invoke Cold War fears of a domestic fifth column. The BJU history cites Winston Churchill's warnings in his Westminster College speech of March 5, 1946, that communists "work in complete unity and absolute obedience to the direction they receive from the Communist center. . . . [they] constitute a growing challenge and peril to Christian civilization."[19] The political and religious right saw the United States as a Christian nation pitted against both godless communism and New Deal socialism. Tensions were exacerbated by the Supreme Court's affirmation in 1947 of the "wall of separation" between religion and the state. In response, beginning with the Eisenhower era, the Pledge of Allegiance affirmed "one nation under God" and coins "in God we trust." The Christian right contended that the American Christian nation was coming undone by secularism. Kevin Kruse has traced how the nineteenth-century Christian nation thesis, amplified by the alliance of evangelicals with business interests in postwar America, deliberately promoted the nation as "Christian" capitalism in opposition to socialism and communism.[20]

A McCarthyite campaign vetted textbooks for "patriotism," altering their content and censoring educational materials. Texas mandated a six credit hour American history requirement for state universities. Such measures attempted to reinstate Christian culture as a bulwark against communist influence.[21] The political right subsequently objected to the civil rights and antiwar movements. These Christian curricula revive many of the issues of McCarthyite surveillance of school curricula during the 1950s, a battle that plays out in various ways to this day. The current efforts of mainline publishers not to offend right-wing school boards as well as their willingness to implement ahistorical state standards replicate the self-censorship of this earlier period.

These Christian histories have no quarrel with McCarthyism. The Abeka history commends McCarthy's efforts to expose communists in government and Hollywood: "He came under severe criticism and personal attack, but many of his conclusions, although technically unprovable, were drawn from the accumulation of undisputed facts."[22] This is a disconcerting notion of both proofs and facts, as not a single communist in the US government was ever found, but it replicates the claim of Billy Graham, who spoke for contemporary evangelicals, when he praised McCarthy for working to expose "the pinks, the lavenders, and the reds who have sought refuge beneath the wings of the American eagle."[23]

In the postwar period, the Christian right became as firmly committed to capitalism's advance as to communism's destruction. It objected to the New Deal and to Eisenhower's enlarging the federal government, particularly its involvement in banking regulation, labor disputes, and specific policies like social security and unemployment insurance, as well as the creation of government offices such as the Department of Health, Education, and Welfare. The right denounced such developments as threats to "the institutions and heritage that made her [America] great." These curricula express strong hostility to these social programs, which remain targets of the Republican Party. They indict Democratic presidents—John F. Kennedy, Lyndon B. Johnson, and Jimmy Carter—for moving the government toward socialism. These Democratic administrations fostered destructive, un-American policies such "as welfare programs [that] sapped the economy and resulted in a heavier tax burden upon the American people."[24]

The economic views of the Christian right during the 1950s were influenced, as they still are, by bestselling author Ayn Rand. A radical libertarian, she believed that selfishness was a virtue, that one should never be restricted by religion, which she dismissed as superstition, and that individuals had an obligation to follow their desires. For her, the state existed solely for law and civil defense. As a result, she rejected the welfare state and celebrated free enterprise. Her maxim was "greed is good."[25] These textbooks do not go that far, but they graft her economic arguments onto their religious views with an important shift: Wealth is not gained by greed but by God's favor.

The Austrian economist Friedrich Hayek also influenced the political right. As we have seen, he was a source for understanding the nineteenth-century working class. Hayek argued that corporations were less coercive than the state, and he celebrated small government, free markets, and private property. Collective action set human beings On the Road to Serfdom and totalitarianism, as his most famous work contended. His disciple, the Austrian economist Ludwig von Mises, believed that bureaucracy constrained creativity. These Austrian economists' views do not simply characterize current right-wing economic orthodoxy, but they also articulate God's intent for the economy and government.[26]

On the international scene, US efforts to rebuild Europe, not explicitly directed against communism, smacked of internationalism and hence were objectionable. The establishment of NATO in 1949 and of the European Economic Community in 1958 were both mistakes, but these textbooks reserve their greatest vitriol for the United Nations: it opposes freedom and favors totalitarian regimes. The Abeka textbook describes the UN as "a colossal failure as a peace-keeping body" and as fundamentally at odds with America—"a threat to freedom around the world." The UN incorporates malign interests, advancing communism and espousing a "collectivist" philosophy, opposed to "the kind of individual freedoms cherished in free nations like the United States." The UN is "contrary to the basic Judeo-Christian concept of law which limits government" and is instead an attempt to found "a totalitarian, one-world government." The UN becomes key to Satan's agenda of one-world government. The Abeka history concludes that "the UN charter . . . threatens religious, and social liberty of all free peoples." It defines the UN as "a collectivist juggernaut that would crush individual freedom and force the will of an elite few on all of humanity."[27]

Attacks on the UN mirror those of the political right at the time. Phyllis Schlafly's Eagle Forum and Beverly La Haye's Concerned Women of America inveighed against the UN as the "headquarters for Soviet espionage" and called for the United States to pull out. They raised the alarm that the UN

Convention on the Elimination of All Forms of Discrimination against Women would undermine "family law, parental rights, religious exercise, education, [and] abortion regulation" and set "employment pay scales, quotas in educational institutions, workplaces and elected offices."[28] The UN's advocacy of women would negatively impact causes the political right sustained in the 1950s and supports still.

These textbooks bemoan the fact that whenever the arms race between East and West led to wars, the West was never wholehearted enough to defeat communism. The fall of China to the communists was not simply a "blow to American interests," as the BJU history puts it, but also a defeat for American efforts to protect Chinese freedom.[29] These textbooks are especially incensed about the treatment of the heroic General Douglas MacArthur by President Truman, who removed MacArthur from his command after he ordered his troops to invade North Korea to the Chinese border, provoking the Chinese, expanding the war, and countering US policy. The Abeka textbook claims, "President Truman feared offending Communist China" and thus failed to support MacArthur. The BJU textbook is incredulous that Truman removed the virtuous MacArthur, whom it identifies as a model of Christian rectitude who brought missionaries to Japan. Japan's development as a prosperous democracy "was one of the remarkable success stories of the postwar era" due, in this retelling, to MacArthur.[30] As Benjamin Lynerd comments, "Nothing chased evangelicals and Republicans into each other's arms faster than President Truman's dismissal of General Douglas MacArthur," even though MacArthur had defied Truman.[31] Truman cut China off from evangelical missionary efforts and was therefore reprehensible. Opposition to Truman's actions led both Republicans and evangelicals to look instead to Eisenhower. The 1952 election intimated the emerging clout of the ballot-box alliance between Republicans and evangelicals.

These curricula criticize US foreign policy for its failure to defeat communism and promote Christianity. After the United States failed to support MacArthur, the US China policy became, according to the Abeka history, a complete failure, as "liberal American journalists promoted Mao Zedong as an 'agrarian reformer' and a 'true man of the people,' while portraying Chiang Kai-shek as 'corrupt' and 'power-hungry.'" The success of communism in China is due to this misbegotten policy: "the United States had deserted a friend in need."[32] ACE is equally unforgiving of America's China policy: it ultimately led to the admission of China into the UN General Assembly. When the United States tried unsuccessfully to have both Taiwan and China seated, ' "Red China' became the legal China." ACE condemns the Cultural Revolution for excising Christian influences from China. This disastrous policy was fully on view in 1978 when Jimmy Carter withdrew diplomatic recognition from Taiwan and recognized the communist People's Republic of China. ACE concludes, "In the name of expediency, America's faithful former allies were unceremoniously discarded like an old shoe."[33]

These curricula cite the Korean War as another American failure. In the postwar period, the United States and the Russians expelled the Japanese from Korea and divided it into north and south with plans for reunification. But two distinct states emerged as North and South Korea, communist and non-communist occupied zones. The North then tried to conquer South Korea. For the Abeka textbook, the Korean conflict amply confirms the inability of the UN to establish peace. The BJU history bemoans that the "failure of the free world to secure a military victory" fostered communist aggression.[34]

American wars in Asia were political and moral failures, but none more so than Vietnam, which remains a glaring indictment of the failure of American will for these curricula.[35] Their account of how the United States came to be involved is straightforward. During World War II, Japan captured French Indochina. After the war, France went to war to regain its former colony, but the communist leader, Ho Chi Minh, declared Vietnam's independence. After the French army was defeated, a settlement divided the country into north and south, but communist guerrillas persisted in attempting to take over the south. In response, SEATO (South East Asia Treaty Organization) member nations agreed to consult over any communist expansion in Asia. In 1955, Eisenhower promised military aid to South Vietnam's President Diem. He believed in the domino theory; if Vietnam fell to communism, all Southeast Asia would follow suit. American advisors took over the training of the South Vietnamese Army from the French.[36] By 1962, the United States had troops there. In 1964, when the United States claimed that North Vietnam attacked its gunboats in the Gulf of Tonkin, Congress empowered Lyndon Johnson to take all necessary action. (Reports of this attack were false.) As the war dragged on without discernible progress and with many American deaths, it became deeply unpopular at home, and Johnson decided not to run for a second term. Nixon officially pursued a policy of "Vietnamization," that is, enlarging the South Vietnamese army while commensurately bringing US troops home. Unofficially, he extended the war by secretly bombing and then invading Cambodia to destroy North Vietnamese bases and supply zones in

Cambodia. But, the BJU textbook reports, "Nixon finally achieved what he called 'peace with honor' by negotiating a peace settlement with the North Vietnamese in January 1973."[37]

Even though these curricula lay out the major transitions in the war, they harshly denounce its denouement. After the US troops left, South Vietnam was quickly overrun by the North. When Laos and Cambodia were also taken over by communists, "the 'domino theory' had proved true," the BJU history concludes.[38] ACE notes that the Vietnam War, though undeclared, was America's longest war. (The current wars in Iraq and Afghanistan now have that dubious distinction.) It concludes that "after three generations of fighting, Vietnam was a unified nation—under the heel of Communist dictators."[39] The BJU textbook contends that "Vietnam [was] America's biggest failure during the Cold War; communism had not been contained; in fact, it had been completely victorious." Defeat led to a loss of American power and provoked opposition to American military interventions, factors that further encouraged communists. By the 1970s, America had lost power and prestige. It was limited by the rise of communist power, the threat of nuclear weapons, and "the lack of resolve of the American people."[40]

These textbooks faithfully convey the positions evangelicals took during the Vietnam War. They supported it as an anti-communist crusade allied to Christian Americanism; Jerry Falwell defended the American soldier as "a champion for Christ."[41] Evangelicals remained staunchly committed to the war long after most Americans no longer were. When these curricula critique the war as a failure of will, they replicate the stance of some evangelicals, many Southern Baptist ministers, and many fundamentalists, including Bob Jones Jr., who had urged more far-reaching military action.[42] For them and many on the political right, the US failure in Vietnam exposed the precipitous decline of America.

The BJU textbook asks students to consider the following questions about the war: "Why do you think God allowed the United States, the most powerful and best equipped military force in the world at the time, to be defeated by the guerilla forces of a backward Third World country? What lessons, if any, do you think Americans learned from that defeat?" This history ultimately questions the wisdom of "fighting a limited war to prevent another global war," but never the rightness of US military intervention. It contends that LBJ's socialist, domestic spending undermined efforts in Vietnam.[43] The Iran policy of the United States too was based on the failure of a Democratic president to sufficiently support its ally, the Shah, in his anti-communist,

EVIL ABROAD AND AT HOME   257

anti-Islamic efforts. In other words, misguided spending on social issues and lack of will frustrated success in the fight against communism, undermined military efforts, and eroded the nation's power and prestige.

These Christian curricula remain committed to a thoroughgoing Cold War narrative, entrenched in the embattled sense of the Christian right at that time. They spell out the ideological contest: the USSR was intent on imposing its political system on the world; the United States wanted to promote democracy and capitalism. These textbooks present the sanguine view that America foreign policy was thoroughly altruistic, intended to advance the self-determination, democracy, and free trade of other countries. These histories uncritically share the view of earlier evangelicals that communism had to be defeated by any means, and thus the textbooks support capitalist dictators and cheer every military coup toppling any left-leaning government, much as US foreign policy did at the time.

While these curricula see this battle as an unrelenting contest between good and evil, as many did at the time, recent histories, written several decades after the end of the Cold War, provide a more nuanced view. Historians recognize that the Cold War shaped US and Soviet policies, but their standoff was not simply or primarily religious. The Soviets wanted to maintain their influence and energy resources, as did the United States. They acknowledge that the Soviet Union grappled with serious political threats, among them the Suez Canal crisis, the Polish election, and the Hungarian uprising. Khrushchev contended with revolts within the Russian sphere of influence as both Hungary and Poland reduced Russia's control over them. Although historical understanding of the Cold War has developed beyond the polemics of the period, these curricula remain entrenched in them.

These textbooks focus primarily on the Cold War and the American response to it as the key to understanding the postwar world, but another significant development was the process of decolonization and its far-reaching implications, as scholars are acutely aware. These curricula are ill positioned to give students sufficient understanding of the complexity of this process. Their criticisms of colonialism are quite muted because they understand it as Christian proselytizing and deplore its end. They see colonial liberation movements as deluded by communists into giving up their freedom. American evangelicals were acutely anxious about US policies as decolonization played out in South Asia and Africa. In contrast, historians typically consider the political and economic issues of those countries seeking liberation from colonial powers more thoroughly and not solely in terms of American interests or evangelical Christianity.

The postwar period saw massive worldwide decolonization, beginning with the Dutch loss of the East Indies (Indonesia) in 1949 and ending with the independence of South Africa in 1994. In 1945, colonial powers governed one-third of the world's population; since then 140 nations have been admitted to the UN. During the interwar period, colonial powers faced revolts and nationalist movements, but World War II fundamentally altered the power dynamic between the colonizer and the colonized. Colonial military forces had joined their home countries to fight the war. After the war, it was clear that the liberal democratic ideals the Allies had fought for accorded ill with colonial control. Furthermore, the United States was inclined to support some independence movements as serving its economic interests. But the Cold War led to worries about emerging nations aligning with the Soviet Union rather than the West. As European powers retreated from empire and former colonies sought their independence, both superpowers, the United States and the Soviet Union, tried to bring former colonies into their spheres of influence.

For these curricula, the impact of the United States on former colonies was unquestionably beneficial: the colonies themselves are passive; they will be saved by the United States or damned by the USSR. Where decolonization does not involve this battle, these textbooks are more objective. Without an ideological ax to grind, they discuss events in more conventional, political terms. For example, these textbooks report the complexities of the Algerian situation with respect to its colonizer, France, dispassionately. They acknowledge that Algeria became part of France by 1848, but that Europeans who settled in Algeria had rights Muslims did not. When celebrations at the end of World War II became violent, the ensuing repression of the Muslim population produced Algerian nationalism. France took a strong stand in Algeria, but the FLN (Front de libération nationale) fought an effective guerilla war against it and forced a strategic retreat in 1962. This even-handed treatment is noteworthy: it discusses the interest of colonized and colonizer and stipulates interests and rights as important to political opposition.[44] This approach does not characterize discussions of other colonial independence movements or political revolts, which are instead understood in terms of Christian or American interests.

Africa's decolonization poses serious problems. As the Abeka textbook describes the process, "Conflicts created by intertribal warfare, witchcraft cults, and Communists and Muslim terrorists resulted in much blood-shed."[45] When African colonies sought independence from colonial powers, they unacceptably looked to communists, who fomented Black discontent and urged revolt. In Kenya, communists influenced Jomo Kenyatta and the Mau [Mau Mau], and the members of one tribe "took a blood oath both terrible and degrading." ACE objects to Kenyatta's seven-year prison sentence as too lenient. It bemoans that this "Communist author of the Mau [Mau Mau] terror" became the first president of an independent Kenya but concedes that Kenyatta later moderated his commitment to communism and even allowed missionaries. The Congo, however, was "rife with chaos, murder, and mayhem" and was "degenerating back into a state of primitive savagery" (no coded language there!) under Patrice Lumumba, castigated as an alleged communist. Katanga broke from the rest of Congo under the leadership of Moise Tschombe, "an educated Christian gentleman" who "soon produced a stable civilized environment." In 1961, the UN sent troops to force Katanga to rejoin the Congo and "committed acts of cruelty and barbarity that were equal to those of Genghis Khan . . . innocent men, women, and children were machine-gunned down in the streets." [46] Such examples corroborate these curricula's indictments of internationalism, especially UN actions. The language of these descriptions of African independence efforts, including "blood oaths," "mayhem," and "primitive savagery," are racially charged and characterize Africa as barbarous—a condition to be redressed through capitalist investment and Christian conversion.

Rhodesia provides another example of misguided internationalism in these histories. When Rhodesia declared independence from Britain in 1965, Britain contested its right to do so because of apartheid. Despite the obvious and well-recognized injustice of this extreme practice of racial segregation and suppression of the Black majority, ACE essentially endorses apartheid: "Rhodesia was accused repeatedly of being an all-white, racist regime, which was totally false." It compares Rhodesia to the American colonies on the eve of the Revolution: white Rhodesians, with the virtues of early Americans, were subjected to "terrorist attacks by Communist guerillas." As "Little Rhodesia stood alone against the world," Robert Mugabe, "a dedicated Marxist, was duly elected as prime minister." Under Mugabe, "the once stable Rhodesia degenerated further into socialism and tribal war."[47] Instead of acknowledging the evils of apartheid, ACE condemns the West for failing to oppose communism in Africa strongly enough. This treatment of Rhodesia is jarring and strikingly at odds with historical consensus. The BJU textbook summarized African decolonization: "Many African countries continued to be plagued by the revolutionary, socialist legacy of communism" even after communist support ended.[48]

Latin America is also problematic for these curricula: within this American sphere of influence, socialism and communism persist. Communists "stir up violence and revolution to create chaos in which desperate people turn to Communism for relief."[49] These textbooks commend the United States for being stronger in resisting communism in Latin America than elsewhere. For example, in 1965 Lyndon Johnson sent troops to prevent a communist takeover of the Dominican Republic and the CIA was effective in Chile. Nonetheless, socialists too often played key roles in Latin America. While claiming to be "of benefit to all," socialists instead were intent on "dominating all mankind," ACE notes. It describes the situation rather strangely: "the tentacles of the social[ist?] octopus have often entangled themselves in the affairs of North and South America."[50] The BJU textbook gives a more nuanced picture, recognizing that extreme inequality, poverty, and limited education made Latin America susceptible to the lure of Soviet assistance against "what they called 'Yankee imperialism.'"[51]

These histories focus on Fidel Castro's rise to political power as a horrifying example of communism in Latin America. Castro was "even involved in some nasty political murders, served time in prison, and then from Mexico organized a rebel army," ACE charges.[52] He seized the government through terror with mass executions. These curricula overlook the role of the infamous military dictator General Fulgencio Batista, who was supported by the United States and, in turn, allowed US companies to control the Cuban economy and exploit its resources. (Abeka even claims inaccurately that the United States did not support Batista.)[53] Batista allowed the Mafia free access to Cuba and used violence and torture to maintain his power. In 1960, then Senator Kennedy recognized Batista as "the culmination of a number of sins on the part of the United States."[54]

When the CIA supported Cuban exiles' desire to overthrow Castro, it conducted the disastrous Bay of Pigs invasion in 1961. The Abeka textbook blames Kennedy for failing "to keep his promise to supply air cover to the Cuban patriots."[55] Castro then asked Russia for missiles to deter another US invasion, provoking the Cuban Missile Crisis. When Kennedy demanded that Russian missiles be dismantled, Khrushchev ultimately agreed. But ACE does not believe they were removed: "Are there still Soviet backed missiles and other sophisticated armament in Cuba? Almost assuredly there are!"[56]

On the other hand, the BJU textbook reports the resolution of the missile crisis as a major victory, as it avoided full-scale war.[57] ACE blames Cuba for promoting "Marxist propaganda and terrorist activities throughout South and Central America."[58]

For these curricula, Chilean President Salvador Allende was a Marxist dictator who nationalized industries and seized foreign holdings and private property. Most despicable, according to ACE, missionaries suffered persecution. The Chilean people begged the military to overthrow the government. When they did so, many freedoms returned to Chile. The overthrow of Allende, ACE notes with approval, was carried out with the support of the CIA.[59]

This narrative is a most striking misrepresentation of Latin American politics and US involvement in Latin America. Allende was democratically elected. The CIA aided the Chilean military coup, installing a military junta under General Augusto Pinochet. Pinochet refused to return authority to a civil government, dissolved Congress, suspended the constitution, and kidnapped, tortured, and murdered thousands who opposed him.

The treatment of India is similarly distorted, viewed through the lens of these curricula's commitment to Christian proselytizing and capitalism. Under British rule, India in the nineteenth century was ripe for religious and political conversion, as we saw. But modern India went astray. According to these curricula, India's leaders are best understood as misguided, influenced by heresies and corrupting political ideas. Gandhi and Nehru were corrupted by "their fanatical devotion to Hinduism" as well as their exposure in British universities to "Fabian socialism." Nehru and his daughter, Indira Gandhi, followed an agenda of government consolidation and social engineering, which damaged its economy and "created more misery and wretchedness for her millions of people."[60]

More balanced histories acknowledge significant problems in the British treatment of India. Indians were required to pay the cost of British administration. Most damaging, Britain pursued a policy of divide and conquer, fomenting ethnic and religious division by pitting Hindus against Muslims. In response, an Indian nationalist movement took root. Other histories recognize that Gandhi had compelling reasons to resist the British and emphasize the distinctive passive resistance he developed, which has inspired others seeking social justice, notably Martin Luther King.

These textbooks find the military successes of Israel inspiring. They appreciate the Six-Day War as a legitimate defensive act by Israel as "over and over again, some Arab leader would raise the cry of 'holy war' to drive the Jews into the sea." The Six-Day War was a stunning Israeli success. It put "Solomon's temple in Jewish hands" for the first time since 70 AD, showing "the hand of God is on His chosen people even to this day." This event was profoundly significant for millenarian expectations that the Jews will rebuild the temple during the Tribulation, and that the "Anti-Christ will commit the Abomination of Desolation in the Temple." ACE asks, "Can we doubt that God had a hand in the outcome of this war?" Events in the Middle East warrant close attention because there "the final events in human culture will one day be enacted in accordance with the plan of God."[61]

When these curricula assess modern Western European governments in the postwar period, the best are the most thoroughly capitalistic. West Germany is a capitalist miracle. (Despite the fact that it is a welfare state!) Its advance stands in notable contrast to the decline of Britain, which adopted illegitimate social programs, including "state-controlled schools, compulsory national health insurance (socialized medicine), nationalized industries, wage and price controls." Conservatives proved too weak "to dismantle the welfare system created by the Labour Party." Social welfare policies produced inevitable decline and exposed British moral decay further evidenced by a falloff in church attendance. France, most directly identified with socialism's evils, declined, while Spain experienced great economic development under Francisco Franco. It is troubling but not surprising that capitalist fascist dictators elicit less criticism from the Abeka textbook than do democratically elected socialists. About Scandinavia, this textbook grudgingly concedes their economies grew, "but the decline of public morality and religious faith and the growing cost of welfare finally took its toll"—the predictable results of socialism.[62]

In fact, European governments recognized the need to provide social security for their citizens to redress recurrent depressions and recessions. The war effort had both mobilized the population and changed the notion of social responsibility. Social insurance was introduced in Germany under Bismarck in the 1880s. But, after the war, European governments recognized social insurance as a right. Britain created the welfare state immediately after the war. France and Germany followed suit in the 1970s.

These curricula are intent on seeing Europe as a failure. They do not recognize that Europe was composed of liberal democracies (except for Spain and Portugal, which remained dictatorships until the 1970s), which recognized that only liberal democracies could resist right-wing, anti-democratic movements. These curricula do not acknowledge that European political parties with disparate interests allied to promote democracy, economic growth, and anti-communism.

In assessing the troubles in Ireland, these textbooks revive anti-Catholicism, exacerbated at that time by the election of America's first Catholic president, John F. Kennedy. In Ireland, when the Catholic minority in Ulster "began to stir up trouble," it was due to "communist agitators" under the guise of a "so-called civil rights program." ACE pronounces that, although most people wanted peace, "Communists and the IRA continue to commit acts of terrorism." It bemoans the fact that "good men like born-again Christian Rev. Ian Paisley are vilified by their Communist enemies."[63]

It is frankly astounding that any curriculum would praise Paisley. The leader of Northern Ireland and an evangelical minister, Paisley crusaded against the union of Ireland and the European Union as a committed nationalist. He railed against Catholicism, homosexuality, ecumenism, and civil rights. Through his relationship with Bob Jones III and service as a member of the BJU Board of Trustees, Paisley had a direct connection to these curricula and American evangelicals.

In treating the rest of the world, these curricula praise countries for rejecting democratic socialism and condemn them for persecuting Christians. For example, China persecutes Christians, and Sudanese Muslims persecute Christians and animists. In distinction to other benighted nations, American democracy shines a beacon for the rest of the world. This praise is somewhat disconcerting, as these curricula emphasize that the United States is a republic, scarcely mention democracy, and consistently disparage attempts to procure democracy such as revolutions and liberation, or reform movements.

As postwar evangelicals took more consistent positions on American domestic issues, those concerns become more overt in these historical narratives. The Abeka textbook points to Planned Parenthood and the UN, which "embrace 'pro-choice,' as a means of population control" and allow "the legally sanctioned practice of physician-assisted suicide, another euphemism for killing the infirm and elderly."[64] They question the rationale and the benefits of the US civil rights movement. The Abeka US history textbook notes that Southerners resented federal officials telling them what to do. "Segregation had become a way of life, and both white and black Southerners had a difficult time changing their ways," it explains.[65] Furthermore, Black Americans "did not believe" they were treated fairly.[66] For these textbooks, social problems are based on the misperception of the aggrieved, who inaccurately believe they suffer and fail to understand sin as the source of their suffering. In presenting the civil rights movement as illegitimate, curricula replicate the stance some evangelicals, particularly Southern evangelicals, took in the 1960s when they denounced the civil rights movement as engineered by communist agitators.[67] The Abeka textbook condemns Martin Luther King: "his teaching that people should break the law in non-violent ways . . . opened the door to other kinds of law breaking."[68]

At that time, the Republican Party developed a Southern strategy to signal that it, not the Democratic Party, would resist the expansion of civil rights. When Barry Goldwater was the Republican nominee in 1964, he connected evangelicals favoring prayer in schools and opposing desegregation to opposition to civil rights. Goldwater subscribed to much of the later Tea Party's platform. He called for the elimination of Social Security, federal aid to schools, welfare, farm programs, and the union shop. He claimed that the Supreme Court's *Brown v. Board* decision was unconstitutional and therefore not the "law of the land." He insisted that the United States must bypass and defund the UN and improve tactical nuclear weapons for frequent use.[69] At the time, these ideas were denounced as extreme. Their reemergence in the present suggests they remained salient. Nixon deployed the Republican Southern strategy even more successfully. In the election of 1968, he gained 80% of the evangelical vote—a figure identical to Trump's success with these voters.

These Christian textbooks condemn the culture of the 1960s, just as evangelicals did then. The Abeka textbook decries its immorality as the young revolted against the old with "long hair, rock music, drugs, and sexual immorality." It attacks antiwar demonstrators: "During the Vietnam years, Soviet influence was growing on college campuses . . . Some protestors burned their draft cards and defaced the American flag to demonstrate their hatred toward America." They were incited "as communist organizations encouraged revolution and defiance of authority across America." About protestors' demands for their rights, this textbook complains, "the Constitutional guarantee of freedom of speech was being abused by a spoiled, selfish society."[70]

Evangelicals were profoundly uneasy about political protest, whether over Vietnam or civil rights. Many considered resistance of any kind illegitimate. The National Association of Evangelicals adopted a resolution condemning all such protests as "The New Treason."[71] As with many disconcerting developments, evangelicals saw the political protests as foreshadowing the apocalypse.

Indictments of the 1960s exposed evangelical antipathy to a changing culture but also their unease about the generational divide in their communities, as younger evangelicals were more receptive to cultural change. Prominent evangelicals described the 1960s as a cultural coup against religion and the Bible engineered by secular humanists who controlled the country. The term "secular humanism" proved an effective umbrella to mobilize opposition to cultural change. Its fears focused on the infiltration of dangerous ideas in universities, public schools, and mainline churches.

These curricula also indict President Johnson's economic policies, noting that "Vietnam did more than divide Americans; it destroyed their prosperity." They see Johnson's Great Society as a continuation of the era of "big government" of FDR. "Johnson assumed that American wealth and government action could solve the nation's problems," and thus his policies were misguided. "He spent billions of dollars on federal health, housing, and education programs to fight what he called the 'war on poverty.'" He was unwilling to curtail "the massive spending needed to build his Great Society" to fund the Vietnam War, the BJU textbook charges.[72] As a result, the United States experienced high unemployment and inflation in the next decade.

While these curricula condemn the Great Society and the War on Poverty as bleeding the treasury, in fact, military expenditure far outpaced domestic spending. For example, in 1966 the War on Poverty had a $2 billion annual budget, while the United States spent $2 billion a month on the Vietnam War. Furthermore, LBJ left office with a budget surplus. Notably, there is no similar indictment of George W. Bush's failure to pay for the massive costs of the war in Iraq or for the financial meltdown of 2008. These curricula denounce spending on social programs but never military expenditure.

While they criticize Johnson, these educational materials exonerate Nixon and dismiss the Watergate burglary. ACE concedes that "the men arrested were part of a group of people who were trying to hinder the legitimate functions of the Democratic Party." It contends that this was common practice for both political parties and wonders whether Watergate would have become an issue if the news media had not greatly "played up the event."[73] This response seems prescient of evangelicals' indifference to Russia's interference in the 2016 elections or to ethical issues in the Trump administration, and a harbinger of current attacks on the media.

These textbooks reflect the disillusionment evangelicals felt when President Jimmy Carter, one of their own, did not advance their causes. He did not oppose abortion, gay rights, or sex education in schools. He was willing to increase welfare programs and to raise taxes. Carter's "failure to recognize man's sinful nature was demonstrated by his weak foreign policy decisions." He did not support African regimes "forced to adopt authoritarian means to fight communism" or recognize that white South Africans were "not preserving apartheid but fighting communism."[74] ACE details the misbegotten policies of the Carter administration, as it "gave away the Panama Canal, downgraded our relationship with Taiwan, pardoned the American draft dodgers, and established the Department of Energy and the Education Department."[75] (The Panama Canal Treaty had been negotiated by Gerald Ford, but signed by Carter.)[76] Many evangelicals viewed the Education Department as "an infringement on local rights." Believers feared that a centralized Department of Education would threaten "the flourishing Christian and homeschool movements," ACE points out. Carter definitively lost evangelicals' support when he withdrew tax-exempt status from religious schools. ACE expresses evangelical disillusionment, "under President Carter, a man who publicly proclaimed himself to be a born-again Christian, government attacks on Christian schools, Christian children's homes, Christian day care centers, and churches rose astonishingly."[77]

What are the implications of this narrative of the postwars world? It revisits the Cold War division of the world between capitalists and communists as a good-versus-evil morality play and espouses positions evangelicals took then. They, like many Americans, fused religion and patriotism to defeat communism. They also began to ally with the Republican Party, to articulate a firm connection between religion and corporate capitalism, and to reject Democrats as New Deal socialists who undermined the nation. They thus aligned with the right in the emerging culture wars. When these textbooks survey the world in this period, they concentrate on whether nations or societies developed collective political actions or social welfare programs—both are deplored as socialism or incipient communism. Their treatment of this period thus corroborates two fundamental principles of these curricula's understanding of history: (1) collective political actions or government welfare programs are illegitimate, invariably inefficacious, and socialist or communist; (2) whether a country and their leaders adhere to the social agenda of Christian conservatives determines whether they are good or evil.

The United States and its interests have become ever more central to these narratives. In the postwar period, the world divided into communist and anti-communist, the one was irredeemably evil and the other unquestionably good. The USSR sought world domination and the United States advanced freedom, democracy, and capitalism. Because these world histories take the perspective of Cold Warriors of an earlier era, they do not emphasize that both blocs of nations intervened across the globe to advance their interests or stymie the other. In contrast, historians acknowledge that both the Soviet Union and the United States were intent on spreading not only their systems of government but also their political and economic influence. With the rise of communist parties in the West, the United States saw a Soviet threat, and the Soviet Union saw the United States as undermining communism in Eastern Europe. Given their mutual hostility, it is astounding that Cold War did not lead to a direct military conflict between the two superpowers and that by 1975 Russia and the United States had signed The Helsinki Accords.

This period also fused the Republican Party and capitalism to evangelical Christianity, as these textbooks document. Among their unquestioned assumptions are that the actions of American Christians are praiseworthy throughout the world. Christianity is inextricably linked to capitalism; those who opposed this alliance were furthering communism or godlessness. The period from World War II to Reagan's presidency was one in which evangelicals were embattled. These present-day textbooks promote their causes with the arguments of this earlier period but with disturbing current resonance for considering America's role in the world and its response to its citizens' concerns.

16

The Righteous Right

"America is great because America is good—and if America ever ceases to be good—America will cease to be great."[1] The Christian right ascribes this quotation to Alexis de Tocqueville's famous *Democracy in America*, which the Abeka textbook pronounces the greatest book written about America.[2] Tocqueville has heroic stature largely because, when he spent nine months of 1831 in the United States, he appreciated the centrality of religion as distinctive of American culture. Despite its rhetorical utility, the statement is not Tocqueville's but rather first used by Richard Nixon and then Ronald Reagan to signal the alliance of the political and religious right as it mobilized into a politically engaged, powerful political force.[3] The Republican Party's efforts to attract evangelical voters have been so successful that they might well now be said to define the party. At that time, the Abeka textbook exults, conservatives "took an active political stand against the tide of socialism, immorality, crime, drug abuse, and Communism threatening the world."[4] These curricula's treatment of recent history celebrates the ascendancy of the religious right in American politics and culture. "The Religious Right hoped to stem the tide of immorality through political action that would reestablish America's traditional standards of morality, standards that reflected the unique contribution of the Christian faith to American history," according to the BJU history.[5]

Ronald Reagan advanced their causes and set the United States on the right course, these textbooks contend. They largely consider world events as they relate to American foreign or domestic concerns. They see admirable political and economic goals and moral values fostered by Republicans and undermined by Democrats.[6] Republican presidents are invariably effective leaders, who support a strong foreign policy and conservative domestic policies. Democratic presidents are inevitably weak leaders, who subvert the character of the American people. On balance, the history of the late twentieth century presents an optimistic morality play with America on the right moral and political path at home and with indisputable power abroad. History records the convergence of two indubitable goods: conservatism and

Hijacking History. Kathleen Wellman, Oxford University Press. © Oxford University Press 2021.
DOI: 10.1093/oso/9780197579237.003.0017

Christianity. Thus when these curricula narrate recent history, they make their political points unequivocally. They no longer shape their narrative to insert evangelical concerns into an overarching narrative, as they did in treating earlier periods. Instead, at the end of the twentieth century, history becomes the story of the Christian right.

How do these textbooks define the recent past? They present Reagan's presidency as the model of Christian values, sound economic policies, and constructive foreign intervention. They consider how well other presidents followed suit and how well other countries adhered to the virtues of Reagan. For them, George W. Bush rose to Reagan's level with stellar accomplishments. But Islam and contemporary culture pose threats to American civilization, they warn: the battle is not won.

The confidence these textbooks express about the 1980 election reflects the Christian right's growing political power. Grassroots mobilizing during the 1970s bore rich fruit. Reagan explicitly appealed to evangelicals, who became significant to his voting bloc. His election established their lasting influence within the Republican Party. Randall Balmer describes this political shift: "rapturous leaders of the Religious Right crawled into bed with the Republican Party in 1980 and heralded Reagan's election as a harbinger of the Second Coming."[7]

This crucial political alliance had solidified during the 1960s and 1970s. Distressed about the sexual revolution, drug culture, the welfare state, government regulations, and Roe v. Wade, evangelicals allied with free-market ideologues, anti-communists, and traditionalists to move into the Republican Party and then, as their influence grew, to move the party to the right. In the late 1970s, evangelicals organized a voting force and entered the political fray, strongly supporting Republicans.[8] The BJU textbook describes their mobilization: "Some state and federal authorities began to call for regulation or even closing of Christian schools. Religious conservatives, realizing that growing governmental power could threaten all constitutional religious freedoms, began to fight back with their dollars and their ballots."[9]

Jerry Falwell, a fundamentalist leader who formerly eschewed politics, became a key figure, especially with his "I Love America" college tour of 1976. Bill Bright's Campus Crusade for Christ reached the same audience. Bright wrote The Spirit of 76 to recruit young evangelicals and form conservative Christian candidates. The most conservative fundamentalists did not welcome the melding of religion and politics, claiming it corrupted religion. Bob Jones III objected vigorously to the movement's alliance with conservative

Catholics, condemning Catholicism as "a movement [that] holds more potential for hastening the church of Antichrist." But he ultimately supported
Reagan in the Republican primary for the election of 1976, with Bob Jones
University even hosting voter registration drives. In 1980, evangelicals again
united behind Reagan.[10] As the Abeka textbook puts it, Reagan had "a sincere desire to return America to biblical values such as moral purity, honesty,
and respect for human life that made America great."[11]

Reagan proved the ideal candidate for a Christian nation committed to
unfettered capitalism. In the 1980s, conservative economists embraced
trickle-down theory and tax cuts funded by reductions in the social safety
net. The Christian right refined the argument these curricula articulate that
both Christianity and limited government defined America's founding and
should be its future. These views were cemented to the Republican ideology
of cutting taxes, undermining the welfare state, reducing governmental
authority over schools and businesses, and appointing judges to uphold
Christian morality—goals evangelicals advocated and these textbooks point
to as signs of Christian resurgence.

To promote Reagan's candidacy, the Christian right adopted effective political strategies to attract evangelicals to the Republican Party. By 1979, Paul
Weyrich, the wealthy Catholic founder of the Heritage Institute, had persuaded Falwell and Schaeffer, the influential Christian Reconstructionist,
to launch voter registration drives targeting evangelicals.[12] They planned
to use abortion as the issue to wrest evangelicals from the Democratic
Party. Falwell's Moral Majority supported Reagan and kept the interests of
the Christian right in the forefront of the Republican Party. Tim La Haye's
popular ministry and fictional works connected secular humanism, which
evangelicals abhorred, to political liberalism and thus made the case that
evangelicals could support only Republicans.

Reagan attracted "values voters" who mobilized against secular humanism, attacking feminism, abortion, and homosexuality. The Republican
platform of 1980 called for a constitutional amendment to overturn *Roe
v. Wade* and the appointment of judges opposed to abortion. It supported
school prayer and school vouchers.[13] These positions resonated with the
emerging Christian right. The evangelical vote was crucial to Reagan's success in 1980; 67% of them voted for him.[14] In 1984, they were again crucial, as
he gained 80% of their votes.[15]

Evangelical supporters were confident that Reagan would restore their
values to the schools. Their battles over curricula consistently advocated

for teaching a heroic, Christian history, in which America was founded as a Christian nation, the Civil War waged primarily over states' rights, and evolution rejected. Public schools, sustaining such beliefs, would be possible only with greater local control and only if evangelicals prevailed in the culture wars over the teaching of history.[16] Evangelicals hoped Reagan would stringently curtail federal oversight of education to enable local control. Imagining that he might even extend their values to the entire nation, they proposed the Family Protection Act to restore school prayer, prevent federal regulation of church-run institutions, and prohibit federal money for institutions supporting the gay community or for educational materials that did not "contribute to the American way of life as it has been historically understood," meaning, of course, as they construed it.[17]

These textbooks credit Reagan with ushering in a new age. He undermined the New Deal, which they denounce as America's failed socialist policies, presumably by cutting taxes and welfare benefits, and undermining labor unions. Reagan was "the first president since the 1930s to question the premise of the welfare state," the BJU history announces.[18] He implemented policies these histories consistently identify with good government—reducing regulations and cutting taxes. Reagan believed, the Abeka history contends, in free enterprise, which it identifies as his commitment to a balanced budget, trade, and deregulation. Reagan put America on the right economic path by undoing "American socialism" and ushering in "the longest period of vigorous and continuous economic growth since World War II." He wins praise for creating 16.5 million jobs, reducing unemployment to a seventeen-year low, bringing inflation down to 4%, and raising the GNP by a third.[19]

These points are central to Republican mythologizing, but this positive assessment of the Reagan economy does not bear scrutiny. While Reagan lowered the marginal tax rate on upper-income Americans from 74% to 38%, he raised taxes on the middle class—payroll and Social Security taxes—eleven times. Moreover, his tax cuts produced growing economic inequality and massive federal deficits. Poverty in the United States rose from 11.7 to 13.5% of the population, the highest in the industrialized world. After Reagan's deregulation of the banking industry led to the savings and loan crisis of the 1980s, American taxpayers bailed out the industry at a cost of $100 billion. The rebound of the economy led to Reagan's landslide victory in 1984.[20] The mythic Reagan resonates with conservatives even though many historians dispute these economic claims as exaggerated or distorted.

These textbooks' uncritical narrative, however, reflects the Republican Party's appreciation of Reagan.

As important for these curricula is Reagan's heroic stature as a cultural warrior. The BJU history praises him for supporting Christian values and for redressing the excesses of the 1960s. The Abeka textbook contends that "the United States experienced the beginnings of a moral and spiritual revival" during his administration.[21] Reagan was not the most likely standard bearer for the religious right; many conservative social positions were new for him. As governor of California, he had signed a bill legalizing abortion as state law.[22]

Indeed, not until the late 1970s did evangelicals themselves espouse the antiabortion cause and mobilize to support it.[23] Only then did abortion become their galvanizing issue. Previously, some accepted it.[24] Even after the passage of *Roe v. Wade*, evangelical leaders, including W. A. Criswell, former president of the Southern Baptist Convention, and W. Barry Garrett, editor of *Baptist Press*, applauded the ruling. The Southern Baptist Convention urged greater access to abortion for "rape, incest, clear evidence of severe fetal deformity, and carefully ascertained evidence of the likelihood of damage to the emotional, mental, and physical health of the mother"—a position it reaffirmed in 1974 and again in 1976. That changed once Weyrich had identified abortion as the issue likely to galvanize evangelicals and attach them to the Republican Party. By 1980, he allied with Falwell and Schaeffer to define antiabortion as *the* evangelical cause. Falwell adopted the Catholic position on abortion, proclaiming "the right to life" and "abortion is murder."[25] The film *Whatever Happened to the Human Race?* was part of a massive media campaign to make abortion a central evangelical concern. Francis Schaeffer Jr., who made the film but has since deplored it as well as his former association with Christian Reconstruction, contended that the decision to mobilize evangelicals around this issue, although almost serendipitous, was fortuitous. It attached Catholics, who had always opposed abortion, to evangelicals and the Republican Party.[26] Leaders of the Christian right used the issue to give its political agenda moral urgency. Abortion became such a single issue for evangelicals that *Christianity Today* warned, it "could lead to the election of a moron who holds the right view on abortion."[27]

Balmer contends that the religious right subsequently constructed what he calls the "abortion myth" that it mobilized in response to *Roe v. Wade*.[28] In fact, the Supreme Court case that galvanized them was *Green v. Connally* (1971), which denied tax-exempt status to institutions practicing racial discrimination. When Bob Jones University lost its tax-exempt status, evangelicals were roused to political action not primarily to prevent abortion but to preserve private, tax-exempt, racially segregated schools.[29] At issue was both race and government control "over God's institution," as Bob Jones Jr. objected.[30]

By 1983, James Dobson's Focus on the Family had advanced evangelical positions by lobbying Congress for legislation against abortion, divorce, homosexuality, and single motherhood. Even though the evangelical movement had frequently been led by women, it opposed feminism and the preceding issues as antithetical to the patriarchal family.[31] Reagan himself neither was religious nor shared many of the religious right's concerns, nor was his personal life the model of family values they asserted. He did, however, espouse their political agenda, asserting that religion must be protected from government. Republican support for that issue has attracted evangelicals ever since, regardless of Mitt Romney's Mormonism or Donald Trump's lack of interest in religion. Reagan deliberately appropriated Jerry Falwell's rhetoric so that evangelicals could readily identify with him, as Republican candidates continue to do.[32]

Although largely symbolic, Congress passed a joint resolution proclaiming 1983 "The Year of the Bible." When it pronounced, "Whereas biblical teachings inspired concepts of civil government that are contained in our Declaration of Independence and the Constitution of the United States," it moved the Christian nation argument into renewed prominence. Although Reagan ultimately did little to promote the conservative social agenda, he made his achievements—tax cuts, deregulation of many industries, and a new arms race—a convincing narrative of American ascendancy.[33] His administration was more effective in implementing a conservative economic agenda by undermining labor and crippling the federal government with massive deficits.

According to these curricula, Reagan restored America's strong international position after weak Democratic presidencies produced defeats in Korea and Vietnam. The Abeka textbook portrays Reagan as a Cold Warrior, whose "strong foreign policy" ended the Cold War by dramatically increasing defense spending and announcing the Strategic Defense Initiative. It condemns liberals for mocking SDI as "Star Wars" and praises Margaret Thatcher for astutely recognizing it as "central to the West's victory in the Cold War."[34] These textbooks find much to praise: Reagan not only toppled a communist regime in Grenada but also stood firm against communism, sending troops into the Dominican Republic and helping the CIA overthrow a Marxist dictatorship in Chile. When he died in 2004, "Reagan's legacy was clear." He had defined a strengthened military and foreign policy, "restoring America's image abroad." Most importantly, "he rejuvenated the freedom philosophy both in the United States and abroad."[35]

Historians do not consider Reagan's interventions against left-wing governments to be the unqualified successes these curricula do. Although Reagan cast US foreign policy in Latin America as a fervent ideological battle against Soviet influence, it often supported opponents of reform or revolutionary change without regard for their human rights violations. The United States supported civil wars in El Salvador, Nicaragua, and Guatemala, which led to thousands of deaths. In 1973, when the CIA helped to remove President Allende of Chile, a democratically elected socialist (not a communist dictator), Nixon was in office. The Reagan administration did try to reduce Chilean popular resistance to General Augusto Pinochet, the military dictator the United States supported.[36] Toward the end of Reagan's administration, US policy focused more on aid and democratization, but some scholars see the current problems in the region as rooted in US policies of the 1980s.[37]

These history textbooks largely dismiss the Iran Contra scandal, in which the Reagan administration disregarded the ban Congress imposed on supplying arms to right-wing rebels in Nicaragua. To disguise its violation of the ban, the Reagan administration supported the rebels with the sale of arms to Iran to carry out its war with Iraq. An independent prosecutor charged seven members of the administration with lying to Congress and destroying evidence but found no evidence that Reagan himself broke the law, although he knew about the diversion of funds and covered up the scandal. The investigation occurred because of "a liberal media plot" and partisanship, as "a Democratic-controlled Congress . . . was eager to pin criminal charges on the president's men," the BJU textbook charges.[38] Reagan also armed the Taliban against the Soviets in Afghanistan and rebels against Soviet-backed forces in Angola. With hindsight, the wisdom of these ventures is dubious.

For these curricula, Reagan was most heroic for bringing about the collapse of communism in Eastern Europe. Reagan said, "Mr. Gorbachev, tear down this wall," and "two years later, it happened," according to ACE. But the end of communism in Eastern Europe is best understood in religious terms. For example, Nicolae Ceausescu's regime in Romania fell because of the heroic efforts of Pastor Láslo Tökés, a Hungarian Reformed Church minister, who brought Scripture to Romanians. When Tökés compared events in Romania to biblical passages, he was suspended by his church. Demonstrations on his behalf led to Ceausescu's trial and execution. The regime fell because "an insignificant pastor had been used by God to spark a revolution that freed a nation."[39]

Although a Hungarian demonstration for human rights and religious freedom did galvanize opposition to the Romanian government, this account is simplistic. It does not mention the political reasons Romanians opposed communism or that a violent overthrow of power proved necessary. Nor does this history reveal that Tökés later became the Vice President of the European Parliament; his internationalism might dim his luster.

When the Berlin Wall fell, the West sold out of Bibles within hours, as East Germans were "more eager to purchase Bibles than food," ACE exults. This inspiring story does not seem supported by evidence, but it may allude to evangelicals' smuggling Bibles into Eastern-bloc countries during the Cold War. The religious implications of the collapse of communism were clear: "God is stronger than any governmental system." The BJU textbook urges students to recognize the fall of the Iron Curtain as "an astonishing answer to prayer and a demonstration of God's power over the nations."[40] Although Soviet communists used repression, "churches grew, and Believers, whose minds were controlled not by the state but by God, faithfully served Him." The fall of communism even made its curriculum more widely used in the CIS (Commonwealth of Independent States), ACE notes.[41]

Historians see the end of the Cold War as more politically complex. Unlike these textbooks, they recognize that the Cold War was a forty-year, bipartisan commitment of Democrats and Republicans dedicated to the cause and willing to fund it. They challenge Reagan's purported role in the fall of the Berlin Wall. (These curricula would never acknowledge the role that Pope John Paul II played in undermining communism in Poland.) Historians acknowledge many factors, including the rise of Solidarity in Poland, the opening of the Hungarian border with Austria, demonstrations in East Germany, and the Velvet Revolution in Czechoslovakia, as well as the violent revolution in Romania. Historians also recognize the crucial roles the citizens of the countries involved played—galvanizing effective opposition and toppling governments. They mobilized, demonstrated in the streets, and voted for opposition candidates. Reagan's sentence "Mr. Gorbachev, tear down this wall," did not bring these events about no matter how much his admirers tout it. The fall of communism was due largely to changes in Soviet policies under Gorbachev, including *Glasnost*, an openness to discussion and critique of Soviet history. (Historical criticism notably played a liberating role.) Gorbachev recognized that the Soviet Union could no longer support communist governments in the Eastern bloc. International horror over the violent Chinese response to the demonstrations in Tiananmen Square likely impelled Russian moderation as well.[42] Ultimately, the citizens of East Berlin were successful only because Gorbachev did not use the Soviet military to suppress them.

The BJU textbook both recognizes that several factors internal to the Soviet Union were significant to the Cold War thaw, especially the economic burden of maintaining its military in Afghanistan, and that political problems continued after communism's fall: despite "a new birth of freedom," conditions for many people did not improve and "shortages and unrest marked the difficult transition from tyranny to freedom."[43]

While these textbooks see the dismantling of formerly state-owned industries after the collapse of communism in the Soviet Union as relatively unproblematic, historians recognize the ensuing capitalist corruption and repressive state that emerged under Vladimir Putin, as leader of the Russian Federation. They note that, while Putin initially improved and stabilized the economy, he has been most intent on asserting Russian power on the world stage and over nations recently independent of Russia. In contrast, some evangelicals praise him for his fight against Islam in Chechnya and Syria and against LGBTQ rights. Other evangelicals expect a powerful Russia to play a role in the coming end times with a possible Russian attack on Israel as the invasion of Gog.[44]

These textbooks subscribe uncritically to the mythic Reagan. His vaunted successes highlight the efficacy of their political engagement. According to ACE, "Many consider the Reagan years to be a high point in American history." His presidency bears out "the truth of Proverbs 29:2, *When the righteous are in authority, the people rejoice.*"[45] Reagan remains the heroic figure against whom these curricula measure subsequent American presidents.

Even Republican presidents occasionally warrant criticism when they deviate from evangelical positions or Republican economic policies. George H. W. Bush undermined the security Americans enjoyed under Reagan because Bush "compromised with a liberal Congress to increase government spending and raise taxes," ACE contends.[46] (Apparently, American security fundamentally rests on low tax rates.) The Abeka curriculum praises Bush for putting generals in charge of the First Gulf War to better indict

Democrats' military failures.[47] But the BJU world history denounces Bush for proclaiming "a new world order."[48] Such a claim ignores human sinfulness and supports one-world government. Only Christ's return will allow unity. Standard histories of George H. W. Bush's administration cite instead The Clean Water Act and The Americans with Disabilities Act as signature achievements and acknowledge that the federal deficit of the Reagan administration forced him to renege on his "no new taxes" pledge to avert a financial crisis.

These textbooks pay scant heed to the Clinton administration. The Abeka history notes his impeachment and his attempt to offer "substandard health care—the hallmark of socialized medicine in every country that has it."[49] When he tried to "impose a socialized medicine under the title 'universal health care,'" the BJU textbook contends, it and he were repudiated in the mid-term elections, and he thereafter "governed as a chastened liberal."[50] The BJU US history textbook treats Clinton more extensively but sees his legislative successes—The Family and Medical Leave Act, The Brady Bill, and The National Voter Registration Act—as "further extensions of the federal government's power over states and individuals." It extols the important Christian "political muscle" exerted by Pat Robertson's Christian Coalition and James Dobson's Focus on the Family.[51] Ultimately, Clinton embodied the country's moral decline; "certainly none (of the presidents) has been accused of as many illegal and immoral actions. Proverbs 14:34 reminds us that *Righteous exalteth a nation: but sin is a reproach to any people,*" as ACE reiterates the refrain common to these curricula.[52]

Under Clinton, the Abeka textbook contends, America declined due to "foreign entanglements." It claims that NAFTA required a $25 billion bailout of Mexico and that the United States ceded its sovereignty to the World Trade Organization. Clinton's commitment to NATO meant that the United States sent troops to Haiti to reinstate the dictator, Jean-Bertrand Aristide.[53] There is something of a disjuncture here: US foreign involvements in support of dictators are reprehensible, if carried out with an international agency, but commendable when unilateral.

Historians assess the Clinton administration more objectively. They note the nation's economic rebound, as spending cuts, tax increases, and declining unemployment led to the first budget surplus since 1969.[54] Job creation, economic growth, and real wages actually made more significant gains during the Clinton administration than under Reagan. The Clinton administration also saw the rise of right-wing, extreme antigovernment activism, including armed militias' stockpiling weapons, best evidenced by the Oklahoma City bombing of 1995, and the rise of white supremacy. The booming economy, propped up by 13 million new jobs, with inflation under control, unemployment down to 4%, and a soaring stock market allowed Clinton to withstand impeachment. In addition, a significant proportion of the population did not consider the charges against him impeachable offences.

The thriving US economy during the Clinton administration and the economic recovery under Barack Obama undermine these histories' story of tax-and-spend Democrats and fiscally responsible Republicans. In discussing another heroic Republican president, George W. Bush, these curricula fail to note how quickly his administration dissipated the Clinton economic gains—by tax cuts, primarily for the rich, and by wars in the Middle East—creating another massive federal deficit.[55] These textbooks' discussions of American presidents highlight Democrats' failures to pursue correct economic policies. Republicans lose elections only when voters are deluded by Democrats' liberal agendas.

These educational materials evaluate the rest of the globe according to how well it conforms to the commendable domestic and foreign policies they define. Just as conservative Republicans provide the model for the United States, so too they set the standard by which other countries are judged. Do they follow the Reagan model of anti-communism, capitalism, and Christianity?

The Abeka history aligns the recent successes or failures of foreign countries with economic positions of the current Republican Party. Our nearest neighbors are troubling examples of anticapitalist policies. Mexico experienced economic and political turmoil because of "incessant demands by farmers for land reform" and because of "the nationalization (government control and operation) of key businesses and industries." Mexico's oil production remains "under government control in an inefficient, socialist bureaucracy."[56] Canada has "moved toward socialism, including the institution of a national health care program ('socialized medicine')." After conservatives were elected, "more free enterprise and more political power to the individual provinces contributed to greater Canadian prosperity."[57] The predominant narrative about Latin America is that in the 1980s and 1990s, Latin America experienced great unrest because of conflict between communists and other parties. When countries did not support capitalism sufficiently, they suffered ill effects, including "political instability, wasteful socialism, and runaway inflation"; governments failed when they did not allow American corporations to invest.

Discussions of specific Latin American countries describe election results and drug trafficking. In Colombia, the United States successfully helped quash the drug trade, but Marxist revolutionaries attacked Christians in Peru. The Abeka history praises the Contra freedom fighters as successful against the Sandinistas in Nicaragua but worries about Marxist rebels' involvement in guerilla war in Mexico.[58] The BJU history notes more optimistically that "the decline of communism and the growth of democratic government have enabled Latin America to shift its focus to pressing economic and environmental problems." This textbook notes criticisms that the West, particularly companies like General Motors and Exxon Mobil, perpetuate "economic imperialism" by taking nations' resources and leaving them in poverty, but dismisses them: "Injustices no doubt exist, [but] the developing nations that are most closely tied to the industrialized West develop the fastest." In Asia, Africa, and Latin America, attracting Western investment measures their success.[59]

Western European governments are good when conservative and bad when they enhance the social safety net or empower certain groups—workers, unions, socialists—against corporate interests. For the Abeka history, modern France is the antithesis of the United States. President François Mitterrand's misguided effort to nationalize France's industries predictably caused the economy to deteriorate badly, leaving him no choice but to implement free-enterprise reforms.[60] The BJU textbook offers another explanation for France's decline: Muslims outnumber Protestants.[61] In treating Britain, it points to increasing welfare benefits and the large Muslim minority as its greatest threats, noting, "Some Muslim leaders in Britain demand the right to practice sharia law" and "some Muslim communities have also become a breeding ground for terrorism."[62] ACE condemns the European Union, as suspect as the United Nations, and sees it as another compelling predictor of end times.[63] Europe, godless and socialist, is destined for doom and a harbinger of the coming apocalypse.

This uncontextualized treatment of recent European history tells students only how countries lined up with American conservative political and economic positions. They neglect key features of European history in the post-1980 period. Europe faced massive Muslim immigration, mostly to fill low-level positions as its economy expanded. Many immigrants expected to return to their homelands, were not well-integrated into European society, and have remained economically disadvantaged. Few Muslim immigrants gained professional positions. After the international recession due to the subprime mortgage crisis in the United States, European unemployment rose significantly, and right-wing politicians blamed immigrants. In response to the economic crisis, politicians adopted austerity measures, exacerbating popular discontent. If these textbooks addressed European economic, political, and social contexts, students would understand European developments as more complex than a series of bad liberal or good conservative governments.

Some Asian countries elicit praise for their commitment to capitalism. Taiwan, "through hard work and free enterprise, developed a modern, industrial economy based upon manufacturing and trade." South Korea too enjoyed "the fruits of capitalism."[64] Japan has a promising future, even though bureaucratic regulation slowed its economy and "the dominance of Liberal Democrats" brought corruption.[65] But communism remains a serious threat in Asia, particularly in China. The BJU textbook condemns Mao's attempts to modernize: the "great leap forward" of the 1950s destroyed the iron industry and produced famine, and the "Cultural Revolution" destroyed Chinese education. Although Mao's successors seemed more moderate, the Chinese government revealed its true character in its crackdown on the Tiananmen Square demonstrators, the BJU history concludes. It condemns China's persecutions of Christians, the Falun Gong, and Tibetan Buddhists but says, most peculiarly, that the fact that Christians outnumber communists explains Chinese repression. It indicts the "one child policy" as state-endorsed abortion.[66]

The growth of communism and the persecution of Christians in Africa are of pressing concern. While the Abeka account optimistically points to the growth of Christian missions in Africa, it harshly condemns Nelson Mandela as brought to power by two evils: communists and the UN. It blames the media for focusing on apartheid rather than on "the communist movement he led." It concludes, "With such unsettling moves toward Communist tyranny, South Africa's future remained uncertain."[67] According to the BJU curriculum, Africa's quest for independence "produced many problems," because they failed to "build their economies with foreign investment, trade, and industrialization." In the absence of European rule, ethnic tensions surfaced in civil wars in Kenya, the Congo, Nigeria, and Rwanda. Other countries succumbed to military dictatorships, and Christians struggled in Nigeria and Sudan, where Muslims tried to impose Muslim law.[68]

The BJU textbook takes a somewhat critical perspective on American involvement in the Middle East, noting that, while the United States supported the Shah of Iran as an anti-communist, he was a tyrannical dictator. Opposition to him brought more radical Islamists to power. It mentions that the Taliban came to power in Afghanistan in the 1990s but not that the United States supported them to challenge the Russians. It worries about the threat of Islamization to the West, explicitly condemns Iranian Muslim extremism, and claims that Iranian suicide bombers are behind the terrorism in Iraq. It sees Iran as the greatest impediment to Western efforts to advance democracy in the Middle East.[69]

The Abeka history places the Middle East conflict in a religious context; it "stems from the contempt that Islamic states, like Iran and Saudi Arabia, have for the Jews and the state of Israel."[70] The BJU curriculum notes that, even though Israel has prevailed against its neighbors, military success has not brought peace. It reminds students that "God promised Abraham that his seed would become a great nation and possess the land that became known as Palestine." Students should consider that "Psalm 122:6 says, 'Pray for the peace of Jerusalem.'" It asks, since the Middle East "will not experience true peace until the coming of the Prince of Peace, how can we reconcile the psalmist's imperative?"[71] Presumably, one should look forward to the Second Coming.

The narrative of modern history, for these curricula, is first and foremost the story of the rise of the Christian right. As they move into the 1990s, they reflect the shift within its leadership. Many of its most popular figures—Jerry Falwell, Jim and Tammy Faye Bakker, Pat Robertson, and Ralph Reed, among others—faced financial or sexual scandals. More extreme members assumed leadership roles, and the ideas they advanced became more characteristic of evangelical political rhetoric and the legislation they promoted. In 1992, the United States Taxpayers Party challenged conventional Republicans by advocating for specific understanding of the Constitution as grounded on biblical law. It argued that the federal government should be abolished in favor of local governments of the godly. Their 1996 platform insisted that government must be tied to God and that the United States was a "republic under God" and not a democracy. Their arguments in favor of states' rights and the free market appealed to libertarians as well. Both groups opposed regulation and wanted the "job creators" to be unconstrained.[72] Even though these ideas were outside the mainstream in the 1990s, they now resonate in right-wing political discourse and might even be considered conventional Republican views.

The next heroic Republican president advancing the Christian right was George W. Bush. The Abeka US history describes the critical choice Americans faced in the 2000 election: "Would they continue on the path toward socialism and moral decline? Would they demand a return to free enterprise capitalism and more traditional moral values?"[73] The BJU history notes Bush's promise to reform education and "restore honor and dignity to the White House" after the Clinton scandal.[74]

Evangelicals recognized Bush's invocation of an "axis of evil" as a direct commitment to their world view and heralded the war on terror as an explicit fulfillment of biblical prophecies of end times.[75] These textbooks claim that the Gulf War was conducted solely to prevent weapons of mass destruction (WMDs) from falling into the hands of terrorists, "thus making the Middle East and the rest of the world safer," even though there was no connection between Saddam Hussein and the attack on the World Trade Center and no weapons of mass destruction. The BJU textbook, nonetheless, proclaims the war in Iraq as an unadulterated success. It cites the trial and execution of Saddam Hussein, Iraqi Parliamentary elections with 60% turnout, and the success of the surge in eliminating violence, temporary as it was, as accomplishments.[76] It is worth noting that by 2016 all contenders for the Republican nomination, even Jeb Bush, repudiated the war.

Other world histories acknowledge, as these Christian curricula do, that the horrifying 9/11 attacks on the United States exposed the vulnerability of the world to terrorist attacks by non-state actors. They, unlike these curricula, do not treat its aftermath as a clash of civilizations. Instead, they recognize the roots of the conflict in the history and politics of the Middle East, specifically in the extremism that produced terrorist attacks.

Islamic extremism initially developed as resistance to both British rule in Egypt in the 1930s and secular Arab nationalism. It opposed undemocratic Middle Eastern governments of monarchs, dictators, and authoritarian military rulers and rejected secularism and Western corruption. Middle Eastern governments have tried to neutralize Islamic fundamentalists. But when Saudi Arabia turned education over to Wahhabism, a form of Islamic fundamentalism, it empowered extremism and jihad against the West. The Iranian Revolution of 1979 united the lower and middle classes to overthrow a modernizing, authoritarian, American-backed state. Revolutionaries saw it as a crusade to reform politics and to purify Islam. In 1979, the United States opposed the Russian invasion of Afghanistan, as did evangelicals as a part of their Cold War battle. The defeat of the Soviets allowed the emergence of the Taliban, whose members had been trained and armed by the United States, which then replaced Russia as the jihad target of Afghani Islamic fundamentalists.

These textbooks do students no favors by presenting the issues in the Middle East as signs of the coming apocalypse divorced from the political, economic, and cultural complexities of the postcolonial world. They neither note the connections between Islamic extremism and religious fundamentalism nor draw the further conclusion that Middle Eastern governments sometimes supported fundamentalism to distract their citizens from social and political grievances.

If these textbooks generally see Bush's foreign policies as legitimate and effective, his domestic policies are unquestionably commendable. He was the Christian culture warrior for whom they hoped. He "identified himself with the traditional values and interests of conservative mainstream America," as the Abeka curriculum puts it.[77] He courted Christian-right groups, notably in South Carolina, where he made his controversial visit to Bob Jones University. His campaign attempted to discredit John McCain with a whisper campaign, inaugurated by Karl Rove, that suggested that his dark-skinned daughter, adopted from Bangladesh, was his illegitimate child. This flagrantly false charge was an explicit racist dog whistle to Southern voters. Had Bush not won the South Carolina primary, his campaign would likely have ended. His primary victory there was only the first sign of the overwhelming evangelical support for him; 40% of his voters were evangelicals.[78]

Bush was sympathetic to the most conservative Christian evangelicals and gave them direct access to him, including Al Mohler, then leader of the Southern Baptist Convention, David Barton of WallBuilders, and James Dobson, whose Focus on the Family effectively promoted the religious right's agenda through mass media. Even Christian nationalists and dominionists had a more prominent place at the political table both because of their growing political clout and Bush's beliefs. Supporters of extreme views about the role of religion in government filled the federal bureaucracy.[79] Bush's administration invoked the "war on believers" (the belief that Christians in America are discriminated against), which played on evangelicals' fears and inspired greater activism.

When Pat Robertson ran for the Republican nomination in 1988, he put dominionism at the center of evangelical politics.[80] He claimed not only that the United States was established as a Christian nation but that it was a republic founded on absolute adherence to biblical law. He maintained that only Christians and Jews could hold office and that the Bill of Rights did not apply to states. He espoused Christian-right social positions, opposing gay marriage and sex education, for example. These views became more central to publicly expressed Christian positions during the Bush administration.[81]

Bush advanced social causes dear to evangelicals' hearts. He took a staunch antiabortion stance and supported school vouchers, sex abstinence programs in the schools, and restrictions on stem-cell research.[82] During his administration, the Justice Department focused on religious rights rather than civil rights. The Christian right exercised tight control over congressional judicial appointments, some of whom opposed the separation of church and state.

Some evangelicals heralded Bush's presidency as divinely inspired. Bush himself told many he had been called by God to serve as President and, after 9/11, that the war was a divine mission.[83] In the attack's aftermath, spokesmen for the Christian right claimed that God had put Bush in the White House and transformed the war into a holy crusade.[84] Bush presented himself as a leader called upon to lead a virtuous nation against evildoers. He did not condemn Islam as a religion and even visited a mosque on 9/12. But leaders of the religious right—Pat Robertson, Jerry Falwell, and Jerry Fines— were not similarly reluctant. They not only condemned Islam but also identified Saddam Hussein as the antichrist. A letter written by Richard Land and signed by prominent evangelicals—Charles Colson, Bill Bright, D. James Kennedy, and Carl Hester among them—urged a preemptive strike on Iran.[85]

The Christian right explicitly looked to events in the Middle East as fulfilling biblical prophecies. The establishment of the state of Israel and the occupation of the West Bank and Jerusalem had been but the first steps in the unfolding of the apocalypse. The battle with Islam, according to modern dispensationalists and some fundamentalists and evangelicals, would lead to Israel's destruction—an essential step in the fulfillment of end times prophecies.

The Christian right's influence was so significant during the Bush administration that historians and popular writers warned of a coming theocracy. They saw disturbing signs of the Christian right's success in asserting that Christians should control all US institutions.[86] Bush's experiment with compassionate conservatism was seen as advancing this goal.

The religious right was initially thrilled when Bush's Office of Faith-Based and Community Initiatives allowed religious institutions to compete for government contracts, essentially directing federal funds to religious institutions. It attempted to replace welfare with private charity but only for the deserving.[87] In his *Tragedy of American Compassion* Marvin Olasky, the strategist behind Bush's faith-based initiatives and greatly influenced by Christian Reconstructionists, attributed America's decline to welfare. He waxed nostalgic for a time before the New Deal when private charity was withheld until the sinner repented. He appreciated that "the early Calvinists knew that time spent in the pit could be what was needed to save a life from permanent debauch."[88]

Faith-Based and Community Initiatives funded Christian and secular groups, but only if they promulgated the "gospel of privatization" with the central belief that the poor need "spiritual uplift" rather than material assistance.[89] These programs appealed to both white conservatives and Black churches. For conservatives, it was a coded call to shred the social safety net and revert to the nineteenth-century practice of private, church-based charity, even though private charity never provided an adequate social safety net before the Social Security Act of 1935.[90] Currently, without Social Security, a minimum of 40% of the elderly would fall below the poverty level.[91] Funds were dispersed through such programs as part of a strategy intended to win Black evangelicals, particularly their pastors, to the Republican Party.[92] Legal experts saw these policies as blurring the separation between church and state, just as courts did then.

Other failures of the Bush administration, which these textbooks do not note, include his subsequently abandoned No Child Left Behind Act. While Bush initiated a subsidy for prescription drugs for the elderly, it was unfunded, as were his tax cuts, which predominantly benefited the wealthiest Americans. These measures, as well as the war on terror, led to a mushrooming federal deficit. Deregulation and the ensuing financial speculation pushed the nation and the world into the greatest financial crisis since the Great Depression.[93] The Environmental Protection Agency was weakened. The appointment of John Roberts and Samuel Alito moved the Supreme Court significantly further to the right, which, not surprisingly, these histories praise.[94]

When the US histories of these Christian publishers consider the Bush administration, they point to those who frustrated his commendable efforts. Hollywood and the liberal media fueled objections to his Middle East policy. Neocons, who supported a new world order, corrupted his foreign policy. The rising debt was due not to Bush's tax cuts but rather to the failure to cut government spending. As the Abeka curriculum insists, "true conservatives believe in reducing payroll taxes rather than funding Social Security."[95]

The BJU textbook presents Barack Obama's election objectively and accurately dates the recession to the Bush administration, but struggles to explain Obama's success: "His charisma, the support of the media, and the support of the black electorate launched him to the presidency."[96] In contrast, the Abeka textbook claims that Americans wanted a change because of the war on terror and the economic decline and, as a result, turnout was unprecedented. But it reassures discomfited readers: with the election of Barack Obama "many people are fearful of what the future will hold for America. . . . Only God holds the future of America in His hands." But it also warns, "only a nationwide revival can preserve America's heritage of freedom."[97] The textbooks reflect the opposition of evangelicals to Obama; 74% of them did not approve of him.[98]

ACE juxtaposes evidence of Christian success to signs of a coming apocalypse but intends both to encourage students. They should cheer the diffusion of Christianity, even as immorality portends end times. A series of questions makes these points clear: "Have modern technological advances improved social conditions? Is the world at peace? . . . Have the humanists converted the world to their belief that man is the only god? Has their philosophy permeated human society and solved all the problems of the past?"[99] Because the answer to all these questions must be a resounding "no," the modern world must return to biblical Christianity.

These textbooks appreciate the recent past when the US government was in the hands of right- (in both senses) thinking Republicans. But contemporary culture remains worrisome. "The humanist educational system media and mind-set is training North Americans to reason away much of the Bible and its teachings."[100] The BJU textbook identifies Protestant ecumenism as an impediment to true Christianity. It condemns the World Council of Churches because it allies with self-designated Christian groups "regardless of *any* false doctrines these groups may hold" and supports "radical social causes." In contrast, British evangelical preacher and member of Parliament D. Martyn Lloyd-Jones commendably refused to compromise with liberal Protestants and urged true Christians to leave those denominations.[101]

The Abeka US history points to disturbing elements in contemporary political culture—most of them hot-button issues for the political right: While "armed citizens could also play a major role in thwarting

Globalism," advocates for gun control instead introduce "a gateway to tyranny." Immigration increases the danger of terrorism, and international trade threatens American sovereignty. Judges continue to reinterpret the Constitution, and the court's ruling against Judge Moore's Ten Commandment monument in the Alabama statehouse "dealt a blow to America's biblical foundation." Elements of mainline culture—the Internet, postmodernism, environmentalism—threaten Christianity. Postmodernism the Abeka history characterizes as an egregious form of humanism, revealing "the degeneration of man-centered ideas" and rejecting "a God-given absolute standard of ethics."[102]

Environmentalism poses a direct threat to Christianity and "has brought many people into a form of earth worship," the Abeka textbook charges. It contends that reputed climate changes reflect ordinary cycles and that any carbon reduction relies on man's belief in his own resources rather than "God's absolute principles."[103] Most importantly, climate science violates the Creation Mandate by "limiting man's ability to subdue the earth and use natural resources." The Abeka textbook aligns with the extreme views of the Coalition on Revival (COR), which defends polluters and insists that Christian stewardship does not apply to caring for the earth but only to maintaining private property. Any broader application of stewardship is "autonomy" and a defiance of God.[104] The Abeka US history claims that "climate fear" fosters government regulation. It cites meteorologist John Coleman, who has denounced global warming as a "SCAM."[105] Only ACE acknowledges that "man has damaged God's creation through pollution and misuse," reflected in more frequent and powerful earthquakes, volcanoes, and hurricanes. But these natural disasters are signs of the coming apocalypse rather than geological shifts or climate change.[106]

Since the 1970s, much of the Christian right and the Republican Party have opposed environmental regulation as articles of political and religious orthodoxy. Opposition began in several Republican strongholds—the mountain West, where ranchers and miners resented regulation, and the South, where farmers and oil men did as well. Reagan's EPA under Anne Gorsuch rolled back regulations. Conservative think tanks like the Heritage Foundation and rural and suburban constituencies, concerned about energy costs, coalesced within the Republican Party against environmentalism. Many evangelicals joined anti-environmentalists because of their expansive reading of the Creation Mandate.[107] But evangelical ranks are beginning to divide as evidence of climate change mounts. In January 2006, the National Association of Evangelicals issued a statement saying there was no consensus on the issue. A month later, eighty-six evangelical leaders issued a "call to action" to address the crisis.[108]

The Abeka textbook is ambivalent about technology and science. The Internet can readily be adapted to nefarious purposes such as identity theft, and on-line pornography by man "to feed his sinful desires." This textbook even endorses the extreme view that innovations such as RFIDs (Radio Frequency Identification) and GPSs (Global Positioning Satellite) are malevolent, confirming the biblical prediction of Revelations 13:16–17 that in the future people around the world will not be allowed to buy or sell without an identifying mark.[109]

In the 1980s, evangelicals revived their vehement attack on the teaching of evolution and promoted the purportedly scientific argument of intelligent design to challenge it. The Abeka curriculum cites Michael Behe's argument that the eye is too complex to have evolved and thus confirms his "theory of irreducible complexity."[110] Christian schools teach this belief, and the Christian right lobbies for its inclusion in public school science curricula as an alternative to evolution.

In treating the world since 1980, these curricula revisit the development of the Christian right and advance ideas the Republican Party has used since the 1960s to attach evangelicals to their cause. In treating topics certainly within the memory of teachers and parents of students, these curricula take positions now part of the "Christian agenda." Their economic arguments resonate in the views of the contemporary political right. As the market is "free," these curricula do not recognize that economic policies favor some at the expense of others, increasingly corporations over citizens and investors over wage earners. The political right generally fails to acknowledge the massive redirection of tax revenue from public interest to corporate welfare or from the economic powerhouses of the Northeast and California to the purportedly self-reliant South and West. The thoroughgoing connection these textbooks draw between any policy intended to advance the public good and inevitable economic, social, and moral decline makes clear why the Christian right anathematizes the former.

These curricula consistently inform students that contemporary Republican economic policies, whenever they have been enacted, invariably led to prosperity. It seems unlikely that the failures of capitalism evident in the Great Recession of 2008 will elicit any reappraisal of the connections between capitalism and virtue. In fact, the Abeka textbook treats the recession as the result of personal failures. People bought "homes they could not afford" and "banks were forced to foreclose," but government policies, like the Stimulus Bill of 2009, "meant that economic recovery was slow and many Americans were left unemployed and receiving government assistance."[111]

Limited government, these textbooks consistently argue, is God's intention for human beings. Since the 1980s, that opinion has been mobilized to undermine government and shred the social safety net. Reagan wins praise for strong government, essentially in the interest of completely undermining government itself. Republican administrations crippled the federal government. These histories endorse such efforts. For them, government programs are socialist and thus evil and unchristian. Reliance on any form of government aid is a clear sign of sin, inevitably leading to personal and social immorality and economic collapse.

So profound is this aversion to government that the ways US citizens, including members of the Christian and political right, depend on it can never be acknowledged. Only the military is defensible. The other services only a central government can provide—from disaster relief, to roads, bridges, monetary policy, diplomacy, and other benefits—go unrecognized. Once government is denounced as antithetical to Christian capitalism, Christians cannot easily see any benefit they receive from government programs they have condemned as unchristian and un-American.[112] This cognitive dissonance contextualizes some peculiarities of contemporary political discourse: Tea Party members crying "hands off my Medicare" or farmers' failing to acknowledge farm subsidies as government support, for example. No student educated with these curricula would likely imagine a government program could be legitimate or beneficial.

As the United States is the key to extending Christianity throughout the world, these educational materials narrow their focus to the United States and to their political causes and goals: the perspective of the American Christian right defines their understanding of the post-1980 world. They essentially issue the rest of the world an American scorecard. With the United States the only remaining superpower at that time, this focus might seem reasonable, but reducing US foreign policy to a religious crusade impedes a more nuanced understanding of it and the political interests of other parts of the world. Because the Christian right and these curricula present post-9/11 wars in the Middle East as a contest between good and evil, they fail to recognize that resistance to the West is often driven by Islamic fundamentalist opposition to secularization and the decline of religion—both seen as the result of Western involvement in their affairs. Ironically, Islamic fundamentalists urge greater influence for religion over government and culture—just what some on the religious right promote for America.

These textbooks deem other nations as good when they accepted US interventions in their affairs or misguided or even evil when they did not. Students educated with these curricula will understand precious little about the interests, concerns, or motivations of citizens of other countries. Foreign countries are mere game pieces in an American quest to spread Christianity and capitalism.

Standard histories offer a more balanced view of both US foreign and domestic policy. They assess Democratic and Republican administrations more evenhandedly. They do not present Republicans as strong, competent, and committed to Christian causes and critique all Democrats as irresponsible and weak at best and as ungodly at worst. They are not completely uncritical of American foreign policy, acknowledging that some policies were controversial and provoked opposition at home and abroad. They do not assess other parts of the world in such starkly ideological terms where US actions are to be emulated and set the standards for other countries. Nor do they look with either delight or foreboding to the coming apocalypse.

What implications does this severely narrowed perspective have beyond its limitations as a history of the world since 1980? These curricula give students a partisan and polemical history of domestic politics and deprive them of a nuanced understanding of American actions in the world. They give students a position from which to judge—a judgment based on divine favor for American Christians, an unquestioned assumption to the point of arrogant superiority. They define US interventions in the affairs of other countries as commendable and as a biblically sanctioned mission to spread Christianity.

The alliance of the Christian right and the Republican Party has become an article of evangelical faith in ways these curricula thoroughly document. Their history makes our partisan divide more comprehensible. The unquestioned virtue of American politics allows foreign-policy decisions to go largely unexamined by the public. Even our military interventions and wars rarely produce intense public scrutiny: early opposition disappears only to occasionally reemerge briefly during election cycles. The historical narrative of these textbooks, despite the interest of evangelicals in proselytizing across the globe, isolates the United States, walling it off from problems we will face as the twenty-first century unfolds—problems that will require both knowledge of the rest of the world and its history and an ability to work globally to solve them.

Conclusion

Toward End Times or Christian Hegemony

"History is a mirror of who we are, where we come from and where we are going," commented historian Gary Nash in response to the furor over history standards during the 1990s.[1] If this is so, what mirror do these world histories from a purported Christian perspective hold up to twenty-first-century Americans? It offers students a bifurcated vision of their future.

While many history curricula end on a positive note, encouraging students' engagement with the world as they come into adulthood better prepared by their understanding of history, these textbooks instead conclude with grim prophesies. The BJU history warns that the twenty-first century began with optimistic hopes for world peace as leaders spoke of a "New World Order," just as they had at the beginning of the twentieth century. Such sanguine hopes are invariably misguided: "Christians must remember that prospects for peace and unity, while left in man's hands will ultimately fail because of the harsh reality of the sinful nature of man."[2] The lessons of history are stark. Peace efforts are doomed, and international cooperation smacks of ungodly, one-world domination. Despite or perhaps because of their grim assessment, these educational materials advise Christians to look forward to end times as the fulfillment of the Book of Revelation's prophecies. Calamitous events in the Middle East should be greeted with cheerful complacency or, more disturbingly, with active hoping for Christ's return, bringing Christ's thousand-year reign of peace "before crushing the final rebellion and ending world history."[3] The last ACE Self-Pac warns, "We are now experiencing many of the natural disasters and lifestyles that Christ and Paul said was [were] to occur in the last days."[4] Nonetheless, the Abeka history insists, "Christians can view current events with confidence, thrilling at the fulfillment of prophecy."[5] Similarly, the BJU textbook reassures, "Christians can face the future with faith and trust, knowing that the end of human history will bring the ultimate victory and true peace of the God of all peace."[6]

Hijacking History. Kathleen Wellman, Oxford University Press. © Oxford University Press 2021.
DOI: 10.1093/oso/9780197579237.003.0018

On the other hand, the Great Commission impels students to recognize that "the Lord of the earth, calls His people to go into every part of the earth teaching the nations to submit to His lordship." The BJU history urges students to promote the history they have learned and seek careers in history to "serve society by preserving or altering that society's sense of cultural identity . . . Only a Christian can do such jobs as they ought to be done. . . . Christians have been given a world view by that Lord [the Lord of the earth] that enables them to study and interpret the events of the past."[7] Students educated with these curricula have privileged knowledge; they should proselytize Christian history.

High school history textbooks more usually cite their intent to inculcate an awareness of research, evidence, and analysis to sharpen critical thinking, appreciate historical complexity, and even challenge received ideas. They attempt to foster the skills of historians. They hope to elicit thoughtful responses to the state of the world and urge students to continue to study history and to understand world events in a rich historical context. They do not cheer the imminent coming of end times. More orthodox textbooks might present positive and negative conclusions about the current state of the world but would not do so in terms of Christian or American hegemony.

Another way to see the mirror these textbooks hold up is to reexamine the terms in which they define themselves. They claim to offer a *Christian* perspective, but what do they show Christianity to be? They insist that the virtuous subscribe to some form of biblical literalism; the sinful question it, deviate from it, or even deny it. They repudiate threats to their notion of biblical truth—evolution, biblical modernism, Protestant ecumenism, social reform movements, even the evangelical Social Gospel movement. They condemn those who accept these reprehensible aspects of modern culture as unchristian.

The Christianity found in these educational materials seems wedded more to capitalism than the New Testament: God rewards Christians with wealth; poverty is His punishment. Any economic development that serves the rich and punishes the poor can be construed as fulfilling God's intentions. Charity, almost entirely absent, is reduced to spiritual solace for the "deserving poor." Proposals to aid the poor are called into question as sinful humanism rather than Christianity—a truly staggering reversal of the Gospel. The Christianity these textbooks avow is devoid of the Gospel and intolerant and inhumane.

The application of the term "Christian" to differentiate the virtuous from the sinful gives these educational materials profound civic implications beyond their obvious role in religious proselytizing. In differentiating America and Americans and Christianity and Christians from all others, they deny the religious pluralism that has characterized the history of the West, at least to some degree, since the Protestant Reformation. They chip away at religious toleration and undermine the separation of church and state. They are dedicated the struggle of Christians against others. They are apocalyptic and see Satan as a player throughout history. Students are taught to identify his work in the ranks of the enemies these textbooks identify—believers in diabolical religions, especially Islam; proponents of evolution or biblical modernism; and socialists of any kind.[8]

These curricula prepare students to identify and denounce the reprobate. This religious test of the virtuous is increasingly salient in modern politics and is being applied as a standard for legitimacy and inclusion in the body politic. Political positions taken by evangelicals, particularly Southern evangelicals, are not simply Christian but also reveal God's intentions for human beings. Any attempt by governments to remediate social ills is unchristian and illegitimate, as these textbooks reiterate evangelicals' historical opposition to such measures from the New Deal to the Affordable Care Act as confirming their commitment to Christianity. By most consistently identifying Islam as the religious "other," these curricula give anti-Islamic sentiment a historical foundation and religious legitimacy. In the culture at large, religion is being used to advocate for increasingly wide application of religious freedom as license to discriminate against those identified as other on the grounds of religious belief, whether the other seeks wedding cakes, contraception, or other prescriptions, or to adopt or foster children.[9]

These educational materials purport to be histories of the *world*. But they are severely constrained by their historical trajectory as a series of providential relationships between God and His people—the Jews of the Old Testament, the first Christians, the Protestants of the Reformation, especially English Protestants, and their descendants in an exceptional America. Their early history of the world reinforces polemical, Christian-right social and political arguments; modern history recounts those who supported or opposed Christian England and America. The rest of the world—its history, and its social, political, or economic concerns—has few points of entry into this narrative except as it responded positively to English and American missionary efforts, political interventions, or capitalist investments, or provides negative examples of failures to do so. These textbooks write a variant of American history, the saga of a mythic Christian nation rewarded with

God-given exceptionalism. If students learn to repudiate Europe as full of dangerous ideas and to reject much of the world as non-Christian, they can see American history as a Christian beacon—in its founding as a Christian nation, in the vigor of its religious revivals, in its military power, in its staunch stances in the culture wars, and in its current ascendancy within the Republican Party. These textbooks advocate Christian hegemony at home and abroad.

Most fundamentally, these materials are *history* curricula for high school students, but they narrow and reshape history as a narrative of faith with the Bible as the key to understanding it. Applying either their understanding of God's intentions or specific biblical quotations supports their historical conclusions. Students are taught to judge whether historical events advanced biblical Christianity. Armed with this ability to judge and with biblical proof texting, they can identify those favored by God.

The study of history allows students to single out the failures of peoples in earlier times to conform to God's intentions for human beings. Those early civilizations that did not accept the one true God are denounced. They reveal their failures to accept biblical values when they failed to endorse patriarchy, condemn homosexuality or abortion, and the broad category of human accomplishments—"humanism." The history of ancient civilizations thus does battle for modern evangelical causes. Staunch political and social messages are easily extrapolated from them. This too is a method of judging other civilizations to dismiss or disparage them, not historical analysis.

History has even more insidious work to do. It, like Christianity, defines the "other" according to religious belief. As the narrative of the Middle Ages more than amply demonstrates, Catholics are not Christians, and Muslims show Satan abroad in the world. There are also political heretics, most notably the French, who contrast with the virtuous, proto-Protestant Anglo-Saxons. The purported Anglo-Saxon foundation of Protestant Christianity and the United States feeds racist and white-supremacist arguments, as it did for some evangelicals, among others, in the past and does more broadly in American culture today.

The Reformation emerges with Christians (meaning Protestants) as the new chosen people. God revealed His support for them from England to America. These textbooks encourage students to see God's work in the Protestant Reformation, the rise of evangelicalism, and the contemporary Christian right. Christians are identified by the social, political, and economic ideas evangelicals held in the past or hold today. The political actions and policies of Christian England and Christian America are imbued with religious significance and authority, as in their colonial or capitalist pursuits, for example.

But these curricula warn that bad ideas challenged biblical truth and posed the greatest dangers in human history. Humanism diverted human beings from God: it proposed alternative relationships between man and gods in ancient or non-Christian civilizations, contested Protestantism before the fact in medieval Catholicism, advocated reason and science during the Enlightenment, and challenged the literal view of creation. Darwinism and theological modernism led the modern world into sin and the disasters of World War I and World War II.

Beginning with their treatment of the post-Enlightenment world, these textbooks take more vehement stances against the predominant culture and articulate more adamant social and political arguments. Reform movements are deplorable signs of hubristic humanism. "Humanism" is their label to condemn human endeavors, especially those intended to remediate the human condition, unless they are motivated by zeal to convert the unbeliever. But these curricula extol the rise of both colonialism and capitalism as God's plan for humanity—the first to spread Christianity and the second to reward the faithful. International diplomatic efforts reflect sinful man's continuous efforts to create one-world government. Scholarship that challenges "biblical truth" is especially dangerous, because, in these curricula, the contest between good and evil is fought in the realm of ideas. Students must study history to identify the ideas they must reject—Darwinism, biblical modernism, socialism, and communism. These curricula juxtapose these evil ideas to essential Christian tenets—biblical inerrancy, Young Earth creationism, evangelical Protestantism.

These curricula convey a somewhat contradictory message to students about how they should respond to such evil ideas. They should reject much of modern culture with the noteworthy exceptions of evangelicalism and capitalism but also spread Christianity and remake a Christian nation. Even though that advice seems contradictory, these educational materials are consistent in making social and political arguments with profound civic implications. As God, not human beings, forms government and ordains rulers, the virtuous nations He favors succeed. As a result, revolution is reprehensible. (Evil Europeans had them; Americans simply had to determine whether crown or colonial magistrates reflected God's will.) Social reform efforts are not only humanist but also lead to socialism or, worse, deny God's endorsement of limited government. Free-market capitalism is God's economic plan and thus intervention by governments or through regulation is illegitimate.

These educational materials deviate sharply from historical consensus on a wide variety of issues, many of which this book has pointed out. Numerous points of divergence are deliberate, reflecting evangelicals' long-standing desire to differentiate themselves from secular education and society. Evangelicalism has long sustained anti-intellectualism in America. Some evangelicals viewed universities with suspicion or overt hostility as purveyors of secularism and established evangelical universities in response. These curricula challenge historians' expertise: it too reflects humanism rather than "biblical truth."

Other differences between these curricula and more standard narratives are rooted in the history of evangelicalism. They tell the story of how America came to occupy its divinely established, privileged position; they signal those who held the "true" religious views and supported the political positions appropriate to Christians. In some cases, these textbooks are simply using very outdated histories or religious writings rather than current scholarship. Their narrative is not one professional historians would generally find credible, although it does resemble some religiously grounded, polemical histories of past centuries. It relies on national origin myths, which have sustained America' idealized identity as white, Anglo-Saxon, and Protestant. These uses of history may not be as clearly articulated as they are in these educational materials, but they are not entirely foreign to other textbooks, particularly those written to implement state standards imposed by conservative state legislatures. The use of high school history textbooks to advance this morally charged, religiously grounded polemical and ideological narrative is disturbing.

Bad history matters. It empowers, as these textbooks do, myths with powerful resonance in contemporary settings. Bad history refuses to tell truths that might embarrass a nation. It empowers nationalism at the expense of a patriotism grounded in a more capacious or measured understanding of a nation's history. Bad history justifies actions that might otherwise be condemned as anathema: for example, repression of religious or ethnic minorities. The mythic founding of a Christian nation has been used to assert white nationalism and has incited hate crimes against Muslims, Jews, immigrants, and ethnic minorities. Neo-Nazis and the alt-right have put bad history from the Lost Cause of the Confederacy to anti-immigrant crusades of the nineteenth century and present-day America back on our streets. Bad history can reshape our national identity by discrediting expert knowledge and mobilizing racism and anti-immigrant sentiment. It can serve explicit political campaigns, including attacks on the need to address climate change or public health care with collective action, by identifying such efforts with sin or by conflating social welfare with totalitarianism, as these textbooks do. The bad history these curricula promote not only reflects the divide in our nation but also plays a role in defining and cementing it.

Adam Laats's comment that "our culture wars are usually fiercest between two groups of people who have been educated in very different ways" seems singularly apt.[10] These curricula stake out specific positions on education, science, politics, and economics and harden them with God's assumed endorsement of their views. It would, of course, be extremely naive to see these curricula as responsible for our current national division or, indeed, to ascribe the national chasm to any educational materials. But it would also be naive to imagine that teaching this narrative for decades and to several generations has had no effect. It would also be illegitimate to see these textbooks as the sole or even primary source of ideas that echo throughout Christian conservative media. Ideas these curricula promote, initially most characteristic of fundamentalism, have attained greater acceptance in the evangelical community, as their voting patterns confirm. Right-wing think tanks, much of Christian media, and many churches promote the firm connections these curricula postulate between Christianity and right-wing politics. But these world histories are the culmination of educational programs that have made these arguments to students in less sophisticated form from kindergarten to twelfth grade. They have benefited from homeschooling networks and advocacy groups that have diffused their materials more widely. Will students educated with them be able to find common ground with others educated differently about what education should be, or what authority science has, or what the role of government or religion should be in our pluralist democracy? In using history to show "the mind of God," has this history become an unquestionable foundation of truth? Would challenging it require apostasy?

This book thus urges readers to pay attention to history curricula in general and to those examined here in particular. It asserts that they are more important than one might have thought. It is worth reemphasizing that these are histories taught to children. But, as the oldest students taught with them would now be in their mid-sixties, they have influenced three generations. Indeed, this history resonates in current political debates, although these textbooks are by no means the only or even the primary sources of the views they advance despite their increasing diffusion over several generations. Those advocating this narrative intend to shape American culture to reflect their view of Christianity and the politics and economics it requires. These curricula are, however, important indications of the fusion of evangelical Christianity to the political right: their historical narrative sheds light on how some fundamental fissures in our understanding of the nation and the world have developed. They conflate the history of American evangelicals with that of the world. They also reveal much about why contemporary evangelicals, almost without question, support Republicans. They contribute to the current, highly partisan, and somewhat inaccurate sense of fundamental political terms, including socialism and liberalism. They even illuminate the salience of some specific charges of the last few election cycles: John Kerry was ridiculed as French speaking, which, as these textbooks suggest, was leveled to convey the undesirable attributes of the non-Christian, un-American, socialist French. Barack Obama was tied to Africans, Muslims, and socialists, characterizations identifying him as both un-American and unchristian.

Many of these textbooks' claims circulate throughout contemporary American culture in large and small ways we can readily see. They can be found in concrete form in the preaching of Robert Jeffress of Dallas First Baptist, an advisor to President Trump who maintained that Trump was chosen by God, and Paula White, Trump's chosen personal pastor, who asserts that Christianity is the source of economic success. They underscore the mission of fundamentalist universities, such as Jerry Falwell's Liberty University, which currently enrolls over 100,000 students, and Bob Jones University, which has dedicated itself to producing school administrators since the mid-1970s.

The legislative agenda of the Christian right also seeks to advance these historical narratives in public schools. Project Blitz, a coalition of Christian right-wing groups, in 2017 sent state legislatures over 300 bills advancing Bible courses in public schools, asserting religious freedom, and repudiating LGBTQ rights. The Bible curriculum, approved by over seventy school districts as an elective and promoted by the conservative National Council on the Bible in Public Schools, shares many of these textbooks' positions. It too emphasizes the impact of the Bible on America, especially on its founding, and presents Thomas Jefferson as proponent of a Christian nation and Mosaic Law as the foundation of moral and civil law.[11] The extracurricular

Good News Clubs in public schools instruct students on how to convert others to evangelical Christianity.[12]

Central ideas of these curricula are readily apparent in public culture. Mike Pompeo, as Secretary of State, asserted claims these textbooks make. When he spoke at a "God and Country Rally," he cited a prayer the Rev. Joe Wright had delivered before the Kansas state legislature: "America had worshipped other Gods and called it multiculturalism. We'd endorsed perversion and called it an alternative lifestyle."[13] In response to a *Harvard Magazine* article of April 2020 on the dangers of homeschooling, Pompeo tweeted, "The risk to children ... is from radical leftist scholars seeking to impose THEIR values on our children."[14] The landing page of the Department of State website on October 11, 2019, featured Pompeo's "Being a Christian Leader" speech. Just off the Mall in Washington, DC, the Museum of the Bible presents the Bible as the foundation of all laws and the American nation, as these curricula do. The Christian nation thesis is broadly diffused in popular histories, and visions of the coming apocalypse fuels "Christian" novels and films.

Many fundamental political ideas these textbooks develop—God forms all governments, human beings cannot contest them, Mosaic Law is the only legitimate foundation of morality and law, central government and internationalism are illegitimate—were far out of the mainstream when they were promoted by Christian Reconstructionists in the mid-twentieth century. Only in the 1980s did proponents of such views as well as dominionists, who believe that Christians must take over society and shape it according to Christian principles, assume prominent political positions. But many organizations now advance such views. To cite a few examples: A Christian think tank, Institute for Faith, Work, and Economics, asserts that biblical economic principles sustain unfettered capitalism. Operation Save America, opposed to abortion, gay rights, and feminism, intends to save America by having it literally conform to the Bible. The Values Voter Summit, an alliance of social conservatives and elected officials, mobilizes voters to support "traditional marriage, religious liberty, sanctity of life and limited government."[15] The Family Research Council (classified as a hate group by Southern Poverty Law Center) attacks the LGBT community and advances the so-called bathroom bills in various state legislatures. These efforts to make laws conform to values defined by these groups (and these textbooks) as Christian have increasing currency in the public sphere—whether in state legislatures, school boards, think tanks, or pulpits.

Recognition of the historical narrative these curricula advance and the diffusion of their ideas in American political culture should provoke a critical response. First, these curricula expose an important public policy issue. As vehicles of religious proselytizing, they should be ruled out of education paid for with public monies, particularly the private schools supported by publicly funded tax-relief vouchers. It is crucial to recognize and oppose these curricula and their like as entirely inappropriate to public history education: they are religious proselytizing.

Second, knowledge of these uses of history should raise concern among educators. While the recent version of the AP exam was widely attacked, notably by conservative state legislators, as an insufficiently heroic narrative of American history, these textbooks present American history as divinely favored. Such claims are ever more frequent in the educational proposals advanced by state legislators across the country or stipulated for inclusion in the state educational standards. In response to the promotion of such a politically motivated, polemical American history, educators can advocate for the strongest possible foundation in history for those who will teach secondary school courses. (Currently, only seventeen states require high school history teachers to have taken any college history courses.[16]) Well-prepared high school history teachers can critically assess curricular materials such as these. High school teachers and administrators could recognize where problematic elements of this narrative have penetrated state standards and textbooks, as in the McGraw-Hill textbook that, as previously discussed in the Introduction, identified slaves in the United States as workers before public exposure forced a correction. Other states could follow California's lead in rejecting courses based on these curricula as fulfilling admission requirements for its state universities because they egregiously violate historical consensus. Other state universities could similarly challenge such standards. University professors, who might mistakenly believe that their students share a rudimentary understanding of a standard historical narrative, should be aware that students entering their college courses might well have this other narrative as their foundation. College courses could address flagrant features of these world histories and teach students to explicitly differentiate history as historians practice it from history as these textbooks "proof text" it. College courses could not only correct misapprehensions but also give students the skills to critically analyze historical materials. Educators should also be aware that the demise of college history requirements means that many university-educated Americans will have these educational materials as their last exposure to history. Educators should recognize these curricula as historical miseducation.

Scholars who study religion in America can continue to refute elements of this narrative in their work, which conveys a broader and more nuanced understanding of religion in history. Christianity in America has never been simply Protestant evangelicalism. Historians can continue to emphasize the ideals that defined the American founding as well as successes and failures in meeting those ideals throughout its history. Law students could be vigilant about questionable uses of history in the law review articles; historical arguments deployed in such articles need a more conscientious vetting than they currently receive.[17] When bad history shapes legal arguments, it can shape our laws.

Recognizing the limits of curricula like these could fuel resistance to the contemporary assault on public education, especially the expansion of voucher programs to private, often religious schools. As Secretary of Education, Betsy DeVos promoted the use of curricula like these in voucher programs and charter schools. Some resistance to this agenda is in play. States that elected Democratic majorities in 2018 professed their intention not to support privatizing public schools and to shut down some of the largest charter school companies.[18] It is worth noting that genuine school reform efforts have, despite good intentions, opened wider and deeper spaces for the dissemination of these materials and others like them.

In addition to professional educators who are likely to be most vigilant in assessing history courses, some evangelicals too might direct their attention to these educational materials as reflecting an unacceptable politicization of their faith. Dissenting evangelical leaders are having a "lover's quarrel" with such manifestations of contemporary evangelicalism. As they both recognize and deplore the connections between evangelicalism and right-wing politics, they might also acknowledge that these educational materials and others like them have exerted an outsized impact in forging that union. They might emphasize that the heritage of nineteenth-century evangelicalism, particularly of its social activism, has been completely subsumed in this alliance between evangelicals and the political right, richly supported by corporate interests and the prominence of evangelical megachurches. Randall Balmer criticizes the political conservatism of contemporary evangelicalism for rejecting the New Testament's message in favor of corporate capitalism, for example.[19] Mark Noll's work, provocatively titled *The Scandal of the Evangelical Mind*, bemoans the fact that modern evangelicalism, unmoored from intellectual foundations, has been unable to articulate a Christian response to pressing contemporary issues.[20] As he put it, "the heritage of fundamentalism was to Christian learning for evangelicals like chairman Mao's 'Cultural Revolution' [was] for the Chinese. Both divorced a generation from mainline academia, thus making reintegration [into larger worlds of learning] a difficult, if not bewildering task."[21] In *Who Is an Evangelical?*, Thomas Kidd argues for a return to the central religious concerns of evangelicalism and presents their history, sharply differentiating its faith from the prosperity gospel and current Republican politics.[22] The work of such scholars attempts to detach "Christianity" from right-wing politics, or evangelicalism from what is now sometimes called "Christian nationalism."[23]

American citizens can contest this historical narrative in a variety of ways. Citizens who become familiar with it can be alert to the challenges it poses to American civic life. Well-informed citizens can get involved in public debates about state standards. These are several examples of the efficacy of such citizen involvement. Even if qualified historians are excluded from review processes, citizens can, as they have done in Texas, protest the exclusion, challenge the process, and pay attention to how such standards are implemented. The work of the Texas Freedom Network provides an admirable model of such advocacy. Parents in Douglas County, Colorado, resisted the imposition of historical inaccuracies on their schools, such as the claim that US history never experienced popular dissent, as did parents in Michigan, who prevented the excision of the word "democracy" from American history materials.[24]

The civic implications of the narrative these textbooks develop should alarm American citizens. Because God forms governments and puts leaders in place, no citizen has the right to question His choice or resist a government. Government should not simply protect religion but also promote it. The capitalist economy is God's reward structure, so no one has the right to question or resist its effects on society, the individual, and certainly not the environment. Appreciation of God's commitment to capitalism cements the allegiance of the religious right to the political right—largely to serve the interests of the latter against the social needs of many of the former. We should be, not as our founding documents assert, citizens of a democratic republic formed by "we the people" living under "government[s] ... instituted among Men, deriving their just powers from the consent of the governed" and with the "right of the people to alter or abolish it." Rather we are and should ever more clearly be a Christian nation God has put in place, according to these curricula. Thus Americans should be compliant and passive, living under a capitalistic Christian government legitimated by biblical law. We should be, as we supposedly were at our founding, a Christian nation looking forward to the Second Coming. This central message of these broadly diffused Christian curricula should not go unchallenged.

Notes

Introduction

1. Arthur Schlesinger Jr., "History and National Stupidity," *New York Review of Books*, April 27, 2004, 1.
2. Stephen Sawchuk, "How History Class Divides Us," *Education Week*, October 23, 2018 . https://www.edweek.org/teaching-learning/how-history-class-divides-us/2018/10
3. James Loewen, "Why Do People Believe Myths about the Confederacy? Because Our Textbooks and Monuments Are Wrong," *New York Times*, July 1, 2015; see Donald Yacovone, "Textbook Racism: How Scholars Sustained White Supremacy," *Chronicle Review*, April 27, 2018, B14–16.
4. *The Diane Rehm Show*, National Public Radio, July 5, 2015.
5. Until 2018, the causes of the Civil War were to be taught as sectionalism, states' rights, and slavery, in that order, 2010 TEKS, 5.b.4.E, 7b.5.A, TEKS, 8b.8B, TEKS, 8.b.17.B.
6. Russell Heimlich, "What Caused the Civil War?," Pew Research Center, May 18, 2011, https://www.pewresearch.org/fact-tank/2011/05/18/what-caused-the-civil-war/.
7. https://www.mcclatchydc.com/news/politics-government/article30101748.html.
8. Manny Fernandez and Christine Hauser, "Texas Mother Teaches Textbook Company a Lesson on Accuracy," *New York Times*, October 5, 2015,
9. See Gary Nash, Charlotte Crabtree, and Ross E. Dunn, *History on Trial: Culture Wars and the Teaching of the Past* (New York: Alfred A. Knopf, 1997).
10. College Board, AP Exam Volume Changes (2005–2015).
11. When Calvary Chapel School and ACSI (Association of Christian Schools International) sued the University of California, the court decided in the state's favor in *Association of Christian Schools International v. Roman Stearns*. ACSI accredits religious schools and homeschooling programs. Schools must submit a form, including a statement of faith, and $1000 membership fee; see https://www. acsi.org/.
12. Slate.com/articles/health_and_science/2014/01/creationism_in_publicschools_ mapped_where_tax_money_supports_alternatives.html provides a map illustrating where and how many public schools teach creationism. Creationism is widely taught in private schools receiving publicly funded vouchers. Arizona has fifteen voucher-supported schools teaching creationism. Colorado, Georgia, Indiana, Ohio, Oklahoma, Utah, and Wisconsin have similar numbers. Outliers are Florida with at least 164 such schools, and Texas with the largest charter program. Tennessee and Louisiana state laws allow the teaching of intelligent design with materials provided by the Discovery Institute.

13. Stephen Jay Gould, "Understanding Fundamentalist Views of Science," in *Science and Creationism*, edited by Ashley Montagu (Oxford: Oxford University Press, 1984), 118–25.

14. In *Edwards v. Aguilars* (1987), the Supreme Court overturned a Louisiana law mandating teaching creationism; see Andrew Hartman, *A War for the Soul of America: A History of the Culture Wars* (Chicago: University of Chicago Press, 2015), 207–9.

15. The chair of the Texas SBOE identified history as its next target in *The Revisionaries*, a documentary, produced by Making History Productions, LLC, Silver Lining Film Group, 2012.

16. Moses is included in world history, TEKS 113.44.8.

17. When these history standards in Texas were adopted in a 9–5 party-line vote, media critics faulted their heavy-handed religious and ideological bias and historical inaccuracy. See Russell Shorto, "How Christian Were the Founders?," *New York Times Magazine*, February 14, 2010, 32–39, 46–47; Mariah Blake, "Revisionaries: How a Group of Texas Conservatives Is Rewriting Your Kids' Textbooks," *Washington Monthly*, January/ February 2010, 13–18. Eagle Forum, a conservative advocacy group, celebrated the changes: "Texas Gives the Boot to Liberal Studies Bias," *Education Reporter* 291 (April 2010) https://www.texasgopvote.com/texas-gives-boot-liberal-social-studies-bias-001119

18. Mark Chancey, "Rewriting History for a Christian America: Religion and the Texas Social Studies Controversy of 2009–2010," *Journal of Religion* 94, no. 3 (July 2014), 325–53; Justine Ellis "Constructing a Protestant Nation: Religion, Politics, and the Texas Public School Curriculum" *Postscripts* 7, no. 1 (2011), 27–58; Keith A. Erekson, ed., *Politics and the History Curriculum: The Struggle over Standards in Texas and the Nation* (New York: Palgrave MacMillan, 2012).

19. Dana Goldstein compared American history textbooks produced by McGraw-Hill and Pearson for the California and Texas markets, "Two States. Eight Textbooks. Two American Stories," *New York Times*, January 13, 2020.

20. State of Arkansas, 91st General Assembly A Bill, Regular Session, 2017 House Bill 1834 prohibited public schools from using any work by Howard Zinn. Purdue University President Mitch Daniel imposed the same prohibition in 2013 as governor of Indiana, Scott Jaschik, "The Governor's Bad List," *Inside Higher Ed*, July 17, 2013. On Michigan's battle over state standards, see Dana Goldstein, "Is the US a Democracy? A Social Studies Battle Turns on the Nation's Values," *New York Times*, April 7, 2019.

21. James C. McKinley, Jr., "Texas Conservatives Win Curriculum Change," *New York Times*, March 13, 2010; "SBOE Politics as Usual: Textbook Review Once Again Corrupted by Lack of Expertise," Texas Freedom Network, July 15, 2014. https://tfn.org/sboe-politics-as-usual-textbook-review-once-again-corrupted-by-lack-of-expertise/

22. Chancey, "Rewriting History for a Christian America," 325.

23. Hartman, *A War for the Soul of America*, 211.

24. The historical content of these textbooks was critiqued in 1993 by Albert Menendez, who called attention to their religious intolerance, *Visions of Reality: What Fundamentalist Schools Teach* (Buffalo, NY: Prometheus Books, 1993); and by

Frances Paterson, who argued that a democratic society should not use public monies for public school educational materials, which are intolerant of all religions except Protestantism, *Democracy and Intolerance: Christian School Curricula, School Choice, and Public Policy* (Bloomington, IN: Phi Delta Kappa Educational Foundation, 2003).

25. James Hudnut-Beumler, *Strangers and Friends at the Welcome Table: Contemporary Christianities in the American South* (Chapel Hill: University of North Carolina Press, 2018), 69.

26. For a history of homeschooling before 1970, see James Dwyer and Shawn Peters, *Homeschooling: The History and Philosophy of a Controversial Practice* (Chicago: University of Chicago Press, 2019), 1–28; Milton Gaither, *Homeschool: An American History,* rev. 2nd edn. (New York: Palgrave Macmillan, 2017), 5–140.

27. Frances FitzGerald, "The Triumph of the New Right," *New York Review of Books*, November 19, 1981.

28. Adam Laats, *The Other School Reformers: Conservative Activism in American Education* (Cambridge, MA: Harvard University Press, 2015).

29. Hartman, A *War for the Soul of America*, 85–86; Adam Laats, *Fundamentalism and Education in the Scopes Era: God, Darwin, and the Roots of America's Culture War* (New York: Palgrave MacMillan, 2010), 195.

30. Paul F. Parsons, *Inside America's Christian Schools* (Macon, GA: Mercer University Press, 1988), x.

31. Bruce Cooper, "The Changing Demography of Private Schools: Trends and Implications," *Education and Urban Society*, August 1984, 432. See National Center for Education Statistics, Private School Universe Survey (PSS), selected years, 2003–2004 through 2013–2014. See the *Digest of Education Statistics 2015. https://nces.ed.gov/pubsearch/pubsinfo.asp?pubid=2016014*

32. See Adam Laats, *Fundamentalist U: Keeping the Faith in American Higher Education* (New York: Oxford University Press, 2018).

33. James Davison Hunter, *Culture Wars: The Struggle to Define America* (New York: Basic Books, 1991), 201; Hartman, *A War for the Soul of America*, 200.

34. James Dobson and Gary Bauer, *Children at Risk: Winning the Battle for the Battle for the Hearts and Minds of Your Children* (Dallas: Word Press, 1990), 37–38..

35. Justin Driver, *The Schoolhouse Gate: Public Education, the Supreme Court, and the Quiet Détente over Religion and Education* (New York: Vintage Books, 2018), 407.

36. Paterson surveyed private schools receiving public funding in the Orlando area. Of those that responded, 52% used Abeka textbooks, 24% used Bob Jones, and 15% used ACE, Paterson, *Democracy and Intolerance*, 12–13.

37. Rachel Tabachnik, "Vouchers/Tax Credits Funding Creationism, Revisionist History, Hostility toward Other Religions," www.Talk2action.org/story/2100/5/25.

38. Leslie Postal, Beth Kassab, and Annie Martin, "Schools without Rules: An *Orlando Sentinel* Investigation," *Orlando Sentinel*, March 18, 2019. When *Newsweek* asked the state for comment on this article, it responded that "private elementary and secondary (nonpublic) schools in Florida are not regulated, controlled, approved or accredited by the Florida Department of Education," Nicole Rojas, "Florida Private

Schools Teaching Students That Humans, Dinosaurs Roamed Earth at the Same Time," *Newsweek*, June 1, 2018.

39. Such schools operate with little oversight or accountability, *NC Private Schools Receiving Vouchers: A Study of the Curriculum*, 3, 14, 16. https://lwvnc.org/wp-content/uploads/2018/04/Voucher-Report-7.2-1.pdf.

40. Of those 7,200 schools receiving public monies for vouchers Klein surveyed, of those who reported to her, 73% were religious, and 44% of them non-Catholic Christian. Of the 5400 schools responding for requests about their curricula, 37% used one of those featured in this book, Rebecca Klein, "Voucher Schools Championed by Betsy DeVos Can Teach Whatever They Want. Turns Out They Teach Lies," *Huffington Post*, December 20, 2017, https://www.huffpost.com/entry/school-voucher-evangelical-education-betsy-devos.

41. Gaither, *Homeschool*, 24.

42. Some 3.4 to 4% percent, or nearly 1.8 million, K–12 students were homeschooled in 2012, J. Redford, D. Battle, and S. Bielick, *Homeschooling in the United States: 2012* (NCES 2016-096), National Center for Education Statistics, Institute of Education Sciences, U.S. Department of Education. Washington, DC, 2012. Brian Ray, founder of the National Homeschool Education Research Institute and the journal *Homeschool Researcher*, contends that 2.5 million K–12 students are homeschooled, Research Facts on Homeschooling, https://www.nheri.org/research-facts-on-homeschooling.

43. Rousas John Rushdoony, *This Independent Republic: Studies in the Nature and Meaning of American History* (Nutley, NJ: Craig Press, 1964), 146–51.

44. Rousas John Rushdoony, *The Nature of the American System* (Fairfax, VA: Thoburn Press, 1965), 11–17; Rushdoony argued the government must be shrunk to meet biblical standards, *Institutes of Biblical Law* (Nutley, NJ: Craig Press, 1973).

45. Rousas John Rushdoony called for the abolition of public schools and social services and the replacement of civil law with biblical law, *The Messianic Character of American Education* (Nutley, NJ: Craig Press, 1963).

46. Dwyer and Peters, *Homeschooling*: 85–86; Elizabeth Bartholet, "Homeschooling: Parent Rights Absolutism vs. Child Rights to Education and Protection," *Arizona Law Review* 62, no. 1 (2020), 42–44.

47. Driver, *The Schoolhouse Gate*, 401; Gaither, *Homeschool*, 142; Bartholet, "Homeschooling," 9; Robert Kuzman and Milton Gaither, "Homeschooling: A Comprehensive Survey of the Research," *Other Education: The Journal of Educational Alternatives*, 2 (2013), no. 1, 4–5; Dwyer and Peters, *Homeschooling*, 66–67.

48. Hudnut-Beumler, *Strangers and Friends at the Welcome Table*, 208; Driver, *The Schoolhouse Gate*, 401.

49. Daniel Turner, *Standing without Apology: The History of Bob Jones University* (Greenville, SC, Bob Jones University Press, 2001), 206.

50. Fritz Dewiler, *Standing on the Premises of God: The Christian Right's Fight to Redefine America's Public Schools* (New York: New York University Press, 1999), 218; Hartman, *A War for the Soul of America*, 200.

51. https://time.com/577765/state-of-the-union-trans-2020/.

52. Hartman, *A War for the Soul of America*, 109, 112.

53. John Holzman, "Christian Education Manifesto," *Home School Digest* (2009) 19, no. 1.
54. Julie J. Ingersoll, *Building God's Kingdom: Inside the World of Christian Reconstruction* (New York: Oxford University Press, 2015), 118.
55. Hudnut-Beumler, *Strangers and Friends at the Welcome Table*, 209.
56. Dwyer and Peters point to the HSLDF as among the most powerful political forces *Homeschooling*, 225.
57. Ingersoll, *Building God's Kingdom*, 100.
58. Chris Klicka, *Home Schooling: The Right Choice; An Academic, Practical, and Legal Perspective* (Nashville, TN: B & H Publishing Group, 2001).
59. Driver, *The Schoolhouse Gate*, 402–3.
60. Bartholet, *Homeschooling*, 40; Watchdog groups like Homeschooling's Invisible Children and support groups like No Longer Quivering and Homeschoolers Anonymous of the formerly homeschooled have arisen, Kathryn Joyce, "The Homeschool Apostates," American Prospect, February 9, 2014 http://prospect.org/article/homeschool-apostates.
61. Only four of more than 300 schools using vouchers in Indiana were not overtly religious, Stephanie Mencimer, "Mike Pence's Voucher Program in Indiana Was a Windfall for Religious Schools," *Mother Jones*, December 2, 2016.
62. During the 1960s, this movement was galvanized in response to perceived threats from the civil-rights and antiwar movements, Laura K. Munoz and Julia Noboa, "Hijacks and Highjinks on the US History Review Committee," in Erekson (ed.), *Politics and the History Curriculum*, 45.
63. CRPE receives Department of Education funding for their network of "portfolio school districts" from New York City to New Orleans, run as stock portfolios. Each district is decentralized and each school autonomous, https://www.crpe.org/research/portfolio-strategy/network.
64. Dina C. Osborn, "Resisting the State: Christian Fundamentalism and A Beka," *Counterpoints* (2010), volume 376, 35–45.
65. *Report and Analysis on Religious Freedom Measures Impacting Prayer and Freedom 2018-2019.*
66. Zahira Torres and Karen Crummy, "Jeb Bush Donated to the Douglas, CO School Board Races," *Denver Post*, November 2, 2016.
67. Mary Bottari, "ALEC Sets the Table for Gerrymandering, Unionbusting, Protecting Fossil Fuels and Privatizing Schools," *Center for Media and Democracy*, August 7, 2018.
68. Valerie Strauss, "Texas GOP Rejects 'Critical Thinking' Skills. Really," *Washington Post*, July 9, 2012.
69. See Susan Jacoby, *The Age of American Unreason* (New York: Random House, 2008), 40–47.
70. Mark Taylor Dalhouse, *An Island in the Lake of Fire: Bob Jones University, Fundamentalism, and the Separatist Movement* (Athens, GA, and London: University of Georgia Press, 1989), 35.
71. Klein, "Voucher Schools."

Chapter 1

1. Adam Laats, "Forging a Fundamentalist 'One Best System': Struggles over Curriculum and Educational Philosophy for Christian Day Schools, 1970–1989," *History of Education Quarterly* 50, no. 1 (January 2010), 55–81.
2. https://www.aceministries.com/about-ace.
3. For a fuller discussion of this issue, see Chapter 4.
4. Laats, "Forging a Fundamentalist 'One Best System,'" 62–63.
5. https://www.aceministries.com/about-ace.
6. Stephen J. Stein, "Millennialism," in *Blackwell Companion to Religion in America*, edited by Philip Goff (London: Wiley-Blackwell, 2010), 220.
7. Laats, *Fundamentalist U*, 40–53.
8. ACE stipulates an inerrant Bible, a literal six-day creation, marriage between a man and a woman, and hell. https://www.aceministries.com/about-ace.See Charles D. Grant and Kirk W. House, "An Evaluation of ACE from a Reformed Perspective," *Journal of Christian Reconstruction* 4 (Summer 1977), 66–67.
9. Patricia Lines, "An Overview of Home Instruction," *Phi Delta Kappan* 68, no. 7 (March 1987), 513.
10. Donald R. Howard, *Rebirth of Our Nation* (Garland, TX: Accelerated Christian Education, 1979), 300, cited in Jonathan Scaramanga, "Systems of Indoctrination: Accelerated Christian Education in England" (PhD dissertation, University College London, Institute of Education, 2017), 13.
11. These numbers, along with ACE's claim that 4743 new ACE schools opened between 2000 and 2009, suggest a high degree of turnover.
12. This curriculum's virtues were advertised in *The Searchlight* (May 1986) and *The Fundamentalist Journal* (May 1986); see Laats, "Forging a Fundamentalist 'One Best System,'" 71.
13. Paul F. Parsons, *Inside America's Christian Schools* (Macon, GA: Mercer University Press, 1988), 40–41.
14. Ibid., 65. Gary Coombs, "ACE, an Individualized Approach to Christian Education," *Interest* (September 1978), 9–10.
15. ACE, Social Studies, *American History*, 2003, rev. 2013.
16. Changes of content are signaled by changing font with few word changes, for example, from Christian to "believer" or "godly" to "biblical."
17. Procedure Manual (ACE 2010a) and Administrative Manual (ACE 2012); Scaramanga, "Systems of Indoctrination," 13.
18. https://www.aceministries.com.
19. Scaramanga, "Systems of Indoctrination," 11, 30. 115, 117, 247–65.
20. Scaramanga, "Systems of Indoctrination," 31, 140–42. Lisa J. L. Kelley, "An Analysis of Accelerated Christian Education and College Preparedness Based on ACT Scores" (unpublished thesis, Marshall University, 2005). Research on the results of Christian schooling is reported by policy advocacy groups, much of it by the National Home Education Research Institute (NHERI), Elizabeth Bartholet, "Homeschooling: Parent

Rights Absolutism vs. Child Rights to Education and Protection," *Arizona Law Review* 62, no. 1 (2020), 21–27.

21. https://www/aceministries.com/media/pageimg/Great_Command_Commission-web.pdf. ACE objectives are explicitly and predominantly religious.

22. https://www.aceministries.com.

23. The science curriculum makes this claim, ACE, 1009. Bruce Wilson, "The Loch Ness monster Is Real: What Students Are Learning from Publicly-Funded Christian Textbooks," *Truth to Action*, January 27, 2015, www.talk2action.org/1/27/15.

24. ACE, 109: 9.

25. Pcci.edu/CollegeInfo/HistoryOfPCC.aspx.

26. Pcci.edu/spirituallife/articlesoffaith.aspx.

27. Ibid.

28. See Beth Bailey, *From Front Porch to Back Seat: Courtship in Twentieth-Century America* (Baltimore: Johns Hopkins, 2013), 13.

29. Laats, *Fundamentalist U*, 80–88.

30. Laats, "Forging a Fundamentalist 'One Best System,'" 68. See A. A. Baker, *The Successful Christian Schools: Foundational Principles for Starting and Operating a Successful Christian School* (Pensacola, FL: Abeka Book Publications, 1979).

31. AbekaUS, 189

32. Abeka's video academy is accredited by the Florida Association of Christian Colleges and Schools (FACCS), by the National Council for Private School Accreditation (NCPSA), and by the Southern Assocation of Colleges and Schools Council on Accreditation and School Improvement (SACSCASI).

33. Thomas Bartlett, "A College That's Strictly Different: Secretive Pensacola Christian Controls Student Life with Tough Regulations and Unwritten Rules," *Chronicle of Higher Education*, April 10, 2006.

34. Gaither, *Homeschool*, 154.

35. Bartlett, "A College That's Strictly Different."

36. Bob Jones, *Annual Bulletin* 3 (April 1929), cited in Laats, *Fundamentalist U*, 78.

37. Bob Jones University Faculty, *Christian Philosophy of Education*, 1–7. Quoted in Dalhouse, *Island in the Lake of Fire*, 141.

38. Daniel Turner, *Standing without Apology*, 163.

39. Ibid., 4. Quoted in Dalhouse, *Island in the Lake of Fire*, 141.

40. Dalhouse, *Island in the Lake of Fire*, 53.

41. Philip Jenkins, *The New Anti-Catholicism: The Last Acceptable Prejudice* (New York: Oxford University Press, 2004).

42. Dalhouse, *Island in the Lake of Fire*, 19, 155. This was a fundamental point of disagreement with religious modernists.

43. Ibid., 148–51.

44. Richard Perez-Peña, "Bob Jones University Blamed Victims of Sexual Assault, Reports Says," *New York Times*, December 11, 2014; Sarah Pulliam Bailey, "Bob Jones University president apologizes to sexual assault survivors on campus, "*The Christian Century*, December 11, 2014. https://www.christiancentury.org/

article/2014-12/bob-jones-university-president-apologizes-sexual-assault-survivors-campus

45. Stephen R. Haynes, *Noah's Curse: The Biblical Justification of Slavery* (New York: Oxford University Press, 2007), 4.
46. Juliet Eilperin and Hanna Rosin "Bob Jones: A Magnet School for Controversy University's Policies Haunt GOP Hopefuls," *Washington Post*, February 25, 2000.
47. Cindy Landrum, "A Brief History of the World's Most Unusual University," *Greenville Journal*, April 12, 2017.
48. Parsons, *Inside America's Christian Schools*, 43.
49. By the mid-twentieth century, some evangelicals thought isolation had gone too far. Billy Graham sought broader appeal, and several fundamentalists developed media empires, including Pat Robertson's Christian Broadcasting network, Jim Baker's PTL News, and Paul and Jan Couch's Trinity Broadcasting Network, Randall Balmer, *The Making of Evangelicalism: From Revivalism to Politics and Beyond* (Waco, TX: Baylor University Press, 2017), 52–53.
50. Turner, *Standing without Apology*, 263, n. 437.
51. Ibid., 263–66.
52. The third edition of the BJU world history credits no author but lists on the copyright page five contributing authors, an editor, a three-person biblical integration team, and a project manager (Greenville, SC: BJU Press, 2009). The fourth-edition title page credits Dennis Bollinger but also lists four of the five contributing authors of the earlier edition with a two-person biblical integration team (Greenville, SC: BJU Press, 2013). Jerry Combee and George Thompson are listed on the copyright page with a list of consultants, *World History and Cultures in Christian Perspective*, 3rd edn. (Pensacola, FL: Abeka, 2012); Jerry Combee is listed on the copyright page with consultants, *History of the World in Christian Perspective*, 5th edn. (Pensacola, FL: Abeka, 2019).. *Social Studies, Self-Pac of Basic Education* credits no author (Garland, TX: Accelerated Christian Education, 2002).
53. Dalhouse, *Island in the Lake of Fire*, 137.
54. https://www.bju.edu/academics/resources-support/catalogs.
55. Dennis Bollinger, *World History Student Activities* (Greenville, SC: BJU Press, 2013).
56. These curricula are highly regarded within the homeschool movement. For example, *Theology Degrees* rates the BJU curriculum as best for critical thinking and the Abeka educational materials receive the highest rating. www.theologydegrees.org/best-christian-homeschool-curriculum.

Chapter 2

1. See Andrew L. Whitehead and Samuel Perry, *Taking America Back for God: Christian Nationalism in the United States* (New York: Oxford University Press, 2020).
2. John Calvin, John Calvin, *Institutes of the Christian Religion*, edited by John T. McNeil, 2 vols. (Louisville, KY: Westminster John Knox Press, 1960), 1: 40–45.

3. Laats, *Fundamentalist U*, 185.

4. Kristin Kobes Du Mez, *Jesus and John Wayne: How White Evangelicals Corrupted a Faith and Fractured a Nation* (New York: Liveright Publishing, 2020), 200.

5. The term "evangelical" initially applied to those who wanted access to the Bible. Catholic Christian humanists were evangelicals in this sense.

6. George Marsden, *Understanding Fundamentalism and Evangelicalism*, (Grand Rapids, MI, Eerdmans, 1990), 2.

7. Randall Balmer, *Thy Kingdom Come: How the Religious Right Distorts the Faith and Threatens American* (New York: Basic Books), 3.

8. Mark Noll bemoans evangelicals' lack of intellectual analysis, *The Scandal of the Evangelical Mind* (Grand Rapids, MI: Eerdmans, 1995).

9. Timothy L. Smith, "The Evangelical Kaleidoscope and the Call to Christian Unity," *Christian Scholar's Review* 15, no. 2 (1986), 125–40.

10. Nicholas Guyatt, *Providence and the Invention of the United States, 1607–1876* (Cambridge: Cambridge University Press, 2007); Brendan Pietsch, *Dispensational Modernism* (New York: Oxford University Press, 2015).

11. *Handbook of Christian Education* (Greenville, SC: Journeyforth, 2017), 124.

12. Kate Bowler, *Blessed: A History of the American Prosperity Gospel* (New York: Oxford University Press, 2013).

13. Dispensationalism developed from interest in biblical prophecy with new biblical institutes, such as the Moody Bible Institute (1886), the Bible Institute of Los Angeles (1907), and the Philadelphia College of the Bible (1914), giving dispensationalism institutional permanence, George Marsden, *Fundamentalism and American Culture: The Shaping of Twentieth-Century Evangelicalism, 1870–1925* (New York: Oxford University Press, 1980), 39–40.

14. Balmer, *The Making of Evangelicalism*, 3, 30–31.

15. Balmer, *The Making of Evangelicalism*, 4–5.

16. Modernism interpreted the Bible through history. Dispensationalists interpreted history exclusively through Scripture; divine intervention explained historical change, Marsden, *Fundamentalism and American Culture*, 41.

17. Ibid., 52. For La Haye, Reconstructionism supported the conspiracy theory that humanists undermined America, Michelle Goldberg, *Kingdom Coming: The Rise of Christian Nationalism* (New York: W. W. Norton, 2007), 39.

18. As Laats notes, fundamentalists defended tradition but created something new. By the 1950s, many called themselves evangelicals, *Fundamentalist U*, 5.

19. According to Marsden, by the 1960s, "fundamentalist" usually meant separatists and no longer included mainline denomination conservatives, Marsden, *Fundamentalism and American Culture*, 1, 4. See also Frank Lambert, *Religion in American Politics* (Princeton, NJ: Princeton University Press, 2008); George M. Marsden and William L. Svelmoe, "Evangelical and Fundamental Christianity," in *Encyclopedia of Religion*, 2nd edn., edited by Lindsay Jones, vol. 5 (Detroit, MI: Macmillan Reference USA, 2005), 2887–94.

20. Don Howard, *Rebirth of Our Nation* (1979), cited in Scaramanga, "Systems of Indoctrination," 21.

21. So BJU historian Carl Adams claimed; see David Gibson "BJU Questions Fundamentalist Label," *HuffPost Religion*, November 21, 2011.
22. James C. Sanford, *Blueprint for Theocracy: The Christian Right's Vision for America, Examining a Radical "Worldview" and Its Roots* (Providence, RI: Metacomet Books, 2014), 54–56.
23. For a thorough exposition, see Abraham Kuyper, Lectures on Calvinism 1931; rpt. (Grand Rapids: Eerdmans, 1983).
24. George Marsden, Mark Noll, and Nathan Hatch all critiqued Francis Schaeffer's intellectual incoherence, Barry Hankins, *Francis Schaeffer and the Shaping of Evangelical America* (Grand Rapids, MI: Eerdmans 2008), 209–27.
25. Ibid., 169–70.
26. See Roussas John Rushdoony, *The Nature of the American* System (Vallecito, CA: Chalcedon/Ross House Books, 2002); *Institutes of Biblical Law* (Phillipsburg, NJ: Presbyterian and Reformed Publishers, 1973).
27. Gary North, *An Introduction to Christian Economics* (Nutley, NJ: Craig Press, 1973) 4–15.
28. Garry Wills, *Under God: Religion and American Politics* (New York: Simon & Schuster, 1990), 174.
29. Jerome Tuccille, It Usually Begins with Ayn Rand (New York: Stein and Day, 1971; Gary North concurred in, "It Usually Begins with Ayn Rand," *Gary North's Specific Answers*, May 2, 2018 https://www.garynorth.com/public/18030.cfm .
30. See Goldberg, *Kingdom Coming*; Sara Diamond, *Roads to Dominion: Right-Wing Movements and Political Power in the United States* (New York: Guilford Press, 1995),
31. Kevin M. Kruse, *One Nation under God: How Corporate America Invented Christian America* (New York: Basic Books, 2015).

Chapter 3

1. Bob Jones University Faculty, *Christian Philosophy of Education*.
2. John Miller, *Early Modern Britain, 1450–1750* (Oxford: Oxford University Press, 2017), 441.
3. ACEUS, 1121: 1.
4. BJU* copyright page; BJU+ copyright page.
5. It intends "a textbook ministry" with the intent to "reach children and young people for the Lord and train them in the Christian way of life," Abeka* copyright page; Abeka+ copyright page.
6. Don Howard, *Rebirth of Our Nation*, 224, cited in Scaramanga, "Systems of Indoctrination," 24.
7. Ronald E. Johnson, vice president of ACE, *Under Tutors and Governors* (Lewisville, TX: Accelerated Christian Education, 1980), 31, quoted in Scaramanga, "Systems of Indoctrination," 26.

8. Bob Jones University Faculty, *The Christian Teaching of History*, cited in Dalhouse, *An Island in the Lake of Fire*, 126.

9. BJU*, 4, 5, 11; BJU+, 7.

10. BJU*, 9; BJU+, 6.

11. BJU*, 10; BJU+, 7; Abeka*, 5.

12. BJU*, 5.

13. Abeka*, 2.

14. BJU*, 10; BJU+, 7; Abeka*, 5.

15. Marsden, *Fundamentalism and American Culture*, 57–58.

16. See James Callahan, "The Bible Says: Evangelical and Postliberal Biblicism," *Theology Today* 53, no. 4 (1997), 449–63

17. Abeka*, 97; Abeka+, 77–78. The fifth edition added several pages to its prior one paragraph about the birth of Christ.

18. These textbooks use BC and AD dating rather the more conventional BCE and CE.

19. BJU*, 5; BJU+, 5.

20. BJU*, 19.

21. Abeka*, +4.

22. Guenter Salter, "The Value of a Christian Liberal Arts Education," in *Some Light on Christian Education*, edited by J. W. Deuink (Greenville, SC: Bob Jones University Press, 1984), 43–48..

23. BJU*, 9; BJU+, 6.

24. ACEUS 1132: 1.

25. BJU* copyright page; BJU+ copyright page.

26. See Michael P. Winship, *Seers of God: Puritan Providentialism in the Restoration and Early Enlightenment* (Baltimore: Johns Hopkins University Press, 1996); Guyatt, *Providence and the Invention of the United States*.

27. Rosalie Slater, *Teaching and Learning America's Christian History* (San Francisco: Foundation for American Christian Education, 1965).

28. Slater's providential history developed seven principles of Christian American history, important for evangelical education, *Teaching and Learning*.

29. ACEUS, 1121: 1.

30. BJU*, 4.

31. Milton Friedman gave capitalism its positive connotation. Previously, it meant the exploitation of the workers, Joseph Stiglitz, "Economic Systems Are Weaponized in a War of Words," *New York Times*, April 30, 2019.

32. As Balmer notes, evangelicalism evolved in response to social and political conditions, *The Making of Evangelicalism*, 4.

33. Susan George, *Hijacking America: How the Secular and Religious Right Changed What Americans Think* (Cambridge, MA: Polity Press, 2008), 50–56.

34. In contrast, the BJU textbook insists that historians interpret by their faith, BJU*, 8; BJU+, 5.

35. See Laats, *Fundamentalist U*, 17–21.

36. Nash et al., *History on Trial*, xi; Joyce Appleby, *A Restless Past: History and the American Past* (New York: Rowman & Littlefield, 2005), 4–5.

37. Ellis, "Constructing a Protestant Nation"; Goldstein, "Two States."
38. Manichaeism, a third-century dualist heresy, posits a force for good and one for evil.
39. BJU*, 8.
40. Noll objects that, by treating the Bible as a code, evangelicals are Gnostics, who neglect the study of nature, history, and world affairs, *The Scandal of the Evangelical Mind*, 51.
41. Abeka*, 2; Abeka+, 3.

Chapter 4

1. The nineteenth-century King James Only movement contested other English translations and divided fundamentalists in the 1970s when other English translations appeared. KJV relied on twelfth-century manuscripts, but in the early seventeenth century, manuscripts a thousand years older were unavailable, *The Bible in Political Debate*, edited by Frances Flannery and Rodney Werline (London: T & T Clark, 2016), 7.
2. Frances FitzGerald, *The Evangelicals: The Struggle to Shape America* (New York: Simon & Schuster, 2017), 78.
3. Abeka+, 45; BJU*, 15; BJU+, 9.
4. FitzGerald, *The Evangelicals*, 102.
5. Fears about the demise of America focused on evolution, Marsden, *Fundamentalism and Evangelicalism*, 59.
6. Ibid., 153.
7. Ingersoll, *Building God's Kingdom*, 122–23; Noll, *The Scandal of the Evangelical Mind*, 153.
8. Laats, *Fundamentalist U*, 77, 248–54, 256.
9. Marsden notes that "inerrancy" was a late nineteenth-century invention. Earlier Christians assumed it, but conservative Protestants made it a test of faith, *Fundamentalism and Evangelicalism*, 75; see also Ronald L. Numbers, *The Creationists: From Scientific Creationism to Intelligent Design* (Cambridge, MA: Harvard University Press, 2006); https://www.pewforum.org/religious-landscape-survey.
10. Barry Hankins, *American Evangelicals: A Contemporary History of a Mainstream Religious Movement* (Lanham, MD: Rowman & Littlefield, 2008), 72–73.
11. By 2011, the book had sold 300,000 copies in forty-eight printings, Arthur McCalla, *The Creationist Debate: The Encounter between the Bible and the Historical Mind* (London: Continuum International, 2006), 172.
12. Hartman, *A War for the Soul of America*, 209; Jacoby, *The Age of American Unreason*, 25.
13. Abeka*, 3. This position is more adamant in the 2016 edition.
14. BJU*, 22; BJU+, 14.

15. See Haynes, *Noah's Curse;* Bob Jones Sr. used the Bible to support his affirmative answer to his question, *Is Segregation Scriptural?* (Greenville, SC: BJU Press, 1960).

16. Abeka+, 5–6; Abeka+, 15–16. The later edition distinguishes the evil descendants of Ham from the virtuous descendants of Abraham. To support this interpretation, Abeka cites Loyal R. Ringenberf, *The Living Word* (Broadview, IL: Gibbs Publishing, 1974), 15–17. Lawrence Kessler, former head of Asian Studies at the University of North Carolina, found extensive errors on its discussion of Asia, *NC League of Women Voters Report*, 10.

17. BJU*, 23; BJU+, 15.

18. See surveys of the alt-right, Patrick Forscher and Nour Kteilly, "A Psychological Profile of the Alt-Right," *Perspectives in Psychological* Sciences January 15, 2020, 1: 90–116..

19. Abeka*, 4: Abeka+, 5–6.

20. Haynes, *Noah's Curse*, 65–105.

21. W. A. Criswell, ed., *Criswell Study Bible* (Nashville: Thomas Nelson, 1981).

22. This apology was posted on the Bob Jones University website on November 2008.

23. Mark Downey identifies the Jews as the most racially mixed and greatest threat to "Christian identity," https://fgcp.org/content/race-mixing-not-christian, mp3, revised 4/14/2013.

24. The Southern Baptist Convention meeting 2018 did not endorse a resolution explicitly repudiating "the curse of Ham," but it did reject white supremacy, Jonathan Merritt, "Southern Baptists Call Off the Culture Wars, *Atlantic*, June 16, 2018. https://www.theatlantic.com/ideas/archive/2018/06/southern-baptists-call-off-the-culture-war/563000/

25. ACE, 98: 10; Abeka*, 4: Abeka+, 5. For these textbooks, all power and authority comes from God alone, as it does for Christian Reconstructionists.

26. Hankins, *Francis Schaeffer and the Shaping of Evangelical America*, 209–27. Hankins notes Schaeffer's contradictory support for a Calvinist ideal of government while rejecting theocracy, *American Evangelicals*, 193–94, 210–11.

27. *Little Sisters of the Poor v. Pennsylvania; Burwell v. Hobby Lobby; Masterpiece Cakeshop, Ltd. v. Colorado Civil Rights Commission.*

28. In the myth of the Last World Emperor, based on an apocalyptic sermon of Pseudo-Methodius (685–690), the king is to lead a war against Islam and abdicate after Gog and Magog are attacked, inaugurating the Second Coming. As the myth requires a flawed leader, it is invoked to legitimate Trump, Thomas Lecaque, "The Apocalyptic Myth That Helps Explain Evangelical Support for Trump," *Washington Post*, November 26, 2019.

29. Many evangelicals insist on obedience to constituted authority as a cardinal principle, Marsden, *Fundamentalism and American Culture*, 362.

30. BJU*, 23–26; BJU+, 15–16.

31. Bob Jones, Sr., *Is Segregation Scriptural?*

32. J. Roussas Rushdoony, "The Tower of Babel: On Work and Confusion," May 25, 1994 https://chalcedon.edu/resources/articles/the tower of babel-work-and-confusion.

33. BJU*, 16, 18; BJU+, 10–11.

34. BJU*, 14, 16, 17; BJU+, 10–11.

35. Carolyn Merchant, *The Death of Nature: Women, Ecology, and the Scientific Revolution* (San Francisco: Harper & Row, 1980), 127–48.

36. Sanford, *Blueprint for Theocracy*, 37.

37. Milton Gaither discusses the involvement of extreme groups in the homeschool movement, *Homeschool: An American History* (New York: Palgrave Macmillan, 2008), 255.

38. See Katheryn Joyce, *Quiverfull: Inside the Christian Patriarchy Movement* (Boston: Beacon Press, 2010).

39. Du Mez, *Jesus and John Wayne*, 188.

40. ACE, 97: 7.

41. Abeka*, 23; ACE, 98: 1.

42. Marsden, *Understanding Fundamentalism and Evangelicalism*, 77.

43. Esther Kaplan, *With God on Their Side: George W. Bush and the Christian Right* (New York and London: New Press, 2004), 26. See also "Religion and Politics: Contention and Consensus," Pew Forum on Religion and Public Life, July 24, 2003.

44. Marsden, *Fundamentalism and American Culture*, 76.

45. Nicholas Guyatt, *Have a Nice Doomsday: Why Millions of Americans Are Looking Forward to the End of the World* (New York: Harper Perennial, 2007), 110–11.

46. Kaplan, *With God on Their Side*, 28–29.

47. Jonathan Weisman, "American Jews and Israeli Jews Break Up," *New York Times*, January 6, 2019.

48. "Proclamation of the Fourth International Christian Congress on Biblical Zionism," February 22, 2001, christianactionforisrael.org/4thcongress3.htlm.

49. See www.cipaconline.org.

50. BJU*, 23; BJU+, 12. Seth (Cain's brother born after Cain murdered Abel) begets "the seed of woman."

51. BJU*, 26; BJU+, 15. This is a nineteenth-century sense of nation and national identity.

52. Abeka*, +4.

53. BJU, *29; BJU+, 19.

54. For Calvin, knowledge of God was available to all, as he believed that God planted an awareness of the divine in each human being—*divinitatis sensum*. Because ignorance of God was no defense, people could be divided into the faithful and the wicked, John Calvin, *Institutes of the Christian Religion*, 1:43–45.

55. Martin Luther, "On the Jews and Their Lies," ed. Helmut T. Lehmann, trans. Martin H. Bertram, *Luther's Works*, vol. 47 (Philadelphia: Fortress Press, 1971). .

56. Calvin, *Institutes of the Christian Religion*, 2: 1502.

57. Mosaic Law, as evangelicals use it, elides the Old Testament God's selection of the Jews as His chosen people, the Ten Commandments, and Paul's comments on the Law. See Jason Meyer, *The End of the Law: Mosaic Covenant in Pauline Theology* (Nashville: B&H Academic, 2009).

58. Abeka condemns Hammurabi's empire as built on lies, deceit, and his selfishness, +13.

59. Abeka*, 19; Abeka+, 14.

60. TEKS 113.44.8.
61. Abeka+, 11–12.
62. BJU*, 43; BJU+, 31.
63. Abeka+, 34.
64. *BJU*, 46, 48; BJU+, +34, 36.
65. *BJU, *113, +97.
66. Abeka*, 48; Abeka+, 27; ACE, 97: 15–18; BJU*, 38; BJU+, 27.
67. Abeka+, 107.
68. BJU +, 129–33; Abeka*, 37, 43; Abeka+, 188–89.
69. Abeka*, 54, 56–57; Abeka+, 276–80.
70. One must "sift out the influence of evolutionary thought from archeological knowledge," Abeka+, 20.
71. BJU*, 33; BJU+, 22.
72. See John Robertson, *A Short Introduction to the Enlightenment* (Oxford and New York: Oxford University Press), 3–26.
73. Donald Kagan, Steven Ozment, Frank M. Turner, and Alison Frank, *The Western Heritage* (Boston: Pearson, 2103), 11th edn., 28.
74. Abeka+, 20.

Chapter 5

1. L. H. Butterfield, Marc Freidlaender, Richard Ryerson, and Hobson Woodward, eds., *Adams Family Correspondence,* 15 vols. (Cambridge, MA: Harvard University Press, 1973), 4:117.
2. Abeka*, 77.
3. As Caroline Winterer notes that classical elitism and democratic egalitarianism proved difficult to unite, *The Culture of Classicism: Ancient Greece and Rome in American Intellectual Life, 1780–1910* (Baltimore: Johns Hopkins University, 2002), 183.
4. D. James Kennedy, *Character and Destiny: A Nation in Search of Its Soul* (Grand Rapid, MI: Zondervan, 1995), 59, cited in Goldberg, *Kingdom Coming,* 43.
5. Abeka*, 76–77; Abeka+, 48; citing Rom 1:25, BJU*, 68; BJU+, 58.
6. Chris Babits, "To Cure a Sinful Nation: Conversion Therapy and the Making of Modern America, 1930 to Present Day," PhD dissertation, University of Texas, 2019.
7. 1 Corinthians 3:19, BJU*, 68.
8. ACE, 99: 16.
9. BJU*, 74; BJU+, 60–61.
10. Abeka*, 65, 67; Abeka+, 51, 53.
11. Abeka*, 74; citing Rom 1:23, BJU*, 58, BJU+, 44.
12. Abeka*, 73; Abeka+, 61.
13. BJU*, 66; BJU+, 54.
14. Abeka*, 75.

15. ACE, 99: 4, 13, 24, 34; ACE, 100: 5.

16. Abeka*, 69.

17. Abeka*, 75. The 2016 edition deletes a section on Greek culture.

18. BJU*, 79; BJU+, 67. Italics are mine.

19. BJU*, 98; BJU+, 84.

20. Abeka*, 74–75, 82, 83, 87.

21. Andrew Klumpp and Jack Levison, "The Bible and Family Values," in *The Bible in Political Debate*, 27.

22. Ronald E. Johnson, *Under Tutors and Governors* (Garland, TX: Accelerated Christian Education), 27, cited in Scaramanga, 29.

23. See Eve d'Ambra, *Roman Women* (Cambridge: Cambridge University Press, 2006); Elaine Fantham, *Women in the Classical World* (Oxford: Oxford University Press, 1995); Mary Lefkowitz and Maureen Fant, *Women's Life in Greece and Rome* (Oxford: Oxford University Press, 2016).

24. Abeka*, 87, Abeka+, 69. Only the second part of the quotation is in the 2013 edition; BJU*, 88–89; BJU+, 102–3.

25. Identifying poverty with moral failing is prominent in Protestantism. See *Thomas Cromwell's Injunctions of 1536*, included in Gerald Bray, ed., *Documents of the English Revolution* (Cambridge: Cambridge University Press, 1994), 176–77. The right's rigid condemnation of poverty developed in the 1970s; see Michael B. Katz, *The Undeserving Poor: America's Enduring Confrontation with Poverty*, 2nd edn. (New York: Oxford University Press, 2013).

26. BJU*, 119; BJU+, 102.

27. Abeka*, 97.

28. BJU*, 119. Many blocks of text raising questions for students are not in the most recent edition; some are in the workbook.

29. BJU*, 77; BJU+, 65.

30. BJU*, 77; BJU+, 65; Abeka*, 93. In the most recent edition, Rome simply prepared the way for Christ's coming.

31. Abeka*, 99–100; Abeka+, 73–74; BJU*, 98; BJU+, 83.

32. BJU*, 109; BJU+, 94.

33. Abeka+, 74.

34. BJU*, 115; BJU+, 99.

35. Abeka*, 100.

36. Abeka*, 105–7; Abeka+, 93.

37. Abeka*, 107; Abeka+, 92.

38. BJU*, 137–41; BJU+, 119–22.

39. Abeka*, 28; Abeka+, 100.

40. BJU*, 139, 140; BJU+, 120, 122.

41. BJU*, 139; BJU+, 121. The second sentence is not included in the most recent edition.

42. The Koran stipulates that other religions be annihilated and that Islamic nations are committed to destroying America as a Christian country, claims AbekaUS, 546.

43. Stephanie McCrummen, "Judgment Days," *Washington Post*, July 21, 2018.

44. BJU*, 140; BJU+, 123.
45. Abeka*, 30. Highly prejudicial views of Islam are included in textbooks for the Texas market; see David Brockman, https://www.bakerinstitute.org/research/religious-imbalance-texas-social-studies-curriculum/.
46. Abeka*, 68; Abeka+, 55. The first part of the quotation omitted in the 2016 edition, which is more antidemocratic.
47. BJU+, 47.
48. BJU*, 99; BJU+, 85.
49. Jennifer T. Roberts, *Athens on Trial: The Anti-Democratic Tradition in Western Thought* (Princeton, NJ: Princeton University Press, 2011).
50. Winterter, *The Culture of Classicism,* 11–12.
51. Carl Richard, *The Founders and the Classics: Greece, Rome, and the American Enlightenment* (Cambridge, MA: Harvard University Press, 1995), 169, 232, 242.
52. See FitzGerald, *The Evangelicals,* 23–25.
53. Jacoby, *The Age of American Unreason,* 184–209.

Chapter 6

1. Abeka*, 120–22; Abeka+, 89–91.
2. Martin Luther urges that the three walls of Romanists be torn down in his "Address to the Christian Nobility of the German Nation" of 1520.
3. BJU*, 183; BJU+, 173.
4. Du Mez, *Jesus and John Wayne,* 210–19.
5. Abeka*, 117.
6. Matthew 16:13–17, Abeka*, 119; Abeka+, 93–94.
7. BJU*, 202; BJU+, 205.
8. This article highlights an illegitimate use of history in legal articles, Richard Schragger and Micah Schwartzman, "Against Religious Institutionalism," *Virginia Law Review,* 99, no. 5 (September 2013), 918–85.
9. Abeka*, 119–121; Abeka+, 92–95; BJU*, 179–82.
10. BJU*, 277–79, 292; BJU+, 249–50, 264–65.
11. ACE, 103: 15–18.
12. BJU+, 251.
13. Abeka+, 105.
14. BJU*, 221. ACE criticizes the crusaders' actions as unchristian, 102: 24. The BJU history acknowledges that the crusades expanded European territory and introduced non-European cultural influences, BJU*, 223–24; BJU+, 199–200.
15. Abeka*, 132.
16. The 2016 edition makes England even more central. It places early English history immediately after the Reformation.
17. Abeka *, 120, 158.

18. BJU*, 213–14; BJU+, 189–190.

19. Merry Wiesner-Hanks, *Early Modern Europe* (Cambridge, Cambridge University Press, 2006), 91.

20. Only after Edward Coke invoked the Magna Carta in the Parliamentary battle with the Stuartswas it consistently used to oppose those in power, Tom Ginsburg, "Stop Revering Magna Carta," *New York Times*, June 14, 2015. See also Nicholas Vincent, *Magna Carta: A Very Short Introduction* (Oxford: Oxford University Press, 2012).

21. ACE, 102: 29, 30.

22. Abeka*, 166.

23. ACEUS, 1122: 13.

24. Abeka*, 163.

25. For a history of Anglo-Saxon racial claims, see Reginald Horsman, *Race and Manifest Destiny: The Origins of American Racial Anglo-Saxonism* (Cambridge: MA, Harvard University Press, 1981).

26. The phrase designates Anglo-Saxon racial superiority as promoted to deny civil rights to others. Founded to support the Lost Cause, the Sons of Confederate Veterans is now a heritage organization, which repudiates white supremacy.

27. Ron Paul used the slogan in his presidential campaign of 2008; Stephen Presser claimed that "Trump and Barr Can Give Us Back Our Constitution," *Newsmax*, February 25, 2019.

28. Matthew Frye Jacobson, *Whiteness of a Different Color: European Immigrants and the Alchemy of Race* (Cambridge, MA: Harvard University Press, 1999).

29. Archeologists have debunked such claims. James M. Harland, "'Race' in the Trenches: Anglo-Saxons, Ethnicity, and the Misuse of the Medieval Past," *Public Medievalist*, February 17, 2017.

30. The proponents included John Wilson, *Our Israelish Origin*, 1840, and Edward Hine, *The British Nation Identified with Lost Israel*, 1871.

31. New England Yankees claimed a proud "Anglo-Saxon Pilgrim" culture unlike that the South; see Grady McWhiney, *Cracker Culture: Celtic Ways in the Old South* (Tuscaloosa: University of Alabama, 1989), 23.

32. A "covenanter" notion of government, rooted in Calvinism, defined the Scots' objection to Charles I. The covenant with God was unconditional but that with the king could be broken if he did not adhere to God's word, Miller, *Early Modern Britain*, 208.

33. Abeka*, 163.

34. Abeka*, 125; Abeka+, 108; BJU*, 186; BJU+, 160.

35. An example of a right-wing use of Martel, Mark Tapson, "Charles Martel: Turning Back the Islamic Tide," *Breitbart*, October 28, 2010.

36. Abeka*, 125–28; Abeka+, 108–11.

37. BJU*, 187; BJU+, 161.

38. BJU*, 230; BJU+, 204; Abeka*, 146.

39. Abeka*, 143. The 2016 edition deletes the discussion of medieval commerce.

40. ACE, 102: 16.

41. Abeka*147; Abeka+, 126. The 2016 edition is more dismissive of Aquinas.

42. Abeka+, 126.

43. Abeka*, 148. The 2016 edition deletes Roger Bacon. See David Lindberg, "The Medieval Church Encounters the Classical Tradition: Saint Augustine, Roger Bacon, and the Handmaiden Metaphor," in *When Science and Christianity Meet*, edited by David C. Lindberg and Ronald L. Numbers (Chicago: University of Chicago Press, 2003); Jeremiah Hackett, "Roger Bacon on *Scientia Experimentalis*," in *Roger Bacon and the Sciences,* edited by Hackett. (Leiden: Brill, 1997), 12–25.

44. Abeka*, 147; Abeka+, 127. The 2016 has only the second quotation.

45. Abeka*, 130; Abeka+, 151. In the 2016 edition, the humanities "became an expression of human pride and vanity."

46. Abeka+, 127.

47. ACE, 103: 3, 4, 7, 8.

48. BJU*, 255.

49. BJU*, 265, 270; BJU+, 237, 242, 244.

50. ACE, 103: 15.

51. BJU*, 274; BJU+, 246.

52. Abeka*, 187.

53. Jonathan Chait, "Trump Chooses Most Ironic Location in the Entire World for Anti-France Rally," *New York Times*, June 3, 2017; Amy S. Kaufman, "Race, Racism, and the Middle Ages," *Public Medievalist*, February 28, 2017. The appropriation of the Middle Ages by white supremacists has been the topic in this online journal for nine months.

54. Dimitri K. Simes, "No More Crusades in the Middle East," *Los Angeles Times*, January 9, 2007; *ABC News*, "Iraq War Raises Suspicion of New 'Crusade,'" January 6, 2006; Matthew Gabriele, "Islamophobes Want to Recreate the Crusades. But They Don't Understand Them at All," *Washington Post*, June 6, 2017; Du Mez, *Jesus and John Wayne*, 217–226.

55. Michael Massa, *Anti-Catholicism in America: The Last Acceptable Prejudice* (New York: Crossword Publishing, 2003), 20.

56. Ibid.

57. See Barry Hankins, *God's Rascal: J. Frank Norris and the Beginnings of Southern Fundamentalism* (Lexington: Kentucky University Press, 1996).

58. Carl F. H. Henry, *The Uneasy Conscience of Modern Fundamentalism* (Grand Rapids, MI: Eerdmans,1947), xv.)

59. Massa, *Anti-Catholicism in America*, 37.

60. Andrew Greeley, *The American Catholic: A Social Portrait* (New York: Basic Books, 1977).

61. In 1960, some evangelicals raised these concerns publicly and with Kennedy, Robert Wuthnow, *The Restructuring of American Religion: Society and Faith since World War II* (Princeton, NJ: Princeton University Press, 1988), 155–57. Even moderate evangelicals wanted Catholic candidates to commit to the separation of church and state, Daniel K. Williams, *God's Own Party: The Making of the Christian Right* (New York: Oxford University Press, 2004, rprnt, 2012), 51–52.

62. Daniel J. Borstin, *The Americans: The National Experience* (New York: Random House, 1965); Gordon S. Wood, *The Idea of America. Reflections on the Birth of the*

United States (New York: Penguin Press, 2011); and *Empire of Liberty: A History of the Early Republic, 1789–1815* (New York: Oxford University Press, 2011).

63. Massa, *Anti-Catholicism in America*, 12.

64. https://www.pewforum.org/wp-content/uploads/sites/7/2017/12/Christmas-Survey-2017-Full.

65. Jimmy Swaggart's video is no longer available.

66. Robert Jeffress, *Pathway to Victory* radio broadcast, Dallas, TX, 2010. https://youtu.be/nI0MBgA7ckA

67. Robert Jones, *The End of White Christian America* (New York: Simon & Schuster, 2016).

68. *The Trump Prophecy*, directed by Stephan Schultze, Reel Works Studio, Brooklyn, New York, 2018.

69. Andrew Elliott, "A Vile Love Affair: Right-Wing Nationalism and the Middle Ages," *Public Medievalist*, February 14, 2017.

70. www.jasoncolavito.blog.

71. Goldberg, *Kingdom Coming*, 45.

72. Hannah Devlin, "First Modern Briton Had 'Dark to Black' Skin: Cheddar Man DNA Reveals," *Guardian*, February 7, 2018. Media widely reported this finding on this date.

73. Mark Bruce, "The Alt-Right Is Hijacking the Middle Ages: Medievalists Aren't Going to Let Them," *Surfingedges*, August 18, 2017; "The Far Right's New Fascination with the Middle Ages," *Economist*, March 7, 2017. For the most thorough exploration, see Andrew B. R. Elliott, *Medievalism, Politics, and Mass Media* (Woodbridge, UK: D. S. Brewer, 2017).

Chapter 7

1. Abeka*, 191; Abeka+, 143; BJU Faculty, *The Christian Teaching of History*) , cited in Dalhouse, *An Island in the Lake of Fire*, 126.

2. Miller, *Early Modern Britian*, 190.

3. Abeka*, 195; Abeka+, 145.

4. Abeka*, 187, 190–91; Abeka+, 139, 141–42.

5. BJU*, 281; BJU+, 253. These curricula do not recognize Anglican theologians, such as Richard Hooker (d. 1600), who balanced Scripture, tradition, and reason.

6. ACE, 103: 23; Abeka*, 188; Abeka+, 139; BJU*, 287; BJU+, 254; Abeka*, 193; Abeka+, 143.

7. ACE, 103: 25–26; BJU*, 285; BJU+, 257.

8. BJU*, 287; BJU+, 259.

9. ACE, 103: 27.

10. ACE, 103: 23.

11. Philippe Mornay du Plessis, *Vindiciae contra Tyrannos* (1589).

12. Abeka*, 202–3; Abeka+, 155.

13. Abeka*, 198; Abeka+, 149.

14. BJU*, 300; BJU+, 271.

15. Abeka cites John Richard Green, *A Short History of the English People*, Abeka*, 211.

16. Abeka+, 160; BJU*, 300.

17. Abeka+, 161.

18. ACE, 103: 28–29, 33; BJU*, 289; BJU+, 261.

19. ACE, 103: 32; Abeka*, 205; Abeka+, 172; BJU*, 293; BJU+, 265.

20. Abeka*, 210; Abeka+, 176; BJU*, 294; BJU+, 266, 268.

21. Rafael E. Tarrago, "Bloody Bess: The Persecution of Catholics in Elizabethan England," *Logos* 7, no. 1 (2004), 117–33.

22. Citing Green, *A Short History of the English People*, Abeka*, 211.

23. Abeka*, 212; Abeka+, 235.

24. Abeka*, 212–13; Abeka+, 235–36; BJU*, 294; BJU+, 268.

25. See Robert Kingdon, *Myths about the St. Bartholomew's Day Massacres, 1572–1576* (Cambridge, MA: Harvard University Press, 1988); Arlette Joanna, *The St. Bartholomew's Day's Massacre: The Mysteries of a Crime of State* (Manchester, UK: Manchester University Press, 2016).

26. Abeka*, 231.

27. Benjamin Lynerd sees the Reformation as promoting "epistemic individualism," and institutional pluralism, *Republican Theology: The Civil Religion of American Evangelicals* (New York: Oxford University Press, 2014), 39.; see also Brad Gregory, *The Unintended Reformation: How a Religious Revolution Secularized Society* (Cambridge, MA: Belknap Press, 2012).

28. Wiesner-Hanks, *Early Modern Europe*, 149. See Eric Metaxas, *Martin Luther: The Man Who Rediscovered God and Changed the World* (New York: Viking, 2017).

29. See Dairmaid MacCulloch, *The Reformation: A History* (New York: Penguin, 2005).

30. Abeka*, 195; Abeka+, 145.

31. Martin Luther, "Admonition to the Peace," in Steven Ozment, *Age of Reform, 1250–1550: An Intellectual and Religious History of Late Medieval and Reformation Europe* (New Haven, CT: Yale University Press, 1981), 283.

32. Martin Luther, "An Open Letter Concerning the Murdering Hoards of Peasants," Ozment, *Age of Reform*, 287.

33. BJU*, 287; BJU+, 259.

34. BJU*, 8.

35. Marsden, *Fundamentalism and American Culture*, 112–13.

36. Abeka*, 195; Abeka+, 145.

Chapter 8

1. Anthony Pagden, *The Enlightenment: And Why It Still Matters* (New York: Random House, 2013).

2. Abeka* 219; Abeka+, 290.

3. See John W. O'Malley, Gavin Bailey, Stephen J. Harris, and T. Frank Kennedy, eds., *The Jesuits: Cultures, Sciences, and the Arts, 1540–1773* (Toronto: University of Toronto Press, 1999).

4. ACE, 104: 10, 11, 12; Abeka*, 220; Abeka+, 288, 289, 290. The 2016 edition puts all discussion of science in a single chapter to tie all science to the Bible.
   Abeka+, 289.

5. Abeka+, 270; BJU*, 381; BJU+, 325.

6. Those who were Catholics questioned the church, Abeka+, 290.

7. BJU*, 383; BJU+, 325; Abeka*, 222; Abeka+, 292.

8. See Betty J. T. Dobbs, *The Janus Faces of Genius: The Role of Alchemy in Newton's Thought* (Cambridge: Cambridge University Press, 2003).

9. BJU*, 383: BJU+, 325.

10. Abeka*, 222, 223–24; Abeka+292, 294.

11. Roger Hahn, *The Anatomy of a Scientific Institution: Paris Academy of Sciences, 1666–1803* (Los Angeles: University of California Press: 1971); Robert K. Merton, "Science, Technology, and Society in Seventeenth-Century England," PhD Dissertation (Harvard University, 1936); I. B. Cohen, K. E. Duffin, and Stuart Strickland, eds., *Puritanism and the Rise of Modern Science: The Merton Thesis* (New Brunswick, NJ: Rutgers University Press, 1990); Steven Shapin, "Understanding the Merton Thesis," *Isis* 79, no. 4 (December 1988), 594–605.

12. Abeka*, 222; Abeka+, 294–95.

13. Abeka*, 225; Abeka+, 314.

14. David Gibson, "Looking for Catholic Art? Fundamentalist BJU Has It," *Christian Century*, November 22, 2011 https://www.christiancentury.org/article/2011-11/looking-catholic-art-fundamentalist-bob-jones-university-has-it.

15. Abeka+, 315. Italic is in the original.

16. BJU*, 309; BJU+, 281.

17. ACE, 104: 1, 2–7.

18. ACE, 104: 9; Abeka+, 199.

19. ACE, 104: 10.

20. Washington Irving, *The Life and Voyages of Christopher Columbus*, edited by John Harmon McElroy (Boston: Qwayne Publishers, 1891), bk. 2, chap. 3, 47–55.

21. ACE, 104: 11–12; Abeka*, 176; Abeka+, 199; BJU+, 277.

22. ACE, 104: 29.

23. ACE, 104: 29; Abeka*, 172; Abeka+, 201; BJU*, 309; BJU+, 281.

24. ACE, 104: 19–20; Abeka*, 234.

25. In the BJU textbook, the period from 1600 to 1800 is "the Enlightened World."

26. BJU+, 357.

27. Abeka*, 251–54; Abeka+, 179–80.

28. ACE, 105: 14, 15.

29. The recent discovery of a 1611 draft of the KJV revealed that six teams of commissioned translators produced a version that favored Anglican over Puritan interpretations, "Early Draft of 1611 Bible Is Revealed," *New York Times*, October 15, 2015.

30. Abeka*, 251.

31. Abeka *, 252; Abeka+, 180; BJU+, 369; BJU+, 311.
32. Abeka+, 181.
33. BJU+, 370; BJU+, 312.
34. Abeka*, 254.
35. Abeka*, 255; Abeka+, 184.
36. ACE, 104: 25.
37. Miller, *Early Modern Britain*, 339.
38. Ibid., 346–47.
39. Abeka+, 184.
40. Louis XIV forced Jansenists to sign *billets de confession*, enforcing the papal ban on five of Cornelius Jansen's propositions in *Augustinus*. Jensen and his supporters adhered to an Augustinian variant of Catholicism resembling Calvinism in specifics the church considered heretical.
41. BJU+, 362, +305.
42. BJU*, 413, BJU+, 354.
43. BJU*, 417, BJU+, 357.
44. Abeka*, 257.
45. BJU*, 362; BJU+, 305.
46. BJU+, 418; BJU+, 357.
47. Abeka*, 210; Abeka+, 205.
48. Abeka+, 205.
49. Ibid., 23. Quotation repeated in AbekaUS, 17.

Chapter 9

1. For historians' debate of the Enlightenment and its legacy, see David Hollinger, "The Enlightenment and the Genealogy of Cultural Critique in the United States," in *What's Left of the Enlightenment? A Post-Modern Question*, edited by Keith Baker and Peter Reill (Stanford, CA: Stanford University Press, 2001), 7–8.
2. Max Horkheimer and Theodor Adorno, *Dialectic of Enlightenment*, edited by Gunzelin Noerr, translated by Edmund Jephcott (Stanford, CA: Stanford University, 2017).
3. The French *philosophes'* efforts to change conventional thinking included a selective and polemical reconstruction of the past. See Jean d'Alembert's *Discours Préliminaire* to the *Encyclopédie*. Ironically, their methods have been used by modern critics to discredit them.
4. Neil H. Buchanan, "Republicans Choose the Dark Ages over the Enlightenment: The Right's Agenda Is Even More Reactionary Than It Had Seemed," *Verdict*, July 25, 2013.
5. Abeka*, 235.
6. BJU*, 387; BJU+, 328–29.
7. BJU*, 388–89.
8. BJU*, 391; BJU+, 332.
9. BJU*, 391.

10. Ibid.
11. Abeka*, 237. The 2016 edition reduces discussion of the Enlightenment to several sentences.
12. Abeka*, 237.
13. BJU*, 392; BJU+, 333.
14. Noll appreciates Edwards as the last great evangelical intellectual, *The Scandal of the Evangelical Mind*, 50.
15. BJU*, 393, 394–95; BJU+, 334, 335–36.
16. Abeka*, 258.
17. Abeka*, 236; Abeka+, 243; BJU*, 387; BJU+, 328.
18. Abeka*, 236; Abeka+, 242.
19. Abeka*, 237.
20. BJU*, 423.
21. James Warden, *Bible Prophecy and Trump: Daniel Prophesied of a Goat Stubborn King of the West* (Independently Published, 2017); Mark Taylor, *The Trump Prophecies: The Astonishing True Story of the Man Who Saw Tomorrow* (Crane, MO: Defender Publishing, 2019).
22. BJU*, 445.
23. BJU*, 387; Abeka*, 236.
24. Amy S. Kaufman, "A Brief History of a Terrible Idea: The 'Dark Enlightenment,'" *Public Medievalist*, February 9, 2017. https://www.publicmedievalist.com/dark-enlightenment/
25. ACE, 105: 34.
26. The 2016 edition changes the wording slightly, Abeka+, 262.
27. These two figures signal that America will displace Europe from the central, historical narrative, as Divine Providence favors America.
28. Immanuel Kant, *What Is Enlightenment*, translated by Ted Humphrey (Indianapolis, IN: Hackett Publishing, 1992).
29. Rushdoony, *By What Standard?*, 48–49; Rushdoony, *Politics of Guilt and Pity* (Nutley, NJ: Craig Press, 1970), 122–23. Sanford develops the implications of Rushdoony's interpretation, *Blueprint for Theocracy*, 100–101.
30. BJU*, 404.
31. Rushdoony, *Politics of Guilt and Pity*, 320.

Chapter 10

1. https://www.abeka.com/SubjectDistinctives.aspx.
2. Cited in Dalhouse, *An Island in the Lake of Fire*, 126.
3. Steven Green's work is especially important in defining these developments, *Inventing a Christian America: The Myth of the Religious Founding* (New York: Oxford University Press, 2005).
4. Slater, *Teaching and Learning America's Christian History*; Verna Hall, *The Christian History of the Constitution of the United States of America* (San Francisco, CA: Foundation for American Christian Education, 1983).

5. Neil Eskelin, *Pat Robertson: A Biography* (Shreveport, LA: Huntington House, 1987), 178–79.

6. See Joseph Ellis, *American Dialogue: The Founders and Us* (New York: Alfred A. Knopf, 2018). The Abeka curriculum make its strongest Christian nation argument with respect to the Constitution.

7. Mid-1980s polemics claimed that lawyers and educators undid the founders' Christian nation, the Bill of Rights did not apply to states, and there was no separation of church and state. See David Brockman, https://www.bakerinstitute.org/research/religious-imbalance-texas-social-studies-curriculum/.

8. Richard T. Hughes, "Why Do We Think of America as a Christian Nation?" in *Politics and the History Curriculum*, 127–47.

9. See David Sekat, *The Myth of American Religious Freedom* (Oxford: Oxford University Press, 2011).

10. Abeka+, 209.

11. "God brought spiritual revival to America," AbekaUS, 57. See Guyatt, *Providence and the Invention of the United States*.

12. Jamestown claimed to be America's failed communism, AbekaUS, 22.

13. ACE, 104: 35, 36; ACEUS, 1122: 10–11. Both texts make identical claims.

14. The original Jamestown Charter gave the colonists veto power over the London Company and the king; see Joseph Kelly, *Marooned: Jamestown, Shipwreck, and a New History of America's Origin* (New York: Bloomsbury, 2019).

15. ACE, 104: 39. The quotations are Exodus 20:9, Genesis 3:19, 1 Thessalonians 4:11–12, 2 Thessalonians 3:10, and Acts 5:1–10. ACE makes the same argument about socialism, ACEUS, 1122: 24.

16. ACE, 104: 40; ACEUS, 1122: 24.

17. Bradford established free enterprise in the colonies, AbekaUS, 28–29.

18. *The First Charter of Virginia*, April 10, 1606, Yale Law School, The Avalon Project, cited in John Fea, *Was America Founded as a Christian Nation?* (Louisville, KY: Westminster John Knox, 2011), 80.

19. Fea, *Was America Founded as a Christian Nation?*, 82, 84.

20. ACEUS, 1122: 13.

21. BJU*, 408; BJU, +348.

22. BJU*, 408; BJU, +348.

23. AbekaUS, 30.

24. See Daniel T. Rodgers, *As a City on a Hill: The Story of America's Most Famous Sermon* (Princeton NJ: Princeton University Press), 2018.

25. War, especially after 9/11, has emphasized Christian America, as reflected in TEKS, Hughes, "Why do We Think of America as a Christian Nation?," 140.

26. ACE, 104: 46; ACEUS, 1122: 25.

27. As Marsden notes, in 1850 most universities had evangelical presidents, but by 1900 most were on a German model with studies grounded in disciplines and objective standards, *Understanding Fundamentalism and Evangelicalism*, 14–15.

28. Fea, *Was America Founded as a Christian Nation?*, 88.

29. Miller, *Early Modern Britain*, 271.

30. Marsden highlights colonial religious tensions between Anglicans and Calvinists and their foreign and domestic implications, *Understanding Fundamentalism and Evangelicalism*, 85–87.

31. BJU+, 284.

32. AbekaUS, 5.

33. Paterson, *Democracy and Intolerance*, 159.

34. ACE, 104: 39.

35. Nancy Isenberg, *White Trash: The 400-Year Untold Story of Class in America* (New York: Penguin, 2017), 28–33.

36. For a lengthy discussion of the Mayflower Compact, see Green, *Inventing a Christian America*, 74–76, 229–34.

37. Separatists and Anglicans got along because they appreciated the Bible and believed in religious freedom, AbekaUS, 25.

38. Green, *Inventing a Christian America*, 229, 352.

39. BJU*, 407–8; BJU+, 347–48.

40. Abeka *, 252; AbekaUS, 28–29.

41. Webster's history ignored slavery and the Southern colonies but remained an important source in high school textbooks into the twentieth century, Donald Yacovone, "Textbook Racism: How Scholars Sustained White Supremacy," *Chronicle Review*, April 27, 2018, B14–16.

42. Abeka+, 229.

43. Citing Noah Webster, *History of the United States to Which Is Prefixed a Brief Historical Account of Our [English] Ancestors, from the Dispersion at Babel, to Their Migration to America and the Conquest of South American, by the Spaniards* (New Haven, CT: Durrie & Peck, 1832), Abeka+, 229.

44. Green, *Inventing a Christian America*, 234–37.

45. See Rousas John Rushdoony, *The Institutes of Biblical Law* (Presbyterian and Reformed Publishing, 1973); Gary North, *Tools of Dominion: The Case Laws of Exodus* (Tyler, TX: Institute for Christian Economics, 1990); Gary De Mar, *God and Government: Issues in Biblical Perspective,* 2 vols. (Brentwood, TN: Woldgemuth & Hyatt, 1989–1990).

46. Gary B. Nash, *Red, White, and Black: The Peoples of Early America* (Englewood Cliffs, NJ: Prentice-Hall, 1973).

Chapter 11

1. John Adams, "Letters of Novanglus," January 23, 1775, in *The Papers of John Adams*, edited by Robert Taylor (Cambridge, MA: Harvard University Press, 1977), 2:230. Cited in Richard, *The Founders and the Classics*, 233.

2. Fea, *Was America Founded as a Christian Nation?*, 3.

3. ACEUS, 1101: 29.

4. Thomas Kidd, *The Great Awakening* (New Haven, CT: Yale University Press, 2007), 174–87. Most converts were farmers and workers, Donald Matthews, *Religion in the Old South* (Chicago: University of Chicago Press), 20–46.

5. See Gary Dorrien, *The Making of American Liberal Theology: Imagining Progressive Religion, 1805–1990* (Louisville, KY: Westminister Press, 2001), 1: 1–3; Edwin Gaustad, *The Great Awakening in New England* (New York: Harper, 1957), 80–101.

6. This lacuna is redressed in their US histories.

7. Henry Steele Commanger, *The Empire of Reason: How Europe Imagined and America Realized the Enlightenment* (New York: Doubleday, 1977), 45, 48.

8. Henry May, *The Enlightenment in America* (Oxford: Oxford University Press, 1978), xi–xii; see also Paul Merrill Spurlin, *The French Enlightenment in America: Essays on the Times of the Founding Fathers* (Athens, GA: University of Georgia Press, 1984); David Hollinger, "The Accommodation of Protestant Christianity with the Enlightenment: An Old Drama Still Being Enacted," *Daedalus* 141, no. 1 (Winter 2012), 76–88.

9. Green, *Inventing Christian America*, 115–19; Fea cites Samuel Sherwood's sermon "The Church's Flight into the Wilderness: An Address on the Times" as an example, *Was America Founded as a Christian Nation?*, 111–13.

10. John M. Murrin. "No Awakening, No Revolution? More Counterfactual Speculation," *Reviews in American History* 11, no. 2 (June 1983), 151–71.

11. Noll, *The Scandal of American Mind*, 71–74. Fea claims their arguments were based on Enlightenment ideas rather than Scripture, *Was America Founded as a Christian Nation?*, 110–112, 119.

12. Green, *Inventing Christian America*, 104–5.

13. Donald S. Lutz, "The Relative Influence of European Writers on Late Eighteenth-Century American Political Thought," *American Political Science Review* 78, no. 1 (March, 1984), 189–97.

14. A religious revolution is, Fea insists, purely wishful thinking, *Was America Founded as a Christian Nation?*, 93–94.

15. Jill Lepore, "A World of Paine," in *Revolutionary Founders: Rebels, Radical, and Reformers in the Making of the Nation*, edited by Alfred F. Young, Gary Nash, and Ray Raphael (New York: Alfred A. Knopf, 2011), 88.

16. Thomas Paine, *Thomas Paine: Collected Works* (New York: Library of America, 1955), 24.

17. Richard, *The Founders and the Classics*, 242.

18. Noll, *The Scandal of the Evangelical Mind*, 85–87.

19. Martin Marty, "Getting Beyond the Myth of 'Christian America,'" in *No Establishment of Religion: America's Original Contribution to Religious Liberty*, edited by T. Jeremy Gunn and John Witte (New York: Oxford University Press, 2012), 274–76.

20. Hughes, "Why Do We Think of America as a Christian Nation?," 129–140.

21. The US history recognizes Locke's influence, BJUUS, 108.

22. Paul Spurlin, *The French Enlightenment in America* (Athens, GA: University of Georgia, 1984), 94.

23. AbekaUS, 104. Green, *Inventing a Christian America*, 89–91.

24. BJU*, 412; BJU+, 352.

25. When Christian Reconstructionist Francis Schaeffer argued this view, evangelical historian Mark Noll countered that founders saw human nature, not sin, as the basis of politics. Hankins details Noll's correspondence with Schaeffer disputing the Christian nation claims, *Francis Schaeffer and the Shaping of Evangelical America*, 211–17.

26. Sehat, *The Myth of American Religious Freedom*, 31–50.

27. BJU*, 411; BJU+, 351.

28. ACE, 105: 26.

29. BJU*, 409; BJU+, 349; government regulations suppress American ingenuity contends, AbekaUS, 48.

30. Gordon S. Wood, *The Radicalism of the American Revolution* (New York: Vintage, 1993).

31. Abeka*, 266.

32. BJU*, 407; BJU+, 347.

33. BJU*, 407; BJU+, 347. Martin Luther, The Freedom of a Christian, edited by Mark D. Tranvik (Minneapolis, MN: Fortress Press, 2008).

34. BJU*, 407; BJU+, 347.

35. Philippe Mornay du Plessis, *Vindiciae contra Tyrannos* (1589). See also Robert Kingdon, "Calvinism and Resistance Theory, 1550–1580," in *The Cambridge History of Political Thought 1450–1700*, edited by J.H. Burns (Cambridge: Cambridge University Press, 1991), 193–218.

36. The extreme claim that it was a Christian Revolution is a dominionist trope. These curricula are more committed to the less extreme argument that the revolution was a religious cause.

37. BJU* 407; BJU+347; Abeka*, 266.

38. For a through discussion of the subtleties in interpreting Washington's religious views, see Green, *Inventing a Christian America*, 146–152.

39. ACEUS, 1123: 39.

40. See Ruth Miller Elson, *Guardians of Tradition: American Schoolbooks of the Nineteenth Century* (Lincoln: University of Nebraska Press, 1971); Green, *Inventing Christian America*, 199–242.

41. Green regrets that the term "deist" has polarized popular discussion, *Inventing a Christian America*, 136–37.

42. Fea, *Was America Founded as a Christian Nation?*, 177–84.

43. Green, *Inventing Christian America*, 205–9.

44. Such claims are based on a highly selective and idiosyncratic understanding of American history, Fea, *Was America Founded as a Christian Nation?*, 139.

45. Ibid., 127–33.

46. BJUUS, 116. See Randy Barnett, *Our Republican Constitution: Securing the Liberty and Sovereignty of We the People* (NY: Harper Collins, 2016).

47. AbekaUS, 103. The Congress issued days of fasting and prayers for deliverance from the British and thanks for victories, Abeka*, 266; Abeka+, 224.

48. BJU* 407; BJU+, 347.

49. Thomas Jefferson, *A Summary View of the Rights of British America*, 122. Electronic Text Center, University of Virginia Library. The italics are mine. They signal the portion of the quote cited by Christian conservatives..

50. David Barton, *The Jefferson Lies: Exposing the Myths You've Always Believed about Thomas Jefferson* (Nashville, TN: Thomas Nelson, 2016).

51. Chris Rodda has documented over 1600 pages of false quotations in the Christian nation argument, many from Barton, in her two-volume *Liars for Jesus Liars for*

Jesus: The Religious Right's Alternate Version of American History, 2 vols.com/bartchro. htm.

52. Peter Marshall and David Manual, *The Light and the Glory* (Ada, MI: Revell, 2009); Michael Novak, *Washington's God: Religion, Liberty, and the Father of Our Country* (New York: Basic Books, 2006); *On Two Wings: Humble Faith and Common Sense at the American Founding* (New York: Encounter Books, 2003).

53. The founders made many statements against religious restrictions on conscience or reason, cited in Candida Moss and Joel S. Baden, *Bible Nation: The United States of Hobby Lobby* (Princeton, NJ, Princeton University Press), 12. Hobby Lobby's Green family has run a full-page ad, featuring founders' quotations to document religion's importance to the nation.

54. The translator of Jefferson's *Koran,* George Sale, intended the text to be used to convert Muslims to Christianity.

55. Fea, *Was America Founded as a Christian Nation?,* 211; Jefferson to William Short, April 13, 1820.

56. See Annette Gordon Reed and Peter Onuf's discussion of the complexity of Thomas Jefferson's religious views, "*Most Blessed of the Patriarchs*": *Thomas Jefferson and the Empire of the Imagination* (New York: Liveright, 2016) 273–82.

57. Some scholars emphasize the Scottish Enlightenment's influence; see Lynerd, *Republican Theology,* 80–82.

58. See Pauline Maier, *American Scripture: Making the Declaration of Independence* (New York: Vintage Books, 2012).

59. Fea, *Was America Founded as a Christian Nation?,* 130.

60. Ibid., 229–33; Spurlin, *The French Enlightenment in America,* 14.

61. For an analysis of the complexities of using these founders, see Green, *Inventing a Christian America,* 138–141.

62. Marsden, *Understanding Fundamentalism and Evangelicalism,* 117–18.

63. Green favors "supernatural rationalism" as more apt, *Inventing a Christian America,* 136. Gregg Frazer labels the founders as adherents of "theistic rationalism," *The Religious Beliefs of America's Founders: Reason, Revelation, and Revolution* (Lawrence, KS: University Press of Kansas, 2014).

64. Green, *Inventing a Christian America,* 158–61.

65. Abeka*, 267; AbekaUS, 107.

66. AbekaUS, 108, 111.

67. BJU*, 412; BJU+, 352.

68. Green, *Inventing a Christian America,* 199–242.

69. Ibid., 181.

70. AbekaUS, 102.

71. Gaillard Hunt, ed., *The Writings of James Madison* (New York: G. P. Putnam & Sons, 1900–1910), 1:324.

72. Fea notes that Madison's argument for strong government to check self-interest in Federalist #10 claimed that societies survive with sacrifices for the common good, to refute the religious right's claim that his argument indicated a Calvinist sense of sin, *Was America Founded as a Christian Nation?,* 157–59.

73. Green, *Inventing a Christian America*, 174–75. See also Derek H. Davis, *Religion and the Continental Congress, 1774–1783* (New York: Oxford University Press) 81–93. In 1785, Congress decided not to offer land grants to support religion.

74. Sekat, *The Myth of American Religious Freedom,* 17–29.

75. The US Supreme Court held that the Establishment and Free Exercise Clauses of the First Amendment applied to states and local governments by virtue of being incorporated in the Fourteenth Amendment Due Process Clause, ratified in 1868.

76. Balmer, *The Making of Evangelicalism*, 17–18.

77. Article VI, clause 3 prohibiting religion test for office holders, Green, *Inventing a Christian Nation*, 182–83.

78. Rob Boston, "D. James Kennedy: Who Is He and What Does He Want?," *Church & State,* April, 1999.https://www.au.org/church-state/april-1999-church-state/featured/d-james-kennedy

79. Green, *Inventing a Christian America*, 191–97.

80. Fea, *Was America Founded as a Christian Nation?,* 147–48.

81. Mark Noll, *America's God: From Jonathan Edwards and Abraham Lincoln* (New York: Oxford University Press, 2002), 170, 197.

82. Lynerd, *Republican Theology*, 20–25. Insistence on the Electoral College with its designation of slaves as three-fifths of a person for purposes of representation was part of this effort.

83. William Blackstone, *Commentaries on the Laws of England,* https://www.laits.utexas.edu/poltheory/blackstone/cle.int.s02.html.

84. Story claimed that "the state was to assist (not interfere with) the church in molding the godly character of the people." David Barton uses Story to assert the Christian nation thesis, *Original Intent: The Courts, the Constitution, and Religion* (Aledo, TX: WallBuilders Press, 2008) 24, 31.

85. Antonin Scalia, "God's Justice and Ours," *First Things* 123 (May 2002), 17–21. In an amicus brief filed against Judge Roy Moore's claim that the Ten Commandments were the source of the US Constitution, forty-one law professors and legal scholars found "no significant references to the 10 Commandments" in the constitutional debates. On November 6, 2018, Alabama approved a ballot measure to put the Ten Commandments on public buildings.

86. See Mark Chancey, "A Textbook Example of the Christian Right: The National Council on Bible Curriculum in Public Schools," *Journal of the American Academy of Religion* 3 (2007), 554–81; "The Bible, the First Amendment, and the Public Schools in Odessa, Texas," *Religion and American Culture: A Journal of Interpretation* 19 (2009), 169–205.

87. Elizabeth W. Sepper, "Making Religion Transparent: The Substance, Process, and Efficacy of Disclosing Religious Restrictions on Care," in *Transparency in Health Care*, edited by Holly Fernandez Lynch, I. Glenn Cohen, Holly Fernandez Lynch, Barbara Evans, and Carmel Shachar (London and New York: Cambridge University Press, 2019);; Elizabeth W. Sepper, "Risky Business of RFRAs after Hobby Lobby," in *The Contested Place of Religion in Family Law*, edited by Robin Fretwell Wilson (London and New York: Cambridge University Press, 2018).

88. The Constitution Restoration Act of 2004. 108th Congress, H.R. 3799 IH, February 11, 2004, drafted by Roy Moore and Herbert Titus, Reconstructionist former dean of Regent University Law School, uses Article III to argue that the Supreme Court cannot enforce its interpretation of the Bill of Rights.

Chapter 12

1. BJU*, 463, 531; BJU+, 397, 442.
2. Abeka*, 287; Abeka+, 264.
3. See Julia Baird, *Victoria: The Queen: An Intimate Biography of the Woman Who Ruled an Empire* (New York: Random Houses, 2016); Susan Kent, *Queen Victoria: Gender and Empire* (London: Oxford University Press, 2015).
4. BJU*, 475; BJU+, 407.
5. Abeka*, 287.
6. BJU*, 466.
7. Abeka*, 291; Abeka+, 269.
8. See Elizabeth Hurrin, *Protesting about Pauperism: Poverty, Politics and Poor Relief in Late-Victorian England, 1870–1900,* Royal Historical Society Studies in History New Series (London: Royal Historical Society, 2015).
9. BJU*, 481; BJU+, 412.
10. On Moody, see FitzGerald, *The Evangelicals*, 83–91; Marsden notes that Moody fused Victorian sensibility to Christianity, *Fundamentalism and Evangelicalism*, 158.
11. Marsden, *Fundamentalism and Evangelicalism*, 22.
12. On Moody Bible Institutes, see FitzGerald, *The Evangelicals*, 93–98.
13. Abeka*, 289; Abeka+, 232.
14. Abeka*, 282. The Industrial Revolution can be explained entirely in economic terms, Wiesner-Hanks, *Early Modern Europe*, 133.
15. David Cannadine, *Victorious Century: The United Kingdom, 1800–1906* (New York: Viking, 2018).
16. Abeka*, 278.
17. BJU*, 469.
18. Abeka*, 275; Abeka+, 306.
19. ACE, 106: 2.
20. Abeka*, 269, 270, 285; Abeka+, 300–301, 310.
21. See Kate Bowler, *Blessed: A History of the American Prosperity Gospel* (New York: Oxford University Press, 2018).
22. Abeka*, 325; the shipping line made this statement after the fact, to express their disabused confidence in the ship; see Richard Howells, *The Myth of the Titanic* (New York: Palgrave McMillan, 1999).
23. BJU*, 464, 467; BJU+, 398, 400.
24. F. A. Hayek, ed., *Capitalism and the Historians* (Chicago: University of Chicago Press, 1954), 20–21 reproduced in Abeka*, 273; Abeka+, 304.

25. Cannadine, *Victorious Century,* 360, 451–52, 498–502.

26. BJU*, 472; BJU+, 404; Abeka*, 291, Abeka+, 269; ACE, 106: 1–4.

27. BJU*, 472–73, 476; BJU+, 405, 408.

28. FitzGerald, *The Evangelicals,* 34–42.

29. Samuel S. Hill, Jr., *The South and North in America Religion* (Athens, GA: University of Georgia Press, 1980), 83; Donald Matthews, *Religion in the Old South* (Chicago: University of Chicago Press, 1977), 153–63; Fitzgerald, *The Evangelicals,* 48–56.

30. BJU*, 501; Abeka*, 288; Abeka+, 266.

31. Abeka*, 297; Abeka+, 274.

32. Abeka+, 274.

33. Marsden, *Understanding Fundamentalism and Evangelicalism,* 13–14, 19–22. Catholic industrial workers challenged the Christian nation.

34. BJU *, 474; BJU+, 408.

35. BJU *, 501; BJU+, 430.

36. Abeka*, 302; Abeka+, 283; BJU*, 513; BJU+, 441. The 2016 BJU edition is stronger, noting "abused the native peoples."

37. BJU*, 513; BJU+, 441.

38. ACE, 106: 14–16; BJU*, 504, 507; BJU+, 433, 435.

39. BJU*, 506–7; BJU+, 434–35.

40. BJU*, 510; BJU+, 438.

41. Abeka*, 282, 285–86; Abeka+, 300, 302–3.

42. The crucial text is Matthew 28:18–20.

43. BJU *, 509; BJU+, 430.

44. BJU*, 505.

45. See Jeffrey Cox, *The British Missionary Enterprise since 1700* (London: Routledge, 2008).

46. BJU*, 498, 653; BJU+, 428–29.

47. BJU*, 514. The block of text praising McKinley was deleted from the 2016 edition.

48. Many Filipinos were Catholics at the time of the American intervention. See https://apjjf.org/2013/11/40/Susan-A.-Brewer/4002/article.html.

49. BJU*, 493; BJU+, 423.

50. Abeka+, 228.

51. BJU*, 492–93.

52. Abeka+, 279.

53. AbekaUS, 177.

54. BJUUS, 283, 291; AbekaUS, 235, 238.

55. AbekaUS, 221.

56. BJUUS, 444.

57. See Paul Finkelman, *Defending Slavery: Proslavery Thought in the Old South* (New York, Bedford/St. Martin's, 2003).

58. Dalhouse, *An Island in a Lake of Fire,* 21–22. The legend pronounced that Southern liberty was the cause and, later, that the civil rights movement was fascist and Jim

Crow was in the nation's interest, Adam Serwer, "The Nationalist's Delusion," *Atlantic*, November 27, 2017.

59. Robert Wuthnow, *The Restructuring of American Religion* (Princeton, NJ: Princeton University Press), 58–62.

60. FitzGerald, *The Evangelicals*, 57–59.

61. Marsden, *Understanding Fundamentalism and Evangelical*, 171–73.

62. Madison Grant, *The Passing of the Great Race, Or the Racial Basis of European History* (New York: Charles Scribner's, 1916).

63. Postwar Confederates' myth that their fight had been for states' rights took hold a generation later and persists. James W. Loewen and Edward Sebesta, *The Confederate and Neo-Confederate Reader: The "Great Truth" about the "Lost Cause"* (Oxford, MS: University of Mississippi, 2010); See Kelly J. Baker, *Gospel According to the Klan: The KKK's Appeal to Protestant America, 1915–1930* (Lawrence, KS: University of Kansas Press, 2017).

64. FitzGerald, *The Evangelicals*, 214.

65. The Christian Reconstructionist Rushdoony legitimated the Southern cause; it favored local government, Calvinist Christianity, and patriarchy. A Northern reorganization of society post Civil War, he believed, would be worse, advancing humanism, not Christianity, Ingersoll, *Building God's Kingdom*, 17.

66. BJU*, 510.

67. Ray Stedman, evangelical pastor and author, argued that employees must give body and mind to employers for the day's work; employee actions such as unions and strikes are illegitimate. Evangelical employer Hobby Lobby does not allow employees to bring suit and requires "religious mediation." Hobby Lobby asserts religious exemptions from many federal employment laws.

68. BJU*, 472.

69. Abeka*, 280: Abeka+, 310.

70. Candida Moss and Joel Baden, *Bible Nation: The United States of Hobby Lobby* (Princeton, NJ: Princeton University Press, 2017), 2. See also Timothy Gloege, *Guaranteed Pure: The Moody Bible Institute, Business, and the Making of Modern Evangelicalism* (Chapel Hill: University of North Carolina Press, 2015).

71. Abeka*, 280.

72. Paterson emphasizes this point in *Democracy and Intolerance*, 11.

73. Ibid. Arguments against welfare revive the myth of the redeeming depression, Alison Collis Greene, *No Depression in Heaven: The Great Depression, the New Deal, and the Transformation of Religion in the Delta* (New York: Oxford University Press, 2015).

74. Abeka*, 281; Abeka+, 312.

75. Abeka, 281; Abeka+, 312. The idealization of Carnegie distinguishes textbooks for the Texas market from those prepared for California, Goldstein, "Two States. Eight Textbooks."

76. BJUUS, 333. This textbook has eight full pages profiling heroic entrepreneurs.

77. Marsden, *Understanding Fundamentalism and Evangelicalism*, 19.

78. Moss and Baden, *Bible Nation*, 11. The emphasis on giving to receive fuels a transactional notion of religion; see Hobby Lobby's David Green, *Giving It All*

Away . . . and Getting It Back Again (Grand Rapids, MI: Zonderven, 2017); Kate Bowler, *Blessed: A History of the American Prosperity Gospel* (New York: Oxford University Press, 2013).

79. Abeka*. 283. The more recent edition simply makes Smith "largely responsible for the rise and triumph of capitalism," Abeka+, 312. Mike Hill and Warren Montag point out diametrically opposed views of Adam Smith from unfettered capitalist of Alan Greenspan to the state-regulated capitalism of the Italian scholar Giovanni Arrighi and attempt to bridge them, *The Other Adam Smith* (Stanford, CA: Stanford University Press, 2014), 2–9.

80. See Spencer J. Peck, *Capitalism as a Moral System: Adam Smith's Critique of the Free Market Economy* (Cheltenham, UK; Edward Elgar, 2010); Emma Rothchild, *Economic Sentiments: Adam Smith, Condorcet, and the Enlightenment* (Cambridge, MA: Harvard University Press, 2005).

81. Adam Smith, *A Theory of Moral Sentiments, I.iii, III.i.32.*

82. Abeka*, 283; Abeka+, 312.

83. BJU*, 477; BJU+, 408.

84. Adam Smith, *The Wealth of Nations*, Book 5, Chapter One, part 3, Article iii.

85. John Maynard Keynes and Owen D. Young, "How Sociopathic Capitalism Came to Rule the World," *Atlantic*, March 18, 2018

86. Abeka*, 282; Abeka+, 312.

87. Sanford, *Blueprint for Theocracy,* 15.

88. Deep state refers to the hidden powerful of unelected career civil servants. This was a marginal conspiracy theory until Breitbart and Trump used it to tar opponents.

89. This example and these textbooks generally assert that God acts and is responsible for any good action, while human beings do evil and thus maintain Calvin's position, John Calvin, "Man, in His Present State Despoiled of Freedom of Will, and Subjected to Miserable Slavery," in *Institutes of the Christian Religion*, translated by John Allen (Philadelphia: Presbyterian Board of Christian Educators, 1930), 410–17.

90. Gary North, *The Dominionist Covenant: Genesis* (Tyler, TX: Institute for Christian Economics, 1982), 10. On the basis of Matthew 18:15–17, some Christian schools assert that teachers may not contest their employers; see Parsons, *Inside America's Christian Schools*, 101. As Molly Worthen noted, evangelical health care ministries guarantee no services and require good behavior. Furthermore, there was no historical golden age when communities solved social problems, "Mutual Aid for Health Care?" *Dallas Morning News*, February 8, 2015.

91. Sanford, *Blueprint for Theocracy,* 192–93.

92. North, *The Dominionist Covenant,* 146.

93. Diana Waring, *World Empires, World Mission, World Wars* (Petersburg, KY: aswersingenesis, 2012) 61, 66–67.

94. Priyamvada Gopal, "Britain's Story of Empire Is Based on Myth. We Need to Know the Truth," *Guardian,* July 6, 2019. See Priyamvada Gopal, *Insurgent Empire: Anticolonial Resistance and British Dissent* (New York: Verso, 2019); Priya Satia, *Time's Monster: How History Makes History* (Cambridge, MA: Belknap Press, 2021).

Chapter 13

1. Marsden, *Understanding Fundamentalism and Evangelicalism* 9.
2. Ibid., 15–16, 32.
3. Dallhouse, *An Island in a Lake of Fire*, 127.
4. BJU*, 463; BJU+, 397.
5. BJU*, 452, 455, 458; BJU+, 388, 393.
6. Wesley was influenced by Romanticism through his exposure to German Moravians in his missionary endeavors.
7. Abeka*, 286.
8. Abeka*, 306.
9. BJU*, 482.
10. FitzGerald, *The Evangelicals*, 64–65.
11. Marsden, *Understanding Fundamentalism and Evangelicalism*, 154.
12. ACE, 106: 6.
13. BJU*, 482–83; BJU+, 414–15; Abeka+, 295.
14. Abeka*, 2; Abeka+, 2.
15. FitzGerald, *The Evangelicals*, 63.
16. As David Brockman points out, Schleiermacher is actually close to modern evangelicals, *No Longer the Same: Religious Others and the Liberation of Christian Theology* (New York: Palgrave Macmillan, 2011), 45–48.
17. Abeka*, 311.
18. Abeka*, 307, 362; Abeka+, 327, 400.
19. Marsden, *Fundamentalism and American Culture*, 112–13.
20. Dalhouse, *An Island in the Lake of Fire*, 12–15.
21. Richard Niebuhr described the evangelical/fundamentalist divide as urban vs. urban, while Richard Hofstadter thought fundamentalism indicated status anxiety, *Anti-Intellectualism in American Life* (New York: Vintage, 1962).
22. FitzGerald, *The Evangelicals*, 66–68, 95.
23. Walter Rauschenbusch, *A Theology for the Social Gospel* (Nashville, TN: Abbington Press, 1917).
24. FitzGerald thoroughly discusses the divergence of liberals and conservatives at the end of the nineteenth century, *The Evangelicals*, 57–94.
25. Abeka*, 362.
26. Marsden, *Evangelicalism and American Culture*, 117.
27. Guyatt, *Have a Nice Doomsday*, 125–27.
28. Abeka*, 362, 363, 364.
29. See William Martin, *With God on Our Side*, rev. edn. (Portland, OR: Broadway Books, 2005), 7–9.
30. BJU*, 460.
31. BJU*, 476; BJU+, 408.
32. BJU*, 476; BJU+, 408.
33. BJU*, 479; BJU+, 411.
34. Abeka*, 306; Abeka+, 340.

35. See Rousas John Rushdoony, *The Messianic Character of American Education* (Nutley, NJ: Craig Press, 1963).
36. Abeka*, 306; Abeka+, 340; BJU*, 478; BJU+, 410.
37. ACE, 106: 4; Abeka*, 346; Abeka+, 342.
38. Abeka*, 343; Abeka+, 341.
39. Abeka*, 343–44; Abeka+, 341–43.
40. Abeka*, 345–46; Abeka+, 340–42.
41. Abeka*, 346.
42. Abeka*, 345.
43. Abeka*, 310; Abeka+, 254.
44. ACE, 105: 40–41.
45. BJU*, 442; BJU+, 379.
46. BJU*, 441–42; BJU+, 378–79.
47. BJU*, 442–23; BJU+, 378–79.
48. ACE, 105: 42.
49. BJU*, 443; BJU+, 380.
50. Abeka*, 317.
51. Louis-Napoleon became Emperor Napoleon III in 1852.
52. ACE, 106: 10.
53. BJU*, 444; BJU+, 381.
54. BJU*, 445, 460.
55. BJU*, 488.
56. Ibid.
57. Abeka*, 320.
58. Marsden, *Understanding Fundamentalism and Evangelicalism* 46–47.

Chapter 14

1. BJU*, 447, 516; BJU+, 460.
2. Abeka*, 318, 326; Abeka+, 327.
3. BJU*, 521.
4. Abeka*, 326.
5. For a more conventional perspective, see Kagan et al., *The Western Heritage*, 837, 861–62.
6. Abeka*, 327–37, 379–97; Abeka+, 327–36, 355–69; BJU*, 519–32, 569–98; BJU+, 447–69, 491–516. u Mez thoroughly discusses this connection in *Jesus and John Wayne*.
7. Abeka*, 332; BJU*, 531.
8. Sidney Ahlstrom, *A Religious History of the American People*, 2 vols. (Garden City, NY: Doubleday, 1975) 2:367–68; FitzGerald, *The Evangelicals*, 95–10.
9. Fea, *Was America Founded as a Christian Nation?*, 32.
10. FitzGerald, *The Evangelicals*, 108.
11. Marsden, *Understanding Fundamentalism and Evangelicalism*, 50.

12. FitzGerald, *The Evangelicals*, 109–10.
13. Boyer, Paul, *When Time Shall Be No More: Prophecy Belief in Modern American Culture* (Cambridge: Harvard University Press, 1992), 156. When Roosevelt recognized the Soviet Union, fundamentalists warned that Soviets were the nation of Gog, Daniel T. Williams, *God's Own Party: The Making of the Christian Right* (NY: Oxford University Press, 2010) 18. See Ron Rhodes, *Northern Storm Rising: Russia, Iran, and the Emerging End-Times Military Coalition against Israel* (Eugene, OR: Harvest House Publishers, 2008).
14. Abeka, *348–49, +339.
15. BJU*, 550.
16. ACE, 106: 24.
17. BJU*, 552.
18. ACE, 106: 25, 32.
19. Abeka*, 351; Abeka+, 344. Italic in the textbook.
20. Abeka*, 352.
21. Citing Herbert Butterfield, *Steps to Christian Understanding*, edited by R. J. W. Bevan (Oxford: Oxford University Press, 1958); Abeka*, 334–37.
22. BJU*, 542, 545.
23. Abeka*, 373; AbekaUS, 447.
24. The Scofield Bible was dispensationalist. Jesus's life was placed in the Old Testament dispensation; the Sermon on the Mount did not apply.
25. Stephen Sizer, *Christian Zionism: Roadmap to Armageddon?* (Downer's Grove, IL: InterVarsity Press, 2004).
26. Joel Carpenter, *Reawakening of American Fundamentalism* (New York: Oxford University Press, 1997), 66.
27. ACE, 106: 26; Abeka*, 339.
28. Abeka*, 339.
29. Ibid.
30. Arno Gaebelein, *The League of Nations in the Light of the Bible* (New York: Our Hope Press, 1919), 3–4. See Markku Ruotsila, "Conservative American Protestantism in the League of Nations Controversy," *Church History* 72, no. 3 (September 2003), 593.
31. Abeka*, 358–59. The 2016 edition omits the discussion of liberalism and conservatism.
32. Abeka*, 360, with emphasis.
33. These associations are so prominent in right-wing, anti-Islamic, antisemitic, and neo-Nazi blogs that classicists and medievalists avoid using the term Western civilization.
34. Abeka*, 360–61. Fears about America's demise focused on evolution, Marsden, *Understanding Fundamentalism and Evangelicalism*, 59.
35. Abeka*, 366–67; Abeka+, 400–402.
36. Abeka+, 352.
37. In July 1938, *Moody Monthly* too blamed the depression on sin, cited in Lynerd, *Republican Theology*, 166.
38. Boyer, *When Time Shall Be No More*, 97–98.
39. Abeka*, 368, 370; Abeka+, 353. The more recent edition claims that the Depression made many susceptible to socialist propaganda.

40. Williams, *God's Own Party*, 11. The election of 1924 began fundamentalists' efforts to reclaim the party, Sanford, *Blueprint for Theocracy* 16.

41. Abeka*, 362.

42. AbekaUS, 189.

43. Nash et al. discuss early-twentieth-century opposition to "treason texts," notably Charles Beard's *An Economic Interpretation of the Constitution of the United States* (1913) in *History on Trial*, 26–32.

44. Abeka*, 362.

45. FitzGerald, *The Evangelicals*, 97–99.

46. Abeka*, 363.

47. Fitzgerald, *The Evangelicals*, 124–26.

48. Marsden, *Making Evangelicalism*, 47, 119–23; FitzGerald, *The Evangelicals*, 98.

49. Lyle Dorsett, *Billy Sunday and the Redemption of Urban America* (Grand Rapids, MI: Eerdmans, 1991).

50. Abeka*, 365.

51. Fea, *Was America Founded as a Christian Nation?* 32–33; Williams, *God's Own Party*, 2. One theory roots the rise of American conservatism in evangelical-inspired movements of the 1920s, Barry Hankins, *Jesus and Gin: Evangelicalism, the Roaring Twenties and Today's Culture Wars* (New York: Palgrave Macmillan, 2010); Allan J. Lichtman, *White Protestant Nation: The Rise of the American Conservative Movement* (New York: Atlantic Monthly Press, 2008).

52. In the 1930s, fundamentalists adopted "premillennial dispensationalism." The world would become increasingly corrupt until Jesus returned for a thousand-year reign, Boyer, *When Time Shall Be No More*, 97–98; Timothy P. Weber, *Living in the Shadow of the Second Coming: American Premillennialism, 1875–1982* (Chicago: University of Chicago Press, 1987), 179–80.

53. Abeka*, 369, 370.

54. BJU*, 545, 546.

55. BJU*, 548–49; Abeka+, 352.

56. Nick Salvatore, *Eugene V. Debs: Citizen and Socialist* (Champagne-Urbana: University of Illinois Press, 2007).

57. Abeka*, 372–73; Abeka+, 349–50.

58. Susanna Heschel and Robert Ericksen, *Betrayal: German Christians and the Holocaust* (Minneapolis, MN: Fortress Press, 1999).

59. Abeka*, 374.

60. BJU*, 548–49.

61. Martin Luther, "On the Jews and Their Lies," ed. Lehmann, *Luther's Works*, vol. 47. . For an analysis, see Thomas Kaufman, *Luther's Jews: A Journey into Antisemitism* (Oxford and New York: Oxford University Press, 2017).

62. Abeka*, 373; Abeka+, 349.

63. BJU*, 562.

64. BJU*, 558.

65. See Susannah Heschel, *The Aryan Jesus: Christian Theologians and the Bible in Nazi Germany* (Princeton, NJ: Princeton University Press, 2008).

66. Timothy P. Weber, "Finding Someone to Blame: Fundamentalism and Anti-Semitic Conspiracy Theories in the 1930s," *Fides et Historia* 24, no. 2 (Summer 1992), 40–55; David A. Rausch, *Zionism with Early American Fundamentalism* (New York: Edwin Mellen, 1979).

67. Fritz Stern, Leo Baeck Institute Award acceptance speech. New York, November 14, 2004.

68. Robert O. Paxton, *The Anatomy of Fascism* (New York: Vintage, 2005), 202.

69. ACE, 106: 34.

70. Abeka*, 375, 377; Abeka+, 353, 355.

71. Abeka*, 379; Abeka+, 372.

72. Abeka*, 375.

73. Abeka*, 455.

74. Abeka*, 386.

75. This conspiracy theory originated in an American First movement opposing American intervention into the war. In September 1994, John Flynn produced *The Truth about Pearl Harbor*, a twenty-five-page document, September 1944. The journalist, Robert Stinnet advanced this view in *Day of Deceit: The Truth about FDR and Pearl Harbor* (New York: Touchstone, 2001), as did Rear Admiral Robert A. Theobald, *The Final Secret of Pearl Harbor—The Washington Contribution to the Japanese Attack* (Greenwich, CT: Devin-Adair Company, 1954).

76. BJU*, 578.

77. Abeka*, 400–401; Abeka+, 372–73.

78. BJU*, 566.

79. Kagan, et al,. *The Western Heritage*, xiv. Horkheimer and Adorno share these curricula's connections between the Enlightenment and totalitarianism, *Dialectic of Enlightenment*.

Chapter 15

1. Williams, *God's Own Party*, 62. See also Laats, "Forging a Fundamentalist 'One Best System,'" 51–81.

2. FitzGerald, *The Evangelicals*, 169–208.

3. Laats, *Fundamentalist U*, 262.

4. Marsden, *Fundamentalism and American Culture*, 29.

5. Recent works credit anti-communism with mobilizing conservative evangelicals; see Lisa McGirr, *Suburban Warriors: The Origins of the New American Right* (Princeton, NJ: Princeton University Press, 2001); Angela M. Lahr, *Millennial Dreams and Apocalyptic Nightmares: The Cold War Origins of Political Evangelicalism* (New York: Oxford University Press, 2007).

6. William G. McLoughlin, Jr., *Billy Graham: Revivalist in a Secular Age* (New York: Ronald Press, 1960), 111–18; Michael G. Long, *Billy Graham and the Beloved Community* (New York: Palgrave Macmillan), 57–58.

7. Abeka*, 352.
8. Kruse, *One Nation under God*, 58–64.
9. BJU*, 605; BJU+, 522.
10. Abeka*, 342; Abeka*, 405.
11. Whittaker Chambers, *Witness* (New York: Regnery History; reprint edn., 2014).
12. Citing Fred C. Schwarz, *Why Communism Kills* (Waterloo, IA: Christian Anti-Communism Crusade Corporation, 1972), Abeka*, 355–57.
13. ACE, 107: 1.
14. BJU*, 554; BJU+, 477; ACE, 106: 25, 32.
15. BJU*, 557.
16. BJU*, 603–4.
17. ACE, 107: 22–24.
18. BJU*, 617–18.
19. BJU*, 602; BJU+, 520.
20. Kruse, *One Nation under God*, 3–65.
21. Gene B. Preuss, "'As Texas Goes, So Goes the Nation': Conservatism and the Culture Wars in the Lone Star State," in *Politics and the History Curriculum*, 22, 34.
22. Abeka*, 406.
23. FitzGerald, *The Evangelicals*, 179.
24. Abeka*, 417, 420.
25. Mark Henderson, *The Soul of Atlas: Ayn Rand, Christianity and the Quest for Common Ground* (N.p.: Reason Publishing, 2013).
26. Abeka*, 304.
27. Abeka*, 403–5, 462; Abeka+, 371–73, 392–94. The UN faced complications in addressing global crises, BJU+, 515–16.
28. Kaplan, *With God on Their Side*, 39.
29. BJU*, 609; BJU+, 525. This claim seems peculiarly anachronistic.
30. BJU*, 626.
31. Lynerd, *Republican Theology*, 172.
32. Abeka*, 412, 414; BJU+, 378–79.
33. ACE, 107: 24–25, 26.
34. ACE, 107: 2; Abeka*, 414; Abeka+, 379; BJU*, 609; BJU+, 525.
35. When he reviewed these curricula, Lawrence Kessler noted that every remark about Vietnam is erroneous, *NC League of Women Voters*, 11. https://lwvnc.org/wp-content/uploads/2018/04/Voucher-Report-7.2-1.pdf
36. ACE, 107: 3.
37. BJU*, 612.
38. BJU*, 613.
39. ACE, 107: 6.
40. BJU*, 613.
41. Du Mez, *Jesus and John Wayne*, 48.
42. Williams, *God's Own Party*, 78–79, 95.
43. BJU*, 613.
44. BJU*, 630–31.
45. Abeka+, 416.

46. ACE, 107: 2, 3, 4.

47. ACE, 107: 22.

48. BJU*, 613.

49. Abeka+, 381–82.

50. ACE, 107: 10.

51. BJU*, 613.

52. ACE, 107: 11.

53. Abeka*, 416; Abeka+, 380.

54. Jean Daniel, "Unofficial Envoy: An Historic Report from Two Capitals," *New Republic*, December 14, 1963, 16.

55. Abeka+, 380.

56. ACE, 107: 11.

57. BJU*, 616; BJU+, 530.

58. ACE, 107: 13.

59. ACE, 107: 14–15.

60. Abeka*, 421.

61. ACE, 107: 6, 8, 9.

62. Abeka*, 409–11.

63. ACE, 107: 28.

64. Abeka*, 461–62.

65. BJUUS, 507.

66. BJU*, 627.

67. On the evangelical movement and civil rights, see FitzGerald, *The Evangelicals*, 203–7, 240–42, 250–51. Carl McIntire, radio host, was one among the evangelicals asserting that communists promoted the civil rights movement, Williams, *God's Own Party*, 7–8.

68. AbekaUS, 507.

69. E. J. Dionne, *Why the Right Went Wrong: Conservativism—From Goldwater to Trump and Beyond* (New York: Simon & Shuster, 2016).

70. Abeka*, 425; Abeka+, 383; AbekaUS, 510, 519.

71. On evangelicals in the 1960s, see Williams, *God's Own Party*, 51–87; ; and FitzGerald, *The Evangelicals*, 233–60.

72. BJU*, 627; BJU+, 539.

73. ACE, 107: 32.

74. AbekaUS, 516, 519.

75. ACEUS, 1132: 21–22.

76. Box 6, folder "Panama Canal Treaty Negotiations: April 17, 1976 (1)" of the White House Special Files Unit Files at the Gerald R. Ford Presidential Library.

77. ACEUS, 1132: 21; ACE 107: 33.

Chapter 16

1. Lynerd, *Republican Theology*, 159. See John J. Pitney, "Tocqueville Fraud," *Weekly Standard*, November 13, 1995.

2. The earlier edition used Tocqueville to warn of republics' dangers, Abeka*, 228; Abeka+, 242.

3. Williams, *God's Own Party*, 2, 130, 266.

4. Abeka*, 430.

5. BJUUS, 567.

6. Their US histories document Democratic failures and Republican successes more extensively.

7. Balmer, *Thy Kingdom Come*, xvii.

8. Lynerd, *Republican Theology*, 183; Williams, *God's Own Party*, 107.

9. BJUUS, 568.

10. See Williams, *God's Own Party*, 187–94; Lynerd, *Republican Theology*, 161.

11. AbekaUS, 522.

12. FitzGerald, *The Evangelicals*, 291.

13. Williams, *God's Own Party*, 129–31.

14. FitzGerald, *The Evangelicals*, 312; Diamond, *Roads to Dominion*, 221–25.

15. A. J. Menendez, *Evangelicals at the Ballot Box* (New York: Prometheus, 1996), 143.

16. Nash et al., *History on Trial*, 22.

17. FitzGerald, *The Evangelicals*, 320; Williams, *God's Own Party*, 169–70.

18. BJU*, 628; BJU+, 540.

19. Abeka*, 431; Abeka+, 388.

20. James L. Roark, *Understanding the American Promise*, 2nd edn. (Boston and New York: Bedford/St. Martin's, 2014), 917.

21. BJU*, 628; Abeka*, 430.

22. Roark, *Understanding the American Promise*, 914.

23. In response to *Humanae Vitae*, "A Protestant Affirmation on the Control of Human Reproduction" located personhood at birth was released as a joint statement by *Christianity Today* and the Christian Medical Society at a symposium on birth control for evangelical leaders in 1968.

24. As David Brockman notes, evangelicals cite passages referring to God's forming a human being in the womb (Job 31:15, Isa. 44:2 and Ps. 139:13–16), although those citations are silent on abortion. Exodus 21:22–25 treats injury to the mother as a person but not the fetus, Brockman, "Religious Freedom Is Only for Christians in Texas," *Texas Observer*, November 1, 2016.

25. Balmer, *The Making of Evangelicalism*, 61–63, 69–71. Balmer notes that abortion allowed evangelicals to focus on sexual sin without emphasizing divorce as the Bible does.

26. Frank Schaeffer, *Crazy for God: How I Grew Up as One of the Elect, Helped Found the Religious Right and Lived to Take It* (Boston: De Capo Press, 2008).

27. "Getting God's Kingdom into Politics," *Christianity Today* 10 (September 19, 1980), 1031.

28. Balmer, *The Making of Evangelicalism*, 61.

29. Candidate Reagan indicated that he would oppose removing tax-exempt status from private schools, Laats, *Fundamentalist U*, 269.

30. Bob Jones Jr. MS, chapel talk, February12, 1965, cited in Turner, *Island in the Lake of Fire*, 224.

31. Balmer, *The Making of Evangelicalism*, 68.

32. FitzGerald, *The Evangelicals*, 9.

33. Lynerd, *Republican Theology*, 189.

34. Margaret Thatcher, *The Downing Street Years* (HarperCollins e-books, 2011), 2, cited in Abeka*, 430; Abeka+, 376.

35. BJU*, 614, 628; AbekaUS, 525, 527.

36. Morris Morley and Chris McGillion, *The Struggle over U.S. Policy toward Chile* (New York: Cambridge University Press, 2015).

37. Policy Roundtable: Reagan and Latin America, https://tnsr.org/roundtable/policy-roundtable-reagan-and-latin-america/.

38. BJUUS, 569, 581–82.

39. ACE, 108: 21, 23.

40. BJU*, 622.

41. ACE, 108: 26, 28.

42. Kagan et al., *The Western Heritage*, 964.

43. BJU*, 623.

44. See   https://www.politico.com/magazine/story/2017/02/how-russia-became-a-leader-of-the-worldwide-christian-right-214755   and   http://theconversation.com/why-putin-is-an-ally-for-american-evangelicals-101504.

45. ACE, 1132: 29. Italic in text.

46. ACE, 108: 29.

47. Abeka*, 439; Abeka+, 393.

48. BJU*, 639.

49. Abeka+, 421.

50. BJU*, 641. The most recent edition blames Hillary Clinton for these policies, BJU+, 545–46.

51. BJUUS, 593–94.

52. ACE, 1132: 39.

53. Abeka+, 453.

54. Roark, *Understanding the American Promise*, 939.

55. Eduardo Porter notes that one of two Americans' incomes fell and those of the top one percent increased disproportionately. The Bush taxes produced negligible benefits for the bottom half of the income scale, "Who Toasted Past Tax Cuts? Take a Guess," *New York Times*, December 27, 2017.

56. BJU*, 629.

57. Abeka*, 451.

58. Abeka*, 451; Abeka+, 398.

59. BJU*, 648, 654; BJU+, 548–53.

60. Abeka*, 410.

61. BJU*, 643; BJU+, 543. In the later edition, France's large Muslim population explains France's failure to support the US effort, BJU+, 548.

62. BJU+, 547.
63. ACE, 108: 19.
64. Abeka*, 456.
65. BJU*, 626; BJU+, 548.
66. BJU*, 646; BJU+, 549.
67. AbekaUS, 526. The world history bemoans Mandela's policy displacing Boers with ANC supporters, Abeka*, 448–50; Abeka+, 416.
68. BJU*, 653; BJU+, 555.
69. BJU*, 659; BJU+, 558.
70. Abeka*, 440.
71. BJU*, 658.
72. Sanford, *Blueprint for Theocracy*, 39–49.
73. AbekaUS, 544.
74. BJU+, 599.
75. Charles Dyer, *The Rise of Babylon: Sign of the End Times* (Carol Stream, IL: Tyndale House, 1991); John F. Walvoord, *Armageddon, Oil, and the Middle East Crisis* (1974; Grand Rapids, MI: Zondervan, 1990, rev. edn.).
76. BJU*, 662–63; BJU+, 559–60.
77. AbekaUS, 545–46.
78. FitzGerald, *The Evangelicals*, 455–56. John C. Green and John DiIulio, "How the Faithful Voted," *Center Conversation, Ethics and Public Policy Center*, March 2001, reprinted in *Religion and Politics in America: A Conversation*, edited by Michael Cromartie (New York: Rowman & Littlefield Publishers, 2005), 125–140.
79. John Ashcroft was perhaps the most prominent among them, Goldberg, *Kingdom Coming*, 16.
80. Ibid., 13.
81. Alan D. Hertze, "Harvest of Discontent: Religion and Populism in the 1988 Election," in *The Bible and the Ballot Box: Religion and Politics in the 1988 Election*, edited by James L. Green and John C. Green (Boulder. CO: Westview Press, 1991), 18–19; William Martin, *With God on Our Side: The Rise of the Religious Right in America* (New York: Broadway Books, 1996), 225–27, 291–92; Kevin Phillips, *American Theocracy: The Peril and Politics of Radical Religion, Oil, and Borrowed Money in the 21st Century* (New York: Viking, 2006), xii–xiv.
82. Kaplan, *With God on Their Side*, 103.
83. Stephen Mansfield, *The Faith of George W. Bush* (New York: Penguin, 2003), 107–11; Kaplan, *With God on Their Side*, 10–11.
84. Dana Milbank, "Religious Right Finds Its Center in the Oval Office," *Washington Post*, December 24, 2001; Kaplan, *With God on Their Side*, 13.
85. FitzGerald, *The Evangelicals*, 476–80.
86. Stephen F. Miller, *The Age of Evangelicalism: America's Born-Again Years* (New York: Oxford University Press, 2014), 95, 140–41; Diamond, *Roads to Dominion*, 221–25. Michelle Goldberg, "Michele Bachmann and Rick Perry's Dangerous

Religious Brand," *Daily Beast*, August 14, 2011; Chip Berlet, "What Is Dominionism? Palin, the Christian Right, and Theocracy," in *The Rise of the Religious Right in the Republican Party*, Political Research Associates, on theocracywatch.com, September 5, 2008; Phillips, *American Theocracy*; and Chris Hedges, *American Fascists: The Christian Right and the War on American* (New York: Free Press, 2006).

87. See Kaplan, *With God on Their Side*, 46–47. House Republicans passed a bill, HR-7, allowing religious institutions receiving government funds to freely proselytize. The Senate did not take it up, FitzGerald, *The Evangelicals*, 461–62.

88. Marvin Olasky, *The Tragedy of American Compassion* (Washington, DC: Regnery Publishing, 1995), 220, 230.

89. Kaplan, *With God on Their Side*, 43–45.

90. Olasky argued this view; Bush himself wrote the introduction to his later work, FitzGerald, *The Evangelicals*, 460.

91. https://www.aarp.org/money/investing/info-2018/seniors-before-social-security.html.

    According to the Center on Budget and Public Policy, Kathleen Rom, "Social Security Lifts More Americans above Poverty Than Any Other Program, February 20, 2020.

92. FitzGerald, *The Evangelicals*, 325–26; 473–75; Kaplan, *With God on Their Side*, 165. Mark Rozell and Clyde Wilcox, eds., *Religion and the Bush Presidency* (New York: Palgrave Macmillan, 2007), 255.

93. Roark, *Understanding the American Promise*, 950.

94. AbekaUS, 550; BJUUS, 606.

95. AbekaUS, 548.

96. BJUUS, 603.

97. AbekaUS, 566.

98. Du Mez, *Jesus and John Wayne*, 248.

99. ACE, 108: 1, 13.

100. https://www.abeka.com/SubjectDistinctives.aspx.

101. BJU*, 638.

102. AbekaUS, 554–56.

103. Abeka*, 462; Abeka+, 425.

104. Sanford, *Blueprint for Theocracy*, 125–28.

105. Abeka*, 462; AbekaUS, 564–65.

106. ACE, 108: 2, 8–12.

107. Christopher Sellers, "How Republicans Came to Embrace Anti-environmentalism," VOX, July 6, 2018.

108. www.ChristiansandClimate.org.

109. Abeka*, 460.

110. Abeka*, 461–62; Abeka+, 422–23.

111. Abeka+, 421.

112. Eduardo Porter, "Where Government Is a Dirty Word, but Its Checks Pay the Bills," *New York Times*, December 21, 2018.

Conclusion

1. Nash, *History on Trial*, 22.
2. BJU*,664. The epilogue has been deleted in the most recent edition.
3. Abeka*, 463.
4. ACE, 108: 1–2.
5. Abeka*, 463.
6. BJU*, 664.
7. BJU*, 667.
8. As Stephen Wertheim argued that Trump's foreign policy was a defense of Western civilization against nonwhite, non-Christian cultures, "A 'Trump Doctrine' Is Born," ' *New York Times*, July 23, 2017.
9. "The Latest Religious Freedom Battleground: Adoption Centers," *Center for Public Integrity/USA Today*, June 21, 2019..
10. These curricula *Fundamentalist U*, 5.
11. National Council on Bible Curriculum in Public Schools, *The Bible in History and Literature* (Greensboro, NC: Ablu Publishing, 2005), 97–101..
12. See Chancey, "The Bible, the First Amendment, and the Public Schools in Odessa, Texas,"), 169–205; Katherine Stewart, *The Good News Club: The Christian Right's Stealth Assault on America's Children* (Philadelphia: Perseus Book, 2012).
13. Michelle Goldberg, "This Evil Is All Around Us," *Slate,* January 12, 2017.
14. @mikepompeo April 26, 2020.
15. William Saletan, "The Trump Commandments," *Slate*, October 19, 2017.
16. As reported by the National History Education Clearing House.
17. Schragger and Schwartzman, "Against Religious Institutionalism," 918–985;; William L. Ramsey and Sean M. Quinlan, "Southern Slavery as It Wasn't: Coming to Grips with Neo-Confederate Historical Misinformation," *Oklahoma City University Law Review* 30, no. 1 (2005), 1–17.
18. Eliza Shapiro, "Blue Wave May Be Charter Schools' Black Cloud," *New York Times*, November 10, 2018.
19. Balmer, *Thy Kingdom Come*, 20.
20. Noll, *The Scandal of the Evangelical Mind*, 22.
21. Nathan O. Hatch, "Evangelical Colleges and the Challenge of Christian Thinking," *Reformed Journal* (September 1985), 12.
22. Thomas Kidd, *Who Is an Evangelical?* (New Haven, CT: Yale University Press, 2019).
23. Andrew Whitehead and Samuel Perry, *Taking America Back for God* (New York: Oxford University Press, 2020).
24. Nicky Wolf, "US 'Little Rebels' Protest against Changes to History Curriculum," *Guardian*, September 26, 2014; Karen Tumulty and Lyndsey Layton, "Changes in AP History Trigger a Culture Clash in Colorado," *Washington Post*, October 5, 2014; Dana Goldstein, "Is the US a Democracy?" *New York Times*, April 8, 2019.

Index

For the benefit of digital users, indexed terms that span two pages (e.g., 52–53) may, on occasion, appear on only one of those pages.

Abeka Academy Video Streaming, 22
Abeka Books
  founding of, 21
  overview of world histories, 17, 21, 22–23, 27, 29–30, 46, 47
  Pensacola Christian College, 2, 21, 22–23, 27, 36
  world history textbooks, 28–29
Abington v. Schempp (1963), 6–7, 247
abolitionists, 181–82, 201–2
"Abrahamic Covenant," 72
Abrams, Carl, 27–28
absolutism, 134, 135
Academy of Home Education, 27
Accelerated Christian Education (ACE)
  founding of, 18
  overview of curriculum, x, 2, 7–8, 14, 17–30, 46
  world histories, 19, 68–69, 130–33, 134–35
Adam and Eve's story in the Bible, 63–65
Adams, John, 79, 169, 173–74, 184, 185
Adams, John Quincy, 79
Adams, Samuel, 182
Affordable Care Act, 295
Afghanistan, 275
Africa, 18, 20–21, 198, 199, 258–59, 266, 281
African Americans, 64–65, 193–94, 263–64
Age of Reason. *See* the Enlightenment
Alexander the Great, 83–84
Alfred the Great, 99–100, 210–11
Algeria, 258
Allah, 89–90
Allende, Salvador, 261, 275
alt-right, 110–11

American anti-intellectualism, 145–46
American Bill of Rights, 137
American Christianity, 2, 6, 49–50, 81. *See also* Christian nation argument
American Educational Products Company, 18
American evangelicals, 32, 37–38, 60, 69–70, 90, 124, 193–94, 195–96, 209, 229, 232, 233–34, 242, 257–58, 263, 299–300
American exceptionalism, 5, 52, 169–70
American Federation for Children, 13
American fundamentalism, 17–18, 214–16
American Historical Association Forum, 169, 187
American Legislative Exchange Council (ALEC), 12, 13–14
American millennialism, 172
American Protestantism, 15, 31–32, 51, 108–9
American Puritans, 22
American Revolution, 92, 107–8, 151, 170–71, 172, 176, 186, 199–200
American socialism, 272
Americans with Disabilities Act, 277–78
American university education, 17–18
Anabaptists, 115, 116, 124
ancient civilizations, 74–75, 79–93
Anglicanism, 32–33, 135, 149–50, 161
Anglocentrism, 189
Anglo-Saxons, 96, 99–102, 110–11, 152, 161–62, 195–96
Annalium pars posterior (Ussher), 60
anti-abortion, 271, 285, 301
anticapitalist policies, 279

anti-Catholicism, 24–25, 32, 96, 107–9, 113, 114–15
anti-communism, 51, 158, 160, 162–63, 219–20, 243, 279
Anti-Federalists, 185
antigovernment activism, 278–79
anti-intellectualism, 92–93
antisemitism, 102, 110–11, 124–25, 241–42
Aquinas, Thomas, ix, 211–12
Arab nationalism, 283–84
arete, Greek notion, 91
Aristotle, 82, 127, 169
Armageddon, 36, 215–16
Armitage, David, 179
Atlantic Slave Trade, 1–2
atomic bomb, 244
Atwood, Margaret, 67–68
Augsburg Confession (Luther), 114–15

Bacon, Francis, 146–47
Bacon, Roger, 104
Bakker, Jim, 27, 282
Bakker, Tammy Faye, 282
Balmer, Randall, 184–85, 270, 273–74, 303–4
Baptists, 38, 92–93, 170, 172, 184–85, 247
Baroque arts, 130
Barton, David, 5–6, 12–13, 180–81, 284
Batista, Fulgenio, 260
Bauer, Gary, 8, 41
Beard, Charles, 237–38
Beecher, Lyman, 108, 185–86
Behe, Michael, 289
Berlin Wall, 276
the Bible
   Book of Exodus, 82–83, 151
   Book of Genesis, 59, 67–69, 83, 151, 203
   Book of Revelation, 25, 109, 159–60, 219, 293
   college codes of conduct based on, 21–22
   Creation Mandate, 67–68
   God's story, 72–74
   historical narratives and, 47–48, 51, 59–78
   New Testament, 48, 89–90, 124, 215
   Noah's story in, 63–65

Old Testament, 27–28, 48, 82–83
Pentateuch, 76
reading in public schools, 6–7
biblical Christianity, 48–49, 65–66, 93, 106–7, 114, 153, 158, 183, 207, 224–25, 231, 245, 287, 296
biblical inerrancy, 59–60, 77–78, 128
Biblical Literacy Act, 12–13
biblical literalism, 23, 61–62, 124, 128–29, 202, 294
biblical modernism, 17, 36–37, 38–39, 61, 122–23, 212–13, 214–16, 218, 227–28, 237–38, 246, 294–95, 297
biblical truth
   in Christian education and curricula, 43, 48–49, 51, 133–34, 137, 207
   early Americans and, 158–59
   of fundamentalism, 93
   Greeks' pursuit of wisdom over, 83–84
   Muhammad and, 90
   Protestantism and, 32, 113–19, 122–25, 127, 129–30, 141–43
   threats to, 209, 214, 294, 297–98
birth control, 67–68
Bismarck, Otto von, 227–28
BJU LINC (Live Interactive Network Classroom), 27
Blackstone, William E., 153, 174–75, 186, 232
Blackstone Memorial (Blackstone), 232
Black student restrictions, 25–26
Bob Jones University (BJU)
   founding of, 17–18, 23, 24, 37
   historical narratives, 45–47, 48
   overview of, 17, 23, 24–30
   political involvement of, 99–100, 216, 222, 240, 280
   world history textbooks, 27–29, 70
Bob Jones University Press, x, 2, 7–8
Bob Jones University v. United States (1983), 26
Bollinger, Dennis, 27–28
Book of Exodus, 82–83, 151
Book of Genesis, 59, 67–69, 83, 151, 203
Book of Revelation, 25, 109, 159–60, 219, 293
Booth, William, 192–93
Boston Massacre, 177

Boston Tea Party, 177
Bourbon kings, 138
Bradford, William, 161
Brady Bill, 277–78
Brazil, 200
Brezhnev, Leonard, 251
Bright, Bill, 96, 285
British colonialism, 111, 145, 160, 194–97, 199, 207, 257–58, 297
British Israelism, 102
Bryan, William Jennings, 36, 60
Buddhism, 244
Bush, George H.W., 25–26, 277–78
Bush, George W., 26, 265, 270, 279, 283, 284–87
Bush, Jeb, 8, 13
Butterfield, Herbert, 231
Byzantine Empire, 89–90

Calas, Jean, 147–48
Calvary Christian Schools, 22–23
Calvin, John, ix, 5–6, 22, 32–33, 35, 237–38
Calvinism
    Christian nation argument, 169–88
    emergence of, 38–42
    evangelical separation from, 34–35
    French nobility and, 120–21
    Old School Calvinism, 238–39
    Protestant Reformation and, 32–33
    Second Great Awakening and, 193–94
    theological positions of, 123–25
Cambodia, 255–56
"Campus Church" TV program, 21
Campus Crusade for Christ, 69–70, 96
Canada, 279
capitalism
    American Protestants and, 15, 40–41
    anticapitalist policies, 279
    in Asian countries, 281
    Bob Jones University on, 204, 206
    "Christian" capitalism, 251, 252
    Christian colonialism and, 189–208
    in Christian historical narratives, 12, 54–55, 138–39, 154, 161–62, 234–35, 239, 246, 248, 262, 294
    Cold War and, 266–67
    of England, 153

fascist dictators and, 262
free-market capitalism, 40–41, 105, 217–18, 223, 297–98
    of Germany, 262
    laissez-faire capitalism, 249
    liberalism and, 236
    Marxism and, 218–19, 230–31
    promotion of, 257, 261
    religious right and, 12, 51–52, 277, 279
    religious virtues of, 249
    Republican Party and, 267, 271
    sin and, 227
Carey, William, 195
Carmichael, Amy, 195
Carnegie, Andrew, 204–5
Carnegie, Dale, 205
Carter, Jimmy, 252, 266
Cartier, Jacques, 133
Castro, Fidel, 260
Catherine de' Medici, 121
Catherine of Aragon, 119
Catherine of Siena, 114–15
Catholic immigrants, 6–7, 35–36, 101–2, 190, 239
Catholicism/Catholic Church. See also Roman Catholic Church/Roman Catholicism
    anti-Catholicism, 24–25, 32, 96, 107–9, 113, 114–15
    baptism, 132–33
    Council of Trent, 118
    the Enlightenment and, 145–56
    Protestant Reformation rejection of, 113–25
    medieval Catholicism, ix, 95, 96–98
    Spanish Catholicism, 117
    Virgin Mary veneration, 97
Catholic Reformation, 118, 130
Catholic schools, 247
Catholics
as heretics, 8, 32
as paganized Christians, 88–89, 109
Ceausescu, Nicolae, 275–76
Center on Reinventing Public Education (CRPE), 12, 13–14
Chambers, Whittaker, 250
Champlain, Samuel de, 133
Charlemagne, Emperor, 102–3

Charles G. Koch Foundation, 12
Charles I, King, 134–35
Charles II, King, 137, 140–41
Charles IX, King, 121
Charles X, King, 222
Chesterton, G.K., 236
child-centered education, 18–19
Child Protective Services, 11
Children at Risk: The Battle for the Hearts and Minds of Our Kids (Dobson, Bauer), 8
Child Welfare Laws, 11
Chile, 260, 274–75
China, 197, 254, 281
China Inland Mission, 197
Christian colonialism and capitalism, 189–208
Christian Congress for Biblical Zionism, 69–70
Christian Constitution argument, 188
Christian day schools, 7–8, 17
Christian Democrats, 237
Christian education and curricula
    biblical truth in, 43, 48–49, 51, 133–34, 137, 207
    capitalism and, 12, 54–55, 138–39, 154, 161–62, 234–35, 239, 246, 248, 262
    on communism, 55–56, 148, 155
    on democracy, 216–17, 304
    historical narratives in, 45–57, 293–305
    homeschooling, 2, 6, 9–11, 217–18
    Protestant Reformation and, 296–97
    racism in, 297–98
    "Schools of Tomorrow" curriculum, 18–19
    world-history curricula distortions, 2, 6
Christian Education Manifesto (Holzman), 10–11
Christian-focused world history, 2, 6
Christian Heritage Week, 12–13
Christian historical narratives
    Abeka Books and, 46, 47
    Accelerated Christian Education and, 46
    ancient civilizations, 74–75, 79–93
    battle between good and evil, 48–49
    the Bible and, 47–48, 51, 52, 59–78
    Bob Jones University and, 45–47, 48

    in Christian education and curricula, 45–57, 293–305
    Christian right-wing historical narrative, 1
    Civil War, 200–3
    of colonial America, 157–68
    as God's story, 45–46, 55–56, 72–74
    Greco-Roman intellectual influence, 79–93
    overview of publishers, 17–30
    slavery narrative by Christians, 1–2, 200–3
Christianity/Christian perspective. *See also* Calvinism; Catholicism/Catholic Church; evangelicals/evangelicalism; fundamentalism; Protestants/Protestantism; Roman Catholic Church/Roman Catholicism
    biblical Christianity, 48–49, 65–66, 93, 106–7, 114, 153, 158, 183, 207, 224–25, 231, 245, 287, 296
    Calvinism emergence of, 38–42
    colonial American historical narratives, 157–68
    defined, 31–43
    evangelicalism, roots of, 32–35, 37–38
    fundamentalism, emergence of, 36–38
    Middle Ages and, 95–111
    on morality, 15, 91, 190, 201–2, 209, 210–11, 247–67, 269–70, 301
Christianity Today, 273
Christian Liberty Academy Schools (CLASS), 18
Christian nationalism, 31, 38, 167, 303–4
Christian nation argument, 169–88
Christian Philosophy of Education (Bob Jones University), 23
Christian publishers, 17–30. *See also* Abeka Books; Accelerated Christian Education; Bob Jones University
Christian Reconstructionism
    democracy and humanism, 206–7
    the Enlightenment and, 154–55
    homeschooling and, 217–18
    introduction to, 9–10, 31–32, 38–42
    negative effect of government funding, 86
    radical characterization of, 68

theological underpinning, 62, 65
Tower of Babel, 66–67
Christian right, 1, 49, 252–53, 269–92. *See also* religious right
Christian school movement, 2, 14–15
Christians' Israel Public Action Campaign, 69–70
The Christian Student Dictionary (BJU Press), 26
The Christian Teaching of History (BJU Press), 113, 209
The Christian View of God and the World (Orr), 38–39
The Christian View of Science and Scripture (Ramm), 62
Churchill, Winston, 251
Cicero, 81
Citizens United case, 13
civil rights, 15, 234–35, 263, 264–65
Civil Rights Act, 26
civil rights movement, 263–64
Civil War, 1–2, 35–36, 51, 54–55, 185–86, 200–3, 271–72
classical education/texts, 80–81
Claude Lambe Foundation, 12
Clinton, Bill, 277–79
Clive, Robert, 196
Clovis, King, 102–3
Coalition on Revival (COR), 288
Code of Hammurabi, 71
Cold War, 4–5, 162–63, 247–48, 257–58, 266, 274–75, 276–77
Colombia, 280
colonial American historical narratives, 157–68
colonialism. *See* British colonialism
colonization
of Africa, 195
English colonization, 133, 157–58, 195
historical consensus about, 207–8
impact of, 199
Spanish colonization, 132–33
Colson, Charles, 41, 285
Columbus, Christopher, 131–33
Combee, Jerry, 28–29
Commager, Henry Steele, 171–72
Commentaries on the Constitution of the United States (Story), 186

Commentaries on the Laws of England (Blackstone), 186
Common Sense (Paine), 172–74
communism
in Africa, 281
anti-communism, 51, 158, 160, 162–63, 219–20, 243, 279
Christian education and curricula on, 55–56, 148, 155
collapse of, 275–77, 280
good *vs.* evil morality and, 247–67
opposition to, 234–36, 239, 241–42, 243, 274–75
Russian Revolution and, 230–31
threat to Christianity, 247–60, 262–63, 266, 269, 281
"Communism: A Negative System" (Abeka Books), 219–20
Confederate symbols, 1
Congregationalist churches, 34
Congressional Prayer Caucus, 12–13
conspiracy theories, 244, 340n.88, 345n.75
Constantine, Emperor, 88–89, 102–3
Constitutional Congress, 185–86
Contra freedom fighters, 280
Convention on the Elimination of All Forms of Discrimination against Women (CEDAW), 20–21, 253–54
Copernicus, 128–29
cosmopolitanism, 210
Council of Trent, 118
COVID-19 virus, 54
creationists, 4
Creation Mandate, 59, 67–68, 206–7
"creation science," 62
Criswell, W.A., 64, 273
Criswell Study Bible (Criswell), 64
critical thinking skills, 14
Cromwell, Oliver, 135–36
Crouch, Paul, 41
Crusaders, 98
crusades, 98, 107, 110–11
crypto-Romanism, 134
Cuba, 260–61
cultural pluralism, 96
Curie, Marie, 212
Czechoslovakia, 249, 251, 276–77

d'Alembert, Jean, 146–47
Dallas Theological Seminary, 36
Dalton, John, 212
Dante, 105
Darby, John, 232
Darby, John Nelson, 215–16
Darrow, Clarence, 36, 60
Darwin, Charles (Darwinism), 23, 60–61,
    209–10, 211–12, 213–14, 224–25,
    235, 237, 238, 239
Das Kapital (Marx), 218–19
Debs, Eugene, 240
Declaration of the Rights of Man of the
    French Revolution, 152–53, 222
decolonization, 247, 257–60
deep state, 340n.88
Deism, 147, 154, 173–74
DeMille, Cecil B., 71
democracy
    Anglo-Saxon commitment to, 195–96
    Christian education and curricula on,
        216–17, 304
    the Enlightenment and, 155–56, 172
    evangelicalism and, 229, 240–41, 282
    French Revolution and, 152–53
    fundamental American
        commitments, 108
    of Greeks, 79, 91–92
    humanism and, 206–7
    liberal democracy, 78, 262–63
    Magna Carta as foundation for, 100
    pluralistic democracy, 15, 299
    Republican Party and, 249, 254
    Rousseau on, 148–49
    Social Gospel movement and, 216
    US promotion of, 257, 262–63,
        267, 281–82
Democracy at Risk: The Rising Tide
    of Illiteracy and Ignorance of the
    Constitution (Abeka Books), 28–29
Democracy in America (Tocqueville), 269
Democratic Party, 264, 269–70, 276–
    77, 279
democratic socialism, 216, 217–18, 235,
    244, 248–49, 263
Descartes, René, 147
The Descent of Man (Darwin), 211
Designed for Destiny (Abeka Books), 28–29

DeVos, Betsy, 13, 303
Dewey, John, 237–38, 248–49
The Diane Rehm Show, 1
Dickens, Charles, 189, 210
Diocletian, Emperor, 86–87
dispensationalism, 35–36
divine intervention theories, 244
divine origin of government, 65–66, 77–78
Divine Providence, 49–51, 136, 178,
    179, 203
divorce, 85
Dobson, James, 8, 85–86, 274, 277–78, 284
Dominican Republic, 260, 274–75
dominionism, 31–32, 41–42
domino theory, 256
"The Donation of Constantine," 102–
    3, 105
Downey, Mark, 64–65
Dunbar, Cynthia, ix, 5–6
Dürer, Albrecht, 130
Dutch Protestantism, 117

Eastern Orthodox Church, 88–89
Edict of Milan, 88
Edict of Nantes, 138
Edison, Thomas, 191–92
Educational Development Zone Act, 13
The Education Savings Account Act, 13
Edward VI, King, 119
egalitarianism, 108–9, 170
Egypt, 74, 75, 76, 198, 199
Einstein's theory of relativity, 212
Eisenhower, Dwight, 249, 252
Eliot, John, 159–60
Elizabeth I, Queen, 120
Ellsworth, Oliver, 182
The Empire of Reason: How Europe
    Imagined and America Realized the
    Enlightenment (Commager), 171–72
end times, 36, 69–71, 73, 159–60, 215–16,
    229, 232, 233–34, 236, 240–41, 277,
    280, 283, 285, 287, 293, 294
Engel v. Vitale (1962), 6–7
English Bill of Rights, 137
English Civil War, 107–8, 134–37,
    142, 159–60
English colonization, 133, 157–58, 195
English exceptionalism, 100–1, 120

English Protestantism, 108, 113, 118, 119, 138, 159–60, 295–96
English Reformation, 99, 118–20, 142–43, 162
the Enlightenment
    Abeka Books and, 149–51, 154
    Accelerated Christian Education and, 152–53
    attacks on, 40–41
    Bob Jones University and, 149–50, 154, 155
    Catholicism/Catholic Church and, 145–56
    Christian nation argument and, 170, 171
    democracy and, 155–56, 172
    Evangelical Christians and, 245
    French Enlightenment, 148, 149–50
    fundamentalism and, 148
    humanism of, 121–22, 146
    influence of, 108–9, 145–56
    Protestants/Protestantism and, 145–56
    rationalism, 210, 213
    Roman Catholic Church/Roman Catholicism and, 150
    Scottish Enlightenment, 182
    thinkers of, 26–27, 90–91, 145
    Thomas Jefferson ties to, ix
The Enlightenment in America (May), 171–72
An Enquiry into the Obligations of Christians to Use Means for the Conversion of Heathens (Carey), 195
entrepreneurial spirit, 103–4
environmentalism and climate science, 288
Environmental Protection Agency, 286, 288–89
Epic of Gilgamesh, 75
Epistle to the Romans (Paul), 66, 81, 114–15
equal protection clause (Fourteenth Amendment), 9–10
Erasmus, Desiderius, 114–15
Erickson, Leif, 130–31
Eric the Red, 130–31
Establishment Clause of Bill of Rights, 8, 247

Ethiopia, 198
European Economic Community, 253
European Union, 280
evangelical Protestantism, 15, 33, 37–38, 42–43
evangelicals/evangelicalism
    American evangelicals, 32, 37–38, 60, 69–70, 90, 124, 193–94, 195–96, 209, 229, 232, 233–34, 242, 257–58, 263, 299–300
    attacks on homosexuality, 82
    attacks on secular education, 80–81
    Christian nation argument and, 180
    community schools of, 2
    divorce and, 85
    George W. Bush and, 285–87
    good *vs.* evil morality, 247–67
    postwar world disquiet, 239
    roots of, 32–35, 37–38
    spread of Christianity and, 209, 214–15
Everson v. Board of Education of Ewing Township (1947), 247
evolutionary biology, 4–5, 6–7
evolutionary theory, 23, 36, 289
exploration of the New World, 130–33
extraterritoriality of China, 197
Ezekiel, 232

Fabians, 217–18, 261
Fairness Doctrine, 218
Faith-Based Initiatives, 285–86
Falwell, Jerry, 5–6, 96, 109, 271, 273, 282, 285
Family and Medical Leave Act, 277–78
Family Protection Act, 271–72
Family Research Council, 301
family values, 85–86
fascism, 145, 241, 242, 243
Fea, John, 161–62, 178, 179
Federal Reserve System, 239
Fellowship of God's Chosen People, 64–65
feminism, 6–7, 271, 301
Fines, Jerry, 285
Finney, Charles, 193–94
First Amendment, 26, 184–85
First Baptist Church in Dallas, 64, 109
First Great Awakening, 38, 92–93, 117, 149, 159–60, 170–73

FitzGerald, Frances, 92–93, 215
fixed beliefs, 14
Florida Department of Education, 8
Focus on the Family (Dobson), 85–86
Ford, Gerald, 266
Foreign Legion, 198
Founding Fathers, ix, 92, 145, 174–75
Fourteenth Amendment, 9–10, 11
France, 102–3, 107, 118–19, 120–22, 138–
    42, 146, 149–53, 177–78, 222–23,
    227–29, 239–40, 258, 280. *See also*
    French Revolution
Francis of Assisi, 114–15
Francke, August, 149
Franco, Francisco, 110–11
Franklin, Benjamin, 179
free enterprise, 161, 203–4, 217–18, 222,
    234, 236, 252–53, 272, 279–81, 283
free-market capitalism, 40–41, 105, 217–
    18, 223, 297–98
free-market education, 12
Fremont, Walter G., 17, 27
French Academy of Sciences, 129
French Christianity, 102–3, 121–22
French Enlightenment, 148, 149–50
French Revolution, 138, 145, 150–53, 176,
    177–78, 222–23
French Wars of Religion, 120–21
Fuller, Charles, 61
fundamentalism
    American fundamentalism, 17–
        18, 214–16
    anti-Catholicism of, 108
    as anti-intellectualism, 93
    attacks on homosexuality, 82
    biblical truth of, 93
    defined, 31
    emergence of, 36–38, 42–43
    the Enlightenment and, 148
    humanism threat, 81
    humanism threat to, 81, 215–16
    modernism threat, 238–39
    orthodox fundamentalism, 23
fundamentalist day schools, 7–8
fundamentalist publishers, 2
fundamentalist universities, 21–22, 61
Fundamentals: A Testimony to the Truth,
    214–15, 238

Gaebelein, Arno, 229, 233–34
Galatians, 216
Galilei, Galileo, 128–29
Garrison, William Lloyd, 185
gay rights, 266, 284–85, 301. *See also*
    LGBTQ rights
The Genesis Flood (Whitcomb, Morris), 62
Gentile, Giovanni, 235
George III, King, 139–40, 173–74
German barbarism, 60–61
German Protestant scholarship, 214
German Reformation, 122–23, 214
Germany, 213–14, 227–29, 233, 241–
    42, 262
G.I. Bill, 52–53
Gilded Age, 80–81
Gladden, Washington, 215
Glorious Revolution, 137, 159–60
Goldwater, Barry, 264
good *vs.* evil morality, 247–67
Gopal, Priyamvada, 207–8
Gorbachev, Mikhail, 276–77
Gould, Stephen J., 4
Graham, Billy, 248, 249, 252
Grant, Madison, 202
grassroots mobilizing, 96
Great Britain, 227–28, 239–40
GREAT COMMANDMENT (ACE), 20
Great Commission, 198, 294
Great Depression, 236–37, 239, 240–
    41, 286
Great Recession, 289–90
Great Society, 265
Greco-Roman culture
    appreciation of, 80–81
    critique of, 79–80, 91
    family values and, 81, 84–87
    Founding Fathers and, 92
    humanism and, 81–82
    intellectual influence, 79–93
Green, John Richard, 120
Green, Steven K., 164–65, 172–73, 178–
    79, 183–84
Green v. Connally (1971), 7–8

Hall, Verna, 158
Hammurabi's Law, 71–72
The Handmaid's Tale (Atwood), 67–68

Hayek, Friedrich, 192, 253
Hegel, Georg Wilhelm Friedrich, 213
Henry, Carl F.H., 108
Henry VIII, King, 118–19
Herodotus, 83–84
Hippocrates, 91
Hiss, Alger, 250
History of the United States (Webster), 166
history standards debate, 6
Hitler, Adolf, 145, 241–44, 246
Ho Chi Minh, 255–56
Holbein, Hans, 130
Holy Roman Empire, 98–99, 117
Holzman, John, 10–11
Home Education Leadership Program
    (HELP), 27
Home Mission Society, 193–94
Homer, 83–84, 91
HomeSat (Home School Access
    Terminal), 27
homeschooling
    Abeka Books and, 22
    Accelerated Christian Education and,
        18, 29–30, 266
    Biblical reasoning in, 49–50
    BJU Press and, 27, 217–18
    Christian publishers and, x, 2, 187
    Christian right and, 299, 301
    expansion of, 9–11, 14–15
    Phillips on, 67–68
    Rushdoony on, 40–41
    voucher programs, 6
Homeschool Legal Defense
    Association, 11
Home School Legal Defense Fund
    (HSLDA), 11, 67–68
homosexuality, 82–83
Horton, Arlin, 21
Horton, Rebekah "Beka," 21
Howard, Donald, 18–19, 37, 46
Howard, Esther, 18
Huguenots, 121, 138–39
humanism
    Christian Reconstructionists
        and, 206–7
    democracy and, 206–7
    the Enlightenment and, 121–22, 146
    ethical dimensions of, 106–7

heathenism and, 106
introduction to, 9–10
the Renaissance and, 105–6
Republican Party against, 237
secular humanism, 7–8, 9–10, 26, 209,
    219, 265, 271
sin of, 48–49
as threat to fundamentalism, 81, 215–16
threat to religion, 81–82, 296, 297
Humanist Manifesto, 81
Hume, David, 153
Hundred Years War, 101
Hungarian Reformed Church, 275–76
Hungarian Revolution, 249
Hus, John, 97–98
Hussein, Saddam, 283, 285
Hutchison, Anne, 163

imperialism, 189, 195, 198
The Independent, 19–20
India, 196, 261
Industrial Age, 192–93
industrialization, 192–94, 272–73
Industrial Revolution, 189, 190–92
Inferno (Dante), 105
Institute for Creation Research (ICR), 62
"intelligent design" creationism, 4
Iran, 275
Iraq, 275
Irish Culdee monks, 130–31
Irving, Washington, 132
Isenberg, Nancy, 164
Islam, 89–90, 93, 98, 236
Islamic terrorists, 90, 285
Israel, 69–70, 72, 75, 76, 229, 261
Italy, 233

Jackson, Stonewall, 201–2
Jacoby, Susan, 93
James I, King, 134–35, 161–62
James II, King, 134–35, 137, 139–40
Jamestown, 135, 160–62, 163–64
Japan, 197, 233, 244, 255–56, 281
Jay, John, 182
Jefferson, Thomas, ix, 158, 173–74, 180,
    185, 300–1
Jeffress, Robert, 109, 300
Jenner, Edward, 212

Jesuits, 128
Jesus Christ, 35–36, 48, 93, 96, 190, 250, 293
Jesus Is Coming (Blackstone), 232
Jewish apocalypticism, 215
Jihad, 90
Jindal, Bobby, 8
John Birch Society, 6–7
John Paul II, Pope, 276–77
Johnson, Lyndon B., 252, 255–56, 260, 265
Johnson, Ronald E., 18–19, 46, 85–86
Jones, Bob, III, 25–26, 96, 263
Jones, Bob, Jr., 25
Jones, Bob, Sr., 23, 24–25, 128, 157–58, 202, 209, 238
Jones, Stephen, 26
Judeo-Christian tradition, 70–71, 79–80, 131, 235–36, 253
July Revolution, 222

Kant, Immanuel, 154, 213
Kennedy, D. James, 185, 285
Kennedy, John F., 25, 108, 252, 263
Kenya, 90, 258–59, 281
Kenyatta, Jomo, 258–59
Kepler, Johannes, 128–29
Kerry, John, 107
Keynes, John Maynard, 192, 239
Kidd, Thomas, 303–4
King, Martin Luther, 261, 263–64
King James Bible, 135
King James Version (KJV), 59–60, 247
Kipling, Rudyard, 198–99
Klein, Rebecca, 9
Klicka, Chris, 11
Klumpp, Andrew, 85
Koch brothers, 12, 13
Korean War, 255
Kossinna, Gustaf, 102
Ku Klux Klan, 108, 201–2
Kuyper, Abraham, 38–39

Laat, Adam, 299
La Haye, Tim, 36, 41, 62, 271
La Hayes, Beverly, 253–54
laissez-faire economics, 205–6
Late Great Planet Earth (Lindsay), 69–70

Latin America, 200, 221, 260–61, 275, 279–80
Law, John, 138–39
League of Nations, 233–34
League of Women Voters of North Carolina, 8
Lee, Robert E., 201–2
Left Behind series (La Haye), 36
Lenin, Vladimir, 230–31
Levison, James, 85
Leviticus, 82–83, 203
Lewis, C.S., 236
LGBTQ rights, 12–13, 266, 271, 300–1. *See also* gay rights
liberal democracy, 78, 262–63
Liberal Democrats, 281
liberalism
    Abeka Books and, 235–36
    capitalism and, 236
    Christianity and, 210, 221, 234–36, 238, 245, 271
    religious liberalism, 213–14, 215, 231–32, 236–37, 243
    theological liberalism, 36–37, 209, 227, 239
Liberia, 198
libertarianism, 86
Liberty Baptist College, 61
Liberty University, 5–6, 26
The Life and Voyages of Christopher Columbus (Irving), 132
Life of Washington (Weem), 178
Lindsay, Hal, 69–70
Livingstone, David, 198
Lloyd-Jones, Martyn, 287
Locke, John, 147, 150, 153, 172–73, 174–75, 179–80, 181–82
Loewen, James, 1
Lost Cause myth, 202–3
Louis XIII, King, 139
Louis XIV, King, 138–41
Louis XV, King, 139–40
Louis XVI, King, 152–53
Lusitania sinking, 228–29
Luther, Martin, 22, 114–16, 122–24, 176–77, 237–38
Lutheranism, 32, 50, 117
Lutz, Donald, 172–73

MacArthur, Douglas, 244, 254–55
Machiavelli, Niccolò, 105–6.
Madison, James, 91–92, 158, 184
Magna Carta, 99–101, 102, 135
Mandela, Nelson, 281
Marsden, George, 33, 36–37, 47–48
Marshall, Peter, 181
Marshall Plan, 249
Martel, Charles, 102–3
Marty, Martin, 174
Marx, Karl, 52–53, 218–20, 230–
    31, 274–75
Marxism, 218, 219–20, 224, 230–31,
    235, 248–49
Mary Tudor, Queen, 119–20
May, Henry, 171–72
Mayflower Compact, 164–66, 167, 168
McCain, John, 284
McCarthy, Joseph, 248, 249, 252
McGraw-Hill textbook, 1–2, 302–3
McGuffey Readers, 209
McKinley, William, 200
McLeroy, Don, 5–6
Mede, Joseph, 159–60
medieval Catholicism, 95, 96–98
Merton, Robert (Merton Thesis), 129
Methodists, 38
Metternich, Klemens von, Prince, 221
Mexico, 279
Middle Ages, 95–111
Middle East, 261–62, 281–82, 283–84,
    286–87, 293
millennialism, 35–36, 232
Mises, Ludwig von, 253
missionaries
    Catholic missionaries, 55–56
    in Chile, 261
    colonialism and, 189, 195–97, 198,
        199, 207
    conservatism and, 235–36
    in Japan, 254
    in Kenya, 258–59
    Middle East challenges, 90
    Protestant, 116, 149, 154
Mitterand, François, 280
modernism, 211, 212–13, 224, 238–39
Mohler, Al, 284
Monroe Doctrine, 199–200, 221

Montesquieu, Charles Secondat
    de, 172–73
Moody, Dwight, 190
Moody Bible Institute, 190
morality in Christianity, 15
Moral Majority, 271
moral relativism, 6–7, 212
Mormonism, 274
Morris, Henry M., 62
Moses/Mosaic Law, x, 9–10, 59, 71, 78,
    123, 187, 300–1
Mugabe, Robert, 258–59
Muhammad, Prophet, 89–90, 93
multiculturalism, 6–7, 91
Murrin, John, 172–73
Muslims, 89–90, 235–36, 280–81
Mussolini, Benito, 242

Napoleonic Wars, 220–21
Nash, Gary, 293
National Association of Evangelicals, 25,
    239, 264–65, 288–89
National Center for Science
    Education, 22–23
National History Standards (1994),
    52, 54–55
National Socialism, 145, 243, 246
National Socialist Party, 243
National Voter Registration Act, 277–78
Native Americans, 133, 159–60, 163–64,
    167, 200–1
Nazism, 102, 110–11, 241–42, 243–44
negative toleration, 127
Neo-Confederate texts, 101–2
Nero, Emperor, 84
Netanyahu, Benjamin, 69–70
New Calvinism, 32–33
new Dark Ages, 152
New Deal, 218, 240–41, 247, 248, 249, 266,
    285–86, 295
New Economic Plan, 230–31
New Testament, 48, 89–90, 124, 215
New Theology, 215
Newton, Isaac, 128–29, 174
New World exploration, 130–33
New Zealand, 196–97
Nicaragua, 275
Nicholas II, Czar, 229–30

Nietzsche, Friedrich, 60–61
19 Kids and Counting (TV
    show), 67–68
nineteenth-century politics, 221–25
Nixon, Richard, 255–56, 269
Noah's story in the Bible, 63–65
No Child Left Behind Act, 286
Noll, Mark, 172–73, 174, 303–4
nondenominational Christian schools, 2
Norris, J. Frank, 108
North, Gary, 41–42, 206–7
Norwegian Equality Board of
    Appeals, 20–21
Novak, Michael, 181

Obama, Barack, 77–78, 90, 279, 287,
    299–300
Office of Faith-Based and Community
    Initiatives, 285–86
Oklahoma City bombing (1995), 278–79
Olasky, Marvin, 285–86
Old School Calvinism, 238–39
Old Testament, 48, 82–83
Old Testament Interpretation, 27–28
one-world government, 46, 240–41, 253,
    277–78, 297
On the Origin of Species (Darwin), 211
On the Road to Serfdom (Hayek), 253
Operation Save America, 301
Order of the Star-Spangled Banner, 108
Orr, James, 38–39
orthodox fundamentalism, 23
Ottoman Empire, 227–28
Oxford University Press, 232

paganized Christians, 88–89, 109
Pagden, Anthony, 127
Paine, Thomas, 172–74
Paisley, Ian, 263
Paris Climate Accord, 107
Paris Peace Conference, 233
parochial schools, 6–7, 247
The Passing of the Great Race (Grant), 202
Pasteur, Louis, 212
Paterson, Frances, 163–64
patriarchal authority, 10–11, 67–68
Paul's *Epistle to the Romans,* 66, 81, 114–15
Pax Romana, 87–88

Paxton, Robert, 242–43
Peace of Westphalia, 127
Pearl Harbor attack, 244
Pensacola Christian College, 2, 21, 22–23,
    27, 36, 59, 60
Pentateuch of Bible, 76
"The Perils of America" (Jones), 24–25
Peru, 280
Peter the Great, 229–30
Pettit, Steve, 24
Pew, J. Howard, 249
Pew Religious Landscape Survey, 61–62
Philip II, 119–20
Philippines, 18, 200
philosophical relativism, 213
Pinochet, Augusto, 261
Pizarro, Francisco, 132–33
Planned Parenthood, 263–64
Plato, 82
pluralistic democracy, 15, 299
Plymouth witch trials, 82–83
Poland, 243–44, 276–77
political criticism, 146
political right, 5, 6–7, 11–12, 51, 86, 101, 125,
    152, 162–63, 171–72, 187–88, 248, 252,
    253–54, 256, 287–88, 289–90, 303–5
Pompeo, Mike, 301
popular vote, 216–17
positivism, 236
postmillennialism, 35–36, 215–16
post-Reformation arts, 130
post-Reformation Christianity, 33
Potter, Beatrix, 236
pragmatism, 236, 237
premillennialism, 36
Presbyterians, 38
Price, George McCready, 61–62
The Prince (Machiavelli), 114
Princeton Theological Seminary, 60, 211–
    12, 213–14
Procedures Manual and Administration
    Manual (ACE), 19
*A Proclamation Recognizing the
    Importance of the Bible in
    History,* 12–13
Prohibition, 24–25
Project Blitz, 12–13
proof texting, 47–48, 56, 181, 296

proselytizing outreach of ACE, 18
prosperity gospel, 34–35, 39–40, 89, 192,
    205, 303–4
Protestant ecumenism, defined, 287
Protestant Reformation
    Abeka Books and, 74, 114, 117, 118
    Accelerated Christian Education and,
        115, 116
    Bob Jones University and, 115, 116
    benefits of, 127–43
    Calvinism and, 32–33
    rejection of Catholicism, 113–25
    in Christian education materials and
        curricula, 296–97
    criticisms of medieval Catholicism, 95,
        96, 97, 106–7
    exploration of the New World, 130–33
    overview of, 113–25
    post-Reformation arts, 127–30
Protestants/Protestantism
    American Protestantism, 15, 31–32,
        51, 108–9
    Anglo-Saxon commitment to, 195–96
    Bible study by, 76
    critiques of Catholicism, 95
    English Protestantism, 108, 113, 118,
        119, 138, 159–60, 295–96
    the Enlightenment and, 145–56
    evangelical Protestantism, 33, 37–38
    introduction to, 6–7, 15, 31
    proto-Protestants, 100, 102, 103, 104
    quasi-Protestants, 99
Protestant work ethic, 207
proto-Protestants, 100, 102, 103, 104, 130–31
Providential History (Slater), 166
providentialism, 34–35
pseudoscience, 62, 248–49
Ptolemy, 128–29
Puritans/Puritanism, 107–8, 115, 129,
    134–36, 166–68

quasi-Protestants, 99
Quebec Act, 176
Quiverfull movement, 67–68

racism, 25–26, 64–65, 110–11, 297–98
The Radicalism of the American Revolution
    (Wood), 176

Ramm, Bernard, 62
Rand, Ayn, 86, 252–53
rationalism, 81, 108–9, 181–82, 210, 213,
    335n.63
rational skepticism, 91
Rauschenbusch, Walter, 215
Reagan, Ronald, 25–26, 251, 267, 269–
    77, 288–89
    economy and, 270–73, 277–79
    foreign policy, 269–70, 274–77
The Reasonableness of Christianity
    (Locke), 174–75
Reed, Ralph, 282
Rejoice Broadcast Network, 21
religious conservatives, 4, 6–7, 12,
    249, 270
religious freedom, x, 12–13, 125, 142–43,
    176–77, 234, 270, 276, 295, 300–1
Religious Freedom Day, 12–13
religious liberalism, 213–14, 215, 231–32,
    236–37, 243
religious revivalism, 34. See also First
    Great Awakening; Second Great
    Awakening
religious right, 4, 38, 155–56, 158, 269–92.
    See also Christian right
religious tolerance, 15, 145, 146,
    154, 159–60
Rembrandt van Rijn, 130
the Renaissance, 105–6
Report and Analysis on Religious Freedom
    Measures Impacting Prayer and
    Freedom 2018-2019 (Project
    Blitz), 12–13
reproductive science, 67–68
Republican Party, 11–12, 14, 86, 145–46,
    237, 264, 266, 267, 269–79, 284–92
Revolutions of 1848, 223
Rhodesia, 258–59
Richard, Carl, 92
Robbing and Murdering Peasants
    (Luther), 123
Robertson, Pat, 27, 41, 277–78,
    282, 284–85
Robespierre, Maximillian, 152–53
Rockefeller, John D., 205
Rockwell, Norman, 236
Rogers, Daniel, 162–63

Roman Catholic Church/Roman Catholicism. *See also* Catholicism/Catholic Church
criticism of, 25
the Enlightenment and, 150
fascism and, 242
Greco-Roman culture and, 88–89, 93
medieval Catholicism and, 96
purgatory and, 105
Roman culture. *See* Greco-Roman culture
Roman *pater familias,* 84–85
Roman Stoicism, 91, 92
Romanticism, 210
Romney, Mitt, 274
Roosevelt, Franklin Delano, 240, 244
Roosevelt Corollary, 199–200
Rousseau, Jean-Jacques, 148
Rove, Karl, 284
Rump Parliament, 135–36
Rushdoony, Rousas John, 9–10, 41–42, 62, 154, 155–56, 202–3
Russia, 18, 227–28, 229–31, 243–44, 265
Russian Revolution, 229–30
Russo-Japanese War, 229–30

Salter, Guenter, 48–49
Salvation Army, 192–93
Satan, 48–49, 70, 78, 87–88, 89, 96, 159–60, 211, 247–48, 250
The Scandal of the Evangelical Mind (Noll), 303–4
Scaramanga, Jonathan, 19–20
Schaeffer, Francis, 39
Schaeffer, Francis, Jr., 273
Schlafly, Phyllis, 253–54
Schleiermacher, Friedrich, 213
Schlesinger, Arthur Jr., 1
Schmitt, Carl, 235
"Schools of Tomorrow" curriculum, 18–19
scientific model of university education, 23, 54–55
scientific racism, 202
Scientific Revolution, 67–68, 127–30, 146–47, 191–92
Scofield Reference Bible, 47–48, 50, 60, 232
Scottish Enlightenment, 182

SEATO (South East Asia Treaty Organization), 255–56
Second Coming of Christ, 35–36
Second Great Awakening, 35–36, 170, 171, 172, 193–94, 207
Second Treatise (Locke), 181–82
sectionalism, 1
secular education, 9–10, 80–81, 298
secular humanism, 7–8, 9–10, 26, 209, 219, 265, 271
secularism, 17, 146, 209, 238–39, 251, 283–84, 298
"seed of Satan," 70, 78
segregation academies, 7–8
separation of church and state, 5–6, 15, 108, 115, 158, 170, 172, 184–85, 285, 294–95
Sepoy Revolt in India, 196
September 11, 2001 attacks, 283–84, 285
Serbia, 227–28
1776 Commission, 4–5
Seventh-Day Adventists, 61–62
Seven Years War, 176
sex education, 6–7, 266, 284–85
Shintoism, 244
A Short History of the English People (Green), 120
sin and spiritual decay, 217–18, 227–46
Six-Day War, 261
sixties (1960s) culture, 264–65
Slater, Rosalie, 158, 166
slavery narrative by Christians, 1–2, 200–3
Smith, Adam, 205–6
Smith, Al, 24–25
Smith, John, 160
Smith, Timothy, 34
Social Contract (Rousseau), 148
social criticism, 146, 150
Social Democrats, 237
Social Gospel, 49, 206–7, 216
socialism
American socialism, 272
democratic socialism, 216, 217–18, 235, 244, 248–49, 263
National Socialism, 145, 243, 246
National Socialist Party, 243
spread of Christianity and, 211, 217–19

Social Security, 234–35, 264, 272–
    73, 286–87
social welfare, 262
social welfare policies of Rome, 86
Socrates, 82
Solzhenitsyn, Alexandr, 251
Sons of Confederate Veterans, 101–2
Sophocles, 83–84
South Africa, 198, 239–40, 258, 266, 281
Southern Baptist Convention, 24,
    273, 284
Southern Baptists, 38, 247
Southern Democrats, 25–26
Southern evangelicals, 209, 225, 295
Soviet Union, 244, 249, 250–51,
    267, 275–77
Spanish colonization, 132–33
The Spirit of 76 (Bright), 96
spiritual programming, 46
Stalin, Joseph, 249, 250
State Board of Education (SBOE) of Texas,
    ix, 1, 5–6, 52
Steps to Christian Understanding
    (Butterfield), 231
Stern, Fritz, 242
Stewart, Lyman, 238
Stoicism, Roman, 91, 92
Story, Joseph, 186
Strong, Josiah, 195–96
A Summary View of the Rights of British
    America, (Jefferson), 180
Sunday, Billy, 229, 238–39
Swaggart, Jimmy, 109
Swanson, Kevin, 10–11

Taiwan, 281
A Tale of Two Cities (Dickens), 189
tax-exempt status and religious schools, 8,
    22–23, 25–26, 266, 273–74
Taylor, J. Hudson, 197
Tea Party, 290
Ten Commandments, 71, 78
terrorism, 280
Texas Education Agency v. Leeper and
    Rushdoony (1994), 9–10
Texas Essential Knowledge and Skills
    (TEKS), ix–xi, 1, 5, 158–59
Texas Freedom Network (TFN), x, 304

theological liberalism, 36–37, 209,
    227, 239
theological modernism, 36–37, 99, 227–
    28, 237, 297
A Theology for the Social Gospel
    (Rauschenbusch), 215
The Ten Commandments (film), 71
Thirty Years War, 141
Thurmond, Strom, 25–26
Titus, Herb, 41
Tocqueville, Alexis de, 269
Tökés, Lásló, 275–76
Tolkien, J.R.R., 236
totalitarianism, 234–35, 241, 245
Tower of Babel, 59, 66–67, 78, 81, 133,
    163–64, 250
Tragedy of American Compassion
    (Olasky), 285–86
Transnational Association of Christian
    Colleges and Schools, 24
Treatise on Tolerance (Voltaire), 147–48
Treaty of Tripoli, 169
Treaty of Versailles, 233
Truman, Harry, 254
Trump, Donald, 4–5, 6, 10, 66, 77–78, 107,
    110, 264, 265, 274, 300
The Trump Prophecy (film), 110

United Kingdom and ACE outreach, 18
United Nations (UN), 253
United States Taxpayers Party, 282
University of California, 3–4
US colonization, 199–200
US Constitution, 100–1, 183–85, 274
US Declaration of Independence, 170,
    179–83, 274
US Department of Education, 303
US invasion of Iraq, 107
Ussher, James, 60

Valla, Lorenzo, 105
values voters, 86
Values Voter Summit, 301
Velvet Revolution in
    Czechoslovakia, 276–77
Verrazano, Giovanni, 133
Victoria, Queen (Victorians), 189–92,
    194, 210–11

Victorians, 101–2, 152, 189–91, 192, 194
Vietnam/Vietnam War, 255–56,
      264, 265
Vins, Peter, 250
Virgin Mary veneration, 97
Vision Forum, 67–68
Voltaire, François Arouet de, 147–48
voucher programs, 8

Waldo, Peter, 97–98
WallBuilders, 5–6, 12–13, 284
Warfield, Benjamin B., 211–12
Waring, Diane, 207
War of the Roses, 100–1
War on Poverty, 265
Washington, George, 170, 173–
      74, 178–79
Watergate burglary, 265
Wealth of Nations (Smith), 205–6
Webster, Noah, 166
Weem, Mason Locke, 178
Wesley, John (Wesleyan revival), 22, 149,
      153, 190–91, 206, 210–11, 237–38
Western civilization courses, 80–81
Weyrich, Paul, 271, 273
Whitcomb, John C., 62

white supremacy, 152, 202, 236, 278–79,
      296, 324n.26
White Trash (Isenberg), 164
Who Is an Evangelical? (Kidd), 303–4
Why Communism Kills (Schwarz), 250
William of Ockham, 104
Williams, Roger, 159–60, 163
William the Conqueror, 99–100
Wilson, Woodrow, 233
Winthrop, John, 162–63, 164
Witherspoon, John, 91–92, 182
Wood, Gordon, 176
World Council of Churches, 287
*World Empires, World Missions, World
      Wars* (Waring), 207
world history textbooks, 28–29
World War I, 223, 228, 229, 231–32, 233
World War II, 223, 231–32, 239–40
Wycliffe, John, 97–98

Xenophanes, 91

Young Earth Creationism/Creationists,
      60–61, 62–63, 232

Zelman v. Simmons-Harris (1994), 8